WORKSHOPS IN COMPUTING

Series edited by C. J. van Rijsbergen

Also in this series

Declarative Programming, Sasbachwalden 1991
PHOENIX Seminar and Workshop on Declarative Programming, Sasbachwalden, Black Forest, Germany, 18–22 November 1991
John Darlington and Roland Dietrich (Eds.)

Building Interactive Systems: Architectures and Tools
Philip Gray and Roger Took (Eds.)

Functional Programming, Glasgow 1991
Proceedings of the 1991 Glasgow Workshop on Functional Programming, Portree, Isle of Skye, 12–14 August 1991
Rogardt Heldal, Carsten Kehler Holst and Philip Wadler (Eds.)

Object Orientation in Z
Susan Stepney, Rosalind Barden and David Cooper (Eds.)

Code Generation – Concepts, Tools, Techniques
Proceedings of the International Workshop on Code Generation, Dagstuhl, Germany, 20–24 May 1991
Robert Giegerich and Susan L. Graham (Eds.)

Z User Workshop, York 1991, Proceedings of the Sixth Annual Z User Meeting, York, 16–17 December 1991
J.E. Nicholls (Ed.)

Formal Aspects of Measurement
Proceedings of the BCS-FACS Workshop on Formal Aspects of Measurement, South Bank University, London, 5 May 1991
Tim Denvir, Ros Herman and R.W. Whitty (Eds.)

AI and Cognitive Science '91
University College, Cork, 19–20 September 1991
Humphrey Sorensen (Ed.)

5th Refinement Workshop, Proceedings of the 5th Refinement Workshop, organised by BCS-FACS, London, 8–10 January 1992
Cliff B. Jones, Roger C. Shaw and Tim Denvir (Eds.)

Algebraic Methodology and Software Technology (AMAST'91)
Proceedings of the Second International Conference on Algebraic Methodology and Software Technology, Iowa City, USA, 22–25 May 1991
M. Nivat, C. Rattray, T. Rus and G. Scollo (Eds.)

ALPUK92, Proceedings of the 4th UK Conference on Logic Programming, London, 30 March – 1 April 1992
Krysia Broda (Ed.)

Logic Program Synthesis and Transformation
Proceedings of LOPSTR 92, International Workshop on Logic Program Synthesis and Transformation, University of Manchester, 2–3 July 1992
Kung-Kiu Lau and Tim Clement (Eds.)

NAPAW 92, Proceedings of the First North American Process Algebra Workshop, Stony Brook, New York, USA, 28 August 1992
S. Purushothaman and Amy Zwarico (Eds.)

First International Workshop on Larch
Proceedings of the First International Workshop on Larch, Dedham, Massachusetts, USA, 13–15 July1992
Ursula Martin and Jeannette M. Wing (Eds.)

Persistent Object Systems
Proceedings of the Fifth International Workshop on Persistent Object Systems, San Miniato (Pisa), Italy, 1–4 September 1992
Antonio Albano and Ron Morrison (Eds.)

Formal Methods in Databases and Software Engineering, Proceedings of the Workshop on Formal Methods in Databases and Software Engineering, Montreal, Canada, 15–16 May 1992
V.S. Alagar, Laks V.S. Lakshmanan and F. Sadri (Eds.)

Modelling Database Dynamics
Selected Papers from the Fourth International Workshop on Foundations of Models and Languages for Data and Objects, Volkse, Germany, 19–22 October 1992
Udo W. Lipeck and Bernhard Thalheim (Eds.)

14th Information Retrieval Colloquium
Proceedings of the BCS 14th Information Retrieval Colloquium, University of Lancaster, 13–14 April 1992
Tony McEnery and Chris Paice (Eds.)

continued on back page...

John Launchbury and Patrick Sansom (Eds.)

Functional Programming, Glasgow 1992

Proceedings of the 1992 Glasgow Workshop on Functional Programming, Ayr, Scotland, 6–8 July 1992

Published in collaboration with the
British Computer Society

BCS

Springer-Verlag
London Berlin Heidelberg New York
Paris Tokyo Hong Kong
Barcelona Budapest

John Launchbury, MA (Oxon), MSc, PhD
Patrick Sansom, BSc (Hons)
Department of Computing Science
The University, Glasgow G12 8QQ, Scotland

ISBN 3-540-19820-2 Springer-Verlag Berlin Heidelberg New York
ISBN 0-387-19820-2 Springer-Verlag New York Berlin Heidelberg

British Library Cataloguing in Publication Data
Functional Programming, Glasgow 1992:
Proceedings of the 1992 Glasgow Workshop on Functional Programming, Ayr, Scotland, 6–8 July 1992. – (Workshops in Computing Series)
I. Launchbury, John II. Sansom, Patrick III. Series
005.1
ISBN 3–540–19820–2

Library of Congress Cataloging-in-Publication Data
Glasgow Workshop on Functional Programming (1992 : Ayr, Scotland)
Functional programming, Glasgow 1992 : proceedings of the 1992 Glasgow Workshop on Functional Programming, Ayr, Scotland, 6–8 July 1992 / John Launchbury and Patrick Sansom, eds.
p. cm. – (Workshops in computing)
"Published in cooperation with the British Computer Society."
Includes bibliographical references and index.
ISBN 3–540–19820–2 (Berlin: acid-free paper). – ISBN 0–387–19820–2 (New York : acid-free paper) : $45.00
1. Functional programming (Computer science) – Congresses.
I. Launchbury, John. II. Sansom, Patrick, *1969* – . III. British Computer Society. IV. Title. V. Series.
QA76.62.G58 1992 93-3308
005.1'1– dc20 CIP

Printed in Great Britain

Typesetting: Camera ready by contributors
Printed by Antony Rowe Ltd., Chippenham, Wiltshire
34/3830-543210 Printed on acid-free paper

Preface

The Glasgow Functional Programming Group is widely recognised for its research in lazy functional languages. Once again this year, for the fifth time, we retreated to a Scottish seaside town to discuss our latest work, this time spending three days in Ayr. We were joined by a number of colleagues from other universities and from industry, with whom we have been enjoying fruitful collaboration.

The workshop serves the dual purpose of ensuring that the whole group remains informed of each other's work, and of providing workshop experience for research students. Most participants presented a short talk about their work, supplemented by papers which appeared in a draft proceedings distributed at the workshop. Since then the papers have been reviewed and the majority are now published here following revision. The workshop also contained a lively discussion session on functional language applications, to which the industrial participants made very helpful contributions.

One interesting feature of this volume is the number of papers addressing practical issues of realistic use of functional languages, from benchmarking and profiling, to user interfaces and file handling. It is perhaps indicative that at last lazy functional languages are being used for significantly larger applications than has been typical in the past. This type of paper is likely to feature prominently in relevant conference proceedings for the next few years. Other papers here continue to address more theoretical topics, such as program logic, semantics of non-determinism, program analysis, and loop detection. It is typical of functional language research that it bears heavily both on practical and theoretical issues.

We would like to thank all the reviewers for their efforts, and especially the programme committee consisting of Cordelia Hall, Nic Holt, John O'Donnell, Simon Peyton Jones, Phil Trinder, and Philip Wadler for their assistance in selecting papers. Many thanks are also due to Teresa Currie, Andy Gill, Cordelia Hall, Simon Marlow, Simon Peyton Jones, Phil Trinder, and Philip Wadler for organising the workshop. We were also very pleased to receive sponsorship and participants from British Telecom, Canon, Harlequin, and International Computers Ltd., all of whose involvement helped to make the workshop possible.

Glasgow University
December 1992

John Launchbury
Patrick Sansom

Contents

High Level Specification of I/O in Functional Languages

Peter Achten, John van Groningen, Rinus Plasmeijer
revised version, November 1992
University of Nijmegen, The Netherlands
peter88@cs.kun.nl, john@cs.kun.nl, rinus@cs.kun.nl

Abstract

The interface with the outside world has always been one of the weakest points of functional languages. It is not easy to incorporate I/O without being allowed to do side-effects. Furthermore, functional languages allow redexes to be evaluated in any order while I/O generally has to be performed in a very specific order. In this paper we present a new solution for the I/O problem which we have incorporated in the language Concurrent Clean. Concurrent Clean offers a linear type system called *Unique Types*. It makes it possible to define functions with side-effects *without violating the functional semantics*. Now it is possible to change any object in the world in the way we wanted: e.g. arrays can be updated in-situ, arbitrary file manipulation is possible. We have used this powerful tool among others to create a library for window based I/O. Using an explicit environment passing scheme provides a high-level and elegant functional specification method for I/O, called Event I/O. Now the specification of I/O has become one of the strengths of functional languages: interactive programs written in Concurrent Clean are concise, easy to write and comprehend as well as efficient. The presented solution can in principle be applied for any other functional language as well provided that it actually uses graph rewriting semantics in the implementation.

1 Introduction

A lot has been said in favour of functional programming [2],[12] but the fact is that functional programming suffers from a paramount lack of appreciation in the established programming society. For one reason this is caused by the fact that only recently functional programs have gained execution speeds comparable to their imperative rivals [13],[18],[8]. Another important reason is that functional programming defected on performing input output (I/O hereafter) with the outer world.

I/O and functional programming doesn't seem to be unifiable: functional languages don't have the notion of *side-effects* and lack a precise *control of the evaluation order*. These are precisely the important aspects for any I/O model. There have been many proposals how to deal with I/O (see section 8) but none of them are completely satisfactory. In particular it is very hard to deal with the side-effect problem.

In this paper we present Clean's *Event I/O*, a new solution for the I/O problem that has been implemented in the lazy functional graph rewriting language Concurrent Clean [5],[13],[17] developed at the University of Nijmegen. This solution not only deals with the problems mentioned above but it also allows the specification of complicated window based I/O on a very high-level of abstraction. Last but not least, the presented solution can be implemented efficiently and is general enough to be applied for other functional languages as well.

The paper is organised as follows. In section 2 we first give a very short description of Concurrent Clean. In section 3 we briefly explain Clean's Unique Types and explain how they can be used to define functions with side-effects. Furthermore we explain how explicit environment passing is used to control the evaluation order. Now we have the tools to change the world. In section 4 we show the world we have created with the I/O library. In section 5 we present as example the Game of Life to demonstrate the resulting high-level specification of Clean's Event I/O. The implementation of the I/O library is discussed in section 6. Section 7 discusses Clean Event I/O and it is compared with other solutions in section 8. Conclusions and future work can be found in section 9.

2 Concurrent Clean

Concurrent Clean [5],[13],[17] is a lazy functional programming language based on Term Graph Rewriting [4]. Here is an example of a Clean function defining the well-known fibonacci function.

```
:: Fib INT -> INT;
   Fib 1 -> 1;
   Fib 2 -> 1;
   Fib n -> + (Fib (- n 1)) (Fib (- n 2)),     IF  > n 2
         -> ABORT "Fib called with argument less than one";
```

Term Graph Rewriting systems are very suited for efficient implementations of functional languages [17]. Graph rewriting is actually used in many implementations. The main difference between Clean and other lazy functional languages is that in Clean graph rewriting is explicitly in the semantics of the language. In Concurrent Clean, the function application to be evaluated is represented by a possibly cyclic graph. Function definitions are actually Term Graph Rewriting rules. For instance, in the right-hand-side of the Fib definition above, actually a graph structure is defined. Each node in the graph contains a symbol (`+`, `Fib`, `-`, `1`) and arguments pointing to other nodes. In Clean, reasoning about programs is reasoning about graphs. It is straightforward to denote cyclic structures and shared computations. For instance, the argument node `n` is shared in the graph constructed on the right-hand side of the example reflecting the call-by-need evaluation of functional languages. Term graph rewriting obeys the functional semantics: given a rewrite rule which left-hand side matches the computation graph, a new graph is created for those nodes of the right-hand side which are new to the computation graph. After this, redirection to the new nodes takes place.

Concurrent Clean provides a type system based on the Milner/Mycroft scheme. There are a number of predefined types: **INT**, **REAL**, etc. and type constructors: lists **[]**, n-tuples **()** and curried functions **=>**. Furthermore there are algebraic types, synonym types and abstract types.

Clean has two types of modules: implementation modules and definition modules. The types and functions specified in an implementation module only have a meaning inside that module unless they are exported in the corresponding definition module. For more information we refer to [17] and [6].

3 Managing Side-effects in Concurrent Clean

In this section we explain how to enforce a specific order of evaluation and how to establish side-effects that are safe (i.e. retaining a pure functional language). First we will shortly introduce the general ideas which underlie the solutions we have found.

3.1 Basic Philosophy

Many of the proposed solutions (see section 8) to model I/O in functional languages have regarded I/O as something alien that in some way had to be incorporated. They all effectively do I/O 'outside' the program. Our starting point has been to do I/O 'inside' the program. We wanted to have a function that reads a character from a file, a function that writes a character to a file, a function that draws a line into a window, etc. So, we wanted to have functions that could change the state (and the contents) of some (abstract) object such as a file or a window.

Such "functions" are very common in imperative languages. There are two problems why this common solution cannot be applied in the functional paradigm. First of all, these functions are not proper functions: they actually perform a side-effect (assignment) to obtain the wanted effect: to change the contents of the abstract object. Assignments are not available in a functional language. The second problem is that functions can be evaluated in any order while functions that perform I/O have to be called in a very specific order.

3.2 Side-effects and Confluence

What kind of problems are caused by functions that perform side-effects? Take for example file I/O. The most obvious and efficient way to perform file I/O is by implementing functions that directly read and write to a file such as is common in imperative languages. However, a naive implementation of such functions in a functional language would conflict with the referential transparency. For instance, assume a function **FWriteC** that upon evaluation directly writes a character to a given file. Assume that such a function is of type `:: CHAR FILE -> FILE`. **FWriteC** takes a character and a file as an argument. However, the character cannot be written into the given file and returned as result because the original file can be shared and used in other function applications. Modification of the argument as a side-effect of the evaluation of a function will therefore also effect the outcome of other computations that share the same argument. The result of a program will now depend on the evaluation order, the Church-Rosser property is lost, the system is no longer confluent. This is illustrated in the following example:

```
:: F FILE -> (FILE, FILE);
   F file -> (FWriteC 'a' file, FWriteC 'b' file);
```

Assume that the function `FWriteC` would actually append, as a side-effect, the given character to the file it receives as an argument. Now, since the file is shared in the function body of `F` the result will be depending on the evaluation order. It either will be `(file++'a', file++"ab")` or `(file++"ba", file++'b')`. And, indeed, such a side-effect is not conform the standard graph rewriting semantics that prescribes to construct a *new* file in the function body with the contents of the given file and the given character. So, each time a character is written a new file has to be constructed and the old ones have to remain intact. Now the result of `FWriteC` are two new files and the result then becomes `(file++'a', file++'b')` independent of the chosen evaluation order. Constructing new files is of course very inefficient and it is not the intention either. One really wants to have the possibility to modify (update) an *existing* file instantaneously. The problem becomes even more obvious when one wants to write to a window on a screen: one would like to be able to draw in an *existing* window. In the standard semantics one would be obligated to construct a new window with each drawing command.

3.3 Unique Types

Fortunately, side-effects *can* be allowed under certain conditions. *If* it can be guaranteed that the offered argument is not used by (shared with) other function applications it becomes garbage when it is not used in the function body. So, in that case one can construct a new object by making use of the old one. This means that one can destructively update such an argument to construct the function result. In Concurrent Clean, a type system is incorporated [6], [17] that guarantees that certain objects (unique objects) can be reused safely.

A node n of a graph G is **unique** with respect to a node m of G if n is only reachable from the root of G via m and there exists exactly one path from m to n. A property of a unique node is the fact that it has a reference count (in-grade) of one. A reference count of one is however not sufficient for uniqueness, the *whole* path from m to n must have reference count one.

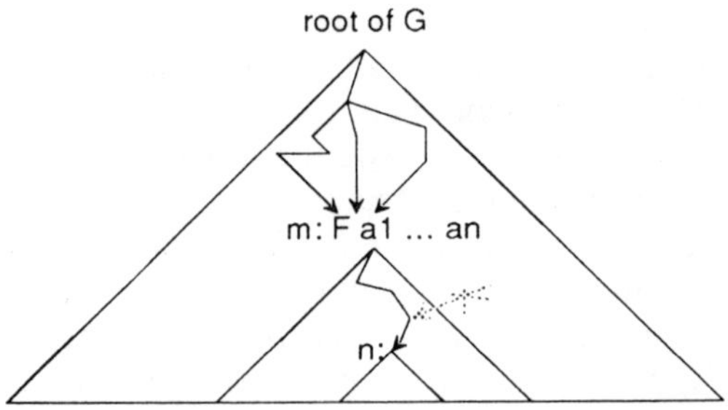

Assume that a node is passed as argument of a certain function application in such a way that the node is unique with respect to that function application: if such a node is accessed via a variable in a pattern of the corresponding rewrite rule and that variable is not used on the right-hand side of that rule, it can be considered as garbage after matching and reused for building the function result. It would be nice if at compile time the uniqueness of arguments and results of functions could be determined. Unfortunately, this is undecidable. In Clean a decidable approximation has been incorporated using **unique types**. Unique types, defined on *graphs*, have many similarities with linear types, defined on *lambda terms* [7],[22]. An important difference is that Clean's unique types give information about the way *a specific function* has to be *applied* (e.g. this function has to be called with an argument that is used in a linear way) while other linear type systems give information about the way expressions are being used in the function body (e.g. this argument of the function is used linear in the function body).

The type of a graph in a rewrite rule can have the **unique type attribute**, i.e. the graph can be of type **UNQ T**. If a graph in a left-hand side or in the right-hand side of a rewrite rule is of type **UNQ T**, it is guaranteed that at run-time the root of the corresponding graph is unique with respect to the root of respectively the function application or function result (see [6], [17]).

The **UNQ** type attribute can be added by the programmer to *any* type to express the restricted use of an object of that type. To verify the correctness of the use of **UNQ** attributes the type system has been extended. This means that all applications on the right-hand side of a function are examined to check that when a parameter or a result of an **UNQ** type is demanded, a unique graph of the demanded type is offered.

An illustrative example is the following. The type of the function **FWriteC** that writes a character to a given file as a side-effect will be **:: CHAR UNQ FILE -> UNQ FILE**. This type specification guarantees that the function will always be called with an object of type **FILE** that is not used somewhere else. That is why the dangerous example given above becomes illegal:

```
:: F UNQ FILE -> (UNQ FILE, UNQ FILE);
   F file -> (FWriteC 'a' file, FWriteC 'b' file);
```

In the function body of **F**, **FWriteC** is in both applications not called with an object of type **UNQ FILE**, but an with an object of type **FILE** (because **file** is shared) and therefore rejected by the type system. The following example is approved:

```
:: F UNQ FILE -> UNQ FILE;
   F file -> FWriteC 'a' file;
```

It is OK to share unique elements. It simply means that the object is not unique anymore and therefore cannot be passed to functions that demand **UNQ** objects. So, the following definition is also fine (although not very useful):

```
:: F UNQ FILE -> (FILE, FILE);
   F file -> (file, file);
```

The **UNQ** type predicate is a powerful tool to enforce programs to use objects in a single threaded way. In Clean the **UNQ** type attribute can be assigned to any type, hence also be used in a user defined algebraic type.

3.4 Controlling the Evaluation Order

So, how can functions be evaluated in a specific order? A well-known method is **environment passing**. The state of the environment one wants to regard is coded into an (abstract) object (e.g. a file in the case of file I/O) on which operations (functions) are defined for creation and manipulation.

Each function that modifies the environment needs the current state of the environment as argument and yields the updated environment as result. In the case of file I/O this means that all functions that perform file I/O need a file as argument and return an updated file as result. So, the abstract object has to be explicitly passed from one function to another.

When a function performs an update of an argument as a side-effect, it must be guaranteed that all previous updates of that argument by other functions have already taken place. So, a function that updates an argument must be **hyper-strict** in this argument, i.e. it must be guaranteed that the argument is always in normal form before the function is applied. This means that functions that perform side-effects on an object that is passed around will evaluate this object in a fixed sequential order: innermost.

4 I/O

Existing environment passing schemes either pass the environment *explicitly* to all functions (explicit environment passing schemes) or *implicitly* to all functions (implicit environment passing schemes) as in the language FL [3]. In both schemes the environment is monolithic: it is one single structure and all access to parts of it must occur via the whole structure. The main disadvantages of using a monolithic environment are over specification of evaluation order and potential loss of parallelism.

In Clean, the Unique Type attribute can be assigned to *any* object. This gives us the possibility to create a "world" that is composed of disjunct sub-worlds. Each of these sub-worlds is an abstract data structure that can be uniquely passed around to those functions that need these sub-worlds to perform I/O. So, we have improved the explicit environment passing scheme by partitioning the monolithic environment in suitable sub-environments (`FILE` for file-I/O, `IOState` for screen-I/O). This avoids over specification of evaluation order and loss of parallelism. The Concurrent Clean I/O libraries offer the following environments to perform I/O: `WORLD`, `FILES`, `FILE` and `IOState`. These environments have the following hierarchic relationship:

```
                    WORLD
          FILES
     FILE ... FILE          IOState
```

4.1 WORLD

The **WORLD** contains all relative information of the concrete environment to programs. In this version these are the concrete file system and the concrete event stream used for screen-I/O.

The **WORLD** is the only monolithic environment in Concurrent Clean. Programs specify their relationship to the world: pure computations ignore the world and its sub-environments, whereas interactive programs need to access and change the world. There are no rules creating **WORLD**s. The only way to get the world in the program is as argument of its initial rule, the **Start** rule. So, the start rule looks as follows:

```
ABSTYPE :: UNQ FILES;
RULE
:: Start WORLD -> any*type
   Start w -> any*computation*yielding*the*indicated*type;
```

Combined with the uniqueness of the **WORLD** it is guaranteed that there is *at most* one world in every program. Contrary to world realisations using linear types the **UNQ** typed world may become garbage during program evaluation. This does not mean that the world has ceased to exist, but it means that the program no longer performs operations on the **WORLD**. If the sub-environments have been retrieved earlier, then these can still be accessed in the program.

4.2 FILES and FILEs

FILES is the unique sub-environment of the **WORLD** containing all the files (the file system). It is a *unique abstract* type defined as follows:

```
ABSTYPE :: UNQ FILES;
RULE
:: OpenFILES WORLD -> (FILES, WORLD);
:: CloseFILES FILES WORLD -> WORLD;
:: FOpen    STRING INT FILES -> (BOOL, UNQ FILE, FILES);
:: SFOpen   STRING INT FILES -> (BOOL,     FILE, FILES);
:: FWriteC CHAR UNQ FILE -> UNQ FILE;
:: SFReadC FILE -> (BOOL, CHAR, FILE);
```

So, the file system is retrieved from the **WORLD** by the rule **OpenFILES** and put back again by the rule **CloseFILES**. Once the **FILES** has been retrieved from the **WORLD**, it can't be retrieved again without closing it first.

A Concurrent Clean file has type **FILE**. To open a file (to read or write) one needs the file system. Only write **FILE**s are opened as **UNQ FILE**; read only **FILE**s don't require the unique attribute. The following example illustrates the use of **WORLD**, **FILES** and **FILE**s:

```
RULE
:: Start WORLD -> UNQ FILE;
   Start w
   -> CopyF sf df,
      (fs, w'): OpenFILES w,
      (source_open, sf, fs' ): SFOpen "Source" FReadData  fs,
      (dest_open,   df, fs''): FOpen  "Dest"   FWriteData fs';
```

```
:: CopyF FILE UNQ FILE -> UNQ FILE;
   CopyF sf df -> df,      IF NOT read_ok
                -> CopyF sf' (FWriteC char df),
                   (read_ok, char, sf'): FReadC sf;
```

The program retrieves the **FILES** from the **WORLD**, after which the **WORLD** becomes garbage. From the **FILES** first the file to be copied is opened followed by the destination file. The resulting **FILES** also becomes garbage. The source file is only being read, so it need not be unique. The destination file is being written and must therefore be unique. After completion of copying, the source file becomes garbage, and the program yields the written file.

4.3 Event I/O

Event I/O is a *different* class of I/O than **FILE** I/O. In Event I/O the objects to be manipulated are graphical interface objects as windows, menus and dialogs. Graphical interface systems operate event driven: the user of a program communicates with that program via the interface objects: with the mouse one draws pictures, selects menu items, activates windows or presses radio buttons in a dialog. One uses the keyboard to fill in text fields in a dialog or to type text in an edit window, or to select menu items. These actions of the user generate *events* to the program. The operating system also uses events to communicate with the program to notify things have been changed. Finally, manipulations of the interface objects by the program may generate events as well. In sequential systems, these events are merged in one globally accessible event stream.

To program event driven applications one basically has to parse the events in the event stream such that the appropriate event handler can be called. However, this is very low level work which gives rise to rather ugly programs due to the complexity of event handling. In the Concurrent Clean Event I/O *all* low level event management is done in the library. The program reasons about interactions on a high abstraction level. In this level the concept of *Devices* is introduced. The aim of a Device is to capture the essence of its real life counterpart. A Device is an object with a consistent behaviour on a precisely defined set of input events. The semantics of the Device is partially fixed by the system, and can be partially specified by the program. Currently there are five devices: the WindowDevice, MenuDevice, DialogDevice, TimerDevice and NullDevice.

The WindowDevice is a real interactive device: its input domain is keyboard-presses and releases and mouse-clicks and releases coupled with the mouse position. The WindowDevice manages all open windows of an interaction. Interactions can have an arbitrary number of open windows. Of all these windows at most one is active: all keyboard events are directed to that window. An interaction can do screen output only by means of windows. A window gives a view on a Picture (an **UNQ** abstract object on which a set of drawing functions are defined). Pictures are finite objects: they have a range defined by the window's PictureDomain.

The MenuDevice conceptualises choosing commands from a set of available commands. A MenuDevice contains a number of pull down menus each holding a number of selectable menu items, sub-menus, menu item groups and menu radio items. Menu items are selected via the mouse or keyboard.

The DialogDevice models structured communication between program and user. The DialogDevice manages property and command dialogs, as well as notices. Property dialogs are always modeless, and are used to set properties of the interaction. Command dialogs can be modal or modeless. Property and command dialogs can contain editable, static and dynamic texts, radio buttons, check boxes, buttons (of arbitrary or standard shape) and program defined controls. Notices are very simple modal dialogs which are used to inform the user about unusual or dangerous situations. The dialog components are accessed by the user via the mouse or the keyboard.

The TimerDevice enables interactions to synchronise every specified time interval. The TimerDevice only responds to timer events. The NullDevice responds only to null events, special events that are generated in case there is no input.

Interactive programs can be regarded as specifications of state transition systems. One part of this state reflects the logical state of the interactive program, the *program state*. Every interaction defines its own program state. The only restriction on the program state is that it has an **UNQ** type. The other part of the state transitions concerns all devices the interaction wants to manipulate, grouped by the *IOState*. The IOState is the *unique abstract* sub-environment for programs that do event I/O. All actual event I/O the program performs, happens via the IOState: the devices themselves are never directly accessed.

```
ABSTYPE :: UNQ IOState UNQ s;

RULE
:: OpenIOState WORLD -> (IOState s, WORLD);
:: CloseIOState (IOState s) WORLD -> WORLD;
```

IOstate is a *unique abstract* type. Analogous to **FILES** it is retrieved from the **WORLD** by the rule **OpenIOState** and put back again by the rule **CloseIOState**. Once an **IOState** has been retrieved from the **WORLD**, it can't be retrieved again without closing it first. The type variable **s** in **IOState s** is the program state **s** of the interaction. When retrieved from the **WORLD** the event stream is set into the IOState which still has to be filled with the devices of an interaction.

Each new event triggers a response of the program: given the event, the program state and the IOState, it is completely determined what the next program state and IOState will be. This implies that in order to fully specify an interaction, it is sufficient to define only the initial program state and the initial IOState. **IOSystem** is a large predefined algebraic type by which a program specifies *what* Devices will engage in an interaction; *how* these Devices will be *initialised* (the look) and which event handler (Clean function) has to be called.

Starting and terminating interactions is handled by two special functions: **StartIO** and **QuitIO**. **StartIO** takes the specification of the set-up of the I/O system as described above, the initial program state s_0 and an **initial_io_state**. The initial I/O state can be obtained from the world by using the predefined function **OpenIOState**. The function StartIO will create the devices as specified and store the characteristics in an I/O state based on the initial I/O state. Then, it starts to 'poll' recursively waiting for input (events). The input event is dispatched to the proper device which computes the next program state and

IOState by applying the proper event handler. In this way a sequence of pairs of program state and **IOState**, starting from the program state s_0 and I/O state $IOState_0$, is computed (below the implementation of **StartIO** is given using internal library functions).

```
StartIO io_system_specification program_state initial_io_state
-> DoIO (program_state, io_state),
   io_state: InitIO io_system_specification initial_io_state;

DoIO states:(program_state, ClosedIO_State) -> states;
DoIO (program_state, io_state)
-> DoIO new_states,
   new_states: event_handler event program_state io_state'',
   (event_handler, io_state''): GetHandler event io_state',
   (event,         io_state' ): GetEvent io_state;
```

The order of evaluation guarantees that the transition triggered by event e_{n+1} is only reduced after the transition triggered by e_n has yielded a complete $IOState_{n+1}$. The interaction obtained in this way can only be terminated by having any of the device functions apply **QuitIO** to their **IOState** argument. **QuitIO** produces a special IOState, **ClosedIO_State**, in which all devices are closed. **StartIO** matches on this special state and produces the final program state.

The program defined Device functions are of type `:: s (IOState s) -> (s, IOState s)` or `:: Event s (IOState s) -> (s, IOState s)` (with **s** the program state). This implies that during an interaction it is straightforward to create *nested* I/O of a completely different program state **t** by calling **StartIO** with an **IOSystem t**, an initial new program state **t** and the current **IOState s**. The currently running interaction is disabled and replaced by the new one until that interaction is terminated.

For the complete definition of the semantics of Clean File and Event I/O we refer to [1].

5 An Example: the Game of Life

In this section we present an example to illustrate a typical interactive Concurrent Clean program. The program describes the interface for a system playing the game of life. This is a 'game' consisting of an infinite two dimensional space (the universe). A cell is identified by a Cartesian position (**LifeCell**) in the universe. A cell is either alive or dead. An initial generation (**Generation**) of alive cells is sown. Each following generation is computed given the current one by two rules: only if an alive cell has two or three alive neighbour cells, it survives in the next generation, and only if a dead cell has three alive neighbour cells, it becomes alive in the next generation.

The module **Life** contains the rules that are not part of the interface. The rule **LifeGame** computes given a **Generation** (**[LifeCell]**) a triplet of the next **Generation**, new-born cells and died cells. **RemoveCell** removes and **AddCell** adds a **LifeCell** to a **Generation**.

The main module **LifeGame** describes the user interface. Apart from module **Life**, it imports the necessary Clean I/O modules and the **delta** modules for basic type computations. In general an interactive program has a type-block in which frequently occurring types are declared. In this program the program state is the tuple **UNQ State**, keeping the current **Generation** and the **Size** in which cells are displayed.

In the rule **StartIO** the **IOSystem** is defined. The interaction uses a **WindowDevice**, a **NullDevice** and a **MenuDevice**. The **MenuDevice** holds all commands the user of the program has at disposal. The menu item **Cell Size** is a sub-menu. Its elements **n * n** change the size of displayed cells into **n**. To warrant one size is valid at all times, the items are organised as **MenuRadioItems**. The initial selected size is **8 * 8**. Note that the items use the same function **SetSize** applied curried in its first argument. The **WindowDevice** manages only one window which ignores all input from the keyboard, but accepts all mouse events. Using the mouse a user can add or remove cells to the current generation. The **NullDevice** calculates the next generation when no action arises from the user. Observe the close relationship between the definitions of the window and menus and their visual appearance on screen.

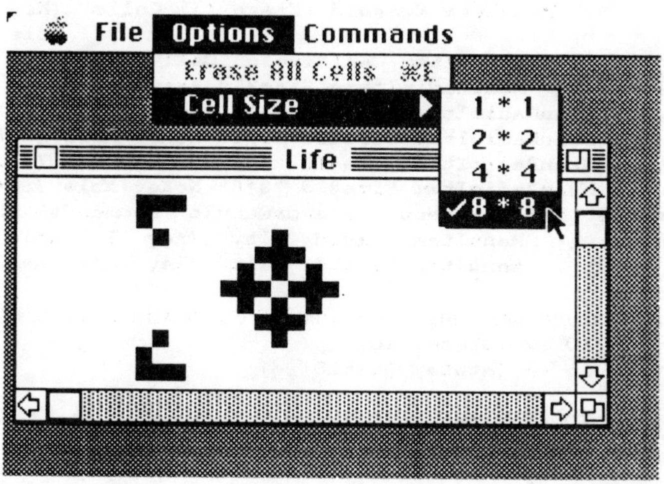

The dynamics of the devices are in control by the **MenuDevice**: initially, the user is allowed to place cells in the universe. This means that the mouse of the window is enabled and the **NullDevice** disabled. As soon as the user selects **Play** the mouse is disabled and the **NullDevice** enabled. **Halt**ing the computations causes the **NullDevice** to be disabled and the mouse enabled.

```
MODULE LifeGame;

IMPORT delta, Life, deltaPicture;
IMPORT deltaEventIO, deltaMenu, deltaNull, deltaWindow;
```

This type-block defines the program state and a shorthand for the IOState.

```
TYPE
:: UNQ State -> (Generation, Size);
:: Size      -> INT;
:: UNQ IO    -> IOState State;
```

RULE

The execution of the program starts here. StartIO initialises the NullDevice, MenuDevice and WindowDevice. *Italic* rules in the device definitions are the program defined event handlers.

```
:: Start World -> (State, IO);
   Start world
   -> StartIO
         [WindowSystem windows,NullSystem null,MenuSystem menus]
         ([], 8) io_state,
      (io_state, world'): OpenIOState world,
      windows: [DocumentWindow LifeWindowId WindowPos "Life"
                     ScrollBarH&V ScrollBarH&V PictureRange
                     InitialSizeOfWindow MinimumSizeOfWindow
                     UpdateWindow [Mouse Able Track]],
      null    : Null Unable Step,
      menus   : [file, options, commands],
      file    : PullDownMenu FileMenuId "File" Able [
                  MenuItem QuitId "Quit" (Key 'Q') Able Quit],
      options: PullDownMenu OptionsMenuId "Options" Able [
                  MenuItem EraseId "Erase All Cells" (Key 'E')
                                                     Able Erase,
                  SubMenuItem CellSizeId "Cell Size" Able [
                    MenuRadioItems Size8Id sizes]],
      sizes: [MenuRadioItem Size1Id "1*1" NoKey Able (SetSize 1),
              MenuRadioItem Size2Id "2*2" NoKey Able (SetSize 2),
              MenuRadioItem Size4Id "4*4" NoKey Able (SetSize 4),
              MenuRadioItem Size8Id "8*8" NoKey Able (SetSize 8)],
      commands: PullDownMenu CommandsMenuId "Commands" Able [
                    MenuItem PlayId "Play" (Key 'P') Able   Play,
                    MenuItem HaltId "Halt" (Key 'H') Unable Halt];
```

Now all device functions are going to be defined. We start with the menu functions.

```
:: Quit State IO -> (State, IO);
   Quit state io -> (state, QuitIO io);

:: Play State IO -> (State, IO);
   Play state io
   -> (state, ChangeIOState [DisableMenuItems [PlayId, EraseId],
                             EnableMenuItems  [HaltId],
                             DisableActiveMouse,
                             EnableNullDevice] io);

:: Halt State IO -> (State, IO);
   Halt state io
   -> (state,
       ChangeIOState [DisableNullDevice,
                      EnableActiveMouse,
                      DisableMenuItems [HaltId],
                      EnableMenuItems  [PlayId, EraseId]] io);

:: Erase State IO -> (State, IO);
   Erase (gen, size) io
   -> (([],size),
       DrawInActiveWindow [EraseRectangle PictureRange] io);
```

SetSize draws the cells in the new size and changes the State accordingly.

```
:: SetSize Size State IO -> (State, IO);
```

```
    SetSize new (gen, cur_size) io
    -> ((gen, new),
        DrawInActiveWindow [EraseRectangle PictureRange |
                             Map (DrawCell new) gen] io);
```

The NullDevice computes the next generation and draws it.

```
:: Step State IO -> (State, IO);
   Step (gen,size) io
   -> ((next,size), ChangeIOState [DrawInActiveWindow erase,
                                    DrawInActiveWindow draw] io),
      erase: Map (EraseCell size) died,
      draw : Map (DrawCell  size) new,
      (next,new,died): LifeGame gen;
```

UpdateWindow draws all cells of the current generation regardless of their visibility.

```
:: UpdateWindow UpdateArea State -> (State, [DrawFunction]);
   UpdateWindow update_area state:(gen,size)
   -> (state,
       [EraseRectangle PictureRange | Map (DrawCell size) gen]);
```

Track is evaluated for all mouse-activities in the window.

```
:: Track MouseState State IO -> (State, IO);
   Track (pos, ButtonUp, modifiers) state io -> (state, io);
   Track ((x,y), down, modifiers) (gen,size) io,
      modifiers:(shift,option,command,control)
   -> ((remove,size), DrawInActiveWindow erase io),  IF command
   -> ((add   ,size), DrawInActiveWindow draw  io),
      remove: RemoveCell cell gen,  erase: [EraseCell size cell],
      add   : AddCell    cell gen,  draw : [DrawCell  size cell],
      cell  : (/ (- x (% x size)) size, / (- y (% y size)) size);
```

Drawing or erasing a cell in a given cell size.

```
:: DrawCell Size Cell -> DrawFunction;
   DrawCell size (x,y)
   -> FillRectangle ((px: * x size, py: * y size),
                     (+ px size,    + py size));

:: EraseCell Size Cell -> DrawFunction;
   EraseCell size (x,y)
   -> EraseRectangle ((px: * x size, py: * y size),
                      (+ px size,    + py size));
```

The program constants to enhance comprehension and maintenance.

```
MACRO
FileMenuId -> 1;     OptionsMenuId -> 2;     CommandsMenuId -> 3;
   QuitId -> 11;        EraseId -> 21;          PlayId -> 31;
                          CellSizeId -> 22;     HaltId -> 32;
                          Size1Id -> 221;
                          Size2Id -> 222;
                          Size4Id -> 223;
                          Size8Id -> 224;
LifeWindowId -> 1;        MinimumSizeOfWindow -> (50,   50);
WindowPos    -> (0,0);    InitialSizeOfWindow -> (1000, 1000);
PictureRange -> ((0,0), (1000,1000));
ScrollBarH&V -> ScrollBar (Thumb 400) (Scroll 8);
```

6 Implementation on Macintosh and X Windows

A few remarks are worth mentioning about the implementation of Concurrent Clean event I/O on Macintosh and X Windows systems.

The I/O system has been designed in such a way that the program only specifies *what* interaction has to be done, never *how*. Interactions are specified in terms of the algebraic data structure IOSystem. All event handling and device handling has been carefully hidden from the program. This approach has made it possible to implement the Concurrent Clean event I/O system on Macintosh and X Windows systems, two quite different systems. Both implementations have been done from the specification down to the respective interfaces. This confirms the suitability of the chosen abstraction level of the Clean devices.

Because interactions are specified in terms of Clean objects, it was possible to write major parts of the library code in Clean, making extensive use of higher order functions (approximately 50% Clean code for the X Windows implementation and 90% for the Macintosh implementation). All device definitions, `IOState` and `Picture` are defined in Concurrent Clean as (abstract) algebraic types. The implementation on the Macintosh uses a thin interface layer which contains Clean rules for most procedures of the Macintosh toolbox. The implementation on X Windows [16] uses an interface layer to the Open Look™ Interface Toolkit (olit) and the general X Windows libraries.

The advantages of this approach are that using algebraic types for all objects of the I/O system allows the use of higher-order functions in the object definitions. Device definitions are ordinary functional objects and can be manipulated the same way as other functional objects. It is easy to experiment with various kinds of devices and system maintenance has become easier.

7 Discussion

We have experienced that Clean's Unique Type system is a very useful tool. We did not have any problems writing the library in Clean itself (5000-7000 lines of code) with the restrictions imposed by the use of unique objects.

With this library many interactive applications have been written in Clean among which some very large ones (a complete Mac-style copy-paste editor and a DBase-like relational database). Due to the high-level of abstraction offered by the I/O-library, it is possible to write compact reliable device independent interactive functional programs in a relatively short time period. The libraries maintain the different look-and-feel of the specific machines.

Of course, not every thinkable bell and whistle has been predefined in the library. But, most of the commonly used I/O gadgets are available and there is a possibility to specify user-defined controls. Furthermore, the library is well structured such that new facilities and devices can be added relatively easy.

Also the large applications written in Clean (together with the library over 10.000 lines of Clean code) still run efficient enough to be used in practice (even on small machines). They behave as good as (or sometimes even better than) their imperative counterparts. It reveals something about the code generated by the Clean compiler as well as about the quality of the libraries of present day object oriented languages.

There are two negative things to be mentioned. Clean programs consume more memory than the imperative programs (typically four times as much). Furthermore, there are some classical and non-classical language features missing in the present version of Concurrent Clean (Clean was designed as intermediate language, not as a full flavoured functional language). We want to solve both problems in the future.

8 Related Work

Other solutions to deal with I/O in functional languages can be divided in a number of categories, each having typical advantages and disadvantages. The (implicit) environment passing approach as taken in the language FL [3] has as main disadvantage that the order of evaluation is fixed. This is problematic for program transformations, introducing sharing of computations and exploitation of parallelism.

The token stream approaches [21],[9],[10],[14] suffer from inefficiency, because programs are obliged to get input by outputting tokens (doing requests). The input can be handled synchronously or asynchronously. When it is handled asynchronously one has to parse the input to determine the corresponding response. When it is handled synchronously an additional synchronisation overhead is introduced. The advantage of synchronised token streams is the control over the domain of input tokens because the program has specified from which devices the input will originate.

With the interaction type of solutions [20],[11] one has to take care that output and input occurs in the right order. The solution to this problem as given by [20] is a predefined set of functions which behave correctly in this respect.

A nice solution is the use of a predefined monad [15] which guarantees the single threaded use of predefined functions with side-effects. A disadvantage is that all functions with side-effects have to be applied on one and the same (hidden) monad. So, for instance it is not possible to define a hierarchy of sub-environments.

9 Conclusions and Future Work

Concurrent Clean's Event I/O provides programmers with a very high-level declarative specification method for writing complex interactive applications in a pure high-order functional language. All low-level I/O handling is done automatically. The library offers most of the commonly used I/O facilities and can easily be extended with new devices and facilities. The device oriented approach yields concise and elegant programs which are easy to understand and maintain.

Currently there is a version of the I/O library for the Sun under X-Windows/Open Look and a version for the Macintosh. These libraries provide the same interface such that a Clean program can run on either of these systems without any modification. Still, the resulting applications will obey the different look-and-feel which is typical for these machines. The library has been used to write several applications. We obtain very good runtime performances even compared with imperative programs.

In the future we want to extend the I/O model for distributed environments. The Unique Type system as well as Clean itself will be refined further to increase flexibility and user-friendliness. Except for type checking, the current Clean system does not yet exploit the full potential of the **UNQ** type predicate, which is a very interesting research for improving the efficiency of Clean programs in both time and space [19].

References

1. Achten PM. Operational Semantics of Clean Event I/O. Technical report - in preparation University of Nijmegen.
2. Backus J. Can Programming Be Liberated from the von Neumann Style? A Functional Style and Its Algebra of Programs.In: Communications of the ACM, Vol.21 Nr.8, 1978.
3. Backus J, Williams J, Wimmers E. An introduction to the programming language FL. In: Turner A (ed) Research topics in Functional Programming, Addison-Wesley Publishing Company, 1990.
4. Barendregt HP, Eekelen van MCJD, Glauwert JRW et al. 'Term Graph Reduction'. In: Proceedings of Parallel Architectures and Languages Europe, Eindhoven, The Netherlands, LNCS 259, Vol.II. Springer-Verlag, Berlin, 1990, pp. 141-158.
5. Brus T, Eekelen van MCJD, Plasmeijer MJ and Barendregt HP. Clean - A Language for Functional Graph Rewriting. In: Proc. of Conference on Functional Programming Languages and Computer Architecture, Portland, Oregon, USA, Springer Verlag, LNCS 274, 1987, pp. 364-384.
6. Eekelen van MCJD, Huitema HS, Nöcker EGJMH, Smetsers JEW and Plasmeijer MJ. Concurrent Clean Language Manual - version 0.8. Technical report No.92-18 Department of Informatics, Faculty of Mathematics and Informatics, University of Nijmegen 1992.
7. Girard J-Y. Linear Logic. In: Theoretical Computer Science 50. 1987, pp. 1-102.
8. Groningen van JHG, Nöcker EGJMH and Smetsers JEW. Efficient Heap Management in the Concrete ABC Machine. In: Proc. of Third International Workshop on Implementation of Functional Languages on Parallel Architectures. University of Southampton, UK 1991. Technical Report Series CSTR91-07.
9. Hudak P. et al (ed) Report on the Programming Language Haskell, - A Non-strict, Purely Functional Language -, Version 1.1 (as made public available in August 1991).
10. Darlington P. Purely Functional Operating Systems. In: Darlington, Henderson, Turner (ed) Functional programming and its applications.
11. Dwelly A. Functions and Dynamic User Interfaces. In: Proc. of ACM 1989. pp. 371-381.
12. Hughes J. Why Functional Programming Matters. In: Turner DA (ed) Research topics in Functional Programming. Addison-Wesley Publishing Company, 1990.

13. Nöcker EGJMH, Smetsers JEW, Eekelen van MCJD and Plasmeijer MJ. Concurrent Clean. In: Proc. of Parallel Architectures and Languages Europe, Eindhoven, The Netherlands. Springer Verlag, LNCS 505, 1990, pp. 202-219.
14. Perry N. Functional I/O - a solution. Department of Computing, Imperial College, London, Draft version, July 1988.
15. Peyton Jones SL, Wadler Ph. Imperative Functional Programming. Extended Abstract, to appear in POPL 1993, University of Glasgow.
16. Pillich L. Portable Clean Event I/O. Department of informatics, Faculty of Mathematics and Informatics, University of Nijmegen. Master Thesis 230, July 1992.
17. Plasmeijer MJ, Eekelen van MCJD. Functional Programming and Parallel Graph Rewriting. Lecture notes. University of Nijmegen 1991/1992. To appear: Addison Wesley 1993.
18. Smetsers JEW, Nöcker EGJMH, Groningen van JHG and Plasmeijer MJ. Generating Efficient Code for Lazy Functional Languages. In: Proc. of Conference on Functional Programming Languages and Computer Architecture Cambridge, MA, USA, Springer Verlag, LNCS 523, 1991, pp. 592-617.
19. Smetsers JEW, Achten PM, Eekelen van MCJD and Plasmeijer MJ. An Unique Type Predicate and its Application for Efficient Code Generation for Functional Languages. Technical report - in preparation. University of Nijmegen.
20. Thompson S. Interactive Functional Programs. A Method and a Formal Semantics. In: Turner DA (ed) Research topics in Functional Programming, Addison-Wesley Publishing Company, University of Kent, 1990.
21. Turner DA. An Approach to Functional Operating Systems. In: Turner DA (ed) Research topics in Functional Programming, Addison-Wesley Publishing Company, University of Kent, 1990.
22. Wadler Ph. Linear types can change the world! In: Broy M, Jones CB (ed) Programming Concepts and Methods, North-Holland, 1990.

GRIT: Guy's RISC Implementation of the Three Instruction Machine

Guy Argo
Tulsa Research Center, Amoco Production Company,
P. O. Box 3385, Tulsa OK 74102. USA.

Abstract

Fairbairn and Wray's Three Instruction Machine [1, 2] has been one of the most influential lazy abstract machine designs in recent years. However, despite its influence, some of the finer details of the implementation technique remain unclear. We hope this paper will help clarify these details. Taking Fairbairn and Wray's Normal Order version of the TIM as a starting point the author has produced two improved TIMs: the G-TIM [3], a simple single stack version; and the A-TIM [4], a more ambitious two stack design. In order to simplify the comparison between the two new TIMs and the original, they are compiled down to μTIM, a RISC microcode for TIMs, which is ultimately translated to native code. The resulting implementation, called GRIT (Guy's RISC Implementation of the Three Instruction Machine), incorporates several novel techniques which simplify the design of the compiler but still produce good quality code. In this paper we describe these techniques and demonstrate that, despite being simpler, they result in performance at least as good as that of the Chalmers' implementation of the G-machine [5, 6, 7].

1. Introduction

In this section, we provide an overview of the compiler's structure. For simplicity, it assumes that the input program is type-correct and contains only simple case expressions. Normally, a robust implementation would contain a scope-checker, a type-checker and a pattern-matching compiler but this technology is well-understood and documented in detail in [6, 7] so we saw little benefit in repeating it. The syntax of the input currently resembles a subset of LML. At some point in the future we may interface our work with an existing compiler for Haskell or LML in order to gain access to more realistic programs like the Nofib suite [8]. The compiler consists of seven phases: parsing, type elimination, argument coercion, μTIM generation, local code elimination, C generation. The output is GNU C version 2.0 or greater - an extension of ANSI C. In the remainder of the paper we highlight some of the novel parts of our compiler.

2. Argument coercion

To allow either the programmer or earlier stages of the compiler to pass on strictness and sharing information to later stages of the compiler, our parse tree data structure includes strictness annotations. These annotations can only occur on the formal parameters on the left-hand side of function definitions[1]. Our current compiler supports the following four annotations: unshared, which denotes that a redex passed in this argument position will be reduced at most once under Normal Order reduction; shared, which denotes that a redex passed in this argument position may be reduced more than once under Normal Order reduction; strict, which denotes that a redex passed in this position is guaranteed to be reduced; unboxed C, which denotes that the argument is strict and once reduced, will produce a C constructor. By default, every bound variable is treated as shared unless annotated to the contrary by % (unshared), ! (strict) or #C (unboxed C). Given these annotations, the purpose of this phase of the compiler is to utilise the information to improve the efficiency of the resulting compiled program. In the remainder of this section we discuss how this is achieved.

To implement the annotations we require two separate operations on expressions. To implement strictness properties properly we must be able to order the evaluation of expressions. To implement sharing properties we must be able to save the results of reductions and re-use them later. We will address these two points in turn.

2.1 Controlling the order of evaluation

The reduction process in the TIM is stack-based. The objects on the stack fall into two distinct categories: arguments, which are accumulated until sufficient are present to initiate a beta reduction; and continuations, which determine the function to be executed when the reduction on the segment of the stack above reduces to weak head normal form. To ease identification, in our future discussion we will annotate continuations explicitly, for instance in the expression:

```
f a b g
```

---

[1]Note as the previous phase of our compiler converts type definitions into groups of constructor functions, it is a simple matter for our system to handle annotations on constructor definitions e.g. head-strict lists.

if `g` is the continuation for the result of the expression `(f a b)`, we denote this by:

```
f a b (Cont h)
```

This gives a simple method to order the evaluation of expressions - `(f x)` and `(x (Cont f))` denote the same value however the latter form causes the argument x to be evaluated before it is passed to f. By noting that the application $(f\ a_1\ a_2 ... a_{n-1}\ a_n)$ can be rewritten as $((... ((f\ a_1)\ a_2) ... a_{n-1})\ a_n)$ we can control precisely which arguments are evaluated before the call by means of this simple transformation on the parse tree. Note that in an abstract machine with a Dump, like our A-TIM [4], Cont-annotated expressions are precisely those which are pushed on the Dump at run-time. Another peculiarity of this transformation worth noting is that strict arguments are evaluated right-to-left rather than the standard left-to-right. Because the language we are implementing is referentially transparent, this non-standard evaluation order is perfectly acceptable.

2.2 Saving the results of lazy expressions

To save the result of a reduction and re-use it later we must set aside a temporary location in memory to store the result. This is achieved by using a locally-defined let expression. Thus in the expression:

$$f\ (g\ a_1 ... a_n)$$

if we wish to treat f's argument as shared we transform it to:

$$f\ (\text{let tmp} = (g\ a_1 ... a_n)\ \text{in tmp})$$

Note that `tmp`'s definition is unannotated and therefore treated as shared, which tells the compiler to allocate a slot for the variable and access that slot via an indirection (rather than directly copying it) to ensure all instances of the variable share the same value. Just before the shared expression is evaluated, a continuation is placed on the appropriate stack which will overwrite the let-bound slot with the expression's weak head normal form. Further details can be found in [3, 4].

2.3 Interpreting the annotations

Now that we have outlined how forcing and sharing is achieved, it is appropriate to discuss how best to make use of these operations to implement the annotations on the formal parameters of functions. A straightforward scheme would be to have a prelude for each function that performed the forcing and sharing operations. The drawback to this approach is that arguments might be unnecessarily forced or shared. The cost of unnecessary forcing a closure is the creation of the return continuation and the two extra context switches. The cost of an unnecessary sharing operation is much higher - moving the closure into the slot, accessing the slot via an indirection each time it is referenced, creating the update continuation when the shared closure is eventually reduced (if ever) and performing the update once it has been reduced to weak head normal form. This difference in cost highlights both the importance of accurate sharing and strictness information and its efficient use. We wish to devise a scheme which eliminates redundant forcing and sharing. The trick required to achieve this is to let the caller decide whether a forcing or sharing operation is required. This makes sense as the caller has information about the actual parameters that is not available to the callee. To achieve this our compiler uses the following table:

	Unshared	Shared	Strict	Unboxed
expression	None	Share	Force	Force Unbox
shared variable	None	None	Force	Force Unbox
strict variable	None	None	None	Unbox
unboxed C variable	Box C	Box C	Box C	None

The columns are the anntotation on the formal parameter; the rows are the form of the actual parameter. Thus if the actual parameter is an expression and the formal parameter is annotated shared, the compiler looks up the table to find that it must share the actual parameter before passing it. From the table we note that this is the only circumstance under which a share operation is applied. This allows us to assert that every shared object is reachable via only one indirection. This is a big improvement over the original TIM which allowed long indirection chains to build up and redundant updates to occur for each shared object. For more details see [3, 4].

2.4 Handling partial applications and unknown functions

Until now we have only discussed function calls which are known and fully applied. We must modify our strategy to accommodate partial applications and unknown functions. A partial application arises when a function is supplied with insufficient arguments. Matters are complicated by the fact that partial applications are treated as values with full civil rights so we must ensure that they can be shared and forced like other values. To simplify the processing of a partial application, a function f of arity n has n+1 entry points labeled f_0 to f_n - the subscript denotes how many arguments have already been transferred to the function's environment (the rest are waiting on the stack). Entry points f_1 to f_n expect the environment to have already been created by the caller. It is unreasonable to expect the caller to know how to construct f's environment if f was passed as a parameter therefore the entry point f_0, which represents f in a higher-order context, constructs the environment instead. So what actions should each entry point perform? It must check to see if the application is partial. This consists of checking if the top item on the stack is a continuation or an argument.

If the top item on the stack is an argument then there is no partial application, all that needs to be done is to perform any strict or unbox coercion, as specified by the formal parameter's annotation, and move the argument into the environment. Note that we do not perform any share coercions - we assume that the caller has performed these. If the caller has no information about called function, he must assume that formal parameters are annotated shared to be safe. This occurs when the function has been passed as a parameter.

If the top item on the stack is a continuation, we have one of two possibilities: either the partial application is shared and we must update its root with its weak head normal form and continue; or the partial application is forced and we must return its weak head normal on top of the stack and resume the continuation. Note the difference in the flow of control - a forced partial application returns to the caller whereas a shared application checks the other argument positions and then executes the function. In the case of the shared partial application, the location of the root node to be overwritten is extracted from the continuation's info table. (Note that continuations which mark shared computations were called *markers* in the original TIM.) The weak head normal form for the shared partial application, when executed, creates a new environment whose first k arguments are copied from the original partial application and then jumps to entry point f_k to process the rest of the arguments waiting on the stack. We name the code for these partial application normal forms f_{0_0} to f_{0_n-1} as they are variants of the f_0 whose second index indicates how many arguments are in the partial application (thus f_0 is the same as f_{0_0}).

3. μTIM

Our goals for the compiler were simplicity, portability and sufficient generality that it could handle a variety of TIM designs. To achieve this we made our intermediate form, which we call μTIM, as simple and RISC-like as possible. As our ultimate target is the C language, the structure of the μTIM code bears a close resemblance to C. We note that our μTIM is very similar to the Abstract C intermediate form used in the Glasgow Haskell Compiler [9]. This is not surprising as both compilers ultimately produce C and their respective abstract machine technology is of a similar sophistication.

One important design feature of the μTIM is that the only instruction to produce a side-effect is the assignment operator, Copy. In earlier designs we experimented with several specialized instructions which performed side-effects but found this complicated the C generator with little benefit to the other modules.

Expressions in the μTIM are entirely side-effect free. Some of our earlier designs allowed expressions to perform side-effects like post-decrement and pre-decrement but this complicated the stack simulator and C code generator to an extent that outweighed their usefulness in expressing stack operations. The small price paid for this decision is that stack operations are slightly clumsier to express. For instance to push an x would be

```
sp = sp + 1; *sp = x
```

instead of

```
*(++sp) = x.
```

Although the μTIM instruction set is simpler than that of the original TIM, it is no harder to generate code for each of the constructs in the parse tree. By far the most complicated instruction in the original TIM was the Take instruction which allocated the function's environment, handled shared partial applications[2] and transferred the arguments on the stack into the environment. As we discussed in the previous section, we break down the task of handling shared (and forced) partial applications by using n separate entry points, f_0 to f_{n-1}. In addition, f_0 to f_{n-1} handle the forcing, unboxing and transferring into the environment of their corresponding argument. The allocation of the environment is performed by the caller, if the identity of the called function is known, otherwise it is performed by the higher-order entry point of the called function, f_0. The check whether a partial application is shared or forced is couched in the form of a case expression which interrogates information in the expression's info-table. This is feasible because our translation of case expressions

[2] Note the original TIM did not handle forced partial applications.

takes care to detect two distinct idioms of pattern matches: scalar, where the object matched is guaranteed to be a nullary constructor, e.g. booleans and integers; and non-scalars, where the object might be a non-nullary constructor, e.g. lists. Further optimizations are possible due to the distinct representations of scalars and non-scalars. Every member of a scalar type shares the same code - the tag which distinguishes members of the type is placed in the environment part of the closure. This allows any instance of a scalar whose type is known and is forced to be represented as an unboxed object thus consuming only half the space. For a non-scalar type the representation is slightly different. The tag field is stored in the object's info-table so each constructor has its own custom code. For a non-scalar type to be unboxed, the constructor must be known - it is insufficient to know the non-scalar's type. It is straightforward matter to have unboxed pairs but unboxed Cons would imply a hyper-strict infinite list which is unlikely to be useful in practice.

4. Stack simulator

In the previous section, we saw that our compiler performs a simple translation from parse tree nodes to μTIM. The quality of code produced from this process is fairly poor. Our justification for this approach is that it keeps a potentially complex part of the compiler, the μTIM generation, relatively simple. The price we pay for this is an extra phase which performs a simple stack simulation. In order to cope with a variety of abstract machine designs, the simulator is passed a list of the machine registers which are used as stack pointers. For each stack it maintains a note of the current simulated state. At context switches, the stack state is flushed and concrete instructions are emitted that will construct the current state. As mentioned in the last section, we have no post-decrement and pre-decrement instructions which simplify the of stack operations. This leads to the following code for stack operations, e.g.

```
sp = sp + 1
*sp = x
sp = sp + 1
*sp = y
sp = sp + 1
*sp = z
...
```

Our experience has been that the GNU C compiler produces poor native code for this style of C. The problem appears to be that the stack pointer is altered between every stack write. A better coding appears to be:

```
*(sp+1) = x
*(sp+2) = y
*(sp+3) = z
```

```
sp = sp + 3
...
```

This style allows the C compiler to do a better job of register allocation and produces a substantial improvement in the speed.

5. Flatten the code tree

As mentioned in section 4, it is extremely convenient to allow the code generator to produce code trees instead of code sequences. Unfortunately, processors deal only with linear sequences of instructions so we must flatten the code trees out. This is simply a matter of traversing the code and replacing literal branches of a code tree with named sequences. In fact this phase is simple enough that it could be merged with the preceding or subsequent phase but we avoided this to keep the structure of the compiler clear and modular.

6. GNU C as an assembly language

Instead of generating native code directly, our implementation produces C which is then compiled using GNU cc version 2.0 or greater. As one of the goals of our project was simplicity this seemed a natural decision. However for this approach to be feasible we must first solve a few technical problems to do with producing efficient code. These problems and our solutions are the subject of this section.

The first of these problems is register allocation. In an abstract machine design there are usually a handful of special purpose registers, which the implementor assumes will be mapped onto concrete registers in the real implementation. If they aren't, the performance penalty would be severe. One of the reasons we use the GNU C compiler is that it has an extension to ANSI C which allows the programmer to keep specific global variables in named concrete registers. This only drawback is that the register name is processor-dependent so a portable implementation must contain a small file of processor-dependent register information. This seems a small price to pay for a threefold increase in speed. I'd like to thank Will Partain and Patrick Sansom of the Glasgow Haskell Compiler Project for pointing out this feature of GNU cc.

The second problem is storing each function's info-table. The info-table of each function contains a variety of information that must be accessed efficiently at run-time. The normal process for doing this is to store the info-table just before a function's code and accessed by negative offsets. This leads to the following structure:

```
f's print routine
f's gc info
other info relating to f...
f: ...
   ...
   ...
```

Unfortunately, C does allow the programmer enough control over the layout of data to specify this kind of arrangement. A compromise is to store all the information relating to f including its code pointer in a record and pass around a pointer to this record instead of the code pointer. The code pointer can be obtained from the record pointer at the cost of an indirection. In C, this arrangement looks like:

```
comb_rec f_rec = { f_code_ptr, "f", f's gc info, ... };
comb_ptr f_ptr = &f_rec;
```

This simple solution costs us an indirection every time we perform a context switch but still achieves respectable performance.

The third problem we tackled was the efficient implementation of context switches. C is very restrictive in how its goto labels may be used. They may not be stored in data structures, passed as arguments or returned as the result of a function. This makes implementing a fast context switch rather awkward. A partial solution to this is to use functions instead of gotos as described by the Glasgow Haskell compiler group in [10]. In this approach each block is modelled by a function. Each such function returns as its result a pointer to the function it wishes to jump to. This is then called at the top-level by a loop of the form:

```
while (1) {
        f = (f->f_code)()
}
```

When I first heard of this solution from members of the Glasgow Haskell Compiler project my first reaction was "Why don't you use a tail-call instead of returning?". Unfortunately, tail-call optimizations are not performed by C compilers so the tail-calls would eventually overflow the call stack. This solution was rejected because we felt the call and return of a function plus the jump around the loop was too expensive. The Glasgow Haskell compiler group have some hacks to circumvent this but it involves using machine code inserts which I felt was unsatisfactory. Earlier we stated that ANSI C does not support labels as first-class objects, however GNU C version 2.0 does. This observation led me to a solution based on first class labels. The only restriction is that the label must be inside a function declaration. To satisfy this constraint, we declare a function for each block which contains the code for the block preceded by a label. The function, when called returns the address of the label. This means our system must have a small initialization phase which calls all the function to obtain the address of their code blocks and store them in their respective info-tables. Thus a typical combinator is mapped into a C function which looks like:

```
comb_label  f_0__12() {
        label f_0__12_label;

        return (&f_0__12_label);
f_0__12_label:
        ...
        code for f_0__12
        ...
}
```

This initialization phase is typically a small fraction of a program's run-time whereas context switches, which are extremely frequent, are cheap and portable so we feel this is a good trade-off

7. Initial results

So how does our system compare with existing implementations ? For our purposes, we will use the Chalmers LML implementation as our yardstick for performance. This LML implementation is the product of at least 8 years refinement and produces native code for several platforms. It is relatively stable and the details of its abstract machine are well-documented in the literature [5, 6, 7]. Our compiler is written in LML and is the product of about six months work. Currently only the one of the three abstract machines that we intend to implement is operational. The following table of benchmarks give a flavour of its performance:

	LML	G-TIM lazy	G-TIM strict	G-TIM unboxed
nfib	6.9	20.6	5.6	4.0
power1	9.3	20.3	3.9	3.0
power2	9.3	13.3	8.2	6.5
power3	5.9	7.6	5.5	4.7
quad	3.6	-	4.8	-
sieve	15.1	-	18.8	18.0
tak	0.6	1.5	0.4	0.2

Nfib is the much-abused modification to the fibonacci function which returns as its result the number of calls it performed. The next three rows are versions of the power function which are respectively lazy, fully lazy and fuller lazy. For a detailed discussion of the distinction see [10]. Note how efficiently the G-TIM handles the strict fragments embedded in lazy code compared with LML. The fifth benchmark, quad, provides a good indication of how well an implementation handles higher-order functions and partial applications. The G-TIM is 33% slower so this is clearly an area for further refinement. We suspect that tuning the mechanism handling shared and forced partial applications could help considerably. The overhead of our context switch mechanism is clearly a factor here. The sixth benchmark is the sieve of Eratostene's which employs higher-order functions, non-scalar types and forced partial applications. In this benchmark our system is 20% slower which leaves us substantial scope for improvement. Our final benchmark is the deeply recursive Takeuchi function. This clearly demonstrates that our system's handling of strict functions involving scalars is very efficient. Although these benchmarks are unrealistically small, we believe these preliminary results give us good cause to be optimistic about the future performance of our compiler on realistic programs.

8. Conclusion

Our compiler is simple and straightforward in its construction. It achieves reasonable efficiency without sacrificing portability by producing C which is then compiler using GNU cc version 2.0. This C compiler was chosen as it has several extensions to the ANSI standard which allow us to produce efficient native code. The initial results from our implementation on unrealistically small benchmarks leads us to believe its performance will be on a par with the Chalmers LML implementation - a heavily-optimizing native code compiler.

Acknowledgements

This work was supported by a SERC studentship and a SERC Research Fellowship. I would like to thank my referees, Andy Gill, Colin Runciman and Duncan Sinclair, and members of the Glasgow Haskell compiler group, especially Cordy Hall, Will Partain and Patrick Sansom for their constructive comments.

References

1. Fairbairn, J. and Wray, S.C. The TIM: a simple abstract machine to execute supercombinators. In: Proceedings of the 1987 Functional Programming and Computer Architecture conference, Portland, Oregon. 1987.
2. Wray, S. C. and Fairbairn, J. Non-strict languages - programming and implementation. Computer Journal. vol. 32 no. 2 April 1989.
3. Argo, G.M. Improving the Three Instruction Machine. In: Proceedings of the 1989 Functional Programming and Computer Architecture conference, London. 1989.
4. Argo, G.M. Efficient laziness. PhD thesis, Glasgow University. to appear 1993.
5. Augustsson, L. and Johnsson, T. The Chalmers Lazy-ML compiler. Computer Journal. vol. 32 no. 2 April 1989.
6. Peyton Jones, S. L. The implementation of functional programming languages. Prentice Hall.. 1987.
7. Peyton Jones, S. L. and Lester D. Implementing functional languages: a tutorial. Prentice Hall.
8. Partain, W. The nofib benchmark suite of Haskell programs. In: Functional Programming, Glasgow 1992, J. Launchbury and P.M. Sansom Eds., Springer-Verlag, Workshops in Computing Science, Ayr, Scotland, 1992.
9. Hall, C. Hammond, K. Partain, W. Peyton Jones, S.L. and Wadler, P. The Glasgow Haskell compiler: a retrospective. In: Functional Programming, Glasgow 1992, J. Launchbury and P.M. Sansom Eds., Springer-Verlag, Workshops in Computing Science, Ayr, Scotland, 1992.
10. Kehler Holst, C. Improving full laziness. In: Functional Programming, Glasgow 1992, S.L. Peyton Jones, G. Hutton and C. Kehler Holst Eds., Springer-Verlag, Workshops in Computing Science, Ullapool, Scotland, 1990.

A Logical Framework for Program Analysis*

Geoffrey Burn
Department of Computing
Imperial College of Science, Technology and Medicine
180 Queen's Gate
London SW7 2BZ
United Kingdom

Abstract

Using logics to express program properties, and deduction systems for proving properties of programs, gives a very elegant way of defining program analysis techniques. This paper addresses a shortcoming of previous work in the area by establishing a more general framework for such logics, as is commonly done for progam analysis using abstract interpretation. Moreover, there are natural extensions of this work which deal with polymorphic languages.

1 Introduction

Kuo and Mishra gave a 'type' deduction system for proving strictness properties of programs, and gave a type inference (sometimes called type reconstruction) algorithm for determining these strictness types [KM89]. The algorithm was proved correct by showing that the types deduced by it were true in an operational model of the language. They observed that their algorithm was not as powerful as one based on the strictness abstract interpretation of [BHA86], and it appeared to be because their type system lacked intersection types.

Both Jensen and Benton have extended this work [Jen91, Jen92, Ben92] by considering the more general notion of a program logic. They use as their language a typed lambda-calculus with fixed points and constants. Given some set of base types, new types can be formed by taking products and function spaces. Both have axiomatised a logic for strictness properties, given a sound and complete model of the logic, defined a deduction system for a typed λ-calculus, and proved the soundness of the deduction system. The main difference between the two pieces of work is that Jensen gives a model for his logic based on an abstract interpretation of the language, and so gets a completeness result for his deduction system, while Benton gives a model based on the standard interpretation of his language. Moreover, Jensen has disjunctions in his logic, where Benton has yet to do this, but Benton has some interesting results on polymorphic invariance. Unlike the work of Kuo and Mishra, neither paper suggests an

*This research was partially funded by ESPRIT BRA 3124 (Semantique) and SERC grant GR/H 17381 ("Using the Evaluation Transformer Model to make Lazy Functional Languages more Efficient").

algorithm for determining the properties that programs satisfy. However, the fact that Jensen established a correspondence between a computable abstract interpretation and his logical system shows that an algorithm must exist.

The main problem with these two pieces of work is that they only give a *strictness* logic; as they stand, all the proofs have to be redone for any other logic describing different properties. This is a bit sad because most of the logical system will stay the same for the new set of properties.

In this paper we take a cue from abstract interpretation and have a first stab at defining a framework for logics for program analysis. We will adopt the approach of Benton, proving correctness against a model based on Scott-closed sets, as we feel this gives a cleaner treatment of disjunction than that given in the paper by Jensen. This has the disadvantage of course that we can no longer state the existence of an algorithm to determine these properties.

The penultimate section will discuss an alternative model and natural extensions to deal with polymorphism.

2 Program Logics: The Key Idea

It is common to write typing judgements for checking the types of programming language constructs. For example,

$$\textbf{App} \quad \frac{\Gamma \vdash E_1 : (\varphi \to \psi) \quad \Gamma \vdash E_2 : \varphi}{\Gamma \vdash E_1 E_2 : \psi}$$

is the typing judgement for application in the typed lambda calculus.

What does it mean? Informally, it means that if we can prove that E_1 has type $(\varphi \to \psi)$ and that E_2 has type φ, then we can conclude that the application $(E_1 E_2)$ has type ψ.

What does it mean for a piece of program to have a *type*? To define this notion, we have to give an *interpretation* of a type (a domain of values for example), and then prove that the semantics of the piece of program lies in the interpretation of the type. For example, if the interpretation of *int* is the flat domain of integers, then E_1 has type $(int \to int)$ if the semantics of E_1 maps any value from the domain of integers to another value in the domain of integers.

To check that the deduction rule above is correct (or *sound*) in the case that $\varphi = int = \psi$, we have to show that whenever E_1 is a function mapping any integer to another integer, and E_2 is an integer, then $(E_1\ E_2)$ is an integer.

There is no reason to restrict ourselves to types such as integers. For example, we could consider the 'type' f_{int} whose interpretation contains only the bottom from the domain of integers. If we could prove that $E_1 : \mathsf{f}_{int} \to \mathsf{f}_{int}$ and that $E_2 : \mathsf{f}_{int}$, then the above typing judgement can be read as saying that applying a strict function to a bottom argument returns bottom. Of course we have to prove that the deduction rule is still true for this new 'type'.

This paper studies alternative types which capture more information about a program than is given by the types usually assigned to programs; gives deduction rules, such as the rule **App** above, for proving programs have particular properties; and proves that these are correct. We do this in a general framework, where the user of the framework can specify the particular types of interest.

Formulae

- $\mathsf{p}_i^\sigma \in \mathcal{L}(\sigma)$ if $\mathsf{p}_i^\sigma \in \mathsf{Con}(\sigma)$
- $\dfrac{\varphi, \psi \in \mathcal{L}(\sigma)}{\varphi \vee \psi \in \mathcal{L}(\sigma)}$
- $\dfrac{\varphi, \psi \in \mathcal{L}(\sigma)}{\varphi \wedge \psi \in \mathcal{L}(\sigma)}$
- $\dfrac{\varphi \in \mathcal{L}(\sigma), \psi \in \mathcal{L}(\tau)}{\varphi \times \psi \in \mathcal{L}(\sigma \times \tau)}$
- $\dfrac{\varphi \in \mathcal{L}(\sigma), \psi \in \mathcal{L}(\tau)}{\varphi \rightarrow \psi \in \mathcal{L}(\sigma \rightarrow \tau)}$

Logical rules

- $\mathsf{p}_i^\sigma \leq \mathsf{p}_j^\sigma$ if $\mathsf{p}_i^\sigma \leq \mathsf{p}_j^\sigma \in \mathsf{Ent}(\sigma)$
- $\varphi \leq \varphi$
- $\dfrac{\varphi \leq \psi, \psi \leq \chi}{\varphi \leq \chi}$
- $\dfrac{\varphi \leq \psi, \psi \leq \varphi}{\varphi = \psi}$
- $\dfrac{\varphi = \psi}{\varphi \leq \psi, \psi \leq \varphi}$
- $\varphi \wedge \psi \leq \varphi$
- $\dfrac{\varphi \leq \psi_1, \varphi \leq \psi_2}{\varphi \leq \psi_1 \wedge \psi_2}$
- $\varphi \wedge \psi \leq \psi$
- $\varphi \leq \psi \vee \varphi$
- $\dfrac{\varphi_1 \leq \psi, \varphi_2 \leq \psi}{\varphi_1 \vee \varphi_2 \leq \psi}$
- $\psi \leq \psi \vee \varphi$
- $\varphi \wedge (\psi_1 \vee \psi_2) = (\varphi \wedge \psi_1) \vee (\varphi \wedge \psi_2)$
- $\varphi \vee (\psi_1 \wedge \psi_2) = (\varphi \vee \psi_1) \wedge (\varphi \vee \psi_2)$

Type–specific rules

- $(\varphi_1 \times \psi) \vee (\varphi_2 \times \psi) = (\varphi_1 \vee \varphi_2) \times \psi$
- $(\varphi \times \psi_1) \vee (\varphi \times \psi_2) = \varphi \times (\psi_1 \vee \psi_2)$
- $(\varphi_1 \times \psi_1) \wedge (\varphi_2 \times \psi_2) = (\varphi_1 \wedge \varphi_2) \times (\psi_1 \wedge \psi_2)$
- $\dfrac{\varphi_1 \leq \varphi_2, \psi_1 \leq \psi_2}{\varphi_1 \times \psi_1 \leq \varphi_2 \times \psi_2}$
- $\dfrac{\varphi_2 \leq \varphi_1, \psi_1 \leq \psi_2}{\varphi_1 \rightarrow \psi_1 \leq \varphi_2 \rightarrow \psi_2}$
- $(\varphi \rightarrow \psi_1) \wedge (\varphi \rightarrow \psi_2) = \varphi \rightarrow (\psi_1 \wedge \psi_2)$
- $(\varphi_1 \rightarrow \psi) \wedge (\varphi_2 \rightarrow \psi) = (\varphi_1 \vee \varphi_2) \rightarrow \psi$

Figure 1: Axiomatisation of program properties

3 Axiomatisation

Figure 1 gives a formal system for reasoning about program properties. In this section we explain this axiomatisation, giving some examples from the strictness logic of [Jen92].

Formulae This describes the set of logical formulae $\mathcal{L}(\sigma)$ for each type σ, where the set of types is defined to be the least set T such that:

$$\{bool, int\} \subseteq T$$
$$\sigma, \tau \in T \Rightarrow (\sigma \rightarrow \tau) \in T$$
$$\sigma, \tau \in T \Rightarrow \sigma \times \tau \in T.$$

The user of the framework must supply a finite set of logical constants, $\mathsf{Con}(\sigma) = \{\mathsf{p}_i^\sigma | i \in I_\sigma\}$ for each type, which represent the basic properties that are to be distinguished at that type (c.f. abstract interpretation where abstract domains are defined so that the points represent the properties of interest).

Example: A strictness analysis may have $\mathsf{Con}(\sigma) = \{\mathsf{f}_\sigma, \mathsf{t}_\sigma\}$ where every term of type σ has property t_σ, whilst only terms with bottom as their denotation have property f_σ. ■

Finite disjunctions and conjunctions are used to build more complicated formulae, and the connectives $\times$ and $\rightarrow$ build formulae for product and function types respectively. Informally, an expression (E_1, E_2) having property $\varphi \times \psi$ can be understood to mean that E_1 has property φ and E_2 has property ψ, whilst E having property $\varphi \rightarrow \psi$ means that E maps all terms with property φ to terms with property ψ.

Logical rules The axiomatisation of program properties falls into two parts: the logical rules define the generic logical connectives $\wedge$ and $\vee$ in terms of the entailment relation $\leq$; and the type-specific rules describe their interaction with properties on product and function types.

The statement $\varphi \leq \psi$ can be understood to mean that whenever a value has property φ, then it also has property ψ, and $\varphi = \psi$ means that φ and ψ are provably equal.

For each type σ, the user of the framework has to give a set $\mathsf{Ent}(\sigma)$ specifying the entailments between the constants in $\mathsf{Con}(\sigma)$. Each of the entailments in $\mathsf{Ent}(\sigma)$ must satisfy a condition which we can only give after discussing models in the next section.

Example: For a strictness analysis we could have the following six rules:

- $\forall \varphi \in \mathcal{L}(\sigma) : \varphi \leq \mathsf{t}_\sigma$ • $\mathsf{t}_{\sigma\rightarrow\tau} = \mathsf{t}_\sigma \rightarrow \mathsf{t}_\tau$ • $\mathsf{t}_{\sigma\times\tau} = \mathsf{t}_\sigma \times \mathsf{t}_\tau$
- $\forall \varphi \in \mathcal{L}(\sigma) : \mathsf{f}_\sigma \leq \varphi$ • $\mathsf{t}_\sigma \rightarrow \mathsf{f}_\tau = \mathsf{f}_{\sigma\rightarrow\tau}$ • $\mathsf{f}_{\sigma\times\tau} = \mathsf{f}_\sigma \times \mathsf{f}_\tau$

■

Let $\varphi, \varphi_1, \varphi_2 \in \mathcal{L}(\sigma)$ and $\psi \in \mathcal{L}(\tau)$.

$[\![]\!]_\sigma : \mathcal{L}(\sigma) \to \mathbf{P}\ \mathbf{S}_\sigma$.

$$\begin{array}{lcll}
[\![\mathsf{p}_i^\sigma]\!]_\sigma & = & \text{some Scott-closed set associated with } \mathsf{p}_i^\sigma & \\
[\![\varphi_1 \wedge \varphi_2]\!]_\sigma & = & [\![\varphi_1]\!]_\sigma \bigcap [\![\varphi_2]\!]_\sigma & \\
[\![\varphi_1 \vee \varphi_2]\!]_\sigma & = & [\![\varphi_1]\!]_\sigma \bigcup [\![\varphi_2]\!]_\sigma & \\
[\![\varphi \times \psi]\!]_{\sigma\times\tau} & = & \{(x,y) \mid x \in [\![\varphi]\!]_\sigma, y \in [\![\psi]\!]_\tau\} & (= [\![\varphi]\!]_\sigma \times [\![\psi]\!]_\tau) \\
[\![\varphi \to \psi]\!]_{\sigma\to\tau} & = & \{f \mid \forall x \in [\![\varphi]\!]_\sigma . f\ x \in [\![\psi]\!]_\tau\} & (= [\![\varphi]\!]_\sigma \Rightarrow [\![\psi]\!]_\tau)
\end{array}$$

Figure 2: Semantics of formulae

Type–specific rules The type-specific rules capture intuitions about properties of compound data types. For example, the first rule says that if either the first element of a pair has property φ_1 and the second has property ψ, or the first element of the pair has property φ_2 and the second has property ψ, then it is certainly the case that the second element of the pair has property ψ and the first element has either property φ_1 or property φ_2. The last rule is as expected because of the contravariance of $\to$.

4 A Model for the Logic

Scott-closed sets are one possible model for the logic:

- the interpretation of a formula in $\mathcal{L}(\sigma)$ is a Scott-closed set;
- conjunction is modelled by set intersection;
- disjunction is modelled by set union; and
- entailment is modelled by subset inclusion.

We denote the interpretation of the type σ by $\mathbf{S}_\sigma$, and $\mathbf{P}\ \mathbf{S}_\sigma$ is the lattice of Scott-closed subsets of $\mathbf{S}_\sigma$. ($\mathbf{P}$ is the Hoare powerdomain functor.)

The interpretation function $[\![\ ]\!]_\sigma : \mathcal{L}(\sigma) \to \mathbf{P}\ \mathbf{S}_\sigma$ is defined in Figure 2, where the user of the framework has to give a Scott-closed set as the meaning of each constant (c.f. defining a concretisation map in abstract interpretation), with the following proviso:

$$\forall \sigma, \forall \mathsf{p}_i^\sigma, \mathsf{p}_j^\sigma \in \mathsf{Con}(\sigma). \mathsf{p}_i^\sigma \leq \mathsf{p}_j^\sigma \iff [\![\mathsf{p}_i^\sigma]\!]_\sigma \subseteq [\![\mathsf{p}_j^\sigma]\!]_\sigma .$$

This is the condition we referred to when discussing the logical rules in the previous section.

Example: If $[\![\mathsf{t}_\sigma]\!]_\sigma = \mathbf{S}_\sigma$ and $[\![\mathsf{f}_\sigma]\!]_\sigma = \{\bot_{\mathbf{S}_\sigma}\}$, then the above condition holds for these constants. ■

The Soundness Theorem states that any entailment that can be proved in the formal system is properly reflected in the semantics as an inclusion between subsets. It is needed in order to prove the soundness of the rule **Weak** in the program logic to be presented in the next section.

The set T of types is the least set defined by:

$$\{bool, int\} \subseteq T$$
$$\sigma, \tau \in T \Rightarrow (\sigma \rightarrow \tau) \in T$$
$$\sigma, \tau \in T \Rightarrow \sigma \times \tau \in T$$

The type system of Λ_T

(1) $x^\sigma : \sigma$ (2) $c_\sigma : \sigma$

(3) $\dfrac{E_1 : \sigma \rightarrow \tau,\ E_2 : \sigma}{(E_1\ E_2) : \tau}$ (4) $\dfrac{E : \tau}{(\lambda x^\sigma.E) : \sigma \rightarrow \tau}$

(5) $\dfrac{E : \sigma \rightarrow \sigma}{\mathbf{fix}_{(\sigma \rightarrow \sigma) \rightarrow \sigma}\ E : \sigma}$ (6) $\dfrac{E_1 : \sigma, E_2 : \tau}{(E_1, E_2) : \sigma_1 \times \sigma_2}$

Abstract Syntax of Λ_T

$\mathbf{true}_{bool}$	$\mathbf{false}_{bool}$	$\mathbf{if}_{bool \rightarrow \sigma \rightarrow \sigma \rightarrow \sigma}$
$\{\mathbf{0}_{int}, \mathbf{1}_{int}, \mathbf{2}_{int}, \ldots\}$	$\mathbf{plus}_{(int \times int) \rightarrow int}$	$+_{int \rightarrow int \rightarrow int}$
$\mathbf{fst}_{\sigma_1 \times \sigma_2 \rightarrow \sigma_1}$	$\mathbf{snd}_{\sigma_1 \times \sigma_2 \rightarrow \sigma_2}$	

The Constants of Λ_T

Figure 3: Definition of the Language Λ_T

Theorem 4.1 (Soundness) *If for all σ, $\mathsf{p}_i^\sigma \leq \mathsf{p}_j^\sigma$ implies $[\![\mathsf{p}_i^\sigma]\!]_\sigma \subseteq [\![\mathsf{p}_j^\sigma]\!]_\sigma$, then for all elements $\varphi, \psi \in \mathcal{L}(\sigma)$:*

$$\varphi \leq \psi \quad \textit{implies} \quad [\![\varphi]\!]_\sigma \subseteq [\![\psi]\!]_\sigma$$

Proof

Each case follows by simple set manipulation.

∎

It is common to prove the converse of the Soundness Theorem (a Completeness Theorem). This is unnecessary for our purposes because we will only be concerned with the soundness of the deduction system given in the next section, not its completeness.

5 A Deduction System for Program Analysis

We use as our programming language a typed λ-calculus with constants, which we call Λ_T, and which is defined in Figure 3. The definition comes in three parts: the type system; the rules for forming terms in the language,

$$
\begin{array}{lcl}
\mathbf{S}_B & = & \text{some domain for the base type } B \\
\mathbf{S}_{\sigma\to\tau} & = & \mathbf{S}_\sigma \to \mathbf{S}_\tau \\
\mathbf{S}_{\sigma\times\tau} & = & \mathbf{S}_\sigma \times \mathbf{S}_\tau
\end{array}
$$

Interpretation of the Types

$$
\begin{array}{l}
\mathbf{S}\ [\![x^\sigma]\!]\ \rho^{\mathbf{S}} = \rho^{\mathbf{S}}\ x^\sigma \\
\mathbf{S}\ [\![c_\sigma]\!]\ \rho^{\mathbf{S}} = \mathbf{K}^{\mathbf{S}}\ [\![c_\sigma]\!] \\
\mathbf{S}\ [\![E_1\ E_2]\!]\ \rho^{\mathbf{S}} = (\mathbf{S}\ [\![E_1]\!]\ \rho^{\mathbf{S}})\ (\mathbf{S}\ [\![E_2]\!]\ \rho^{\mathbf{S}}) \\
\mathbf{S}\ [\![\lambda x^\sigma.E]\!]\ \rho^{\mathbf{S}} = \lambda d\epsilon\mathbf{S}_\sigma.\mathbf{S}\ [\![E]\!]\ \rho^{\mathbf{S}}[x^\sigma := d] \\
\mathbf{S}\ [\![\mathbf{fix}_{(\sigma\to\sigma)\to\sigma}\ E]\!]\ \rho^{\mathbf{S}} = \bigsqcup_{i\geq 0} (\mathbf{S}\ [\![E]\!]\ \rho^{\mathbf{S}})^i\ \bot_{\mathbf{S}_\sigma} \\
\mathbf{S}\ [\![(E_1, E_2)]\!]\ \rho^{\mathbf{S}} = (\mathbf{S}\ [\![E_1]\!]\ \rho^{\mathbf{S}}, \mathbf{S}\ [\![E_2]\!]\ \rho^{\mathbf{S}})
\end{array}
$$

Interpretation of Language Terms

Figure 4: The Semantics of Λ_T

including a rule for constants, where c_σ stands for an arbitrary constant; and some example constants. The semantics of Λ_T is given in Figure 4, where for all c_σ, $\mathbf{K}^{\mathbf{S}}\ [\![c_\sigma]\!]$ is the usual meaning of the constant.

Note that we now have two concepts of constants in this paper: logical constants, which we have been denoting by p_i^σ, and programming language constants, denoted by c_σ.

A disjunctive program logic is given in Figure 5, where the user has to give deduction rules $\mathsf{Ded}(c_\sigma) = \{\mathbf{c}\text{-}\mathbf{j} | j \in J_{c_\sigma}\}$ for each constant c_σ.

Example: The deduction rules for $\mathbf{if}_{bool\to\sigma\to\sigma\to\sigma}$ for a strictness analysis are:

$$
\textbf{If-1}\quad \frac{\Gamma \vdash E_1 : \mathsf{f}_{bool}}{\Gamma \vdash \mathbf{if}\ E_1\ E_2\ E_3 : \mathsf{f}_\sigma} \qquad \textbf{If-2}\quad \frac{\Gamma \vdash E_2 : \varphi_1 \quad \Gamma \vdash E_3 : \varphi_2}{\Gamma \vdash \mathbf{if}\ E_1\ E_2\ E_3 : \varphi_1 \vee \varphi_2}
$$

The first one says that if the expression E_1 is undefined, then the result of the application is undefined. The the second captures the fact that either E_1 evaluates to true and E_2 has property φ, or E_1 evaluates to false and E_3 has property ψ, or the evaluation of E_1 fails to terminate, and so the result in all cases must has either property φ or property ψ (with this holding when E_1 fails to terminate because $\mathsf{f}_{bool} \leq \varphi \vee \psi$ in the strictness logic). ■

Theorem 5.3 gives a soundness result for the deduction system. It states that whenever we can prove that an expression E has property φ, then the semantics of E is in the Scott-closed set given as the interpretation of φ. Before we state and prove this theorem, we define some notation and then give a simple lemma which will make our job easier for the case of λ-abstraction.

c-j if **c-j**$\in$ Ded(c_σ)

Conj $\dfrac{\Gamma \vdash E : \psi_1 \quad \Gamma \vdash E : \psi_2}{\Gamma \vdash E : \psi_1 \wedge \psi_2}$ **Weak** $\dfrac{\Gamma \leq \Delta \quad \Delta \vdash E : \varphi \quad \varphi \leq \psi}{\Gamma \vdash E : \psi}$

Disj $\dfrac{\Gamma[x \mapsto \varphi_1] \vdash E : \psi \quad \Gamma[x \mapsto \varphi_2] \vdash E : \psi}{\Gamma[x \mapsto \varphi_1 \vee \varphi_2] \vdash E : \psi}$

Var $\Gamma[x \mapsto \varphi] \vdash x : \varphi$ **Pair** $\dfrac{\Gamma \vdash E_1 : \varphi_1 \quad \Gamma \vdash E_2 : \varphi_2}{\Gamma \vdash (E_1, E_2) : \varphi_1 \times \varphi_2}$

Abs $\dfrac{\Gamma[x \mapsto \varphi] \vdash E : \psi}{\Gamma \vdash \lambda x.E : (\varphi \rightarrow \psi)}$ **App** $\dfrac{\Gamma \vdash E_1 : (\varphi \rightarrow \psi) \quad \Gamma \vdash E_2 : \varphi}{\Gamma \vdash E_1 E_2 : \psi}$

Fix $\dfrac{\Gamma \vdash E : \varphi \rightarrow \varphi}{\Gamma \vdash \mathbf{fix}(E) : \varphi}$

Figure 5: Disjunctive program logic

Definition 5.1 *We say that*

- $d \models \varphi \equiv d \in [\![\varphi]\!]$
- $\rho^{\mathbf{S}} \models \Gamma \equiv \forall x : \rho^{\mathbf{S}}\ x \models \Gamma\ x$
- $\Gamma \models e : \varphi \equiv \forall \rho^{\mathbf{S}} \models \Gamma : \mathbf{S}\ [\![E]\!]\ \rho^{\mathbf{S}} \models \varphi$

Lemma 5.2 $\rho^{\mathbf{S}} \models \Gamma$ *implies* $\forall d \models \varphi :\ \rho^{\mathbf{S}}[x := d] \models \Gamma[x \mapsto \varphi]$.

Theorem 5.3 *Suppose that each deduction rule for each constant c_σ in Λ_T is sound. Let E be a term of type σ and let Γ be an environment of formulae for E. For φ a formula belonging to $\mathcal{L}(\sigma)$ we then have:*

$\Gamma \vdash E : \varphi$ *implies* $\forall \rho \models \Gamma . \mathbf{S}\ [\![E]\!]\ \rho^{\mathbf{S}} \models \varphi$

Proof

This is proved by a simple induction over the length of a deduction proof. We give the case for the **App** rule as an example. Suppose that the theorem holds for E_1 and E_2. Then we have that $\mathbf{S}\ [\![E_1]\!]\ \rho^{\mathbf{S}} \models \varphi \rightarrow \psi$ and $\mathbf{S}\ [\![E_2]\!]\ \rho^{\mathbf{S}} \models \varphi$ implies that $\mathbf{S}\ [\![E_1\ E_2]\!]\ \rho^{\mathbf{S}} = \mathbf{S}\ [\![E_1]\!]\ \rho^{\mathbf{S}}\ (\mathbf{S}\ [\![E_2]\!]\ \rho^{\mathbf{S}}) \in [\![\psi]\!]$ (by the definition of $[\![\varphi \rightarrow \psi]\!]$). But this means that $\mathbf{S}\ [\![E_1\ E_2]\!]\ \rho^{\mathbf{S}} \models \psi$ as required.

■

6 An Example: Extending a Strictness Logic to Deal With Lists

In this section we show how to use the framework to give a logic that can express the same set of properties as the four-point domain which is often used in abstract interpretation [Wad87]. We do this by extending the strictness logic, which has been presented as an example throughout the paper, with the (logical) constants: $\bot_\sigma \leq \infty_\sigma \leq \bot\in_\sigma \leq \top\in_\sigma$, for each type σ, that informally have the meanings: the bottom list; infinite lists or lists with a bottom tail at some point; all lists except finite ones with no bottom elements; and all lists. To define this formally we use the following functions:

$$
\begin{array}{lcll}
P_\sigma : list\ \sigma \rightarrow list\ \sigma & & & \\
P_\sigma . \bot_{\mathbf{S}_{list\,\sigma}} & = & \bot_{\mathbf{S}_{list\,\sigma}} & \\
P_\sigma\ \mathbf{nil} & = & \mathbf{nil} & \\
P_\sigma\ (\mathbf{cons}\ u\ v) & = & \left\{ \begin{array}{ll} \bot_{\mathbf{S}_{list\,\sigma}} & \text{if } P_\sigma\ v = \bot_{\mathbf{S}_{list\,\sigma}} \\ \mathbf{cons}\ u\ v & \text{otherwise} \end{array} \right. & \\
F_\sigma : list\ \sigma \rightarrow list\ \sigma & & & \\
F_\sigma\ \bot_{\mathbf{S}_{list\,\sigma}} & = & \bot_{\mathbf{S}_{list\,\sigma}} & \\
F_\sigma\ \mathbf{nil} & = & \mathbf{nil} & \\
F_\sigma\ (\mathbf{cons}\ u\ v) & = & \left\{ \begin{array}{ll} \bot_{\mathbf{S}_{list\,\sigma}} & \text{if } u = \bot_{\mathbf{S}_\sigma} \text{ or } F_\sigma\ v = \bot_{\mathbf{S}_{list\,\sigma}} \\ \mathbf{cons}\ u\ v & \text{otherwise} \end{array} \right. &
\end{array}
$$

and so we can give the semantics of the logical constants:

$$
\begin{array}{lcl}
[\![\bot_\sigma]\!]_{list\,\sigma} & = & \{\bot_{\mathbf{S}_{list\,\sigma}}\} \\
[\![\infty_\sigma]\!]_{list\,\sigma} & = & \{l \mid P_\sigma\ l = \bot_{\mathbf{S}_{list\,\sigma}}\} \\
[\![\bot\in_\sigma]\!]_{list\,\sigma} & = & \{l \mid F_\sigma\ l = \bot_{\mathbf{S}_{list\,\sigma}}\} \\
[\![\top\in_\sigma]\!]_{list\,\sigma} & = & \mathbf{S}_{list\,\sigma}
\end{array}
$$

We extend Λ_T by including the constant $\mathbf{case}_{list\,\sigma \rightarrow \tau \rightarrow (\sigma \rightarrow list\,\sigma \rightarrow \tau) \rightarrow \tau}$, with the usual semantics:

$$
\begin{array}{lcl}
\mathbf{K^S}\ [\![\mathbf{case}]\!]\ \bot_{\mathbf{S}_{list\,\sigma}}\ s\ f & = & \bot_{\mathbf{S}_\tau} \\
\mathbf{K^S}\ [\![\mathbf{case}]\!]\ \mathbf{nil}\ s\ f & = & s \\
\mathbf{K^S}\ [\![\mathbf{case}]\!]\ (\mathbf{cons}\ u\ v)\ s\ f & = & f\ u\ v
\end{array}
$$

The following deduction rules can easily be proved to be sound with respect to $\mathbf{K^S}\ [\![\mathbf{case}]\!]$:

$$
\textbf{case-1} \quad \frac{\Gamma \vdash E_1 : \bot_\sigma}{\Gamma \vdash \mathbf{case}\ E_1\ E_2\ E_3 : \mathsf{f}_\tau}
$$

$$
\textbf{case-2} \quad \frac{\Gamma \vdash E_1 : \infty_\sigma \quad \Gamma \vdash E_3 : \mathsf{t}_\sigma \rightarrow \infty_\sigma \rightarrow \varphi}{\Gamma \vdash \mathbf{case}\ E_1\ E_2\ E_3 : \varphi}
$$

$$
\textbf{case-3} \quad \frac{\Gamma \vdash E_1 : \bot\in_\sigma \quad \Gamma \vdash E_3 : (\mathsf{f}_\sigma \rightarrow \top\in_{list\ \sigma} \rightarrow \varphi) \wedge (\mathsf{t}_\sigma \rightarrow \bot\in_\sigma \rightarrow \psi)}{\Gamma \vdash \mathbf{case}\ E_1\ E_2\ E_3 : \varphi \vee \psi}
$$

$$
\textbf{case-4} \quad \frac{\Gamma \vdash E_1 : \top\in_\sigma \quad \Gamma \vdash E_2 : \varphi \quad \Gamma \vdash E_3 : \mathsf{t}_\sigma \rightarrow \top\in_\sigma \rightarrow \psi}{\Gamma \vdash \mathbf{case}\ E_1\ E_2\ E_3 : \varphi \vee \psi}
$$

As an example, we will deduce that the length function:

$$\mathbf{fix}\ (\lambda g.\lambda x.\mathbf{case}\ x\ \mathbf{0}\ (\lambda y.\lambda z.\mathbf{1} + (g\ y\ z))),$$

where $g : list\ int \rightarrow int$, has the property $\infty_{int} \rightarrow \mathsf{f}_{int}$, that is, it is tail-strict. The derivation will require the following rule for $+$:

$$\textbf{+-1}\quad \frac{\Gamma \vdash E_2 : \mathsf{f}_{int}}{\Gamma \vdash +\ E_1\ E_2 : \mathsf{f}_{int}}$$

Let $\Gamma_0 = \{g \mapsto \infty_{int} \rightarrow \mathsf{f}_{int}, x \mapsto \infty_{int}\}$ and $\Gamma_1 = \Gamma_0 \bigcup \{y \mapsto \mathsf{t}_{int}, z \mapsto \infty_{int}\}$. Then we have the following derivation:

$$\cfrac{\cfrac{\cfrac{\cfrac{\cfrac{\cfrac{\Gamma_1 \vdash g : \infty_{int} \rightarrow \mathsf{f}_{int} \qquad \Gamma_1 \vdash z : \infty_{int}}{\Gamma_1 \vdash g\ z : \mathsf{f}_{int}}\ \textbf{App}}{\Gamma_1 \vdash \mathbf{1}{+}(g\ z) : \mathsf{f}_{int}}\ \textbf{+-1}}{\Gamma_0 \vdash \lambda y.\lambda z.\mathbf{1}{+}(g\ z) : \mathsf{t}_{int} \rightarrow \infty_{int} \rightarrow \mathsf{f}_{int}}\ \textbf{Abs,Abs}}{\Gamma_0 \vdash \mathbf{case}\ x\ \mathbf{0}\ (\lambda y.\lambda z.\mathbf{1}{+}(g\ z)) : \mathsf{f}_{int}}\ \textbf{case-2}}{\vdash \lambda g.\lambda x.\mathbf{case}\ x\ \mathbf{0}\ (\lambda y.\lambda z.\mathbf{1}{+}(g\ z)) : (\infty_{int} \rightarrow \mathsf{f}_{int}) \rightarrow \infty_{int} \rightarrow \mathsf{f}_{int}}\ \textbf{Abs,Abs}}{\vdash \mathbf{fix}\ (\lambda g.\lambda x.\mathbf{case}\ x\ \mathbf{0}\ (\lambda y.\lambda z.\mathbf{1}{+}(g\ z))) : \infty_{int} \rightarrow \mathsf{f}_{int}}\ \textbf{Fix}$$

7 Extensions

7.1 Different Models for the Logic

One of the limitations of the development so far is our use of Scott-closed sets to model properties. It is well-known that some properties, head-strictness and constancy for example, cannot be represented using a finite number of Scott-closed sets ([Kam91, Hun91]), because they are *relational* properties. Hunt has suggested using *complete pers* (*complete partial equivalence relations*) as models of properties [Hun91]. This suggestion has been discussed at length in [Bur92]. For our current purposes it is sufficient to note that most of the development of this paper can be repeated using complete pers to model properties in the following way, where **CPER** D is the set of complete pers on D:

Let $\varphi, \varphi_1, \varphi_2 \in \mathcal{L}(\sigma)$ and $\psi \in \mathcal{L}(\tau)$.
$[\![]\!]_\sigma : \mathcal{L}(\sigma) \rightarrow \mathbf{CPER}\ \mathbf{S}_\sigma$.

$$\begin{aligned}
[\![\mathsf{p}_i^\sigma]\!]_\sigma &= \text{some per associated with } \mathsf{p}_i^\sigma \\
[\![\varphi_1 \wedge \varphi_2]\!]_\sigma &= [\![\varphi_1]\!]_\sigma \bigcap [\![\varphi_2]\!]_\sigma \\
[\![\varphi_1 \vee \varphi_2]\!]_\sigma &= ?? \\
[\![\varphi \times \psi]\!]_{\sigma\times\tau} &= [\![\varphi]\!]_\sigma \times [\![\psi]\!]_\tau \\
[\![\varphi \rightarrow \psi]\!]_{\sigma\rightarrow\tau} &= [\![\varphi]\!]_\sigma \twoheadrightarrow [\![\psi]\!]_\tau
\end{aligned}$$

where, if Q and R are pers, then $f(Q \twoheadrightarrow R)g$ if and only if $\forall q\ Q\ q', (f\ q)\ R\ (g\ q')$.

The only exception is that we do not know what to do with the disjunction of properties because the union of two complete pers is not necessarily a complete per.

7.2 Polymorphism

One of the nice things about a logic-based approach to program analysis is that there are obvious ways to extend the logic to deal with polymorphism. In a program logic, there are two types of polymorphism:

- polymorphically typed logical constants; and
- polymorphically typed terms, which comes from adding (logic) variables to $\mathcal{L}(\sigma)$.

By allowing polymorphically typed logical constants, Benton is able to show that, if some property holds at one instantiation of a type, then it holds at all instantiations of the type for which the property makes sense. This is analogous to the polymorphic invariance results of Abramsky and Jensen [Abr85, AJ91]. We imagine that similar results could be proved for the more general framework of this paper.

A second type of polymorphism is opened up if we introduce variables into the set of logical formulae. There are two levels at which this can be done: a set of variables for each type σ, standing for arbitrary formulae of that type; and a set of variables representing formulae of any type. The latter would allow us to write that $\lambda x.x$ has the property $\varphi \rightarrow \varphi$ for any property φ at any type. Providing a soundness result for such a system would involve working with models of the polymorphically-typed λ-calculus, itself a research area.

8 Conclusion

Using logics to express program properties, and deduction systems for proving properties of programs, gives a very elegant way of defining program analysis techniques. This paper addressed a shortcoming of previous work in the area by establishing a more general framework for such logics, as is commonly done for progam analysis using abstract interpretation. The following table gives some informal intuitions about how the two frameworks are related:

Abstract Interpretation Framework	Logical Framework
abstract domain point for a base type	logical constant
ordering on abstract domain	relation $\leq$ on logical formulae
concretisation function on base types	interpretation of logical constant
interpretation of constructed types	interpretation of constructed types
abstract interpretation of a function	deduction of some property of a function
correctness theorem for an abstract interpretation (predicated on the correctness of the abstract interpretations given to programming language constants)	soundness of a deduction system for a program logic (predicated on the soundness of the deduction rules for programming language constants)

Jensen discusses the relationship in much more detail for a strictness logic [Jen91].

It is encouraging that the logical system can be extended in a natural way to handle polymorphism as this has proved to be a difficult problem in other frameworks for the analysis of higher-order languages.

Acknowledgements

I have appreciated many useful discussions with my colleagues on the Semantique project, Sebastian Hunt, Thomas Jensen and Dave Sands in particular. Since the original draft of this work I have had very helpful discussions with Nick Benton. Phil Wadler and Kei Davis have made helpful comments on improving the presentation of this paper.

References

[Abr85] S. Abramsky. Strictness analysis and polymorphic invariance. In H. Ganzinger and N.D. Jones, editors, *Proceedings of the Workshop on Programs as Data Objects*, number 217 in LNCS, pages 1–23. Springer-Verlag, 17–19 October 1985.

[AJ91] S. Abramsky and T.P. Jensen. A relational approach to strictness analysis for higher-order functions. In *Proceedings of the Symposium on Principles of Programming Languages*, pages 49–54, Orlando, Florida, 21–23 January 1991.

[Ben92] P.N. Benton. Strictness logic and polymorphic invariance. In A. Nerode and M. Taitslin, editors, *Proceedings of the International Symposium on Logical Foundations of Computer Science*, pages 33–44, Tver, Russia, 20–24 July 1992. Springer-Verlag LNCS620.

[BHA86] G.L. Burn, C.L. Hankin, and S. Abramsky. Strictness analysis of higher-order functions. *Science of Computer Programming*, 7:249–278, November 1986.

[Bur92] G.L. Burn. Properties of progam analysis techniques. Technical Report DOC92/19, Imperial College of Science, Technology and Medicine, Department of Computing, June 1992. Submitted to ACM TOPLAS.

[Hun91] L.S. Hunt. *Abstract Interpretation of Functional Languages: From Theory to Practice.* PhD thesis, Department of Computing, Imperial College of Science, Technology and Medicine, University of London, 1991.

[Jen91] T.P. Jensen. Strictness analysis in logical form. In J. Hughes, editor, *Proceedings of the Conference on Functional Programming and Computer Architecture*, pages 352–366, Cambridge, Massachussets, USA, 26–28 August 1991. Springer-Verlag LNCS523.

[Jen92] T.P. Jensen. Disjunctive strictness analysis. In *Proceedings of the 7th Symposium on Logic In Computer Science*, pages 174–185, Santa Cruz, California, 22–25 June 1992. Computer Society Press of the IEEE.

[Kam91] S. Kamin. Head-strictness is not a monotonic abstract property. *Information Processing Letters*, 1991. To appear.

[KM89] Tsung-Min Kuo and P. Mishra. Strictness analysis: a new perspective based on type inference. In *Proceedings of the Conference on Functional Programming Languages and Computer Architecture*, pages 260–272, London, 11–13 September 1989. ACM.

[Wad87] P.L. Wadler. Strictness analysis on non-flat domains (by abstract interpretation over finite domains). In S. Abramsky and C.L. Hankin, editors, *Abstract Interpretation of Declarative Languages*, chapter 12, pages 266–275. Ellis Horwood Ltd., Chichester, West Sussex, England, 1987.

Analysing Functions by Projection-Based Backward Abstraction

Kei Davis
Department of Computing Science, University of Glasgow
Glasgow G12 8QQ, UK

Abstract

Various techniques for strictness analysis by non-standard interpretation have been proposed in which the basic non-standard values are projections. We show that continuous functions can be completely characterised by appropriate forward and backward abstractions.

1 Introduction

Strictness analysis by non-standard (or abstract) interpretation allows significant optimisation by compilers for lazy functional languages ([1], [2], [3]). Research continues in both the development of strictness analysis techniques and their practical exploitation. In projection-based *backward* analysis, abstract values in the form of projections are propogated from the leaves of an expression to the root, and such analyses are able to determine not just ordinary strictness but more elusive properties such as head strictness, even when working in finite domains of abstract values ([4]). We are concerned with the theoretical power of such analyses, without much consideration of such practical considerations restriction to finite abstract domains; in particular we show that continuous functions can be completely determined by both forward and backward abstract values from appropriate domains.

This works brings together and expands on ideas from several sources, most notably [4], [5], and [6].

2 Projections

A *projection* is a continuous idempotent function that approximates the identity. The set of all projections on a given domain, ordered by the usual function ordering, forms an ω-algebraic complete lattice, with the identity ID as the greatest element, and the constant bottom function BOT as the least. Since the glb of a set of projections in the domain of continuous functions is not necessarily a projection, the glb in the lattice of projections is defined to be the greatest projection approximating every element of the set. This projection necessarily approximates the glb in the continuous function space. A projection is *finitary* if its image is a domain. The set of finitary projections on any domain U also forms an ω-algebraic complete lattice, and will be denoted by $|U|$. All projections herein are finitary, though no essential use is made of this fact. The symbols α, β, γ, and δ will always denote projections.

3 Projections and Strictness

Projections may be used to specify upper and lower bounds on the definedness of values—a semantic interpretation, and upper and lower bounds on the degree of evaluation of expressions—an operational interpretation. Though it is possible to formalise the operational interpretation [3], here it is used only as an informal source of intuition. We give three examples. Let `f` denote $f \in U \rightarrow V$ such that $f = f \circ BOT$. This equation makes clear that f requires no information from its argument, that is, the argument may be completely undefined; operationally this says that any argument of `f` need never be evaluated: if evaluation of an application of `f` requires evaluation of the argument, evaluation of the argument may safely diverge or return a dummy value. Here we say that f is BOT strict.

As another example, let **swap** denote *swap*, a function on pairs, such that $swap(x, y) = (y, x)$. Define projections F and S by $F = ID \times BOT$, and $S = BOT \times ID$. Then $S \circ swap = swap \circ F$, indicating that if the second component of the result of *swap* need not be defined, then the first component of its argument need not be defined. Operationally, if the second component of the result of **swap** will not be evaluated, then the first component of any argument of **swap** need never be evaluated. Here we say that *swap* is F strict in an S-strict context. In the previous example, we could have said that f was BOT strict in an ID-strict context. In both examples, projections only specified upper bounds on required definedness (by discarding unnecessary information) and therefore only upper bounds on evaluation.

Finally, consider the projection H on lists defined by

$$\begin{array}{lcl} H \perp & = & \perp , \\ H \, [] & = & [] , \\ H \, (\perp : xs) & = & \perp , \\ H \, (x : xs) & = & x : (H \; xs), \;\; x \neq \perp , \end{array}$$

where $[]$ denotes the empty list and infix : denotes the cons operation. Then H is the identity on finite, partial, and infinite lists not containing bottom elements, but truncates other lists at their first bottom element. For example,

$$H \, (1:2:3:\perp:4:[]) \;=\; 1:2:3:\perp .$$

If function f has the property $f = f \circ H$ then f is head strict; we take this as the *definition* of (semantic) head strictness. Operationally, if `f` denotes f, and f is head strict, then whenever evaluation of an application of `f` demands evaluaton of a cons cell of its argument it is safe to evaluate the head of the cons cell as well. Again, the projection H has specified only an upper bound on required definedness, though in a conditional manner: if the head of any cons cell is not defined, then the tail need not be defined either.

In projection-based backward strictness analysis, the central problem is, given γ and f, to find δ such that $\gamma \circ f = \gamma \circ f \circ \delta$, or equivalently, $\gamma \circ f \sqsubseteq f \circ \delta$. More generally, given f we seek to determine a *projection transformer* τ, a function from projections to projections, such that for all γ we have $\gamma \circ f \sqsubseteq f \circ (\tau \; \gamma)$. This inequality is the *safety condition* for τ, and any τ satisfying the safety condition will be called a *backward abstraction* of f. Taking τ to be $\lambda\alpha.ID$ is always safe, but tells nothing about f; smaller τ is more informative, and greater τ is always safe.

As the following example shows, we cannot in general hope to choose τ small enough that we get equality instead of inequality in the safety condition. Let $f \in \mathbf{1}_{\bot\bot} \rightarrow \mathbf{1}_{\bot\bot}$, and $\gamma,\ \delta \in |\,\mathbf{1}_{\bot\bot}\,|$, where $\mathbf{1}_{\bot\bot} = \{\bot,\ \mathit{lift}\ \bot,\ \mathit{lift}^2\ \bot\}$, and

$$\begin{array}{lll} f\ \bot = \bot\ , & \gamma\ \bot = \bot\ , & \delta\ \bot = \mathit{lift}\ \bot\ , \\ f\ (\mathit{lift}\ \bot) = \bot\ , & \gamma\ (\mathit{lift}\ \bot) = \mathit{lift}\ \bot\ , & \delta\ (\mathit{lift}\ \bot) = \mathit{lift}\ \bot\ , \\ f\ (\mathit{lift}^2\ \bot) = \mathit{lift}^2\ \bot\ , & \gamma\ (\mathit{lift}^2\ \bot) = \mathit{lift}\ \bot\ , & \delta\ (\mathit{lift}^2\ \bot) = \mathit{lift}^2\ \bot\ . \end{array}$$

Then δ is the least projection such that $\gamma \circ f \sqsubseteq f \circ \delta$, but

$$\begin{array}{ll} (\gamma \circ f)\ \bot = \bot\ , & (f \circ \delta)\ \bot = \bot\ , \\ (\gamma \circ f)\ (\mathit{lift}\ \bot) = \bot\ , & (f \circ \delta)\ (\mathit{lift}\ \bot) = \bot\ , \\ (\gamma \circ f)\ (\mathit{lift}^2\ \bot) = \mathit{lift}\ \bot\ , & (f \circ \delta)\ (\mathit{lift}^2\ \bot) = \mathit{lift}^2\ \bot\ , \end{array}$$

that is, $\gamma \circ f \neq f \circ \delta$.

A continuous function may not even have a *least* backward abstraction. For example, there is no least backward abstraction of *parallel or*, defined by

$$\begin{array}{lcl} \mathit{Bool} & = & \{\mathit{true},\ \mathit{false}\}_\bot \\ \mathit{por} & \in & \mathit{Bool}\ \rightarrow\ \mathit{Bool}\ , \\ \mathit{por}\ (\bot,\ \mathit{lift\ false}) & = & \bot\ , \\ \mathit{por}\ (\mathit{lift\ false},\ \bot) & = & \bot\ , \\ \mathit{por}\ (\mathit{lift}\ u,\ \mathit{lift}\ v) & = & \mathit{lift}\ (u\ \vee\ v)\ . \end{array}$$

To see this, let δ_1 be the greatest projection such that $\delta_1\ (\mathit{lift\ true},\ \mathit{lift\ true}) = (\mathit{lift\ true},\ \bot)$, and δ_2 be the greatest projection such that $\delta_2\ (\mathit{lift\ true},\ \mathit{lift\ true}) = (\bot,\ \mathit{lift\ true})$. Then $\mathit{ID} \circ \mathit{por} \sqsubseteq \mathit{por} \circ \delta_1$ and $\mathit{ID} \circ \mathit{por} \sqsubseteq \mathit{por} \circ \delta_2$, but since $(\delta_1 \sqcap \delta_2)\ (\mathit{lift\ true},\ \mathit{lift\ true}) = (\bot,\ \bot)$, it is not true that $\mathit{ID} \circ \mathit{por} \sqsubseteq \mathit{por} \circ (\delta_1 \sqcap \delta_2)$. As will be discussed in Section 4, existence of least backward abstractions can be guaranteed by restricting the space of functions under consideration; in the meantime, we nonetheless try to find as small backward abstractions as possible.

Even when a function does not have a least backward abstraction, it may have *minimal* backward abstractions: a backward abstraction is minimal if no other backward abstraction approximates it. For example, *por* above has two minimal backward abstractions, determined by whether *ID* is mapped to a projection that maps (*lift true*, *lift true*) to ($\bot$, *lift true*), or to (*lift true*, $\bot$).

A minimal backward abstraction of a continuous function may not be monotonic. For example, the function $f = \lambda((x, y), (z, t)).(\mathit{por}\ x\ y,\ \mathit{por}\ z\ t)$ has non-monotonic minimal backward abstractions. To see this, let δ_1 be the least projection mapping (*lift true*, *lift true*) to ($\bot$, *lift true*) so that $\mathit{ID} \circ f \sqsubseteq f \circ \delta_1$, and δ_2 be the least projection mapping (*lift true*, *lift true*) to (*lift true*, $\bot$) so that $\mathit{ID} \circ f \sqsubseteq f \circ \delta_2$. Then δ_1 and δ_2 are incomparable, and there is a minimal backward abstraction of f that maps $\mathit{ID} \times \mathit{ID}$ to $\delta_1 \times \delta_2$ and $\mathit{ID} \times \mathit{BOT}$ to $\delta_2 \times \mathit{BOT}$.

A continuous function might not even have a minimal backward abstraction. Let f map infinite lists of $\mathbf{1}_\bot$ to $\mathbf{1}_\bot$, such that f returns *lift* $\bot$ if any element of its argument is *lift* $\bot$ and $\bot$ otherwise. (The function f is in fact computable: it is the least upper bound of the functions f_i, $1 \leq i \leq n$ where f_i returns the ith element of its argument. Operationally, this can be realised by simulating parallel reduction by diagonalisation: for each $i \geq 1$ starting with 1, reduce the ith cons cell and perform a single reduction step on the head of each of the first through i^{th} cons cells. If at any point a head cell reaches normal form (has value *lift* $\perp$), stop and return that value.) Now for each $i \geq 0$, let l_i be the list with the first i elements equal to $\perp$ and all subsequent elements equal to *lift* $\perp$, and let l_∞ be the infinite list of $\perp$. Define γ_i to be the greatest projection that maps l_0 to l_i, and γ_∞ to be the greatest projection that maps every l_i to l_∞. The important property of each γ_i is that it maps no list other than l_∞ to l_∞, so $ID \circ f = f \circ \gamma_i$ for all i. However, $\sqcap_{i\geq 0}\gamma_i = \gamma_\infty$, so $f \sqsupset f \circ \gamma_\infty$. Hence f has no minimal backward abstraction. We note that this is not a consequence of glb on projections differing from glb on continuous functions—here the glb is the same.

The following states that if we restrict ourselves to monotonic backward abstractions, then nothing is lost by the further restriction to continuous backwards abstractions.

Proposition 3.1
If τ is a monotonic backward abstraction of a continuous function f then there is a continuous backward abstraction $\tau' \sqsubseteq \tau$ of f.

Proof
In the following we write $f\ X$ to mean $\{f\ x \mid x \in X\}$ and similarly for functions of more than one argument. Let τ be a monotonic backward abstraction of a continuous function f. Then there is a unique continuous projection transformer τ' such that $\tau'\ \gamma = \tau\ \gamma$ for all finite γ, and $\tau' \sqsubseteq \tau$. To show that τ' is a backward abstraction of f we need only show that τ' meets the safety condition at infinite arguments. Now every infinite γ is the lub of some directed set X of finite elements, and $\bigsqcup(X \circ f) \sqsubseteq \bigsqcup(f \circ \tau'\ X)$, so $(\bigsqcup X) \circ f \sqsubseteq f \circ \tau'\ (\bigsqcup X)$ since τ', f, and function composition are continuous. $\square$

Corollary 3.2
Every minimal monotonic backward abstraction of a continuous function is continuous.

Henceforth we will only consider continuous backward abstractions.

Even when a strict function has a least (that is, most informative) backward abstraction, it may not be possible to determine that the function is strict from this backward abstraction. Consider all of the monotonic functions from $\mathbf{1}_\perp$ to $\mathbf{1}_\perp$, defined by

$$\begin{array}{lll} bot\ \perp = \perp, & id\ \perp = \perp, & top\ \perp = lift\ \perp, \\ bot\ (lift\ \perp) = \perp, & id\ (lift\ \perp) = lift\ \perp, & top\ (lift\ \perp) = lift\ \perp. \end{array}$$

There are only two projections on $\mathbf{1}_\perp$, namely *ID* and *BOT*. The least backward abstractions of *bot* and *top* are the same, the function that maps both *ID* and *BOT* to *BOT*, though *bot* is strict and *top* is not. (The least backward abstraction of *id* is the identity.) Further, so long as the result domain is not $\mathbf{1}$, no single backward abstraction can determine that a function is strict, since any backward abstraction of any function is a backward abstraction of $\lambda x.v$ for any v. This example also shows that the least backward abstraction (or set of all backward abstractions) of a function sometimes determines that function (here *id*) and sometimes does not (here *bot* and *top*).

Interestingly, if a function is head strict, then this fact is determined by some backward abstraction: the function that maps every projection to H is a backward abstraction of a head-strict function.

As shown in [4], by defining the projection STR on every lifted domain $U_\perp$ by

$$\begin{array}{lcl} STR\ \perp & = & \perp\,, \\ STR\ (\mathit{lift}\ \perp) & = & \perp\,, \\ STR\ (\mathit{lift}\ v) & = & \mathit{lift}\ v,\ \text{if}\ v \neq \perp\,, \end{array}$$

we have that f is strict if and only if $STR \circ f_\perp \sqsubseteq f_\perp \circ STR$. Put another way, a continuous function f is strict if and only if there is a continuous backward abstraction τ of $f_\perp$ such that $\tau\ STR \sqsubseteq STR$ (define $\tau\ \alpha = STR$ if $\alpha \sqsubseteq STR$, and $\tau\ \alpha = ID$ otherwise).

Besides ID, BOT, and STR, there is one further projection ABS defined on every lifted domain:

$$\begin{array}{lcl} ABS\ \perp & = & \perp\,, \\ ABS\ (\mathit{lift}\ v) & = & \mathit{lift}\ \perp\,. \end{array}$$

For all f we have $ABS \circ f_\perp \sqsubseteq f_\perp \circ ABS$.

So long as U differs from the one-point domain, projections ID, ABS, STR and BOT on $U_\perp$ are all distinct, and form a lattice in which ABS and STR are incomparable. All other projections on any lifted domain lie between ID and ABS, or between STR and BOT. In fact, there is an isomorphism between the lattice of projections between ID and ABS and the projections between STR and BOT. This isomorphism maps each projection between STR and BOT to its least upper bound with ABS; its inverse maps each projection between ID and ABS to its greatest lower bound with STR. Further, every projection in $|\,U_\perp\,|$ between ID and ABS is of the form $\gamma_\perp$, $\gamma \in |\,U\,|$. Hence every projection in $|\,U_\perp\,|$ is either of the form $\gamma_\perp$ or $\gamma_\perp \sqcap STR$. (A revealing observation is that $|\,U_\perp\,|$ is isomorphic to $|\,U\,| \times \mathbf{2}$, where $(\gamma,\ \perp)$ and $(\gamma,\ \mathit{lift}\ \perp)$ in the latter domain correspond to $\gamma_\perp \sqcap STR$ and $\gamma_\perp$ in the former, respectively.) To get the effect of lifting a projection and then taking its glb with STR we introduce the operator $\cdot_{\underline{\perp}}$, pronounced "strict lift", defined by

$$\begin{array}{lcl} \gamma_{\underline{\perp}}\ \perp & = & \perp\,, \\ \gamma_{\underline{\perp}}\ (\mathit{lift}\ \perp) & = & \perp\,, \\ \gamma_{\underline{\perp}}\ (\mathit{lift}\ v) & = & \mathit{lift}\ (\gamma\ v),\ \text{if}\ v \neq \perp\,. \end{array}$$

Then $\gamma_{\underline{\perp}} = \gamma_\perp \sqcap STR$, and $\gamma_\perp = \gamma_{\underline{\perp}} \sqcup ABS$. Further, we have $STR = ID_{\underline{\perp}}$ and $ABS = BOT_\perp$; together with the facts $BOT_{\underline{\perp}} = BOT$ and $ID_\perp = ID$ we can dispense with the special names STR and ABS.

As was shown for por, it does not follow from $\gamma \circ f \sqsubseteq f \circ \delta_1$ and $\gamma \circ f \sqsubseteq f \circ \delta_2$ that $\gamma \circ f \sqsubseteq f \circ (\delta_1 \sqcap \delta_2)$. However in the case when δ_1 is $ID_{\underline{\perp}}$ this does follow. This is trivially true if $\delta_2 \sqsubseteq ID_{\underline{\perp}}$. Otherwise:

Proposition 3.3
For continuous $f \in U_\perp \to V_\perp$ and projection γ, if $\gamma \circ f \sqsubseteq f \circ \delta_\perp$ and $\gamma \circ f \sqsubseteq f \circ ID_{\underline{\perp}}$, then $\gamma \circ f \sqsubseteq f \circ \delta_{\underline{\perp}}$.

Proof
Suppose that $\gamma \circ f \sqsubseteq f \circ \delta_\perp$ and $\gamma \circ f \sqsubseteq f \circ ID_{\underline{\perp}}$, then we need to show that $\gamma\ (f\ v) \sqsubseteq f\ (\delta_{\underline{\perp}}\ v)$ for all v. This clearly holds if $\delta_\perp\ v = \delta_{\underline{\perp}}\ v$. Suppose that $\delta_\perp\ v \neq \delta_{\underline{\perp}}\ v$. Then it must be that $lift\ \perp \sqsubseteq v$, and $\delta_\perp\ v = lift\ \perp$ and $\delta_{\underline{\perp}}\ v = \perp$. From $\gamma \circ f \sqsubseteq f \circ \delta_\perp$ and $\delta_\perp\ v = lift\ \perp$ we have $\gamma\ (f\ v) \sqsubseteq f\ (lift\ \perp)$; by monotonicity and $lift\ \perp \sqsubseteq v$ we have $\gamma\ (f\ (lift\ \perp)) \sqsubseteq \gamma\ (f\ v)$ and $f\ (lift\ \perp) \sqsubseteq f\ v$; all together:

$$\gamma\ (f\ (lift\ \perp)) \sqsubseteq \gamma\ (f\ v) \sqsubseteq f\ (lift\ \perp) \sqsubseteq f\ v\ .$$

Idempotence of γ requires that $\gamma\ (f\ (lift\ \perp)) = \gamma\ (f\ v)$. From $\gamma \circ f \sqsubseteq f \circ ID_{\underline{\perp}}$ we have $\gamma\ (f\ (lift\ \perp)) \sqsubseteq f\ \perp$, then by the last equality $\gamma\ (f\ v) \sqsubseteq f\ \perp$; finally since $\delta_{\underline{\perp}}\ v = \perp$ we have $\gamma\ (f\ v) \sqsubseteq f\ (\delta_{\underline{\perp}}\ v)$ as desired. □

Then we can show the following.

Corollary 3.4
If f is a strict continuous function and τ is any continuous backward abstraction of $f_\perp$, then there is a continuous backward abstraction τ' of $f_\perp$ such that $\tau' \sqsubseteq \tau$ and $\tau'\ ID_{\underline{\perp}} \sqsubseteq ID_{\underline{\perp}}$.

Proof
Since f is strict, $ID_{\underline{\perp}} \circ f_\perp \sqsubseteq f_\perp \circ ID_{\underline{\perp}}$. Define $\tau'\ \alpha$ to be $\tau\ \alpha$ if $BOT_\perp \sqsubseteq \alpha$, otherwise $(\tau\ \alpha) \sqcap ID_{\underline{\perp}}$. Then τ' is continuous, and by Proposition 3.3 and the previous discussion τ' is a backward abstraction of $f_\perp$. □

For any continuous function f, the function $f_\perp$ is strict and bottom reflecting. This follows from the fact that for all domains U and V, the operator $\cdot_\perp$ is an isomorphism between the domain of continuous functions $U \to V$ and the domain $U_\perp \stackrel{\text{sb}}{\to} V_\perp$ of continuous, strict, bottom-reflecting functions. Though the function $f_\perp$ contains no more information than f, projections on the argument and result domains of $f_\perp$, and hence a backward abstraction for $f_\perp$, may contain more information than those for f since the projections on the lifted domains have the additional degree of freedom to map values to the new bottom element. Intuitively, a value that is mapped to the new bottom element may be thought of as 'not sufficiently defined', or 'unacceptable'. Projections on lifted domains may then be regarded as giving lower bounds on the definedness of values in the corresponding unlifted domain, and thus lower bounds on the degree of evaluation of expressions that take values in the unlifted domains. For example, $STR \in |\,U_\perp\,|$ maps $lift\ \perp$ (which corresponds to $\perp$ in U) to $\perp$, indicating that $\perp$ in U is not an acceptable value. If expression `f` denotes function f, then $STR \circ f_\perp \sqsubseteq f_\perp \circ STR$ may be interpreted as "if the result of f must be more defined than $\perp$, then the argument of f must be more defined than $\perp$", that is, f is strict. Operationally, in any context in which it is safe (and in particular, necessary) to evaluate an application of `f`, then it is safe to evaluate its argument.

The backward abstractions of a function $f_\perp$ can reveal more than just simple strictness in f, as the following shows.

Proposition 3.5
Every continuous strict bottom-reflecting function is determined by its continuous backward abstractions.

In order to prove this theorem, we need some results regarding what we will call projection-based *forward analysis*, wherein the goal is, given function f and projection δ, to find projection γ such that $\gamma \circ f \sqsubseteq f \circ \delta$. Projection-based forward analysis is interesting in its own right, for example, Launchbury uses it in his study and implementation of partial evaluation [7]. Some further details on the power of forward analysis may be found in [6].

A projection transformer τ is a *forward abstraction* of f if for all δ we have $(\tau\ \delta) \circ f \sqsubseteq f \circ \delta$. Then

Proposition 3.6
Every continuous function has a greatest forward abstraction, and it is continuous.

Proof
Let f and δ be fixed. Let X be the set of projections γ such that $\gamma \circ f \sqsubseteq f \circ \delta$. Since X is not empty (it always contains BOT), $\bigsqcup X$ always exists. So

$$\begin{array}{rcll} (\bigsqcup X) \circ f & = & \bigsqcup(X \circ f) & \text{[continuity } \circ] \\ & \sqsubseteq & f \circ \delta & \text{[safety condition]} \end{array}$$

Since lub in the lattice of projections and lub for projections in the domain of continuous functions is the same, $\bigsqcup X$ is the greatest projection satisfying the safety condition.

Now we show that the greatest forward abstraction τ of f is continuous. It is clear that τ is monotonic. Let X be a directed set of projections on the argument domain of f. The image of a directed set under a monotonic function is directed, so $\tau\ X$ is directed, and $\bigsqcup(\tau\ X) \sqsubseteq \tau\ (\bigsqcup X)$. On the other hand, by the definition of τ we have $\tau\ (\bigsqcup X) \sqsubseteq f \circ (\bigsqcup X)$, so by the continuity of composition $\tau\ (\bigsqcup X) \sqsubseteq \bigsqcup(f \circ X)$, hence by algebraicity there is some $\delta \in X$ such that $\tau\ (\bigsqcup X) \sqsubseteq \bigsqcup(f \circ \delta)$, so $\tau\ (\bigsqcup X) \sqsubseteq \tau\ \delta$, hence $\tau\ (\bigsqcup X) \sqsubseteq \bigsqcup(\tau\ X)$. We conclude that $\bigsqcup(\tau\ X) = \tau\ (\bigsqcup X)$, and hence that τ is continuous. □

Proposition 3.7
Every continuous strict bottom-reflecting function is determined by its greatest forward abstraction.

Proof
Let $f \in U \rightarrow V$ be continuous, strict, and bottom reflecting, and let τ be the greatest forward abstraction of f. Then $\tau \in |U| \rightarrow |V|$. Given domain T, For all $c \in T$ let $\gamma_c \in |T|$ be defined by

$$\begin{array}{l} \gamma_c\ x = \bot, \text{ if } x \sqsubseteq c\ , \\ \gamma_c\ x = x, \text{ if } x \not\sqsubseteq c\ . \end{array}$$

It is not hard to see that for $x \in U$, it must be that $\tau\ \gamma_x = \gamma_{(f\ x)}$. Since $\gamma_c = \gamma_d$ iff $c = d$, it is straightforward to reconstruct f from τ. □

Proposition 3.8
The greatest forward abstraction of a continuous function is determined by its continuous backward abstractions.

Proof
First we observe that $\gamma \circ f \sqsubseteq f \circ \delta$ if and only if there exists a continuous backward abstraction τ such that $\delta = \tau\ \gamma$ (define $\tau\ \beta$ to be δ if $\beta \sqsubseteq \gamma$ and ID otherwise). Second, if X is the set of projections γ such that $\gamma \circ f \sqsubseteq f \circ \delta$, then as shown in the proof of Proposition 3.6, the greatest forward abstraction of f maps δ to $\bigsqcup X$. □

Proof of Proposition 3.5
That a continuous strict bottom-reflecting function is determined by its continuous backward abstractions follows from the fact that function is determined by its greatest forward abstraction, which is in turn determined by its continuous backward abstractions. □

Often we work with functions with argument domains that are finite (e.g. *Bool*) or of finite depth (e.g. $Int = \mathbf{Z}_\bot$).

Corollary 3.9
Every monotonic, strict, bottom-reflecting function $f \in U \to V$ such that U is of finite depth is determined by its minimal backward abstractions.

For example, $por_\bot$ is determined by its two minimal backward abstractions.

Following we show a dual to the fact that the greatest forward abstraction of a function is determined by its backward abstractions.

Proposition 3.10
The set of backward abstractions of a continuous function is determined by its greatest forward abstraction.

Proof
Let τ' be the greatest forward abstraction of a function f. Then the projection transformer τ is a backward abstraction of f if and only if $\tau' \circ \tau \sqsupseteq id$. □

Hence the greatest forward abstraction of a function contains the same information as its set of backward abstractions.

We now briefly relate this to reversal of abstract interpretations [9]. If τ' is any forward abstraction of a continuous function f then any τ such that $\tau' \circ \tau \sqsupseteq id$ is a backward abstraction of f. Similary, if τ is any backward abstraction of f then any τ' such that $\tau \circ \tau' \sqsubseteq id$ is a forward abstraction of f. In particular, when τ' is the greatest forward abstraction of f, the set of projection transformers τ such that $\tau' \circ \tau \sqsupseteq id$ is a *relational reversal* of τ', and contains the same information as τ'. In general this set cannot be characterised by a single element, that is, a value τ such that $\tau' \circ \tau \sqsupseteq id$ and $\tau \circ \tau' \sqsubseteq id$—such a τ would be the least backward abstraction of f. When a least backward abstraction τ exists, τ' and τ form a *Galois connection*. Propositions 3.7 and 3.10 can be shown to follow in part from the more general theory of reversal of abstract interpretations—the only significant difference is that we work with infinite rather than finite lattices and so consider continuity in addition to monotonicity.

In general, when we wish to determine strictness properties of some function f we will find backward abstractions of $f_\bot$ rather than of f. Following is a first step in this direction.

Fact 3.11
For all f we have $\gamma \circ f \sqsubseteq f \circ \delta$ iff $\gamma_{\perp} \circ f_{\perp} \sqsubseteq f_{\perp} \circ \delta_{\perp}$.

So, given a backward abstraction of a function f we may readily derive a backward abstraction τ of $f_{\perp}$—we may safely take $\tau\gamma_{\underline{\perp}} = \delta$ when $\tau\ \gamma_{\perp} = \delta$. Though this takes no advantage of the lifting, it does say that no information available via a backward abstraction is lost by lifting, since $\cdot_{\perp}$ on functions is an injection. That $BOT \circ f \sqsubseteq f \circ BOT$ allows the following improvement. For any monotonic backward abstraction τ of f, and τ' defined by $\tau'\ BOT = BOT$ and $\tau'\ \gamma = \tau\ \gamma$ for $\gamma \neq BOT$, we have τ' is a monotonic backward abstraction of f and $\tau' \sqsubseteq \tau$.

Proposition 3.12
If τ is a continuous backward abstraction of a continuous function f, then there is a strict continuous backward abstraction τ' of f such that $\tau' \sqsubseteq \tau$. Hence every minimal monotonic backward abstraction of a continuous function is strict and continuous.

Since every monotonic backward abstraction of a continuous function is approximated by a strict continuous backward abstraction, we restrict our attention to the strict continuous projection transformers, which form a sublattice of the lattice of projection transformers.

The following proposition and its proof come from [4].

Proposition 3.13
If $\gamma_{\underline{\perp}} \circ f_{\perp} \sqsubseteq f_{\perp} \circ \delta$ then $\gamma_{\perp} \circ f_{\perp} \sqsubseteq f_{\perp} \circ (\delta \sqcup BOT_{\perp})$.

Proof

$$
\begin{array}{lll}
 & \gamma_{\perp} \circ f_{\perp} & \\
= & (\gamma_{\underline{\perp}} \sqcup BOT_{\perp}) \circ f_{\perp} & [\text{defn } \cdot_{\underline{\perp}}] \\
= & (\gamma_{\underline{\perp}} \circ f_{\perp}) \sqcup (BOT_{\perp} \circ f_{\perp}) & [\text{defn } \sqcup] \\
\sqsubseteq & (f_{\perp} \circ \delta) \sqcup (f_{\perp} \circ BOT_{\perp}) & [BOT_{\perp} \circ f_{\perp} \sqsubseteq f_{\perp} \circ BOT_{\perp}] \\
= & f_{\perp} \circ (\delta \sqcup BOT_{\perp}) & [\text{defn } \sqcup]
\end{array}
$$

□

Thus, in defining a backward abstraction τ of a function $f_{\perp}$, if $\gamma_{\underline{\perp}} \circ f_{\perp} \sqsubseteq f_{\perp} \circ \delta$ then it is safe to take $\tau\ \gamma_{\perp} = \delta \sqcup BOT_{\perp}$. Not only is this safe, but as we show, it is the right choice. Let a projection transformer τ have the *guard property* if when $\tau\ \gamma_{\underline{\perp}} = \delta$, then $\tau\ \gamma_{\perp} = \delta \sqcup BOT_{\perp}$. (In [4], an operator "guard" is defined to facilitate definition of strict projection transformers with the guard property. Here we have separated the issues.)

Fact 3.14
If τ is a backward abstraction of a continuous function $f_{\perp}$, then for all γ the projection $\tau\ \gamma_{\perp}$ has the form $\delta_{\perp}$ for some δ.

Proposition 3.15
If τ is a continuous backward abstraction of a continuous function $f_{\perp}$, then there is a strict continuous backward abstraction τ' of f with the guard property such that $\tau' \sqsubseteq \tau$.

Proof
Let τ be a continuous backward abstraction of a continuous function $f_\perp$, and define τ' by

$$\begin{array}{lll} \tau'\ BOT_{\underline{\perp}} & = & BOT_{\underline{\perp}} \\ \tau'\ \gamma_{\underline{\perp}} & = & \tau\ \gamma_{\underline{\perp}},\ \text{if}\ \gamma \neq BOT \\ \tau'\ \gamma_{\perp} & = & \tau\ \gamma_{\underline{\perp}} \sqcup BOT_{\perp}\ . \end{array}$$

Then τ' is a strict continuous backward abstraction of $f_\perp$ with the guard property. Now for all γ we have

$$\begin{array}{lll} & \gamma_{\underline{\perp}} \sqsubseteq \gamma_{\perp} & [\text{defns } \cdot_{\perp},\ \cdot_{\underline{\perp}}] \\ \Rightarrow & \tau\ \gamma_{\underline{\perp}} \sqsubseteq \tau\ \gamma_{\perp} & [\text{monotonicity } \tau] \\ \Rightarrow & (\tau\ \gamma_{\underline{\perp}}) \sqcup BOT_{\perp} \sqsubseteq (\tau\ \gamma_{\perp}) \sqcup BOT_{\perp} & [\text{monotonicity } \sqcup] \\ \Rightarrow & (\tau\ \gamma_{\underline{\perp}}) \sqcup BOT_{\perp} \sqsubseteq \tau\ \gamma_{\perp} & [\text{Fact 3.14}] \\ \Rightarrow & \tau'\ \gamma_{\perp} \sqsubseteq \tau\ \gamma_{\perp} & [\text{defn } \tau'] \end{array}$$

So $\tau' \sqsubseteq \tau$ as required. □

Corollary 3.16
Every minimal monotonic backward abstraction of a continuous function $f_\perp$ is strict, continuous, and has the guard property.

We conclude that for continuous functions, it is sensible to restrict attention to strict continuous backward abstractions, and for continuous, strict, bottom-reflecting functions from lifted domains to lifted domains, to restrict attention to strict, continuous backward abstractions with the guard property. Just as the space $U_\perp \overset{sb}{\to} V_\perp$ of strict and bottom-reflecting continuous functions is a subdomain of the domain of continuous functions $U_\perp \to V_\perp$, the space $|\,V_\perp\,| \overset{sg}{\to} |\,U_\perp\,|$ of strict continuous projection transformers with the guard property is a sublattice of the continuous projection transformers $|\,V_\perp\,| \to |\,U_\perp\,|$: it is isomorphic to $|\,V\,| \overset{s}{\to} |\,U_\perp\,|$, where $\overset{s}{\to}$ contructs the domain of strict continuous functions.

4 Stability and Backward Analysis

As shown, an arbitrary continuous function may not have a least backward abstraction, or even a minimal backward abstraction. However, least backward abstractions always exist for *stable* functions. The theory of stability was developed by Berry [8] in an attempt to extend the characterisation of *sequential* functions to include higher order functions. At first order the stable functions are a superset of the sequential functions, and this is hypothesised to be the case at higher order.

Definition
A continuous function f is *stable* if for all x and y such that $y \sqsubseteq f\ x$, there exists a least value $M(f,x,y) \sqsubseteq x$ such that $y \sqsubseteq f\ (M(f,x,y))$.

The simplest function that is continuous but not stable is $f \in \mathbf{1}_\perp \times \mathbf{1}_\perp$ where f maps $(\perp,\perp)$ to $\perp$ and all other arguments to *lift* $\perp$—here *lift* $\perp \sqsubseteq f\ (\mathit{lift}\ \perp, \mathit{lift}\ \perp)$ but there is no least x such that *lift* $\perp \sqsubseteq f\ x$. However, parallel-or is regarded as the archetypical non-stable function, and it plays an important role in the development of the theory of stability. In fact, at first order the stable functions are a superset of the sequential functions: an example (due to Berry) of a function that is stable but not sequential is the least monotonic function h such that h (*lift true*, *lift false*, $\bot$) $=$ h ($\bot$, *lift true*, *lift false*) $=$ h (*lift false*, $\bot$, *lift true*) $=$ *lift true*. Note that h is not the three-argument analog of parallel-or (which is not stable), since h (*lift false*, *lift true*, $\bot$) $= \bot$.

A well-known and useful consequence of the definition of stability is the following.

Proposition 4.1
Given stable f, for all x_1, x_2 such that there exists y such that $x_1,\ x_2 \sqsubseteq y$, we have $f\ (x_1 \sqcap x_2) = (f\ x_1) \sqcap (f\ x_2)$.

Proof
We have $f\ x_1 \sqcap f\ x_2 \sqsubseteq f\ y$ (monotonicity of f), so there is a least $x' \sqsubseteq y$ such that $f\ x_1 \sqcap f\ x_2 \sqsubseteq f\ x'$. Since $x_1,\ x_2 \sqsubseteq y$ it must be that $x' \sqsubseteq x_1,\ x_2$ and hence $x' \sqsubseteq x_1 \sqcap x_2$, so $f\ (x_1 \sqcap x_2) \sqsupseteq (f\ x_1) \sqcap (f\ x_2)$. However, $f\ (x_1 \sqcap x_2) \sqsubseteq f\ x_1,\ f\ x_2$, so $f\ (x_1 \sqcap x_2) \sqsubseteq (f\ x_1) \sqcap (f\ x_2)$. We conclude that $f\ (x_1 \sqcap x_2) = (f\ x_1) \sqcap (f\ x_2)$.
□

Proposition 4.2
Every stable function has a least backward abstraction.

Proof
Let $f \in U \to V$ be a stable function and $\gamma \in |V|$ be fixed. Since f is stable there is a least function δ such that $\gamma \circ f \sqsubseteq f \circ \delta$. Clearly δ is weaker than the identity; to show that it is a projection we show that it is monotonic, continuous, and idempotent, in that order.

Let $x,\ y \in U$, with $x \sqsubseteq y$. Now

$$\begin{array}{rcll} \gamma\ (f\ x) & \sqsubseteq & \gamma\ (f\ y) & [\text{monotonicity } f \text{ and } \gamma] \\ & \sqsubseteq & f\ (\delta\ y) & [\text{definition } \delta] \end{array}$$

Since $\delta\ a$ is the least value below a such that $\gamma\ (f\ a) \sqsubseteq f\ (\delta\ a)$, it cannot be that $\delta\ a$ is larger than $\delta\ b$. If $\delta\ a$ were incomparable to $\delta\ b$, then $\delta\ a \sqcap \delta\ b$ would be strictly smaller than $\delta\ a$ or $\delta\ b$, and

$$\begin{array}{cll} & f\ (\delta\ a \sqcap \delta\ b) & \\ = & f\ (\delta\ a) \sqcap f\ (\delta\ b) & [\delta\ a \sqsubseteq a,\ \delta\ b \sqsubseteq b,\ f \text{ stable}] \\ \sqsupseteq & \gamma\ (f\ a) \sqcap \gamma\ (f\ b) & [\text{definition } \delta, \text{ property } \sqcap] \\ = & \gamma\ (f\ a) & [\text{monotonicity of } f] \end{array}$$

contrary to $\delta\ a$ being least. Hence $\delta\ a \sqsubseteq \delta\ b$ and we conclude that δ is monotonic.

Let $X \subseteq V$ be a directed set. Since δ is monotonic, $\delta\ X$ is directed, and $\delta\ (\bigsqcup X) \sqsupseteq \sqcup\ (\delta\ X)$ again since δ is monotonic. Now

$$\begin{array}{cll} & \gamma\ (f\ (\bigsqcup X)) & \\ = & \sqcup\ (\gamma\ (f\ X)) & [\text{continuity } f,\ \gamma] \\ \sqsubseteq & \sqcup\ (f\ (\delta\ X)) & [f,\ \delta \text{ monotonic},\ \gamma \circ f \sqsubseteq f \circ \delta] \\ = & f\ (\sqcup\ (\delta\ X)) & [f \text{ continuous}] \\ \sqsubseteq & f\ (\delta\ (\bigsqcup X)) & [\delta \text{ monotonic}]\ . \end{array}$$

Since $\delta\ (\bigsqcup X)$ is by definition the least value weaker than $\bigsqcup X$ such that $\gamma\ (f\ (\bigsqcup X)) \sqsubseteq f\ (\delta\ (\bigsqcup X))$, and $\sqcup\ (\delta\ X) \sqsubseteq \bigsqcup X$ (since δ is weaker then the identity), it must be that $\sqcup\ (\delta\ X) = \bigsqcup X$. We conclude that δ is continuous.

Let $x \in V$, then $\gamma\ (f\ x) \sqsubseteq f\ (\delta\ x)$. Now $\delta\ (\delta\ x)$ is by definition the least value bounded above by $\delta\ x$ such that $\gamma\ (f\ (\delta\ x)) \sqsubseteq f\ (\delta\ (\delta\ x))$. Since $\gamma \circ f \circ \delta = \gamma \circ f$, it must be that $\delta\ (\delta\ x)$ is the least value bounded above by $\delta\ x$ such that $\gamma\ (f\ x) \sqsubseteq f\ (\delta\ (\delta\ x))$. However, $\delta\ x$ is the least value bounded above by x such that $\gamma\ (f\ x) \sqsubseteq f\ (\delta\ x)$; hence it must be that $\delta\ x = \delta\ (\delta\ x)$, and we conclude that δ is idempotent.

Thus the projection δ is the least function such that $\gamma \circ f \sqsubseteq f \circ \delta$. It follows that there is a least function τ such that $\gamma \circ f \sqsubseteq f \circ (\tau\ \gamma)$ for all G. It is clear that τ is monotonic; Proposition 3.1 tells us that τ is continuous. □

We write $|\,f\,|$ to denote the least backward abstraction of f.

Proposition 4.3
Every stable function f is determined by the least backward abstraction of $f_\perp$.

Proof
Proposition 3.8 tells us that the greatest forward abstraction of a stable function is determined by its least backward abstraction. If f is stable then so is $f_\perp$, so by Proposition 3.7 f is determined by the least backward abstraction of $f_\perp$. □

The safety condition for backward abstractions of continuous functions is not monotonic in the following sense. Recall the definitions *bot*, *id*, and *top*. The least backward abstractions of *bot* and *top* are $\lambda\alpha.BOT$, and the least backward abstraction of *id* is $\lambda\alpha.\alpha$, so there are backward abstractions of both *bot* and *top* that are not safe for *id*. More generally, if τ is a backward abstraction of f and τ' is a backward abstraction of f', and $f \sqsubseteq f'$, then it is not generally the case that either τ' is a backward abstraction of f or that τ is a backward abstraction of f'. Since *bot*, *id*, and *top* are stable, this example shows that the mapping to least backward abstractions is not monotonic under the usual function ordering. However, the mapping is monotonic when the ordering on the argument domain is the *stable* ordering.

Definition
For stable f and g the stable ordering $\sqsubseteq_s$ is defined by $f \sqsubseteq_s g$ iff $f \sqsubseteq g$ and for all x, y, if $y \sqsubseteq f\ x$ then $M(f,x,y) = M(g,x,y)$.

Proposition 4.4
For all stable functions f and g, we have that, $f \sqsubseteq_s g$ implies $|\,f\,| \sqsubseteq |\,g\,|$.

Proof
Let $f,\ g \in U \to V$ be stable functions with $f \sqsubseteq_s g$, and let $\gamma \in |\,V\,|$. Then by the definition of $\sqsubseteq_s$ we have $f \sqsubseteq g$ and for all x we have $M(f,x,\gamma\ (f\ x)) = M(g,x,\gamma\ (f\ x))$. Now since $f \sqsubseteq g$ we have $\gamma\ (f\ x) \sqsubseteq \gamma\ (g\ x)$, so that $M(f,x,\gamma\ (f\ x)) \sqsubseteq M(g,x,\gamma\ (g\ x))$, since M is monotonic in its third argument. Since $M(f,x,\gamma\ (f\ x)) = |\,f\,|\ \gamma\ x$, and similarly for g, we have that $f \sqsubseteq_s g$ implies $|\,f\,| \sqsubseteq |\,g\,|$ □

For example, for *bot*, *id*, and *top* as defined before we have $bot \sqsubset_s id$, $bot \sqsubset_s top$, but $id \not\sqsubseteq_s top$ and $top \not\sqsubseteq_s id$.

5 Two Implications for Real Analyses

We identify two sources of imprecision in the first-order projection-based backward strictness analysis of Wadler and Hughes [4] and show how they can be eliminated by making the analysis relational. In essence, given a function definition denoting a function f in the standard semantics, their analysis determines a projection transformer that is (isomorphic to) a backward abstraction of $f_\perp$.

The first source of imprecision is the the treatment of non-stable functions such as *por*. As we have seen two backward abstractions are required to determine $por_\perp$, and in general a continuous functions from domains which are finite (as are all of the abstract domains in implemented analysers) have more than one minimal backward abstraction. Equivalently, a continuous function f is determined by a function τ mapping projections γ to sets of projections $\{\delta_i\}$ such that $\gamma \circ f_\perp \sqsubseteq f_\perp \circ \delta_i$ for all i, and for functions from finite domains these sets are finite and are characterised by their minimal elements. Taking the upward closures of these sets gives functions from domains of projections to powerdomains of projections.

A second source of imprecision is the treatment of products. Ignoring for the moment the issue of lifted domains, given a projection γ on pairs from $U_1 \times U_2$ we seek to find δ_1 and δ_2 satisfying the safety condition $\gamma\ (x_1, x_2) \sqsubseteq (\delta_1\ x_1, \delta_2\ x_2)$. Their solution is to define

$$
\begin{aligned}
\delta_1\ x &= \sqcup_y\ \mathit{fst}\ (\gamma\ (x, y))\ , \\
\delta_2\ y &= \sqcup_x\ \mathit{snd}\ (\gamma\ (x, y))\ .
\end{aligned}
$$

In fact $\delta_1 \times \delta_2$ is the least element of $|\,U_1\,| \times |\,U_2\,| \subseteq |\,U_1 \times U_2\,|$ such that $\gamma \sqsubseteq \delta_1 \times \delta_2$. Factoring the projection in this way makes defining the non-standard semantics straightforward since it allows projections to be propogated 'backward' down expressions, but it loses information. However, every element of $|\,U_1 \times U_2\,|$ is characterised by a set of elements from $|\,U_1\,| \times |\,U_2\,|$ as follows.

Proposition 5.1
Let $\gamma \in |\,U_1 \times U_2\,|$. Let $\gamma' = \bigsqcup\{\delta_1 \times \delta_2 \in |\,U_1 \times U_2\,|,\ \delta_1 \times \delta_2 \sqsubseteq \gamma\}$ Then $\gamma = \gamma'$.

Proof
Certainly $\gamma' \sqsubseteq \gamma$. For any x and y let $(x', y') = \gamma\ (x, y)$. For any z and z' such that $z' \sqsubseteq z$ define $p(z, z')$ to be the least projection such that $p(z, z')\ z = z'$. Then $p(x, x') \times p(y, y')\ (x, y) = (x', y')$. Define

$$
q(x, y) = p(x,\ \mathit{fst}\ (\gamma\ (x, y))) \times p(y,\ \mathit{snd}\ (\gamma\ (x, y)))\ .
$$

Then $\gamma = \sqcup_{x,y} q(x, y)$, and since for all x and y we have $q(x, y) \sqsubseteq \gamma$, it must be that $\gamma' = \gamma$. A similar construction may be done using glb instead of lub. □

Let us call projections on products that can be expressed as products of projections *independent* projections. Then any projection transformer can be characterised by a function from sets of independent projections to sets of independent projections. Putting these two observations together, we have that any continuous, strict, bottom-reflecting function is determined by a function from a power domain of independent projections to a power-power domain (sets of sets) of projections. In fact we can do better than this; the construction of least backward abstractions of stable functions in [6] shows that every stable, strict, bottom-reflecting functions is determined by a function from a domain of independent projections to a powerdomain of independent projections, and every continuous, strict, bottom-reflecting functions is determined by a function from a domain of independent projections to a power-power domain of independent projections. Though this might greatly increase the sizes of the domains involved, it is conceivable that these ideas could be practically exploited in a restricted form, e.g. in a *locally relational* analysis [9].

References

[1] Wray, S. "A new strictness detection algorithm." In *Proceedings of the Workshop in Implementation of Functional Languages* (Aspenäs, Sweden). L. Augustsson et. al., eds. Report 17, Programming Methodology Group, Department of Computer Sciences, Chalmers University of Technology and University of Göteborg, Göteborg, Sweden.

[2] Augustsson, L. and Johnson, T. "The Chalmers Lazy ML Compiler." Department of Computer Science, Chalmers University of Technology, Göteborg, Sweden, 1988.

[3] Burn, G.L., "Using Projection Analysis in Compiling Lazy Functional Programs", *Proceedings of the 1990 ACM Conference on Lisp and Functional Programming,* ACM, 1990.

[4] Wadler, P., and Hughes, J. "Projections for Strictness Analysis." In *Proceedings of Functional Programming Languages and Computer Architecture* (Portland, Oregon). G. Kahn, ed. LNCS 274. Springer-Verlag, Berlin, 1987.

[5] Hunt, S. *Projection analysis and stable functions.* Unfinished manuscript.

[6] Davis, K. "A Note on the Choice of Domains for Projection-Based Program Analysis." In *Functional Programming: Proceedings of the 1991 Glasgow Workshop, 13-15 August 1991, Isle of Skye, Scotland.* P. Wadler *et al.*, eds. Springer Workshops in Computing. Springer-Verlag, 1992.

[7] Launchbury, J. *Projection Factorisations in Partial Evaluation.* PhD Thesis, Glasgow University, Nov 89. Distinguished Dissertation in Computer Science, Vol 1, CUP, 1991.

[8] Berry, G. "Stable models of typed lambda-calculi." In *Proceedings of the 5th ICALP* pp 375-387, LNCS 62. Springer-Verlag, Berlin, 1978.

[9] Hughes, R.J.M. and Launchbury, J. "Relational Reversal of Abstract Interpretation." In ??.

Abstract Interpretation of Higher Order Functions using Concrete Data Structures (Summary)

A. B. Ferguson
University of Glasgow
Scotland

John Hughes
Chalmers University of Technology
Göteborg, Sweden

Abstract

An implementation of abstract interpretation is outlined, which uses techniques taken from work on semantics of sequential languages. For a familiar example, analysis is much faster than with the frontiers method.

1 Introduction

The high computational cost of abstract interpretation is almost proverbial. This is unfortunate, since such techniques are often vaunted as being of potentially great practical value in compilers; in particular strictness analysis, which it is hoped will reduce the not inconsiderable overhead of lazy evaluation.

A key difficulty in implementing abstract interpretation is testing approximations to fix-points for convergence. It is not sufficient to test for equality at the desired points, since these may depend on other parts of the fix-point. Thus in general, each approximation must be completely evaluated to test for equality. Where a large higher-order type is involved, these may become very expensive to compute. This is a common drawback of other techniques, such as the frontiers method [4], which we seek to overcome.

Our idea is as follows: if we choose a representation which makes the dependencies of a function on its argument explicit, this will enable us to annotate each approximation to a fix-point with the parts of the previous approximation on which it depended. This information is sufficient to allow a local test for convergence, potentially allowing earlier convergence in some places, and avoid evaluating unused portions of the fixpoint.

2 Concrete Data Structures

Concrete data structures (CDSs) are a model of programming language terms, developed in the context of constructing fully abstract semantics for sequential languages. We will assume the reader has a working knowledge of this work, although we shall reprise some key points. See for example, the work of Berry and Curien [1], hereafter B&C. A particularly significant class of CDSs are those for function types which represent *sequential algorithms*. The CDSs we consider are restricted to a similarly defined class, although not equivalent for reasons discussed later.

Following B&C, we define a CDS to be a 4-tuple $(C, V, E, \vdash)$, of *cells* (C), *values* (V), *events* $(E \subseteq C \times V)$, and an *enabling relation* $(\vdash \subseteq \mathcal{P}(E) \times C)$ between sets of events, and cells. A cell is said to be *enabled* by one of a number of possible sets of events, if such a set and the cell are in the enabling relation. A *state* x of type T is a *consistent* set of events, that is, for all c, if $(c, v), (c, v') \in x$ then $v = v'$, of which every cell is enabled: if c is filled in x, then $x' \vdash c$ for some $x' \subseteq x$. We will say a cell c is *filled* in a state x, if for some v, $(c, v) \in x$, and define $access_T\, x$ to be the set of c not filled in x such that for some v, $x \cup \{(c, v)\}$ is a state of T.

All states we consider are trees, which is important in that it will allow a convenient representation in our implementation. A term is here represented by a state, each constituent event of which may be thought of as being an atom of information: the cell represents how much is known, the value, what is known. Descending the tree therefore corresponds to increasing knowledge about the value represented. When we come to consider the CDS for a function type, discovering more may mean either finding out more of the result, or of dependency on its argument.

We will consider the particular example of strictness analysis, using the framework of B.H.A. [2], and Wadler's four point domain for lists [8]. We will represent a state of the CDS for each of the requisite abstract types as follows: for the type $\mathbf{2}$, we use a single cell, containing $\mathbf{0}$ or $\mathbf{1}$; and for $T_\perp$, a state of the CDS for T, plus a new root cell, containing $\perp$ or $\top$. A product of type $T \times U$ will be represented by a state of T paired with a state of U. Finally, for function types, a decision tree is used, in which each event may be filled by either a question about the argument (a *valof* value), or production of part of the result (*output* value).

Firstly, we define the following language of values and cells.

$$\begin{array}{rcl} \textit{value} & ::= & \mathbf{0} \mid \mathbf{1} \mid \perp \mid \top \mid \text{output } \textit{value} \mid \text{valof } \textit{cell} \\ \textit{cell} & ::= & \bullet \mid \diamond \mid \text{lift } \textit{cell} \mid \text{fst } \textit{cell} \mid \text{snd } \textit{cell} \mid (\textit{state}, \textit{cell}) \\ \textit{event} & ::= & (\textit{cell}, \textit{value}) \end{array}$$

For each abstract type T, the corresponding CDS is given by $(C_T, V_T, E_T, \vdash_T)$:

$$\begin{array}{rcl} C_{\mathbf{2}} & = & \{\bullet\} \\ V_{\mathbf{2}} & = & \{\mathbf{0}, \mathbf{1}\} \\ E_{\mathbf{2}} & = & C_{\mathbf{2}} \times V_{\mathbf{2}} \\ & \vdash_{\mathbf{2}} & \bullet \end{array}$$

$$\begin{array}{rcl} C_{T_\perp} & = & \{\diamond\} \cup \{\text{lift } c : c \in C_T\} \\ V_{T_\perp} & = & \{\perp, \top\} \cup V_T \\ E_{T_\perp} & = & \{(\diamond, \perp), (\diamond, \top)\} \cup \{(\text{lift } c, v) : (c, v) \in E_T\} \\ & \vdash_{T_\perp} & \diamond \\ (\diamond, \top) & \vdash_{T_\perp} & \text{lift } c, \text{ iff } \vdash_T c \\ (\text{lift } c', v) & \vdash_{T_\perp} & \text{lift } c, \text{ iff } (c', v) \vdash_T c \end{array}$$

$$
\begin{array}{rcl}
C_{T\times U} & = & \{\text{fst } c : c \in C_T\} \cup \{\text{snd } c : c \in C_U\} \\
V_{T\times U} & = & V_T \cup V_U \\
E_{T\times U} & = & E_T \cup E_U \\
 & \vdash_{T\times U} & \text{fst } c, \text{ iff } \vdash_T c \\
 & \vdash_{T\times U} & \text{snd } c, \text{ iff } \vdash_U c \\
(\text{fst } c', v) & \vdash_{T\times U} & \text{fst } c, \text{ iff } (c', v) \vdash_T c \\
(\text{snd } c', v) & \vdash_{T\times U} & \text{snd } c, \text{ iff } (c', v) \vdash_U c
\end{array}
$$

$$
\begin{array}{rcl}
C_{T\to U} & = & \{(x, c') : x \text{ a (finite) state of } T, c' \in C_U\} \\
V_{T\to U} & = & \{\text{valof } c : c \in C_T\} \cup \{\text{output } v' : v' \in V_U\} \\
E_{T\to U} & = & \{((x, c'), \text{valof } c) : c \in \mathit{access}_T\, x\} \\
 & & \cup\{((x, c'), \text{output } v') : (c', v) \in E_U\} \\
((x, c'), \text{valof } c) & \vdash_{T\to U} & (y, c'), \text{ iff for some } v, y = x \cup \{(c, v)\} \\
 & \vdash_{T\to U} & ((\emptyset, c'), \text{output } v), \text{ iff } \vdash_U c' \\
((x, c''), \text{output } v) & \vdash_{T\to U} & (x, c'), \text{ iff } c'' \vdash_U c'
\end{array}
$$

Note that the function and product CDSs are simply those of B&C, restricted to at most a single event in the enabling relation, which slightly simplifies the latter, since we do not have to consider a non-tree result CDS.

It is worth commenting on our choice of CDS for the type **2** (and similarly, the values in the root cell of lifted states). The more usual construction would be that with one cell, and only one value (**1**), with **0** being represented by an empty state, that is, the empty set of events. Firstly this is because we require an explicit representation of bottom values to effectively represent abstract functions. Furthermore, some abstract functions would not be representable if we were to choose to merely introduce a special constant to represent bottom as a state, although this would be a perfectly valid choice in the world of concrete (that is, in the usual sense of 'non-abstract') functions. This is indeed the approach we have taken in such a context [3].

The principle example of such a function is *lub*, that is $\mathit{lub}\,\mathbf{0}\,\mathbf{0} = \mathbf{0}; \mathit{lub}\,\mathbf{1}\,b = \mathbf{1}; \mathit{lub}\,a\,\mathbf{1} = \mathbf{1}$. The presence of this construct amongst our primitive operations means that (abstract) functions may inspect part of their argument, discover it to be bottom, and yet still return a non-bottom result. This might the represented by the following state of the CDS of type $(\mathbf{2} \times \mathbf{2}) \to \mathbf{2}$:

$$
\begin{array}{l}
\{((\emptyset, \bullet), \text{valof}\,(\text{fst}\bullet)), \\
\qquad ((\{(\text{fst}\bullet, \mathbf{0})\}, \bullet), \text{valof}\,(\text{snd}\bullet)), \\
\qquad\qquad ((\{(\text{fst}\bullet, \mathbf{0}), (\text{snd}\bullet, \mathbf{0})\}, \bullet), \text{output}\,\mathbf{0}), \\
\qquad\qquad ((\{(\text{fst}\bullet, \mathbf{0}), (\text{snd}\bullet, \mathbf{1})\}, \bullet), \text{output}\,\mathbf{1}), \\
\qquad ((\{(\text{fst}\bullet, \mathbf{1})\}, \bullet), \text{output}\,\mathbf{1})\}
\end{array}
$$

One consequence of this is that although our CDSs have the form of sequential algorithms, they are sequential only on *representations*: the functions they represent may be non-sequential, such as *lub*.

To illustrate how a state of a function type CDS represents a function, we now give a definition of CDS application:

$$apply\ x\ y = \{(c', v') \mid ((z, c'), \text{output } v') \in x \text{ for some } z \subseteq y\}$$

3 Finding Fixpoints (Outline)

For the most part, we may proceed as if we were defining a CDS interpreter. Only for the fixpoint operation need we be concerned with any special treatment of non-termination (assuming all recursion has been removed).

We might define, for F of some type $T \to T$, where $|T|$ is finite:

$$fix F = \bigsqcup_{i=0}^{\infty} F^i \perp$$

where $F^0 \perp = \perp$; $F^{(n+1)}\perp = apply\ F\ (F^n \perp)$.

This gives the desired result, but suffers from the usual flaw of requiring a global test for convergence of successive approximations. For a local test to be possible, we must know what other parts of the fixpoint any given cell may depend upon. We can do this by annotating each event with a set of dependencies: those cells which it requires, either directly, or through any number of others.

We now test for convergence by, for each cell, requiring only that the cell itself and those annotated as its dependencies need be stable at two successive approximations, rather than that all cells agree. We further require that the sets of dependencies themselves be similarly stable. Stability for some cells may therefore be detected after fewer iterations than with global convergence, but that the two agree is assured by the closure under dependency of the tested cells.

4 Provisional Results

Our initial results, from an admittedly very small range of examples, are encouraging. Our objective to date has been to attempt to show significant gains on other methods which implement full higher-order analysis, rather than purely first-order techniques, or methods which have been extended to deal with higher order-cases by means of semi-decidable procedures for function equality (such as Young's pending analysis [7]), or by use of a closure analysis. Such means may worsen the result, as do those which perform an analysis at some lower type, which is not the case with our technique.

To our knowledge, the best known such technique is the frontiers method [4]. This achieves a very considerable improvement on naïve implementations, but is still sufficiently expensive for certain quite simple examples as to constitute a fairly severe deterrent to one hoping to use such an analysis in a compiler. A notorious example is the definition `append = foldr (++) []`, requiring that the `foldr` function be analysed at the type $\mathbf{2}_{\perp_\perp}$, in both type parameters. We are assured that the frontiers method can perform this calculation in about 15 minutes [5, 6].

Our implementation is able to analyse the above definition in approximately 0.5s, running in LML-0.997.5 on a Sun 4/75. We wish to offer a number of caveats here however. Firstly, our timings compare computing those parts of the CDS necessary for a particular application with finding the entire frontier. Thus if the application of `foldr` at the same type instance to many different functions were to be computed, the cost using CDSs would rise in approximate proportion to the number of instances, while with frontiers it remains essentially the same. In fact, the cost to compute the whole of the `foldr` CDS is considerably in excess of that for frontiers — several hours of CPU time. We believe that this is not a close upper bound on any practical worst case cost though.

A second concern is that of use of heap space. Using our original representation of CDSs, involving general trees branching with an association list, the above analysis consumed 0.5Mb of heap at peak residency, representing almost half of the storage allocated in total. Calculating the whole `foldr` state was not possible in a heap size of 120Mb(!). We have made significant improvements to this by making some use of an alternative representation (see [3]), in which a branching function is used, leading to a certain amount of redundant computation, when some part of a CDS is demanded more than once, but eliminating a great deal of the excessive heap residency. We are currently carrying out experiments to determine a favourable trade-off between these properties, and also investigating other aspects of space usage.

5 Acknowledgements

We would particularly like to thank Sebastian Hunt, for both his help in making comparisons with frontiers, and his observations about an earlier presentation of this work; and Phil Wadler, for his comments on this paper.

References

[1] G. Berry and P.-L. Curien, Theory and practice of sequential algorithms: the kernel of the applicative language CDS, *Algebraic Methods in semantics*, 35-87, Cambridge University Press (1985).

[2] G. L. Burn, C. L. Hankin and S. Abramsky. Strictness Analysis for Higher-Order Functions. *Science of Computer Programming*, 7, 1986.

[3] John Hughes and A. B. Ferguson, A Loop-detecting Interpreter for Lazy, Higher-order Programs, *Functional Programming, Glasgow 1992*, Springer-Verlag, Workshops in Computing (1992).

[4] Sebastian Hunt, Frontiers And Open Sets in Abstract Interpretation.

[5] Sebastian Hunt, personal communication.

[6] Julian Seward, presentation, Strictness Day, May 1992, Strathaven.

[7] J. H. Young, The Theory and Practice of Semantic Program Analysis for Higher-Order Functional Programming Languages. *Yale University Research Report* YALEU/DCS/RR-669.

[8] Phil Wadler, Strictness Analysis on Non-Flat Domains (by Abstract Interpretation over Finite Domains).

The Glasgow Haskell Compiler: A Retrospective

Cordelia Hall, Kevin Hammond, Will Partain,
Simon L. Peyton Jones, Philip Wadler
University of Glasgow *

1 Introduction

We've spent much of our time over the last two years implementing a new compiler for the functional language Haskell [HPW91]. In this effort, we've been joined by Andy Gill, who has implemented a strictness analyser, Andre Santos, who has contributed a 'simplifier', and Patrick Sansom, who wrote garbage collectors for our runtime system.

This paper describes some of the things we have learned, what we might do differently, and where we go from here.

2 Design decisions

There are three major design decisions that have influenced virtually all of the construction of the Glasgow Haskell compiler. First, the compiler is written in Haskell. We anticipated several benefits from this:

1. The typechecker could be written to fit very closely with the static semantics being developed at the same time [PJW91]. This would ensure that it checked the semantics and vice versa.
2. The compiler would be easier to write and modify.
3. Each time it was modified to produce better target code, the fact that it could compile itself would reduce compile time as well.
4. The advantages and disadvantages of the new Haskell language would become clear very quickly, leading to faster and better language design.
5. The code would be compact, and easy enough to read to be part of a book on the compiler.

In actual fact:

*This work is supported by the GRASP Project. Authors' address: Computing Science Dept, Glasgow University, Glasgow, Scotland. Email: {cvh, kh, partain, simonpj, wadler}@uk.ac.glasgow.dcs

1. The static semantics did indeed make writing the typechecker easier, but there were still many tricky corners that had to be handled at a low level.

2. The compiler is easy to write and modify, but we've had to be careful when dealing with lazy evaluation and circular programming. In fact, these techniques have sometimes cost time rather than saved it.

3. It is an advantage to write a compiler in the language it compiles, and this is an excellent test of the compiler which finds subtle bugs.

4. Using overloading, we've developed a general approach to such things as writing pretty printers for the abstract syntaxes of various passes, or forcing functions which evaluate the results of a pass so that they can be timed. We've also exercised a variety of techniques for maintaining abstract data types using the Haskell module design. These experiments will probably help us in suggesting new paths for the development of the Haskell language.

5. The size of the code is rather larger than expected. There are some 50,000 lines of text and about 230 modules. This means that a book containing the code is no longer very likely.

In general, it appear to have been a good idea to write the compiler in Haskell. Will Partain developed facilities for making literate Haskell documents which have been very useful to us in documenting the compiler and writing papers.

The second decision was to have the compiler produce C target code. This was to have the following benefits:

1. The compiler could produce code for any machine that supported the C language.

2. The target language was quite abstract, allowing us to pay attention to producing the best C code we could and allowing experts like Richard Stallman who build C compilers to optimise it.

This worked out well. One advantage of using C was that we got a low-level debugger virtually for free. In order to handle tail calls, each piece of code produced is a C function without arguments which returns the address of the next piece of code to be executed. An interpreter then simply dispatches these calls, which when traced form the output of a simple debugger.

Recently, we have been using the GNU C compiler, which allows us to implement the registers of our abstract machine directly as registers, rather than global variables.

The final major design decision we made was to use monads [W90, W93] wherever they were appropriate. The benefits we expected were:

1. IO calls could be implemented at a very low level in the functional language itself, rather than by a special purpose 'wrapper', and the order in which they were performed could be controlled directly by monads. In fact, general calls to functions written in C could be written and controlled using similar techniques.

2. Compiler passes which manipulated abstract types, such as a name supply for unique new variable names or a substitution, could be written so that they were both easier to read and had far fewer errors.

Both of these have proven to be very useful. In particular, monads made it possible to implement the typechecker so that the code looked much like the static semantics in many places.

The most important decision has proven to be the use of monads, and for that reason much of the rest of this paper is devoted to describing how we used monads in writing the compiler as well as for handling IO [PJW93]. The last sections describe some of the other features of the compiler and give some timings, as well as how to get a copy of it by ftp.

3 Monads

Compiler passes can be thought of as having two parts. There is the part that does the essential work of the pass, such as dependency analysis. Then there is the bookkeeping, such as making fresh variable names or propagating errors. With monads, these two parts can be separated, so that the bookkeeping is done invisibly by combining forms. The programmer is then free to worry about the algorithm itself. Without monads, functional programmers often find themselves peering through the underbrush at the interesting code somewhere within.

A monad is an abstract data type with a set of operations, typically 'return', and 'then'. In other work [W90, W93, W92], these have been called 'unit' and 'bind'; categorists will know 'bind' as the Kleisli operator.

We'll refer to 'functions which use monads' as monad functions. If `f` has type `a -> b`, then the corresponding monad function `f'` has type `a -> M b`. These functions are given access to the monad state only by monad operations.

Here is a typical compiler monad which passes around unique variable names. The supply must be passed in and out of each monad operation.

```
type NameSupply = [Int]
type M result   = NameSupply -> (NameSupply, result)
```

The name supply is seen only by the monad operation `getName` which removes one name and passes the depleted supply back to the monad.

```
getName :: M Name
getName (n:name_supply) = (name_supply, n)
```

The operations 'return' and 'then' do the plumbing; the simplest of these is 'return'.

```
return :: result -> M result
return result name_supply = (name_supply, result)
```

The most complex monad operation is 'then'. In general, its type shows that it takes a computation of type `a`, and a function (continuation) from a value of type `a` to a computation of type `b`, yielding a computation of type `b`. It works as follows:

1. perform the first computation to yield a value of type a;
2. apply the continuation to this to get a value of type b;
3. this value is combined with the effects of the two computations in an appropriate way, and this combination is a computation of type b.

For example, the implementation of 'then' for this particular monad is:

```
then :: M a -> (a -> M b) -> M b
then e k name_supply
 = case (e name_supply) of
    (next_name_supply, result) -> k result next_name_supply
```

The expression e receives the name supply, which it can access and update, returning the new supply. Its value is passed to the continuation, which gets the new name supply. Since nothing needs to be done to combine the value of the continuation with the monad state, the result of 'then' is just the application of the continuation. Another monad might look at the state returned by this application and combine it with the first state which was returned by evaluating e.

Suppose we have a function which passes around a name supply explicitly, such as part of a pass which renames variables:

```
f :: Exp -> NameSupply -> (NameSupply, Exp)
f (Lambda x e) (n:name_supply)
 = (next_name_supply, Lambda (new_name x n) e')
   where (next_name_supply, e') = f e name_supply
```

We can now write this as the monad function

```
f' :: Exp -> M Exp
f' (Lambda x e)
 = getName                'then' (\ n ->
   (f' e)                  'then' (\ e' ->
   return (Lambda (new_name x n) e')))
```

reading the infix 'then' as syntax which binds the value on the left to the name on the right.

One particularly useful feature of monads is that they can also propagate errors. To do this, we alter M as follows:

```
type ErrorType
        = String
data MaybeErr res err
        = Succeeded res | Failed err
type M result
        = NameSupply
            -> MaybeErr (NameSupply, result) ErrorType
```

The corresponding monad operations are:

```
return :: result -> M result
return result name_supply = Succeeded (name_supply, result)

then :: M a -> (a -> M b) -> M b
then e k name_supply
 = case (e name_supply) of
    Succeeded (next_name_supply, result)
         -> k result next_name_supply
    Failed err -> Failed err
```

Notice that if evaluation of `e` fails, then the continuation is never applied.

We add a new monad operation to introduce failures:

```
fail :: ErrorType -> M a
fail err = Failed err
```

Suppose that we had wished to add error messages to the pass which renames variables. The rest of the code would have had to be changed substantially, to something like this:

```
f :: Exp -> NameSupply -> MaybeErr (NameSupply, Exp) ErrorType
f (Lambda x e) (n:name_supply)
 = case (f e name_supply) of
    Failed err -> Failed err
    Succeeded (next_name_supply, e')
     -> Succeeded (next_name_supply, Lambda (new_name x n) e')
```

The corresponding monad function doesn't have to be changed at all.

3.0.1 IO using monads

The basic idea behind using monads to handle IO is this: if we use monads to specify the order in which we allow interactions with the outside world to be performed, then we can treat IO commands as having ordinary values, just like any other expression. These may be evaluated to weak head normal form in whatever order is specified by the implementation of the language, so referential transparency is preserved. However, the order in which they are *performed* is controlled by the monad operations, which ensure that execution takes place sequentially (notice that 'thenIO' is strict in the value of its first argument before it applies the continuation).

The IO monad is implemented by providing a series of IO monad operations, or *actions*, which are written in C and passed to Haskell via a 'C call', a new function which has been added to the language. The IO system is implemented by IO monad functions, which use these operations, together with the operations 'thenIO' and 'returnIO'.

We can now define functions which handle IO entirely in Haskell. For example, here is the `readLine` function, which reads and writes one line:

```
readChar :: FileHandle -> IO Char

readLine :: FileHandle -> IO [Char]
readLine f =       readChar f `thenIO` (\c ->
```

```
                    -- Check for end of file
                if c == eofChar then
                        returnIO []
                else

                    -- Check for end of line
                if c == '\n' then
                        returnIO ['\n']
                else

                    -- Read rest of line
                readLine f `thenIO` (\cs ->
                returnIO (c:cs)
        ))
```

Performing **readLine** causes the following sequence of events:

1. A character c is read from the file.
2. The character is checked to see if it is the end of file character or a newline. If either case is true, **readLine** terminates that line, otherwise it reads the rest of the line.
3. **readLine** returns the string c:cs, which contains the rest of the line and the character.

IO operations may need to report failures, and this can also be dealt with using monads. For more information about using monads to implement IO, see [PJW93].

4 Distinctive features

The Glasgow Haskell Compiler has a number of characteristics which distinguish it from others we are aware of. We've discussed three that have heavily influenced the development of the compiler, but there are many others. These include

- Pervasive use of the second order polymorphic lambda calculus in both the typechecker and the back end;
- Unboxing of integers, booleans and other primitive data types;
- An unusually high level abstract machine language called STG code;
- A highly configurable runtime system;
- Time and space profiling tools;
- A validation suite which is built into the 'make world' system managing compilation.

Except for the validation suite, none of these has really paid off yet, in comparison to the potential we believe they have. One of the things we plan to do in the future is exploit them further.

4.1 The second order polymorphic lambda calculus

We originally decided to include types as values in our compiler's intermediate code simply because types are so important that we thought they would eventually be useful. So far, they have mainly served to harass us when writing code for intermediate code and the back end. However, there are several ways we could take advantage of them:

- Some strictness analysers which look at non-flat domains must know the type of the code they analyse. So far, little work has been done on exploiting this analysis, but we are working on this.
- The code generator can generate specialised closure code if it knows the type of the object in the closure. This is already done to some extent.

4.2 Unboxed types

An unboxed type is one which can be represented directly, without a pointer. For example, a character can be an unboxed type, as can an Int. This has significant space and time implications - fewer 'boxes' need to be created, and functions on these types needn't open the boxes to get at the value inside. Currently, some transformations made by Santos' simplifier and Gill's strictness analyser take advantage of unboxed types [PJL91]. A strictness analyser for general polymorphic data types was implemented for the Semantique project by a researcher from Poland, Ryzard Kubiak [KHL92]. We are currently planning to allow the user to define unboxed types, and to use the Semantique strictness analyser to discover where list and recursive data type boxing can be reduced.

4.3 STG code

When the STG language was originally designed [PJ92], it was intended to be an abstract machine language which was at a high enough level of abstraction to allow program transformation as well. As anticipated, this has turned out to be useful. For example, the STG expression

```
let x = (let y = e in y:ys) in ...
```

requires an update for `x`, which can be avoided by the following equivalent code:

```
let y = e in (let x = y:ys in ...)
```

4.4 Profiling tools

Patrick Sansom and Simon Peyton Jones have developed profiling tools which allow the user to annotate an expression with a *cost centre* and receive information about the cost incurred when evaluating it [SPJ92]. One of our goals in future is to explore applications of these tools.

test name	ghc real	ghc user	ghc sys	hbc real	hbc user	hbc sys
bspt	**1228.4**	976.8	115.4	**337.3**	262.0	63.6
cichelli	**147.1**	104.4	23.5	**71.6**	46.1	14.9
clausify	**78.1**	60.0	6.4	**25.0**	18.2	4.2
compress	**919.5**	827.9	34.0	**89.8**	48.4	14.6
infer	**421.3**	307.7	61.8	**199.4**	131.0	39.6
lift	**403.8**	335.1	31.6	**119.4**	87.9	18.7
minimax	**193.0**	139.9	28.4	**90.6**	62.5	17.9
pretty	**125.5**	95.5	14.4	**55.7**	37.5	9.7
reptile	**889.1**	721.0	77.0	**304.5**	215.9	46.6
rewrite	**443.6**	377.0	24.4	**149.5**	131.3	9.4
scc	**60.2**	33.1	9.4	**24.0**	15.4	5.0
sorting	**108.4**	82.7	10.8	**41.1**	30.5	6.7

Figure 1: Compilation timings for *ghc* compared with *hbc*

4.5 A configurable runtime system

The current release comes with three different garbage collectors: two-space, one-space compacting and an Appel-stype generational collector. It's easy to add fields to heap objects for profiling or debugging - this just involves altering C macros without having to recompile Haskell source code.

4.6 Make World

This is a vital part of the compiler implementation with a special feature - it allowed us to run the compiler over a substantial validation suite every night. This is helpful when a project is being implemented by several people. For example, a bug recently turned up in an obscure portion of the suite which had been silent for several months because the parser had been altered a few days before. When major changes were made to the front end to handle renaming, the validation suite caught a large number of the errors. Boot-strapping the compiler was a good test as well. Now, the compiler often is recompiled overnight as part of the test suite.

5 Test results

Here, we give a couple of tables (Figure 1, Figure 2) which compare the performance of the Glasgow Haskell compiler (*ghc*) with that of *hbc*, version 0.998.5, written by Lennart Augustsson at Chalmers University in Goteborg, Sweden. These tests were run by Will Partain on a Sun 4 with 24 MB of memory at the end of August, 1992.

It's easy to see that while the run times of code produced by *ghc* are sometimes faster than that of *hbc*, the compile times need a lot of tuning.

test name	ghc real	ghc user	ghc sys	hbc real	hbc user	hbc sys
bspt	**12.5**	9.4	1.7	**9.3**	6.0	1.4
cichelli	**104.8**	95.9	2.5	**138.7**	130.7	2.7
clausify	**8.1**	4.5	1.5	**8.6**	5.7	1.1
compress	**8.8**	5.5	1.6	**11.9**	9.9	0.9
infer	**1.9**	0.5	0.8	**3.8**	0.5	0.9
lift	**2.0**	0.5	0.7	**1.8**	0.5	0.6
minimax	**5.5**	2.8	1.6	**4.0**	2.6	0.7
pretty	**2.5**	0.2	0.6	**1.4**	0.1	0.5
reptile	**11.2**	7.7	2.1	**6.4**	4.0	1.4
rewrite	**4.5**	2.4	1.5	**4.1**	2.1	0.7
scc	**1.4**	0.2	0.6	**1.2**	0.2	0.5
sorting	**2.7**	1.0	1.2	**2.9**	0.6	0.7

Figure 2: Run times for *ghc* compared with *hbc*

6 How to get a copy of the Glasgow Haskell compiler

Our latest release is a 'hackers' release, intended for implementors. Please report bugs to `glasgow-haskell-bugs@@dcs.glasgow.ac.uk` and make general queries to `glasgow-haskell-request@@<same>`.

This release is available, in whole or in part, from the usual Haskell anonymous FTP sites, in the directory pub/haskell/glasgow:

```
nebula.cs.yale.edu      (128.36.13.1)
ftp.dcs.glasgow.ac.uk   (130.209.240.50)
animal.cs.chalmers.se   (129.16.225.66)
```

(Beleaguered NIFTP users within the UK can get the same files by using a `<FP>/haskell/glasgow` prefix, instead of `pub/haskell/glasgow`.)

These are the available files (for the ON DEMAND ones, please ask):

```
ghc-0.06-src.tar.Z
              the basic source distribution; assumes you
              will compile it with Chalmers HBC, version
              0.997.3 or later.

ghc-0.06-proto-hi-files.tar.Z
              An "overlay" of .hi interface files, to be
      used when compiling with the *prototype*
      Glasgow Haskell compiler (version 0.411 or
      later).

ghc-0.06-hc-files.tar.Z
              An "overlay" of .hc generated-C files; used
      either to save you the trouble of compiling
      the prelude, or because your only interest is
      porting the C.
```

```
ghc-0.06-tests.tar.Z
          Some of our test files we have used in getting
     the compiler going.  We hope to grow them into a
     semi-respectable benchmark suite.
```

References

[HPW91] Hudak, P., S. L. Peyton Jones, and P. Wadler, editors, Report on the Programming Language Haskell, version 1.2, *ACM Sigplan Notices*, 27(5), 1992.

[KHL92] Kubiak, R., J. Hughes and J. Launchbury, A projection-based strictness analyser for a Haskell compiler, in preparation.

[PJ92] Peyton Jones, S. L., Implementing lazy functional languages on stock hardware: the Spineless Tagless G-machine, *Journal of Functional Programming*, Vol. 2, No. 2, April 1992, pp. 127-202.

[PJW93] Peyton Jones, S. L. and P. Wadler, Imperative functional programming. To appear in *Proceedings of the 20'th Annual Symposium on Principles of Programming Languages*, January 1993.

[PJL91] Peyton Jones, S. L. and J. Launchbury, Unboxed values as first class citizens, *Conference on Functional Programming and Computer Architecture*, 1991.

[PJW91] Peyton Jones, S. L. and P. Wadler, A static semantics for Haskell. Department of Computing Science, Glasgow University, May 1991.

[SPJ92] Sansom, P. and S. L. Peyton Jones, Profiling lazy functional programs, in *Functional Programming, Glasgow 1992*, Springer Verlag Workshops in Computing Science, 1992.

[W92] Wadler, P. The essence of functional programming. In *Proceedings of the 19'th Annual Symposium on Principles of Programming Languages*, Albuquerque, New Mexico, USA, January, 1992.

[W93] Wadler, P., Comprehending monads, To appear in *Math. Struct. in Comp. Science.*

[W90] Wadler, P., Comprehending monads, In *ACM Conference on LISP and Functional Programming*, Nice, France, June, 1990.

Improving Persistent Data Manipulation for Functional Languages

Kevin Hammond
University of Glasgow

Dave McNally
University of St. Andrews

Patrick M. Sansom
University of Glasgow

Phil Trinder
University of Glasgow*

Abstract

Although there is a great deal of academic interest in functional languages, there are very few large-scale functional applications. The poor interface to the file system seems to be a major factor preventing functional languages being used for large-scale programming tasks. The interfaces provided by some widely-used languages are described and some problems encountered with using these interfaces to access persistent data are discussed. Three means of improving the persistent data manipulation facilities of functional languages are considered: an improved interface to the file system, including a good binary file implementation; an interface to a database; and the provision of orthogonal persistence. Concrete examples are given using the functional programming language, Haskell.

1 Introduction

Modifying a file is a common operation in application programs. Frequently, a program needs to change only small parts of a large file or files. For example, to record the arrival of a shipment, a program controlling an inventory might update the information about a single item in the stock file. We term reading or writing part of a file without needing to read or write the entire file *incremental read/write*.

There are some inherent problems associated with modifying files in a functional language. Firstly, when any data structure is modified, the original data structure must be preserved and a new copy constructed[1]. If this is not done, then referential transparency may be lost. The cost of replication may be high for large data structures such as files. Secondly, the order in which update and read operations are performed is significant. In a functional language the new logical versions provide a handle on the sequencing, but may force an unnatural style on the programmer.

The following sections critique several existing languages before discussing means of improving file-handling within functional programs. There appear to

*This work is supported by the SERC GRASP and Bulk Data Types Projects, a Royal Society of Edinburgh Fellowship, and a Commonwealth Scholorship.
Authors' address: Dept of Computing Science, Glasgow University, Glasgow, Scotland.
Email: {kh,trinder,sansom}@dcs.glasgow.ac.uk, djm@cs.st-andrews.ac.uk

[1] It may be possible to avoid this for unshared data structures [3].

be two broad generations of file interfaces in current functional languages. The first generation includes the interfaces provided by LML[2], Miranda[13], KRC [12] and Orwell[14]. These interfaces present several difficulties, including the lack of incremental read/write, evaluation-order issues, type issues, the loss of type information, the loss of sharing within stored data structures and even the loss of referential transparency. More recent languages such as Hope+[7], Haskell[4], or Concurrent Clean[9] have improved second-generation file interfaces, based on continuations, response/request and event I/O, respectively. None of these interfaces provides incremental read/write primitives, though they may be added in each case[2].

It is worth distinguishing between problems which are fundamental to manipulating persistent data and those which arise simply because features have been omitted from current languages. Incremental read/write and loss of sharing within persistent data structures are problems that can be solved by careful re-design and implementation. Indeed preliminary proposals for both are included in Section 4. Preserving type security over files appears to be more difficult with the static type systems based on name equivalence which are used in most functional languages.

Three means of improving the persistent data manipulation facilities of functional languages are investigated. Firstly, and in the short-term, a language can be better integrated with the file system. Secondly, for large amounts of data or concurrent access a language can be grafted onto a database: Software AG's Natural Expert[10] is an example of this approach. Thirdly, and in the longer-term, a language can be made fully persistent, as has been done with Staple or Poly/ML [5, 6].

The remainder of this paper is structured as follows. Section 2 describes file-handling in non-persistent languages. Section 3 outlines the problems encountered using these constructs. Section 4 investigates the means of improving the file manipulation facilities of functional languages. Section 5 concludes.

2 Current File Constructs

2.1 Read/Write Operations

All non-trivial functional languages provide some mechanism for reading and writing files. These mechanism are not necessarily functional, however. For example, KRC's well documented *read* and *write* functions have the following specification.

- *write fname x* will print the value of *x* into the file called *fname*.
- *read fname* will return the contents of the file *fname*.

This means that a program that copies the contents of a file "old" to a file "new" can be written as simply:

```
write "new" (read "old")
```

[2]In fact, we have been informed that incremental I/O primitives have now been added to Concurrent Clean, in response to an earlier draft of this paper.

The semantics of *read* and *write* are not so simple. The *read* function is lazy: the contents of the file are retrieved when demanded by the program. The *write* operation is hyper-strict: a single write is performed when the result of the *write* function is demanded. Data is written to the file using the normal printing function, so the integer 103 would be written as the string "103", for example. Nothing prevents written data being read as a value of a different type. In addition, the evaluation order may determine the result of a series of reads and writes. This is undesirable since referential transparency may be lost.

2.2 Response/Request Streams

Haskell uses streams of responses and requests to communicate with the file system, and indeed with the operating system in general. A Haskell program that interacts with the file system is a stream-processing function that produces a stream of requests for file operations and receives a stream of responses corresponding to the requests. More formally, file manipulating programs the have type `[Response] -> [Request]` and, if `Name` and `IOError` are some sensible values,

```
data Request =   ReadFile Name | WriteFile Name String | ...

data Response =  Success | Str String | Failure IOError | ...
```

The operations have the obvious meanings, for example the program that copies "old" to "new" files can be written:

```
main resps = [ReadFile "old", WriteFile "new"
     (case head resps of Str contents  -> contents
                         Failure error -> "Error Reading old")]
```

The body of `main` is the list containing the `ReadFile` and `WriteFile` requests. The parameter is the list of responses, with the first response giving the result of the `ReadFile` request.

The Haskell file interface is much more elaborate than described here. However, the only significant difference from the viewpoint of persistent data is that files may contain data of type `Bin` instead of `String`. This type is an implementation-defined, space-efficient representation, which can be used for most data types. It is described further in Section 3.3.

3 Issues

3.1 Incremental Read/Write

Compilers are generally the largest programs written in most functional languages. A compiler reads the entire source file and generates a complete target file, possibly repeating this process in several passes. Most functional languages manage this type of interaction well.

However, many file application programs do not have this pattern of interaction. Instead they retrieve and modify only a small part of a file or files. For example to record the delivery of an item of stock in a warehouse, the record associated with just that item is modified. Staple[5] is the only functional language which the authors are aware of that permits the modification of part of a file (or persistent data structure) without rewriting the entire file. In the warehouse example this would require rewriting the entire stock file just to record the delivery of a single item, a clearly undesirable effect.

Both the `read` operation and the `ReadFile` request provide incremental reading, in part because the contents of the file are only retrieved when demanded by the program. Hence a query about some item in the stock file would only need to read the stock file until the item was encountered. The remainder of the file need not be read, and so only half of the file is read on average. In contrast, in a language with random access files, only the desired item would be read.

3.2 State

The state, or contents, of a file may change during the execution of a program: the file may be written by this or another program. Without care, referential transparency may be lost in a program which reads a file that could change.

The `read` operation in KRC and other languages can either not observe the changing state of a file or is not referentially transparent. It is possible to define functions that do not permit the observation of state changes. Hence when the KRC function

```
getold = read "old"
```

is first called it returns the contents of the file named "old". Even if the contents of "old" are changed, subsequent invocations of `getold` will return the original value.

Miranda's `read` operation apparently allows the changing state of a file to be observed. This option violates referential transparency as the same expression `read "new"` can return different values when evaluated at different times. Programmers are admonished: "users who write Miranda programs that read and write the same file are warned that they are treading on dangerous ground and that the behaviour of such programs is unlikely to be reliable"[13].

In Haskell every `ReadFile` request notionally retrieves the entire file and so must, at least logically, duplicate the file to prevent subsequent writes to the same file from changing the value read. If the file is long, duplicating it might be an expensive operation.

Duplication of the file by requests like `ReadFile` can be avoided by read-locking the file. In the prototype Glasgow Haskell implementation, a write to a read-locked file causes the file to be renamed. The renamed file is deleted if the program terminates normally. This has the (significant) advantage that no file duplication need occur. However, under an OS such as Unix, the applications are responsible for maintain these locks.

3.3 Printable Representation

The type of the file contents in both the `write` operations and the `WriteFile` request is `String`. Non-string data is typically coerced into a string by a `show` function, for example 130 becomes "130". Storing a printable representation has some serious disadvantages.

- The file must be reparsed on input.
- A text file is marginally less secure as it is easily edited.
- Typically the data expands in size. For example a 4-byte real 3.1789E12 becomes the 9-byte string "3.1789E12".
- Type information may be lost. In particular type abstractions may be breached. For example was "160" a height or a weight? See also Section 3.5
- Without explicit efforts to preserve it, sharing within data structures is lost.

To avoid these problems Haskell introduced the Binfile construct. `Bin` is a primitive abstract data type and values of type `Bin` are implementation-dependent representations of values in the language. There is a class `Binary` of types that can be coerced into type `Bin`. The coercions to and from `Bin` are performed by `showBin` and `readBin` respectively. The request `WriteBinFile` is identical to `WriteFile` except that the file contents are of type `Bin`. Because an internal representation has been used,

- The file does not need to be reparsed on input,
- The file is slightly more secure, and
- Data expansion is reduced.

There are some serious limitations with current implementations, however.

- A Binfile can only be used within a single implementation, i.e. one that uses the same internal representation.
- Sharing within data structures may still be lost by current implementations.
- Type information is still lost, including the breaking of type abstraction.

In section 4.2 we argue that both the sharing and type abstraction problems can be overcome by a suitable modification of the Binfile implementation.

3.4 Hyperstrict Writes

Both the `write` operation and the `WriteFile` request are hyperstrict in the value written to the file. Hyperstrictness precludes the preservation of

- Partially evaluated, and hence any potentially infinite data structures.
- Data structures containing functions.

It has been argued that, to make error detection easier, only completely evaluated values should be stored in data files. If unevaluated values are stored, then a program may encounter an erroneous closure that is the legacy of an unknown program that was evaluated at some unknown time [11]. In contrast, the Staple persistent functional language permits the storage of partially evaluated values.

3.5 Type Issues

Preserving all of the type information associated with persistent values is difficult. Section 3.3 described how type abstractions could be broken if structural type equivalence is used. Our preferred solution is to use dynamic name equivalence, similar to the static name equivalence used for internal types in most functional languages, and to provide a mapping between the static and dynamic types. This design avoids loss of type abstraction, without needing to modify the type system (as may be necessary with full dynamic types). There are still several problems, however:

1. It must be possible to convert any stored value into its equivalent internal form, and no other. This can be achieved by suitable mappings between the static and dynamic types, as suggested above.

2. It is impossible to communicate data between two independent programs unless they share identical types. This is a consequence of requiring strong type abstraction.

3. Since there is no strong connection between a program and its data, a programmer may change a type without changing the persistent data which uses that type. In this case, some mechanism must be provided to convert between old and new type representations, if the existing data is still to be used.

Although we believe these are very important issues we will not consider them further here, since they are general issues which apply to all persistent systems and not to functional languages per se. Instead, we concentrate our attention on proposals to improve the underlying facilities for persistent data manipulation.

3.6 Summary

The Haskell Binfile and response/request constructs overcome or ameliorate many of the problems with read and write operations. However, some problems remain. The most important of these is the lack of incremental read/write. Coping with state changes, and preserving both type information and sharing within data structures are also desirable.

4 Improvements

4.1 Indexed File System

Incremental Read/Write

As argued above (in Section 3.1) any serious functional language requires support for incremental file read/write. This section outlines one possible design based on indexed files.

A new, *optional*, indexed file type could be added to Haskell's existing text and binary file types. The associated requests are similar to the existing `ReadVal` and `WriteVal` optional requests. The model underlying indexed files is that of an indexed sequential file that stores key, value pairs. Strings have been used to represent keys because they have a complete order and also because values of most data types can be easily converted into a string using `show`. The stored values must be of type `Bin`. Finally, the present Haskell file mode (a Boolean) is generalised to include a mode which allows both reading and writing.

```
type Index = String

data Mode = RMode | WMode | RWMode

data Request =  ...
      | OpenIxFile Name Mode
      | ReadIx File Index
      | DeleteIx File Index
      | InsertIx File Index Bin
      | ReplaceIx File Index Bin
      | ReadNextIx File
      | ReadPrevIx File

data Response =  ...
      | IndexBin Index Bin
```

`OpenIxFile` is analogous to `OpenFile`, and the existing `CloseFile` is generalised to also close indexed files. `ReadIx` returns a key, value pair corresponding to the least key greater than or equal to the key supplied. This facilitates programs that, for example, list all names beginning with "D". `InsertIx` of an existing key value is an error. `DeleteIx` or `ReplaceIx` of a key that does not exist is an error. `ReadNextIx` (`ReadPrevIx`) returns the key, value pair with the next (previous) greatest key, on a newly opened file it returns the first key, value pair

While indexed files do allow incremental read/write, they provide no more type security than the existing file types. In fact, because values may be stored incrementally they allow the creation of heterogeneous files, that is a file might contain an `Integer` and a `String`.

4.2 Improved Binfile Implementation

An alternative approach is to provide an improved Binfile implementation. We believe that a carefully constructed implementation of the Haskell Binfile can provide a file system which preserves sharing and enables incremental read/write. Such an implementation may provide many of the benefits of a persistent system without the high implementation cost of providing fully orthogonal persistence (as described in Section 4.4).

The idea is to give the runtime system the task of moving the data between the heap and the file. This process can be made to preserve the structure within the file and restore it in the heap when the data is subsequently read. It is initiated by modified `WriteBinFile` and `ReadBinFile` requests:

- The new `WriteBinFile` request forces evaluation of the data and writes it into the file. File offset pointers are used within the Binfile to preserve

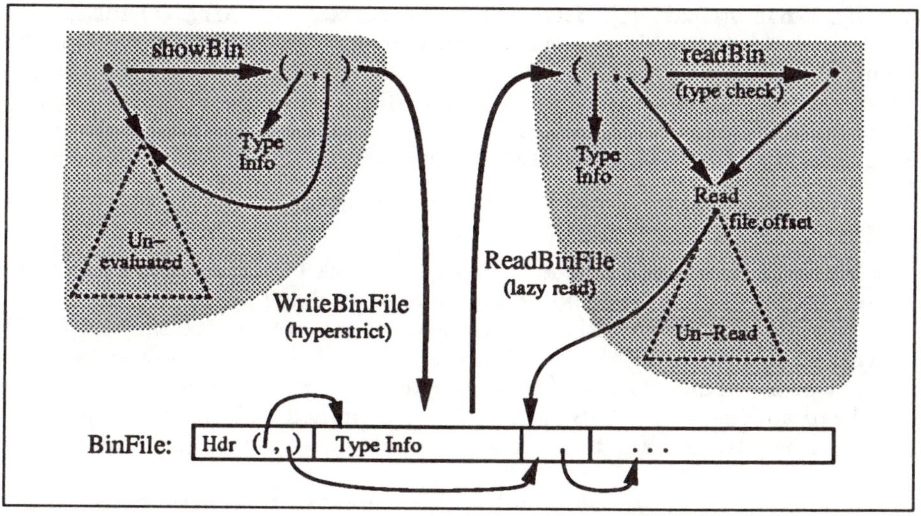

Figure 1: Improved BinFile implementation

the structure of the original data.

- The new **ReadBinFile** request opens the file and reads the first closure. Rather than reading the entire data structure, special "read" closures are constructed which contain the *file* and an *offset* within the file for each data item which should be read (see figure 1). This constitutes an "address" which can be used to access the data in the file. When the program demands the value of a "read" closure the runtime system reads the file and constructs the closure. A random access file facility, like the Unix *seek* system call, is required to provide efficient *file/offset* access.

Preserving Sharing

Sharing is preserved by maintaining two mappings: (heap address → *file/offset*) and (*file/offset* → heap address)[3]. Before a closure is written into a file the heap address is looked up in the (heap address → *file/offset*) mapping: If the closure already resides in the file being written the offset returned is used to reference the file copy of the closure. If the closure does not reside in the file being written it is written into the file. Entries are added to both mappings indicating the new *file/offset* for this heap address, and the new offset used to reference the file copy of the closure. A similar process occurs when a closure is read except that the (*file/offset* → heap address) mapping is used to determine if the *file/offset* is already in the heap.

This process of transferring data between the heap and a file is very similar to the transfer between the local and global memories described for the

[3]These are address translation tables. Persistent systems may refer to the latter mapping as the PIDLAM — Persistent Identifier to Local Address Mapping.

parallel GRIP machine[8]. Here the (heap address → *file/offset*) mapping is implemented by attaching an extra word to every closure containing its global memory address (if present). GRIP does not yet implement the (*file/offset* → heap address) mapping so sharing is lost when reading from global memory, with multiple copies being created in the local memory. A similar technique to that described above could be used to preserve sharing.

Incremental Read/Write

If a Binfile is read modified and then written back to the same file one might expect the old file to be removed and a new modified version created. This need not happen. Instead the runtime system can extend the existing Binfile writing back the modified data structure. Now any part of the data which has not been modified already resides in the file. This will be detected when the (heap address → *file/offset*) mapping is examined and the unmodified data need not be written back to the file — the file offset given by the mapping is used.

By making use of appropriate data structures, such as trees, modified versions of the data can be built and the changes written. Consider the following batch update transaction processor:

```
main ~(Str upd: ~(Bn oldbin: _))
  = [ReadFile "update", ReadBinFile "datafile",
                        WriteBinFile "datafile" newbin]
  where olddata       :: Tree Key Data
        (olddata, _) = readBin oldbin
        newbin       = showBin (update upd olddata) nullBin
```

The `Bin` data structure stored in the file, `"data"`, is a tree. Only the path(s) modified by the updates will be written back to the file. This program makes use of irrefutable pattern-matching (~) to match the response lazily.

The final step of the `WriteBinFile` request is to update the file header to reference the new data. This commits the entire write. Subsequent `ReadBinFile` requests will now return the new data. If an error occurs before the header is written, the old version of the data remains intact and will be accessed by subsequent `ReadBinFile` requests instead. Transaction processing can be simulated by performing a `WriteBinFile` request data after each committed transaction.

Unfortunately this scheme causes fragmentation: Binfiles increase monotonically in size with old data cluttering the file. The *file* itself must be garbage collected to recover this unused space. A simple utility program which copies exactly the live data from the old Binfile to a new file would suffice for a basic implementation. For example, the following Haskell program could be used:

```
main ~(Bn old: _) = [ReadBinFile "old", WriteBinFile "new" old]
```

The actual copying would be performed by the runtime system with the strict `WriteBinFile` request forcing the lazy read from `"old"`.

One Persistent File

Instead of implementing Binfiles as multiple files in the operating system, all Binfiles could be written into a single file. This file could itself be a Binfile containing a single value of type `Tree String Bin`. The tree provides an index implementing the logical file naming structure. The actual `Bin` values are stored at the leaves. All Binfile requests would then access this one file directly, using the index to perform the necessary filename → `Bin` mapping.

This idea could be extended to make the single file a persistent store. The runtime system would then allocate objects in this store rather than manipulating the file directly. The store would provide the required garbage collection and locking facilities. Such a scheme would not pay the runtime cost of implementing the entire language on top of the store as with the Staple system[5]. Local computations are still executed in the local heap with data being transferred between the program and the store by Binfile requests. In particular, the runtime garbage collection costs (which are large for Staple) would be no greater than for a normal functional program.

This is still not an orthogonally persistent system, however: neither functions nor suspensions could be stored in the persistent store.

Type Checking

Dynamic type checking needs to occur when the data is extracted from a `Bin` value by `readBin`. This `Bin` value may have been read from a file or created in the heap by a `showBin` during the run of this program. In either case suitable type information can be attached to the `Bin` value by `showBin` (see figure 1). In fact, the principal purpose of these functions is to provide type security when coercing data to and from `Bin` values.

The fact that `showBin` and `readBin` are incremental (e.g. `showBin :: Binary a => a -> Bin -> Bin`) adds some complication when using these functions[4]. It would be preferable to use non-incremental versions instead (e.g. `showBin :: Binary a => a -> Bin`), and define `readBin` to return a suitable error if the dynamic type check fails.

Any developments in dynamic type checking could be incorporated into this scheme by attaching appropriate type information to `Bin` values. Indeed we hope that such a Binfile implementation would encourage further research into this area.

4.3 Database

To implement real applications with large amounts of data, many programming languages have been integrated with a database. For example, C with embedded Ingres SQL. A functional language that has been integrated with a database is Software AG's Natural Expert [10]. Their model directs certain requests to the database in addition to handling the standard operating system requests.

The advantages of this approach are as follows:

- Incremental read/write are provided.
- Sharing within data structures is preserved by the referential integrity of the database.

[4] An incremental `showBin` might also cause loss of sharing in some circumstances.

- Concurrent access to data is provided by transactions.
- A `DoQuery` request permits efficient interrogation of the database.

The disadvantages are as follows:

- The type problem is compounded by the mismatch between the higher-order type system in the functional language and the data types supported by the database (e.g. tuples and relations in a relational database).
- The `DoQuery` request requires meta-programming to construct the string representing the query.
- Portability might be lost as the databases may not be available on some architectures.

This approach would seem most suitable for applications that require incremental read/write of, efficient queries over, or concurrent access to large quantities of data.

4.4 Orthogonal Persistence

Conventional languages only allow certain types of data to persist, e.g. strings in LML or sequences of most types in Pascal. Languages with orthogonal persistence permit data of any type to persist. Staple[5] is a functional language with orthogonal persistence, and Poly/ML[6] is a near-functional language with orthogonal persistence.

The advantages of this approach are as follows.

- Incremental read and write can be implemented on persistent data structures, but the programmer must explicitly reconstruct a new version of the data structure. New versions of only some data structures can be cheaply constructed. For example a new version of a tree can be cheaply constructed, but a new version of an association-list cannot. There are several data structures that are useful for storing persistent data but cannot be cheaply copied[11].
- Sharing within a data structure can be preserved.
- Concurrent and lazy evaluation are both possible. See Section 3.4.
- Persistence is elegant: transfer to and from persistent storage is performed without explicit programmer control.

The disadvantages are as follows.

- Persistent languages use structural type equivalence and it is not clear how to integrate this with the name equivalence used in most functional languages.
- At present persistence is a new technology, and not well understood. Implementations are slow, small and experimental. Considerable effort is required to make a language persistent. In contrast, much less effort is required to produce a good Binfile implementation, as described in Section 4.2.

It is conceivable that the structural versus name equivalence issue can be resolved, and that persistent language technology will become well-established. In this case orthogonal persistence appears to offer the most elegant means of manipulating persistent data in a functional language.

5 Conclusion

The file system interfaces provided by current functional languages have been described, and some problems have been identified. Many of these problems are resolved or alleviated by the Haskell Binfile and response/request constructs. Some outstanding problems with the Haskell interface have been identified, the most important being the lack of incremental update. Following an earlier version of this paper, incremental I/O has now been implemented in at least one functional system (the Concurrent Clean compiler mentioned earlier). We hope that other implementors will be similarly motivated to improve their file system interface.

Three approaches to resolving the remaining problems with a response/ request interface have been investigated. We conclude that, in the short term, an improved file system interface with a better implementation of Binfiles will make it easier to implement many application systems. For applications requiring access to large quantities of data, concurrent access or efficient queries, a database interface may be necessary. In the long term, if the type equivalence issues can be resolved and persistent language technology becomes well-developed, orthogonal persistence appears to offer the most elegant means of manipulating persistent data in a functional language.

6 Acknowledgements

We would like to thank John Launchbury, John O'Donnell and Rinus Plasmeijer for reading and commenting on earlier versions of this paper.

References

[1] Atkinson M.P. Programming Languages and Databases, in *Proceedings of the 4th International Conference on Very Large Databases*, 1978.

[2] Augustsson L. A compiler for lazy ML, in *Proceedings of the ACM Symposium on Lisp and Functional Programming*, Austin Texas, USA, August 1984.

[3] Bloss A. Update analysis and the efficient implementation of functional aggregates, in *Proceedings of the 1989 IFIP Conference on Functional Programming Languages and Computer Architecture*, London, September, 1989.

[4] Hudak P. Wadler P. Peyton Jones SL. (Eds) Report on the Programming Language Haskell, Version 1.2, *ACM SIGPLAN Notices*, 27(5), May 1992.

[5] McNally D. Joosten S. Davie A. Persistent Functional Programming, in *Proceedings of the 4th International Workshop on Persistent Object Systems*, Martha's Vineyard, Mass., USA, September, 1990.

[6] Matthews D.C.J. A Persistent Storage System for Poly and ML. University of Cambridge Technical Report 102, January, 1987.

[7] Perry N. Hope+C - a continuation extension for Hope+. Internal Report, Department of Computing, Imperial College London, October, 1987.

[8] Peyton Jones S.L. Clack C. Salkild J. Hardie M. GRIP - a high-performance architecture for parallel graph reduction, in *Proceedings of the IFIP conference on Functional Programming Languages and Computer Architecture*, Portland. Kahn G. (Ed), Springer-Verlag LNCS 274, September, 1987.

[9] Achten P.M., van Groningen J.H.G. and Plasmeijer M.J. High-level specification of I/O in functional languages, in *Functional Programming, Glasgow 1992*, Launchbury J. Sansom P.M. (Eds), Springer-Verlag, Workshops in Computing Science, 1992.

[10] Software A.G. NATURAL EXPERT Reference Manual, Version 1.1.3, 1990.

[11] Trinder P.W. A Functional Database. D.Phil. Thesis, Oxford University, December, 1989. Available as: Technical Monograph PRG-82, Programming Research Group, 8-11 Keble Road, Oxford OX1 3QD, England; Technical Report CSC 90/R10 Dept. of Computing Science, University of Glasgow, Scotland.

[12] Turner D.A. Recursion Equations as a Programming Language in *Functional Programming and its Application.* Darlington J. Henderson P. Turner D.A. (Eds), Cambridge University Press, 1982.

[13] Turner D.A. Miranda System Manual, Research Software Limited, 1987.

[14] Wadler P. An Introduction to Orwell 4.07, Internal Document, Oxford University Programming Research Group, December, 1987.

A Loop-detecting Interpreter for Lazy, Higher-order Programs

John Hughes
Informationsbehandling, Chalmers Tekniska Högskola
S-41296 GÖTEBORG, Sweden

A.B. Ferguson
Department of Computing Science, University of Glasgow
Glasgow G12 8QQ

Abstract

Interpreters that detect some forms of non-termination have a variety of applications, from abstract interpretation to partial evaluation. A simple and often used strategy is to test for a repeated state, but this cannot handle infinite values (such as first-class functions) or unevaluated states such as arise in lazy programs. In this paper we propose using Berry and Curien's theory of sequential algorithms as a semantic foundation for loop detection: we obtain straightforwardly a loop detector for lazy higher-order functional programs, which is more effective than the simple strategy even for strict first order cases.

1 Introduction

We normally expect an interpreter, given a non-terminating program to interpret, to fail to terminate itself. But there are applications in which it is useful for an interpreter to stop in such cases, with a report that the interpreted program is in an infinite loop.

One such application is *abstract interpretation*[1], a method of compile-time analysis in which the program to be analysed is interpreted over abstract data, representing sets of possible concrete data. The result of an abstract interpretation may frequently be $\perp$, but this conveys definite information and we certainly do not expect the compiler to loop in such cases. Another application is *partial evaluation*[2], in which a program is interpreted given some of its data, yielding a 'residual program' consisting of the operations on the unknown data. In this application a loop generates an infinite residual program, and loop detection is used to express the result as a recursive program instead.

The very simplest loop-detecting strategy for functional programs is to compare the actual arguments of each function call with the arguments of any enclosing call of the same function. If they are the same, the interpreted program is looping. This strategy is used in Young's pending analyser[3] (an abstract interpreter), and in Jones' partial evaluator MIX[2]. But it suffers from serious disadvantages: since function arguments must be compared, they cannot be functions, or infinite or partial data structures. Thus the strategy is applicable only to strict, first-order functional languages, not the lazy, higher-order languages that are most interesting. Moreover, even in the strict case this strategy fails to detect some quite obvious loops — for example, consider

```
let rec f m n = if m=0 then 1 else f m (n+1)
```

Clearly if `m` is non-zero, then `f` loops, but the loop is not detectable because no two calls of `f` have the same second argument.

Holst and Hughes presented a loop-detecting interpreter which keeps track of the parameters that the control flow depends on, and thereby detects the loop in the example above[4]. That interpreter also delays the comparison of arguments until they are needed in the normal course of evaluation, and thereby supports lazy evaluation. But it is limited to first-order programs operating on atomic data. More recently Holst has generalised that work to programs operating on lazy data-structures, but higher-order functions still present a problem.

This paper takes a new approach based on Berry and Curien's theory of sequential algorithms[5]. A sequential algorithm encapsulates more information than a mapping from inputs to outputs: it tells us also how each *part* of the output depends on the parts of the input. This extra information makes it possible to define an efficient fix-point finder, which detects self-dependent parts of the fixpoint and substitutes an explicit representation of $\perp$ — that is, detects loops. By representing functions as sequential algorithms we have constructed a loop-detecting interpreter for lazy higher-order programs.

Naturally no loop-detecting interpreter can detect all loops — we cannot solve the halting problem. This need not matter in the applications we have in mind. Let us call a program whose interpretation terminates (perhaps by detecting a loop) *quasi-terminating*. An abstract interpreter may exploit the fact that all programs operating over finite domains are quasi-terminating to guarantee termination. A partial evaluator may simply require the programmer to supply a quasi-terminating program for partial evaluation — this is the approach taken by MIX. Alternatively, we may use a *quasi-termination analysis* to check that a program is quasi-terminating before interpreting or partially evaluating it. No such analysis can recognise all quasi-terminating programs, but one may recognise a large and useful class. Of course, each loop-detection strategy needs its own quasi-termination analysis. Such an analysis for the simple strict strategy was developed by Holst[6]; we have not yet begun to investigate an analysis corresponding to the loop-detection strategy presented here.

2 Concrete Data Structures and Sequential Algorithms

Berry and Curien's theory is an alternative framework for denotational semantics, which makes the *sequentiality* of terms in the λ-calculus explicit. In place of Scott domains, we use *concrete data structures*. In place of continuous functions, we use *sequential algorithms*. In this section we give a simplified presentation of the theory.

2.1 Concrete Data Structures

Concrete data structures (CDSs) correspond to types or domains, and their elements represent values. An element of a CDS is a *tree*, with labelled nodes and edges. Consider a few examples:

- 23 is an element of the CDS `Int` (it is a tree with a single labelled node).
- 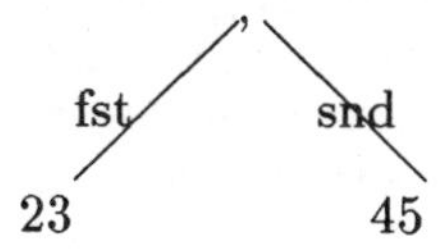

is an element of the CDS `Int`$\times$`Int`.
- 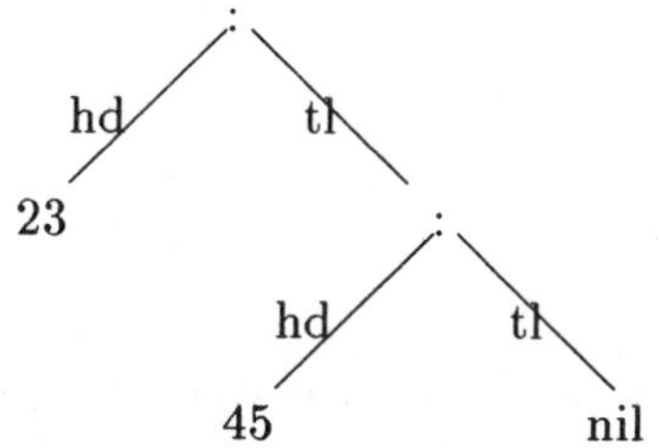

is an element of the CDS `List Int`.

We can think of the node labels as constructor names, and the edge labels as selector names. A little nomenclature: we will call the node labels *values* and the edge labels *selectors*. Any node can be identified by the sequence of selectors on the path to it from the root of the tree, and we will call such a sequence a *cell*. For example, the value 45 in the element of the list CDS above is in the cell `[tl,hd]`.

The elements of a CDS can be ordered to form a domain. The least element is the empty tree with no nodes or edges, and an element approximates another if the larger can be obtained from the smaller by adding nodes and edges. The pictures above illustrate total elements: partial elements look like total ones with some subtrees missing. For example,

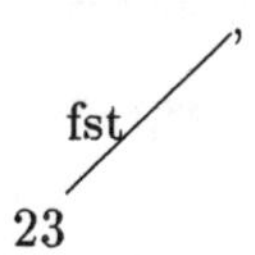

represents a pair with an undefined second component.

2.2 Sequential Algorithms

The corresponding notion to a function from one CDS to another is a sequential algorithm. This is just a program in a very restricted language. Sequential algorithms are constructed from a **case** construct to inspect the input, and an **out** construct to produce the output.

```
case cell of              out val then
   val: ...                  sel: ...
   val: ...                  sel: ...
   ...                       ...
```

The cell referred to in a **case** must be a cell of the input, and the value in that cell must be one of the values listed. A **case** construct is executed by inspecting the input and continuing to execute the branch corresponding to the value found. If the input cell does not exist (because the input is a partial element) then execution stops and no output is produced. An **out** construct writes the value supplied to the root node of the output CDS, and then attaches subtrees with the given selectors to the root, using the algorithm labelled by each selector to construct the corresponding subtree. As an example, the algorithm below computes the conjunction of a pair of booleans:

```
case [] of
  ,: case [fst] of
       true:  case [snd] of
                true:  out true
                false: out false
       false: out false
```

Recall that cells are sequences of selectors — so `[]` refers to the root of the input (which since it is a pair must contain the pair constructor `,`), `[fst]` refers to its first component, and `snd` refers to its second. As another example, here is an algorithm to compute a pair of the boolean input and its negation:

```
out , then
  fst: case [] of
         true:  out true
         false: out false
  snd: case [] of
         true:  out false
         false: out true
```

Well-formed sequential algorithms must obey two rules:

- A **case** construct may not inspect the same cell as any enclosing **case**.
- A **case** construct may only inspect a cell whose parent was inspected by an enclosing **case**[1].

One pleasant consequence is that there are only finitely many sequential algorithms between finite CDSs.

2.3 The CDS of Sequential Algorithms

A sequential algorithm may be regarded as a decision tree — and therefore may itself be represented as an element of a CDS! The nodes represent **case** and **out** constructs, and so are labelled either **case** c or **out** v, where c is a cell of the input type and v is a value of the output type. The edges emanating

[1] It is this rule that forces the algorithm for conjunction to inspect the root of its argument, even though it can only contain the pair constructor.

from a **case** node are labelled with values, and the edges from an **out** node are labelled with selectors.

For example, there are six sequential algorithms from `Bool` to `Bool`, represented by the following trees (the third picture represents four different trees).

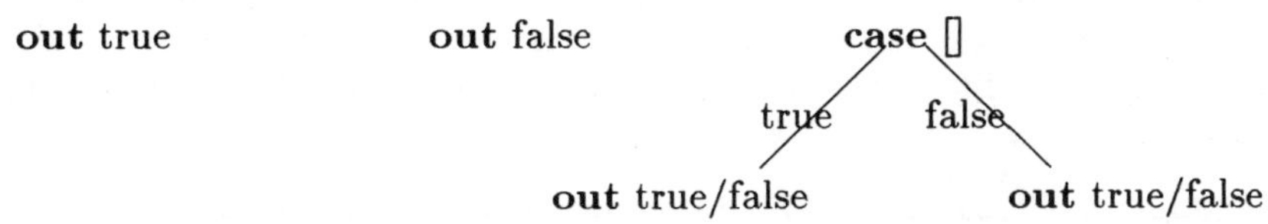

Since functions can be represented as elements of CDSs, *higher-order* functions can be represented as sequential algorithms. Below is the algorithm for **`apply`**, defined by

```
apply :: (Bool->Bool) X Bool -> Bool
apply (f,x) = f x
```

The algorithm first inspects the root node of its (pair) argument, as it must, and then inspects the root node of its function argument. Looking at the diagrams above, we see the value found there must be one of **out** true, **out** false, or **case** []. In the first two cases **`apply`** can output its result at once, but in the third case it must inspect its second argument. The value of the second argument must be true or false, and **`apply`** can then inspect the corresponding node of its function argument, and produce the appropriate output.

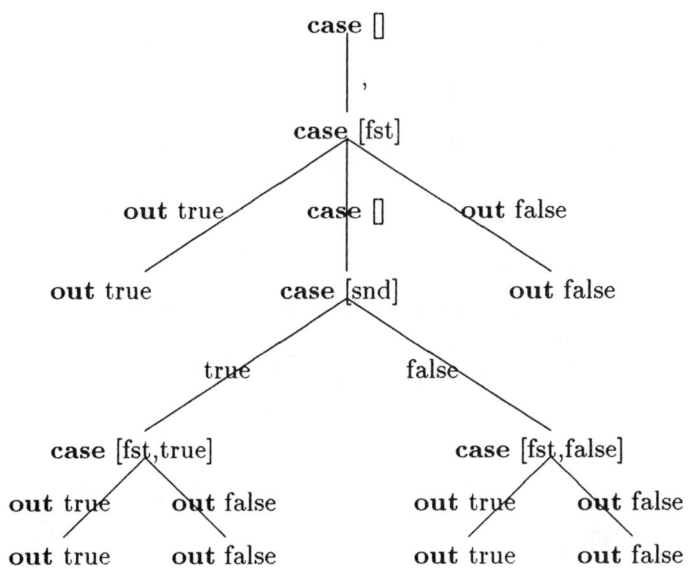

As this example shows, we can think of higher-order sequential algorithms as containing an interpreter for decision trees.

3 A Lazy Fixpointing Algorithm for Sequential Algorithms

The fixpoint of a sequential algorithm f can be constructed in much the same way as the fixpoint of a continuous function. Starting from the empty tree, we can repeatedly run f to construct a sequence of better and better defined partial trees. The fixpoint of f is then the union of all of these. For example, consider the function

```
f :: (Bool X (Bool X Bool)) -> (Bool X (Bool X Bool))
f p = (true,(fst p,snd(snd p)))
```

which corresponds to the sequential algorithm

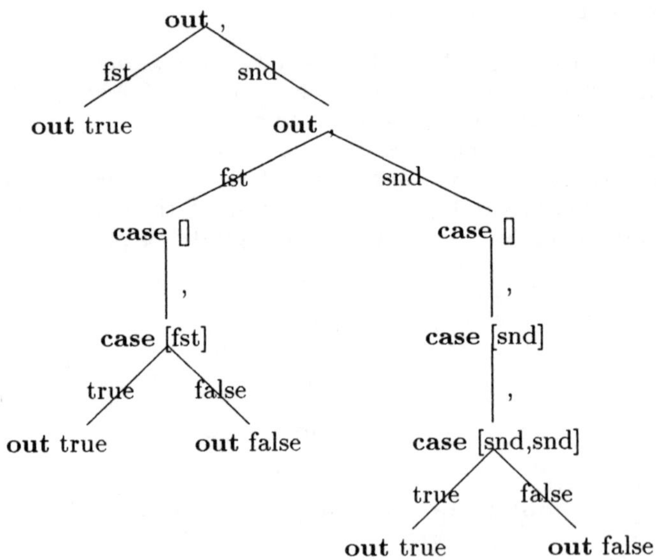

Interpreted as a continuous function, the approximations to its fixpoint are $\bot$, $(true, (\bot, \bot))$, and $(true, (true, \bot))$, the last of these being the fixpoint. Running the sequential algorithm repeatedly, starting with the empty tree, produces the corresponding partial trees

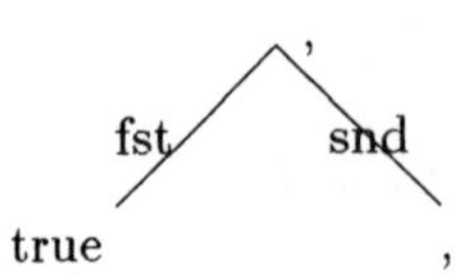

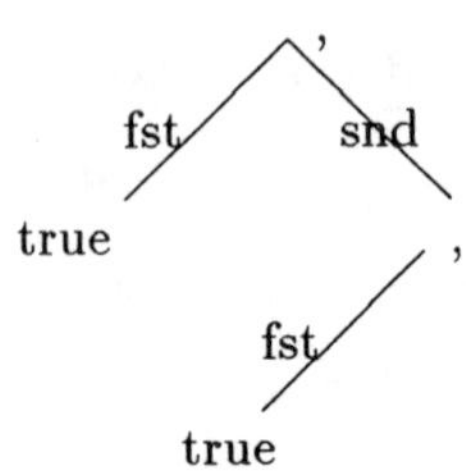

In each case the first approximation has two undefined components, while the fixpoint has only one. Consider the following question: how many approximations must we compute to be certain that a component of the fixpoint is really undefined? When finding the fixpoint of a continuous function, we cannot be certain of this until two successive approximations are equal *everywhere*, because the putative undefined component might depend on any other component. Thus in this example both components of the nested pair appear to be undefined after one iteration, but in fact the first component depends on a part of the fixpoint which is now available, and so becomes defined after the second iteration. Just in case the remaining undefined component depends on the first, we must compute a third iteration and verify that the result is exactly the same as after the second. This comparison of complete approximations is always expensive, may be impossible if the fixpoint is a function, and in any case may be pointless since in general we do not reach the fixpoint after finitely many iterations.

In contrast, when finding the fixpoint of a sequential algorithm we can decorate the nodes of the approximations with the cells in the previous approximations that they depend on. When a node cannot be computed, we can tell which missing cell of the previous approximation it depended on. In the example, the cell `[snd,snd]` cannot be computed in the second iteration because it depends on itself! It's now clear that this cell will remain undefined in every future iteration, so we can immediately conclude that it is undefined in the fixpoint also. It is this ability to conclude that parts of the fixpoint are undefined after finitely many iterations, even if the fixpoint itself is never reached after any finite number, that makes loop detection possible.

In the implemented algorithm, there is no need to construct a series of approximations explicitly. Instead we use *circular programming*: we give a recursive definition of an annotated tree representing the fixpoint, in which nodes are decorated with the transitive closure of the cells they depend on, and in which nodes that depend on themselves are replaced by an explicit representation of an empty tree.

4 An Implementation of Sequential Algorithms

In our implementation, elements of CDSs are represented using the following type:

```
rec type CDS = Event Val (Sel -> CDS)
             + Depend (List Sel) CDS + Empty
and type Val = Num Int + Comma + Case (List Sel) + Out Val
and type Sel = Fst + Snd + Value Val
```

Empty trees are represented by **Empty**, non-empty trees are represented as **Events**, and nodes that depend on other cells are represented during fixpointing using **Depend**.

Since the decision tree for a function on integers will contain infinite branching, we have chosen to represent the collection of sub-trees of a node as a *function* from a selector name to a sub-tree. As a result, if the same cell of a CDS is inspected more than once, our implementation must normally recompute it.

We regard this as reasonable since inspecting a cell of a function's decision tree corresponds to calling it.

The implementations of sequential algorithms resemble programs in continuation passing style. For example, the addition algorithm + is represented by

```
+ :: Int X Int -> Int

plusA = Event (Case []) (\(Value Comma).
        Event (Case [Fst]) (\(Value (Num m)).
        Event (Case [Snd]) (\(Value (Num n)).
        Event (Out (Num (m+n))) (\_. errA))))
```

The composition **f o g** of two sequential algorithms can be constructed from the algorithm **f** by replacing **case** nodes by the code in **g** that computes the corresponding cell. Some care is needed since, although the code in **g** for computing any particular cell of its output will read each cell of **g**'s input at most once, it is possible that the algorithms for computing two different cells of **g**'s output will both read the same cell of **g**'s input. If **f** uses both cells together then the value read from **g**'s input must be saved at the first use, so that it need not be re-read for the second.

As an example, we compute the composition of the two algorithms given as examples in section 2.2: the algorithm for conjunction, and the algorithm taking a boolean input and computing a pair of the boolean and its negation. We refer below to these algorithms as **f** and **g** respectively. We are computing

<table>
<tr>
<td><pre>
case [] of
  ,: case [fst] of
       true: case [snd] of
               true: out true
               false: out false
       false: out false
</pre></td>
<td>o</td>
<td><pre>
out , then
  fst: case [] of
         true: out true
         false: out false
  snd: case [] of
         true: out false
         false: out true
</pre></td>
</tr>
</table>

The outermost **case** in **f** reads the comma produced by the first **out** of **g**, so no computation in the composed algorithm is produced from this **case**. To compute the **[fst]** cell of **g**'s result, we copy the **case []** from **g** and then compose the **true** and **false** branches of **f** with **g**:

case [] of

<table>
<tr>
<td>true:</td>
<td><pre>
case [snd] of
  true: out true
  false: out false
</pre></td>
<td>o</td>
<td><pre>
out , then
  fst: case [] of
         true: out true
         false: out false
  snd: case [] of
         true: out false
         false: out true
</pre></td>
</tr>
</table>

```
false: [out false] o  [out , then
                         fst: case [] of
                                true: out true
                                false: out false
                         snd: case [] of
                                true: out false
                                false: out true]
```

The `false` branch simply outputs `false`; in the `true` branch we must compute the `[snd]` cell of `g`'s result. The algorithm for doing so begins with a `case []`, but this cell of the input has been read by an enclosing `case`! The value read was `true`, so we compute the `[snd]` cell of `g`'s output as `false`. The final composition is

```
case [] of
  true: out false
  false: out false
```

As another optimisation, rather than find the code for computing each cell of `g`'s result by starting from the root each time, our implementation records the subtree of `g` at every cell inspected. Since no cell can be inspected until its parent has been, we are guaranteed to find every cell inspected in one step from this cache. Because components of trees are normally recomputed each time they are used in our implementation, this optimisation brings a very large improvement in performance.

We have also implemented currying and uncurrying of algorithms, the projections `fst` and `snd`, pairing and conditional choice of algorithms satisfying

```
(pairA f g) x = (f x, g x)
(ifA p f g) x = if p x then f x else g x
```

and the identity algorithm — in short, we have implemented a family of categorical combinators operating on sequential algorithms.

5 A Loop Detecting Interpreter

We have used the implementation of sequential algorithms described above to construct a loop-detecting interpreter for a small subset of LML. The syntax of the interpreted language is shown in Figure 1. The language is untyped and higher-order, with three kinds of data: numbers[2], pairs, and functions. In addition to the built-in operators, `fst` and `snd` are provided as primitive functions. If recursive types such as lists are required they must be modelled using pairs.

Toy LML programs are translated into categorical combinators in the standard way: each expression denotes a function from the environment to its value. An environment binding n values is represented as nested pairs of the form

[2]Booleans are modelled by 0 and 1.

```
program ::= let rec def {and def}* in expr
def ::= identifier identifier* = expr
expr ::= if expr then expr else expr
       | expr op expr
       | expr expr
       | number
       | identifier
       | (expr)
       | (expr, expr)
op ::= = | < | + | - | * | /
```

Figure 1: The Syntax of Toy LML

$((\ldots(\bot, x_1), \ldots), x_n)$, with the result that currying a denotation corresponds to λ-abstraction in the source. Each definition denotes a function from the (recursively defined) top-level environment to the value defined. By combining the denotations of the definitions we construct a function from the top-level environment to itself, and take its fixpoint. This supplies the environment used to evaluate terms.

The implemented interpreter reads a Toy LML program from a file, and then interactively evaluates expressions using the functions defined.

6 Practical Results

6.1 First-Order Examples on Atomic Data

We begin with some examples from [4].

- `let rec x = x+1`
  This loop is detected by most functional language implementations.

  ```
  x
  ** loop **
  ```

- `let rec f x y = if x=0 then f x (y+1) else y`
  This function loops if `x` is zero, but not otherwise. The loop cannot be detected by the simple strict strategy since no two recursive calls have the same second argument.

  ```
  f 0 0
  ** loop **
  ```

- `let rec h x y = if x=0 then h y (y+1) else y`
  This function does not loop — but its first two calls have the same parameters as the first two calls of `f` above, making it appear to be looping at first.

```
h 0 0
2
```

- `let rec j x y = if x=0 then j (j x y) y else 0`
  This function loops if **x** is zero.

  ```
  j 0 0
  ** loop **
  ```

6.2 First-Order Examples on Lazy Data-structures

The following examples illustrate the detection of looping components of partial structures.

- `let rec k x = (x,fst(k x))`
  This function doesn't loop, despite the recursive call with an identical argument.

  ```
  k 1
  (1,1)
  ```

- `let rec l x = (x,snd(l x))`
  This very similar function does loop, in its second component.

  ```
  l 1
  (1,** loop **)
  ```

- `let rec ones = (1,ones)`
  This definition does not loop — it defines an infinite structure. Our interpreter implements this lazily.

  ```
  fst ones
  1
  fst (snd ones)
  1
  ```

- `let rec len xs = if xs=0 then 0 else 1+len (snd xs)`
  This is the standard length function, operating on pairs with nil coded as zero. It works on finite lists

  ```
  len (1,(2,0))
  2
  ```

  but the following loop is *not* detectable.

  ```
  len ones
  ^C
  ```

  The reason that this loop cannot be detected is that the CDS representation of `ones` is as an infinite tree, not as a cyclic graph. We therefore cannot verify that `len` is applied to the same argument in each recursion.

6.3 Higher-order Examples

- `let rec g x = g x`
  This function loops whatever its argument

  ```
  g 0
  ** loop **
  ```

  but our interpreter can in actually discover more than this:

  ```
  g
  ** loop **
  ```

  g is the undefined function.

- ```
  let rec fix f = f (fix f)
  and     id x = x
  and     g p = (1, snd p)
  ```
  It's possible to define a fixed-point operator in Toy LML. Loop detection works just as well if loops are constructed using this operator rather than by explicit recursive definitions.

  ```
  fix id
  ** loop **
  fix g
  (1,** loop **)
  ```

- ```
  let rec upd f x y z = if z=x then y else f z
  and f g = if g 0=0 then 1 else f (upd g 1 (g 1+1))
  and g x = x+1
  ```
  Here the higher-order function `f` loops if it is passed a function mapping zero to anything but zero. But no two recursive calls of `f` have the same function parameter, so no method which relies on spotting identical parameters can detect the loop. Yet all that matters is that `f`'s parameter maps zero to the same value in each call, which it does.

  ```
  f g
  ** loop **
  ```

6.4 Performance

The loop-detecting interpreter is slow. Running the `nfib` benchmark on a SPARCstation 1 it performs 60 calls per second. This is about 25 times slower than a comparable non-loop-detecting interpreter for the same language. It also uses a lot of memory: `nfib 14` cannot be computed in an 8MB heap. The present interpreter is very much a prototype, however, and we may hope to improve on these figures.

We did compare the fixpoint algorithm described with another, based on Young's pending analysis. Rather than compute a tree annotated with dependencies, the pending algorithm passes a list of 'pending cells' which are in the process of being computed, and returns an empty tree if an attempt is ever made to inspect one of them. The pending algorithm is not amenable to memoisation since there is no obvious relationship between a cell of the fixpoint evaluated with one pending list, and the same cell evaluated with another. Nevertheless, in view of the success of pending analysis (which works in a very similar way) one might expect this algorithm to perform well. We found that, for first-order programs, it is slightly more efficient (the `nfib` number rises to 68). But for higher-order programs it is disastrously slow. For example, consider

```
let rec fix f = f (fix f)
and facf f n = if n=0 then 1 else if 0<n then n*f(n-1) else f n
and fac = fix facf
```

which defines the factorial function as the fixpoint of a higher-order functional. This function runs thirty times faster on our present interpreter than on the 'pending' one.

7 Conclusions and Future Work

The theory of sequential algorithms provides a simple framework within which a loop-detecting fixpoint operator can be defined. Sequential algorithms can model the λ-calculus, so we can thereby construct a loop-detecting interpreter for higher-order, lazy programs operating on structured data. Such an interpreter is slow, but not hopelessly so.

There may be some mileage in extending the language of sequential algorithms. In particular, the identity function, and functions such as `fst` and `snd` are quite inefficient at present since they must essentially *copy* the appropriate part of the input to the output. The addition of a **copy** construct to the language, allowing the output of a sequential algorithm to share an entire subtree with the input, might potentially yield a significant improvement in time and space behaviour. The disadvantage is that every new construct must be interpreted by the sequential algorithms for higher-order functions.

Given a **copy** construct to create them, it might make sense to use *graphs* rather than trees as the fundamental data structure. This would permit cyclic structures such as the 'infinite' list of ones to be represented explicitly, and might enable the detection of loops such as `len ones`.

So far we have no quasi-termination analysis for any lazy loop-detecting interpreter. It will be interesting to see whether the relatively simple framework of sequential algorithms is helpful in developing such an analysis.

Finally, the loop-detecting interpreter is of little use in isolation. We plan to integrate it into a CDS-based partial evaluator. In comparison with current systems, such a partial evaluator should be able to evaluate programs lazily, unfold higher-order functions more aggressively without risking non-termination, and create fewer unnecessary versions of residual functions. We are developing a CDS-based abstract interpreter[7], which can analyse some reasonable higher-order programs over a thousand times faster than competing frontier-based systems[8].

Acknowledgements

It has been a pleasure to work on another approach to loop detection with Carsten Kehler Holst.

References

[1] Patrick Cousot and Radhia Cousot, *Abstract interpretation: a unified lattice model for static analysis of programs by construction or approximation of fixpoints*, ACM Principles of Programming Languages, 1977.

[2] Neil D. Jones, Peter Sestoft and Harald Søndergård, *Mix: a self-applicable partial evaluator for experiments in compiler generation*, Lisp and Symbolic Computation, 2(1):9-50, 1989.

[3] Jonathon Young and Paul Hudak, *Finding fixpoints on function spaces*, Research Report YALEU/DCS/RR-505, Dept. of Computer Science, Yale University (December 1986).

[4] Carsten Kehler Holst and John Hughes, *A Loop Detecting Interpreter for Lazy Programs*, Proc. Glasgow 1991 Workshop on Functional Programming, Springer-Verlag Workshops in Computing, 1992.

[5] G. Berry and P.-L. Curien, *Theory and practice of sequential algorithms: the kernel of the applicative language CDS*, in Algebraic Methods in semantics, 35-87, Cambridge University Press (1985).

[6] Carsten Kehler Holst, *Finiteness analysis*, in ACM Conference on Functional Programming Languages and Computer Architectures, Cambridge MA, 1991.

[7] A.B. Ferguson and John Hughes, *Abstract Interpretation of Higher Order Functions using Concrete Data Structures*, in Functional Programming, Glasgow 1992, eds. J. Launchbury and P. M. Sansom, Springer Verlag Workshops in Computing, 1992.

[8] Sebastian Hunt, personal communications, 1992.

A The CDS Implementation

LML implementation of CDS operations for an UNTYPED langauge
types to represent CDSs

```
rec type CDS = Event Val (Sel -> CDS)
             + Empty
             + Depend (List Sel) CDS
and type Val = Num Int + Comma + Case (List Sel) + Out Val
and type Sel = Fst + Snd + Value Val
```

operations on sequential algorithms
functions which copy a part of their input.

```
and     idA = copy []
and     fstA = Event (Case []) (\(Value Comma). copy [Fst])
and     sndA = Event (Case []) (\(Value Comma). copy [Snd])
```

copy c constructs an algorithm for copying the tree rooted at cell c.

```
and     copy c = Event (Case c) (\(Value v).
                 Event (Out v) (\s.
                 copy (c@[s])))
```

primitives, constant functions, and pairing.

```
and     errA = fail "type error"
and     primA op = Event (Case []) (\(Value Comma).
                   Event (Case [Fst]) (\(Value (Num m)).
                   Event (Case [Snd]) (\(Value (Num n)).
                   Event (Out (Num (op m n))) (\_. errA))))
and     numA n = Event (Out (Num n)) (\_.errA)
and     pairA f g = Event (Out Comma)
                       (\s. case s in Fst: f || Snd: g end)
```

currying and uncurrying. Application is easily defined in terms of uncurry.

```
and     curA (Event (Case []) f) = curA (f (Value Comma))
||      curA (Event (Case (Fst.c)) f) =
                Event (Case c) (\v. curA (f v))
||      curA (Event (Case (Snd.c)) f) =
                Event (Out (Case c)) (\v. curA (f v))
||      curA (Event (Out v) f) =
                Event (Out (Out v)) (\v. curA (f v))
||      curA Empty = Empty

and     uncA f = Event (Case []) (\(Value Comma). uncA' f)
and     uncA' (Event (Case c) f) =
                Event (Case (Fst.c)) (\v.uncA' (f v))
||      uncA' (Event (Out (Case c)) f) =
                Event (Case (Snd.c)) (\v.uncA' (f v))
||      uncA' (Event (Out (Out v)) f) =
                Event (Out v) (\s.uncA' (f s))
||      uncA' Empty = Empty

and     apA = uncA idA
```

composition. comp' composes f and g, copying outputs from f and replacing cases in f by the appropriate computation from g, using the function findA to locate it. The first parameter of comp' is an association list mapping the previously inspected cells of g's result to their subtrees. The function memoise removes any multiple reads of the same cell of the input.

```
and     compA f g = memoise [] (comp' [] f g)
and     comp' m (Event (Out v) f) g =
                Event (Out v) (\s. comp' m (f s) g)
||      comp' m (Event (Case c) f) g =
```

```
                findA m c g (\m'.\v. comp' m' (f (Value v)) g)
||      comp' m Empty g = Empty
```

find m c g k finds the cell c of g's result and applies k to a new memory and the value found there. The memory contains all the cells previously inspected, which is guaranteed not to include c, but to include c's parent. The root cell is therefore a special case.

```
and     findA [] [] g k = compute g (\v.\f. k [([],f)] v)
||      findA m c g k = compute (assoc m (init c) (last c)) (\v.\f.
                            k ((c,f).m) v)
```

compute root of argument's result and apply continuation to val and successors found there.

```
and     compute (Event (Out v) g) k = k v g
||      compute (Event (Case c) g) k =
            Event (Case c) (\s. compute (g s) k)
||      compute Empty k = Empty
||      compute (Depend c g) k = Depend c (compute g k)

and     memoise m (Event (Case c) f) =
        if member (map fst m) c then memoise m (f (assoc m c))
        else Event (Case c) (\v. memoise ((c,v).m) (f v))
||      memoise m (Event (Out v) f) =
        Event (Out v) (\s. memoise m (f s))
||      memoise m Empty = Empty
||      memoise m (Depend c f) = Depend c (memoise m f)
```

conditional

```
and     ifA p f g = memoise [] (compute p (\v.\_.
                            if v = Num 0 then g else f))
```

The fixpoint algorithm computes a cds in which each node is labelled with the cells it depends on, and self-dependent nodes are Empty. The dependencies are stripped to give the final result. This is not the standard fix: its type is $(Env \times \tau \rightarrow \tau) \rightarrow (Env \rightarrow \tau)$.

```
and     fixA f =
        stripD (let rec x = blackhole [] (compF f (pairA idA x))
                in x)

and     stripD (Depend c f) = stripD f
||      stripD (Event v f) = Event v (stripD o f)
||      stripD Empty = Empty
```

blackhole c cds maps to Empty any states of the CDS that depend on themselves. c is the cell of the root of the cds given.

```
and     blackhole c (Depend c' f) =
                if c=c' then Empty else Depend c' (blackhole c f)
||      blackhole c (Event (Out v) f) =
```

```
            Event (Out v) (\s. blackhole (c@[s]) (f s))
||      blackhole c (Event (Case c') f) =
            Event (Case c') (\s. blackhole c (f s))
            -- in this case we shouldn't add s to the cell being
            -- computed.
||      blackhole c Empty = Empty
```

compF composes f and g, where g produces a "dependant" CDS, and introduces dependencies of f on g to the result.

```
and     compF f g = memoise [] (compF' [] f g)
and     compF' m (Event (Out v) f) g =
            Event (Out v) (\s. compF' m (f s) g)
||      compF' m (Event (Case (Snd.c)) f) g = -- reading the fixpoint
            Depend c (findA m (Snd.c) g
                        (\m'.\v. compF' m' (f (Value v)) g))
||      compF' m (Event (Case c) f) g = -- reading the env or root
            findA m c g (\m'.\v. compF' m' (f (Value v)) g)
||      compF' m Empty g = Empty
```

A Semantics for Locally Bottom-Avoiding Choice

John Hughes
Chalmers University of Technology and University of Göteborg
Göteborg, Sweden

Andrew Moran
Chalmers University of Technology and University of Göteborg
Göteborg, Sweden

Abstract

We present a small step reduction semantics for the untyped lazy lambda calculus plus a non-deterministic choice. The addition of a fair scheduler enables the choice operator to avoid divergence, and so the semantics implements locally bottom-avoiding choice and not erratic choice. A big step semantics that is sound and complete with respect to the small step semantics is also presented. It includes inference rules for both convergent and divergent behaviour. The operational equivalence that is derived from the big step semantics is much more discriminating than that arising in current denotational models. The semantics is suitable as a basis for reasoning about non-deterministic functional programs.

1 Introduction

Non-determinism is a very interesting and useful programming tool. It greatly simplifies program transformation and refinement, and is crucial for implementing functional operating systems [Tur90]. Non-determinism also leads to natural implementations of many parallel algorithms. Interesting parallel operators, like parallel condition and Plotkin's existential quantifier [Plo77], may be simulated using an appropriate non-deterministic choice operator:

$$\begin{aligned} \mathit{pcond}\ b\ t\ e &\triangleq (\mathit{if}\ b\ t\ e) \,[\!]\, (\mathit{if}\ (t = e)\ t\ \bot) \\ \exists\, f &\triangleq (f\ \bot) \,[\!]\, (\mathit{foldr}\ (\mathit{por})\ (\mathit{map}\ f\ [0..])) \end{aligned}$$

where *por* is parallel or, defined by parallel condition in the manner described in [Plo77], and $[\!]$ is McCarthy's *amb* operator.

Typically, we add non-determinism to a language by including a some kind of non-deterministic choice operator. There are a few binary non-deterministic choice operators to consider. Of these, the most interesting and difficult to model is McCarthy's *amb* [McC63], also known as locally angelic choice or locally bottom-avoiding choice.[1] It can converge if *either* operand can, and can only diverge when *both* operands can. Most current operational semantics for non-determinism implement *erratic* choice, which can diverge if *either* operand can.

[1] We prefer the latter term, for we feel it is more descriptive. See section 2 for our reasons.

We would like to reason about and perform program analyses upon programs written in functional languages with McCarthy's *amb* added. To do so, we require an equivalence relation that reflects distinctions we make in practice. Current denotational semantics for non-determinism identify too many programs we consider distinct and are therefore unsatisfactory.

The small step semantics presented here implements McCarthy's *amb*, not erratic choice. We also present a simple and elegant big step semantics that contains inference rules for both convergent and divergent behaviour of terms, and prove the two semantics equivalent. The derived equivalence discriminates between expressions that current denotational models identify. It is able to do this because the equivalence can distinguish between expressions that differ only on their divergent behaviour. The resulting framework is well suited to equational reasoning.

The rest of the paper is organised as follows. First, we present a small step reduction semantics for the untyped lazy lambda calculus plus McCarthy's *amb*. This can be viewed as an *implementation* of the language and gives a clear operational intuition for the behaviour of $[]$. A big step convergence semantics is then described and shown to be sound and complete (with respect to finite reduction sequences in the small step semantics). Since there are expressions that we wish to distinguish that differ only on their divergent behaviour, we then add big step divergence rules. These are also shown to be sound and complete (with respect to infinite reduction sequences in the small step semantics). Together, the convergence and divergence big step semantics provide a framework for proving properties of terms in this language. Next, the operational approximation and equivalence relations are presented and their use is illustrated with examples. Related work is then discussed, after which our conclusions are presented.

NOTE: No proofs are given in this paper. An extended version of this paper containing all proofs will be published as a CTH/GU technical report.

2 Small Step Reduction Semantics

In this section we present the small step reduction semantics for the untyped lazy lambda calculus[2] plus McCarthy's *amb*. Terms are of the form

$$M \;::=\; x \mid \lambda x.M \mid MN \mid M[]N.$$

We will call this language $\mathcal{L}_A$, the set of all terms Λ_A, the set of all closed terms Λ_A^o, and the set of expressions in weak head-normal form, or values, Λ_A^{NF}. Choice expressions are not considered to be in weak head-normal form.

McCarthy's *amb* can converge if either operand can converge but may only diverge when *both* operands do. For the remainder of the paper we call it locally bottom-avoiding choice because we feel that this is a more descriptive term. We call it *locally* bottom-avoiding because it ignores context when avoiding divergence. For example, consider $e = recip(1[]0)$. If $[]$ is locally bottom-avoiding choice, e may diverge because 0 may be the value of the choice expression. However, Hoare's angelic (or *globally* bottom-avoiding) choice will always lead

[2] In the sense of Abramsky [Abr90] : $\bot \neq \lambda x.\bot$. Our semantics does not capture sharing.

$$\frac{e_1 \to e_1'}{e_1\, e_2 \to e_1'\, e_2} \quad Fun_{\to} \qquad (\lambda\, x.e)\, e_2 \to e[e_2/x] \quad Subst_{\to}$$

$$v_1 \;{}^{m+1}\Box^{n}\; e_2 \to v_1 \quad Amb_{\to_1} \qquad e_1 \;{}^{m}\Box^{n+1}\; v_2 \to v_2 \quad Amb_{\to_2}$$

$$\frac{e_1 \to e_1'}{e_1 \;{}^{m+1}\Box^{n}\; e_2 \to e_1' \;{}^{m}\Box^{n}\; e_2} \quad Red_{\to_1} \qquad \frac{e_2 \to e_2'}{e_1 \;{}^{m}\Box^{n+1}\; e_2 \to e_1 \;{}^{m}\Box^{n}\; e_2'} \quad Red_{\to_2}$$

$$e_1 \;{}^{0}\Box^{0}\; e_2 \to e_1 \;{}^{m}\Box^{n}\; e_2, \quad m, n > 0 \quad Sched_{\to}$$

Figure 1: The small step reduction semantics

to convergence because it avoids divergence for the program as a whole (in effect, it considers context).

In this paper, we consider what is known as *run-time* choice: choice expressions are copied when substituted. When sharing is present, as in many current implementations of functional languages, choice expressions are also shared, resulting in *call-time* choice. This has wide-ranging consequences for non-deterministic programs. Consider the classic example involving the *double* function:

$$(\lambda\, x.x + x)(5 \Box 7).$$

Without sharing, this may result in 10, 12, or 14. With sharing, it may only result in 10 or 14. Call-time choice is more useful in practice, and is also more complex to model. This is the subject of current work and is not considered in this paper.

We first define an immediate reduction relation $\to$, between terms of $\mathcal{L}_A$. This is a *weak* reduction scheme, meaning that the rules do not apply inside λs. The small step reduction semantics is defined as the reflexive, transitive closure of this relation, written $\overset{*}{\to}$. We write $e \overset{*}{\to} v$ to mean that there exists a reduction sequence from term e to value v. We write $e \overset{\omega}{\to}$ to mean that e has an infinite reduction sequence, i.e. possible non-termination. Note that for all values v, $v \overset{*}{\to} v$. Also, since non-determinism is present, the same expression may have many finite and infinite reduction sequences.

A first attempt at giving an operational semantics to $\Box$ might be to evaluate each operand until one reaches a value:

$$\frac{e_1 \to e_1'}{e_1 \Box e_2 \to e_1' \Box e_2} \qquad \frac{e_2 \to e_2'}{e_1 \Box e_2 \to e_1 \Box e_2'}$$

$$v_1 \Box e_2 \to v_1 \qquad e_1 \Box v_2 \to v_2$$

However, this allows a diverging branch to cause the choice to diverge also. In fact, these rules define erratic choice, not $\Box$. We need a mechanism for ensuring that converging branches always get a chance to finish, even if their companion is divergent.

We do this by assigning to each branch a finite amount of *evaluation resources*, allocated by a fair scheduler. The expression $e_1 \;{}^{m}\Box^{n}\; e_2$ means that the left branch has m reductions allocated to it, while the right branch has n. A branch may only reduce if it has resources remaining. When both branches have used their allocation, the scheduler allocates non-zero positive resources to both. Choice expressions $e_1 \,[]\, e_2$ are represented by $e_1 \;{}^0[]^0\; e_2$.

The rules that express this scheduling are given in figure 1. By ensuring that each branch gets non-zero reductions in each allocation phase, the rules allow divergence only when both branches have infinite reduction sequences. The rules $Fun_{\rightarrow}$ and $Subst_{\rightarrow}$ define function application and normal order β-reduction in the usual way.

The following two theorems characterise the convergent and divergent behaviour of $[]$.

Theorem 2.1 *For all closed expressions e_1 and e_2,*

$$e_1 \overset{*}{\rightarrow} v_1 \vee e_2 \overset{*}{\rightarrow} v_2 \Leftrightarrow \exists\, i . e_1 \,[]\, e_2 \overset{*}{\rightarrow} v_i .$$

Theorem 2.2 *For all closed expressions e_1 and e_2,*

$$e_1 \overset{\omega}{\rightarrow} \wedge\, e_2 \overset{\omega}{\rightarrow} \Leftrightarrow e_1 \,[]\, e_2 \overset{\omega}{\rightarrow} .$$

3 Big Step Semantics

The small step reduction semantics implements locally bottom-avoiding choice well, but it is cumbersome to use as the basis for program transformation or for proving equivalences and other properties of expressions. This section presents a big step operational semantics that is more suited to these tasks. First, we present rules describing convergent behaviour in the language and prove those sound and complete with respect to the small step semantics. Then, to allow the big step semantics to properly describe the choice operator we add rules for divergent behaviour. Since the choice operator *avoids* divergence where possible, and we wish to reason about programs involving this operator, we need to have rules for divergent behaviour. The divergence rules are also proven sound and complete with respect to the small step semantics.

3.1 Convergence Rules

The convergence rules are presented in figure 2. The notation

$$e \Downarrow v$$

is used to denote that closed expression e may converge to some value v (i.e. in weak head-normal form). The $Lam_{\Downarrow}$ rule states that values converge to themselves. The $App_{\Downarrow}$ rule defines convergent normal order β-reduction. The two $Choice_{\Downarrow_i}$ rules state that choice expressions may converge whenever either operand can. The i refers to which of e_1 and e_2 is chosen.

The convergence judgements are labelled with a $+$ to indicate that they form an *inductive definition* (after [CC91]).

$$\lambda x.e \Downarrow \lambda x.e \qquad Lam_{\Downarrow} \quad +$$

$$\frac{e_1 \Downarrow \lambda x.e \quad (e[e_2/x]) \Downarrow v}{(e_1\, e_2) \Downarrow v} \qquad App_{\Downarrow} \quad +$$

$$\frac{e_i \Downarrow v}{(e_1 \,[]\, e_2) \Downarrow v}\; i \in \{1,2\} \qquad Amb_{\Downarrow_i} \quad +$$

Figure 2: The convergence rules for the big step semantics

3.1.1 The Set of Convergent Terms

The rules given in figure 2 define a subset of Λ_A^o: the set of all convergent terms. To show this, it is necessary to start with some definitions, which we borrow from [Acz77] and [CC91].

Let Φ be a set of rule instances. We say $\Phi : X \mapsto x$ to mean that the *rule instance* with set of premises X and conclusion x is in *rule set* Φ. There is a monotone operator ϕ associated with Φ, given by

$$\phi(Y) = \{x \mid \Phi : X \mapsto x \text{ for } X \subseteq Y\}.$$

A set X is Φ-closed if and only if $\phi(X) \subseteq X$. The set *inductively defined* by ϕ, $I(\phi)$, is given by

$$I(\phi) = \bigcap\{X \mid \phi(X) \subseteq X\}.$$

This is the least fixed point of ϕ, and is the smallest Φ-closed set.

Calling the rules in figure 2 Φ^+, and the associated operator ϕ^+, the set of all valid convergence judgements is then $I(\phi^+)$. The set of all convergent terms, Λ_A^+, is the set of terms of the elements of $I(\phi^+)$.

3.1.2 Soundness and Completeness

We now prove that the big step convergence semantics is *sound* and *complete* with respect to convergent behaviour in the small step semantics.

Theorem 3.1 *For all closed expressions e,*

$$\forall v \in \Lambda_A^{NF}. e \Downarrow v \Rightarrow e \xrightarrow{*} v.$$

Theorem 3.2 *For all closed expressions e,*

$$\forall v \in \Lambda_A^{NF}. e \xrightarrow{*} v \Rightarrow e \Downarrow v.$$

Theorems 3.1 and 3.2 yield the soundness and completeness result for convergent behaviour.

Corollary 3.3 *For all closed expressions e,*

$$\forall v \in \Lambda_A^{NF}. e \Downarrow v \Leftrightarrow e \xrightarrow{*} v.$$

$$\frac{e_1 \Uparrow}{(e_1\ e_2) \Uparrow} \quad App_{\Uparrow_1} \quad -$$

$$\frac{e_1 \Downarrow \lambda\, x.e \quad (e[e_2/x]) \Uparrow}{(e_1\ e_2) \Uparrow} \quad App_{\Uparrow_2} \quad -$$

$$\frac{e_1 \Uparrow \quad e_2 \Uparrow}{(e_1 \,\square\, e_2) \Uparrow} \quad Amb_{\Uparrow} \quad -$$

Figure 3: The divergence rules for the big step semantics

3.2 Divergence Rules

Consider the following expressions:

$$\begin{aligned} e_1 &= 1 \,\square\, \bot \\ e_2 &= ((\lambda\, x.1) \,\square\, (\lambda\, x.\bot))2 \end{aligned}$$

Both e_1 and e_2 may converge to 1. However we don't consider them to be equivalent, because e_2 may diverge. Since they differ only on divergent behaviour, if our equivalence is to distinguish between them (and similar expressions), it must refer to divergent behaviour. Therefore we need divergence rules in the semantics.

We write

$$e \Uparrow$$

to mean that closed expression e may diverge. The divergence rules are presented in figure 3. An application may diverge if the function itself does, or if substitution leads to divergence. A choice expression may only diverge if both of its operands can diverge. The last rule is crucial, because it distinguishes the choice described in the big step semantics from erratic choice.

The divergence judgements are labelled with a — to indicate that they form a *co-inductive definition* (after [CC91]).

3.2.1 The Set of Divergent Terms

The rules in figure 3 also define a subset of Λ^o_A: the set of all divergent terms, Λ^-_A. To show this, we need to add some definitions to those given in section 3.1.1.

We say set X is Φ-dense if and only if $X \subseteq \phi(X)$. The set *co-inductively defined* by ϕ, $K(\phi)$, is given by

$$K(\phi) = \bigcup\{X \mid X \subseteq \phi(X)\}.$$

This is the greatest fixed point of ϕ, and is the largest Φ-dense set.

Calling the rules in figure 3 Φ^-, and the associated operator ϕ^-, the set of all divergence judgements is then $K(\phi^-)$. The set of all divergent terms, Λ^-_A, is the set of terms of the elements of $K(\phi^-)$. Note that the $App_{\Uparrow_2}$ rule has as a premise a convergence judgement. Since the set of convergent terms is constructed without reference to divergent terms, we can use convergence judgements to construct the set of divergence judgements. In effect, ϕ^- is indexed on $I(\phi^+)$.

A consequence of the co-inductive definition of Λ_A^- is that we can use structural co-induction to prove that a term diverges. To prove that $e\Uparrow$, we have to show that it is a member of some Φ^--dense set, called it's *judgement* set. For example, to show that $\Omega = (\lambda\, x.xx)(\lambda\, x.xx)$ diverges, we need only show that the set

$$\{(\lambda\, x.xx)(\lambda\, x.xx)\Uparrow\}$$

is Φ^--dense, which is easily done.

3.2.2 Soundness and Completeness

We now prove that the big step divergence semantics is *sound* and *complete* with respect to divergent behaviour in the small step semantics.

Theorem 3.4 *For all closed expressions e,*

$$e\Uparrow \Rightarrow e\stackrel{\omega}{\rightarrow}.$$

Theorem 3.5 *For all closed expressions e,*

$$e\stackrel{\omega}{\rightarrow} \Rightarrow e\Uparrow.$$

Theorems 3.4 and 3.5 yield the soundness and completeness result for divergent behaviour.

Corollary 3.6 *For all closed expressions e,*

$$e\Uparrow \Leftrightarrow e\stackrel{\omega}{\rightarrow}.$$

4 Equivalence

We use program contexts to define operational approximation and equivalence on our language.

Definition 4.1 *Expression* e_1 *operationally approximates* e_2, *written* $e_1 \precsim e_2$, *if and only if for all contexts* $C[\cdot]$

$$(C[e_1]\Downarrow \Rightarrow C[e_2]\Downarrow) \wedge (C[e_2]\Uparrow \Rightarrow C[e_1]\Uparrow).$$

So $e_1 \precsim e_2$ if and only if all program contexts which converge for e_1 do so for e_2, and those which diverge for e_2 also do so for e_1. $\precsim$ is a pre-congruence (a result of it's contextual definition). We don't require $C[e_1]$ and $C[e_2]$ to converge to the same value when they do both converge; such distinctions can be made within the context. Thus only values which the language itself can distinguish may be distinguished by the ordering and the equivalence.

Definition 4.2 *Expression* e_1 *is operationally equivalent to* e_2, *written* $e_1{\simeq}e_2$, *if and only if* $e_1{\precsim}e_2$ *and* $e_2{\precsim}e_1$.

4.1 Distinguished Expressions

We begin our examination of the pre-order and the equivalence by giving examples that demonstrate that they are more discriminating than those found in current denotational models of non-determinism. In the following examples, we assume the standard type-free λ-calculus definitions of numbers and lists of numbers. We use Ω to denote the always divergent expression, defined by $(\lambda\, x.xx)(\lambda\, x.xx)$.

Example 1. $1 \,\|\, \Omega \not\lesssim ((\lambda\, x.1) \,\|\, (\lambda\, x.\Omega))2$.
A witnessing context (one that violates the conditions above) is the trivial context, $[\cdot]$. These two expressions differ only on their divergent behaviour. Of the current powerdomain models, only the Hoare powerdomain construction leads to these expressions being identified.

Example 2. $(1 : \Omega) \,\|\, (1 : 1 : 1 : \Omega) \not\lesssim (1 : \Omega) \,\|\, (1 : 1 : \Omega) \,\|\, (1 : 1 : 1 : \Omega)$, where : is the list constructor.
A witnessing context for these two expressions is *tl* $((tl\ [\cdot]) \,\|\, (1 : 1 : \Omega))$. These expressions have equal denotations in all of the current powerdomain models.

Example 3. $1 \not\lesssim 1 \,\|\, 2$.
Any context which converges when its argument converges to 1 and diverges otherwise will distinguish these expressions.

Example 4. $\Omega \not\lesssim 1 : \Omega$.
An appropriate context in this case is *tl* $([\cdot] \,\|\, (1 : 1 : \Omega))$. This means that we don't have partial elements in our operational semantics, which makes it difficult to construct the standard fix-point semantics for recursion or the usual denotational model of infinite quantities. However, as will be shown below, since we have a valid semantics for Y, we have a semantics for recursion and infinite structures.

Example 5. $\Omega \not\lesssim 0$.
A witnessing context in this case is *if* $(1 \,\|\, [\cdot]) = 1$ *then* 1 *else* Ω. This example illustrates that Ω isn't really the least element of our semantics as we may have expected; in fact, we have no such element. Indeed, it seems that the reason choice is bottom-avoiding is that the semantics itself avoid "bottom" altogether.

These examples lead to a natural question: Are expressions only comparable when they have the same set of possible normal forms? In other words, is $\lesssim$ equivalent to $\simeq$?

It isn't, as a simple counter-example shows. Taking example 1 above, the trivial context demonstrates that $1 \,\|\, \Omega$ does not approximate $((\lambda\, x.1) \,\|\, (\lambda\, x.\Omega))2$. But $((\lambda\, x.1) \,\|\, (\lambda\, x.\Omega))\, 2$ approximates $1 \,\|\, \Omega$, so $\lesssim$ is not identical to $\simeq$.

4.2 Interesting Equivalences

The following equivalences hold:

$e \simeq e \,\|\, \bot$	$\bot$ is the identity
$e \simeq e \,\|\, e$	idempotency
$a \,\|\, b \simeq b \,\|\, a$	commutativity
$a \,\|\, (b \,\|\, c) \simeq (a \,\|\, b) \,\|\, c$	associativity
$(\lambda\, x.e)e_2 \simeq e[e_2/x]$	β-equivalence
$Y\, f \simeq f\,(Y\, f)$	recursion via unfolding

Powerdomain	$[\![(1:\bot)\,[\,]\,(1:1:1:\bot)]\!]$
Smyth	$\{\!\!\{1:t \mid \text{any } t\}\!\!\}$
Hoare	$\{\!\!\{\bot, 1:\bot, 1:1:\bot, 1:1:1:\bot\}\!\!\}$
Plotkin	$\{\!\!\{1:\bot, 1:1:\bot, 1:1:1:\bot\}\!\!\}$
Big Set	$(\{\!\!\{\bot, 1:\bot, 1:1:\bot, 1:1:1:\bot\}\!\!\},$ $\{\!\!\{1:t \mid \text{any } t\}\!\!\})$
Mix/Small Set	$(\{\!\!\{\bot, 1:\bot, 1:1:\bot, 1:1:1:\bot\}\!\!\},$ $\{\!\!\{1:t \mid \text{any } t\}\!\!\})$

Figure 4: e's denotation in some of the powerdomain constructions

The last two equivalences are very important, and their proofs are given in the full paper. The last gives us a semantics for recursion, via the Y combinator. This is important, because example 4 in section 4.1 shows that we do not have partial values (making the standard least fixed point semantics difficult to construct).

5 Related Work

The big step semantics we have presented is reminiscent of one written in the G^∞SOS style presented in [CC91]. G^∞SOS is a generalization of Plotkin's structural operational semantics [Plo81] developed by Cousot and Cousot. We use substitution instead of the Cousots' environments, and we do not allow judgement relations to be negated.

The major difference is that in G^∞SOS, the + and − subsets of the universe (i.e. Λ_A^+ and Λ_A^- in our semantics) are constructed simultaneously. This requires a very complicated theory of well-founded systems of inductive definitions. The main benefit is to allow + rules to use − judgements in their premises (both styles allow − rules to refer + judgements in their premises). Since the convergence of terms in the lambda calculus never depends on the divergence of sub-terms, this extra expressiveness is not required in our case. As a result, our big step semantics and its theoretical justifications are much simpler and more understandable.

Much of the work on the semantics of non-determinism in functional languages has concentrated on the use of powerdomain constructions. In the denotational framework, we typically characterise a non-deterministic expression by a set containing its possible denotations (which may include $\bot$). The domain in which these sets reside is constructed using one of various powerdomain constructions. However, to be a valid member of one of these domains, a set must satisfy the closure requirements specific to the construction being used. For example, a member X of a domain constructed with the Hoare construction [Smy83] must be *lower-closed*, i.e. if x is in X, then so are all the values that approximate x. It is these closure requirements that leads to expressions that we do not consider equivalent being identified in the semantics.

Figure 4 gives the denotations of $(1 : \bot) \,[]\, (1 : 1 : 1 : \bot)$, where : is list cons, in domains constructed with the Smyth [Smy78], Hoare, Plotkin [Plo76], Big Set [Hec90], and Small Set or Mix [Hec90, Gun90] powerdomain constructions. All of the current powerdomain constructions lead to e being identified with expressions that our semantics considers distinct. For example, the Plotkin powerdomain construction (which performs *convex-closure*, i.e. if x and y are in X, then so are all the values "in between" x and y) identifies e with $(1 : \bot) \,[]\, (1 : 1 : \bot) \,[]\, (1 : 1 : 1 : \bot)$. As we saw in example 2 section 4.1, our semantics is able to distinguish these expressions.

In [HA80], Hennessy and Ashcroft show that the lambda calculus plus choice is fully abstract with respect to the Plotkin construction for flat domains, but not in the non-flat case. However, the choice defined is erratic choice (due to the simple rewrite rules for the operator).

de'Liguoro and Piperno examine the use of *must converge* rules in [dP92], rather than *may converge* as we have used. They show that the untyped lambda calculus plus erratic choice is fully abstract with respect to an interpretation using the Smyth powerdomain construction. However, the orderings involved identify all expressions that may diverge, which results in an equivalence that is not very discriminating. Though not investigated in [dP92], it is possible to describe the divergent behaviour of locally bottom-avoiding choice (and so distinguishing it from erratic choice) using must converge rules in conjunction with may converge rules. In fact, the must converge rules form the inductive dual of the may diverge rules. However, to reason about divergent behaviour as we would like to, we have to negate the must converge judgements. The resulting rules are not compositional and not easy to use.

6 Conclusion

We have presented a small step reduction semantics that correctly implements locally bottom-avoiding non-deterministic choice. A big step semantics using both may converge and may diverge inference rules that is sound and complete with respect to the small step semantics was also given. This big step semantics is simple and elegant. The operational equivalence is arguably the most discriminating of current equivalences and distinguishes many expressions that are identified in current denotational models. As such, it is suitable as the basis for reasoning about non-deterministic functional programs.

Acknowledgements

The authors would like to thank John Launchbury for his vociferous participation in discussions, and Fritz Henglein for helping to clarify the situation with $\lesssim$ and $\simeq$.

References

[Abr90] S. Abramsky. The lazy lambda calculus. In D. Turner, editor, *Research Topics in Functional Programming*. Addison Wesley, 1990.

[Acz77] P. Aczel. An introduction to inductive definitions. In J. Barwise, editor, *Handbook of Mathematical Logic*, pages 739–782. Elsevier, 1977.

[CC91] P. Cousot and R. Cousot. Inductive definitions, semantics and abstract interpretation. In *POPL '91*, Albuquerque, New Mexico, USA, January 1991.

[dP92] U. de'Liguoro and A. Piperno. Must preorder in non-deterministic untyped λ-calculus. In *CAAP '92*, volume 581 of *LNCS*, pages 203–220, February 1992.

[Gun90] C. A. Gunter. Relating total and partial correctness interpretations of non-deterministic programs. In *POPL '90*, San Francisco, California, USA, January 17–19 1990.

[HA80] M. A. B. Hennessy and E. A. Ashcroft. A mathematical semantics for a nondeterministic typed λ-calculus. *Theoretical Computer Science*, 11:227–245, 1980.

[Hec90] R. Heckmann. Set domains. In *ESOP '90*, volume 432 of *LNCS*, pages 177–196, May 1990.

[McC63] J. McCarthy. A basis for a mathematical theory of computations. In P. Braffort and D. Hirschberg, editors, *Computer Programming and Formal Systems*, pages 33–70. North-Holland, 1963.

[Plo76] G. D. Plotkin. A powerdomain construction. *SIAM Journal of Computing*, 5(3):452–487, 1976.

[Plo77] G. D. Plotkin. LCF considered as a programming language. *Theoretical Computer Science*, 5:223–255, 1977.

[Plo81] G. D. Plotkin. A structural approach to operational semantics. Tech. Rep. DAIMI FN–19, Aarhus University, 1981.

[Smy78] M. B. Smyth. Power domains. *Journal of Computer and System Sciences*, 16(23–26):23–35, 1978.

[Smy83] M. B. Smyth. Power domains and predicate transformers: A topological view. In *ICALP '83*, volume 154 of *LNCS*, pages 662–676, 1983.

[Tur90] D. Turner. An approach to functional operating systems. In D. Turner, editor, *Research Topics in Functional Programming.* Addison Wesley, 1990.

A Certain Loss of Identity

Geraint Jones
Oxford University Computing Laboratory
Oxford, England

Mary Sheeran
Informationsbehandling, Chalmers Tekniska Högskola
Göteborg, Sweden

Abstract

For pragmatic reasons it is useful to exclude the identity relation from the 'implementable subset' of Ruby. However there are many expressions in the relational calculus whose natural meaning is just this identity relation. This note gives an identity-free account of some of these expressions, and shows that there is no satisfactory identity-free account of some others. This is an exercise in writing about Ruby without drawing any pictures, in part because it is about those expressions which would correspond to blank pictures.

What there is when there is nothing there

In Ruby* one uses relations to represent circuit components, and the composition $R ; S$ of relations corresponds to some connection of two components in which the parts of the R represented by its range are connected to the parts of the S represented by its domain. With this interpretation, the repeated composition R^n naturally represents a 'pipeline' of n components, each an R, connected in a linear array. At least, this is the natural interpretation for $n > 0$.

For strictly positive n and m it is clearly the case (and can be shown by induction) that R^{n+m} is the composition $R^n ; R^m$ of smaller powers of R. This suggests that it might be desirable for any definition of R^0 to be consistent with $R^n = R^n ; R^0 = R^0 ; R^n$. One possible choice of a value for R^0 consistent with these equations would be the identity (or equality) relation, id, for which $x \; id \; x$ for all possible x.

Sub-expressions whose values are as 'big' as the identity relation are generally undesirable in Ruby expressions which might be classed as 'implementations'. These expressions are the *results* of refinements, ones which we expect to be able to pass to an implementor, perhaps a silicon manufacturer, with the expectation that they will be accurately represented by some (probably finite) machine operating on a physical data representation. For example, in refining to a design to be implemented in digital electronics, we would not want to say that we had completed the design until all the components in the expressions were relations between tuples of binary signal values.

*This paper is not meant to be self-contained, and should be read in the context of an introduction to Ruby, such as reference [1].

If a circuit contains, for example, a component which is $\mathsf{fst}\,R$ for some R, where $\mathsf{fst}\,R = [R, id]$ is the parallel composition of an R with an instance of the identity, we should not necessarily expect a manufacturer to know how to implement the id which this requires. In fact we would normally not be too concerned about this particular case: so long as it appears in a composition, such as $S;\mathsf{fst}\,R$ it can be read as an instruction to the manufacturer to construct an S, and to attach an R to the first connection (of the pair) in its range. On its own, with nothing connected to the second wire in either the domain or range of $\mathsf{fst}\,R$, it is just as unrealistically unimplementable as was id alone.

If asked we could give an account of this in the refinement: suppose we know that the type of the data handled by the troublesome identity relation is T, that is suppose that there is some partial equivalence relation (per) T for which $S = S\,;\mathsf{snd}\,T$. We can calculate that $S\,;\mathsf{fst}\,R = S\,;\mathsf{snd}\,T\,;\mathsf{fst}\,R = S\,;[R, T]$, and we are asking the implementor to provide us with an S, and an R alongside a T. The specification of a T can usually be read as a request for 'a wire capable of carrying signals of type T', and would be feasible for those types T that had physical representations.

In a similar way, we could choose to say that an expression is only implementable if it contains no instances of R^n for which n is zero. This is unpleasant, both because it adds an arithmetic side-condition to the calculation, and because we find R^0 in some expressions that we certainly do want to be able to call implementable. In particular, the relation $\mathsf{tri}\,R$ constructs a triangular array of successively higher powers of R which are applied in parallel to tuples of signals, that is $\mathsf{tri}\,R = [R^0, R^1, R^2, \ldots]$, but we would often want to call $\mathsf{tri}\,R$ an implementable relation.

Although we could treat $\mathsf{tri}\,R$ in the same way as $\mathsf{fst}\,R$ it turns out to be more convenient to change the definition of R^0 so that $\mathsf{tri}\,R$ can often be called implementable even when not in a composition. For example, if we know that R is a component which only deals with Ts, it would be convenient to be able to say that $\mathsf{tri}\,R$ deals only with lists of Ts.

An idea of type, and an ideal type

First let us introduce some notation for type judgements. We write R^{-1} for the converse of a relation, and R^{-n} for $(R^{-1})^n = (R^n)^{-1}$. Our types are the partial equivalence relations, and we note that the following are equivalent: $\mathsf{per}\,T \Leftrightarrow (T^{-1} \subseteq T \supseteq T^2) \Leftrightarrow (T \supseteq T^2 \cup T^{-1}) \Leftrightarrow (T^{-1} = T = T^2) \Leftrightarrow (T = T\,;T^{-1})$.

We write $R \vdash T$ for $R = R\,;T$, and $U \dashv R$ for $U\,;R = R$, and say that 'T is a right type for R', and 'U is a left type for R'. Notice that since $T = T^{-1}$ for any per T, left types of R are just right types of R^{-1} and vice versa, $T \dashv R \Leftrightarrow R^{-1} \vdash T$. For conciseness, we write $R : U \sim T$ for $U \dashv R \,\&\, R \vdash T$. We will only use these symbols for type judgements when the relations in the positions of T and U are pers.

The idea is to define R^0 in such a way that if $R : T{\sim}T$, then $R^0 : T{\sim}T$, and it would follow that $\mathsf{tri}\,R : \mathsf{map}\,T \sim \mathsf{map}\,T$. Because R^0 is going to be absorbed on either side by (non-zero) powers of R, it seems that we should choose it to be both a right type and left type for R. The identity relation is certainly a candidate, but is too big to be implementable. We need to find a smaller left and right type.

A suitable value for R^0 would be the unique per for which $R : R^0 \sim R^0$ and $R : T \sim T \Rightarrow R^0 : T \sim T$. It is in fact the composition of all those pers T for which $R : T \sim T$. Of course it is not immediately plain that R^0 is well defined by either of these characterisations: it needs to be shown that there is such an optimal type; and it is not always going to be possible to give a meaning to the composition $\boldsymbol{;}\, S$ of the elements of some set S, because composition is neither commutative nor idempotent.

Looking at one side of the problem

Let us begin with the simpler problem of justifying the use of the term '*the* right type' of a relation R. We say that a per T is *a* right type of R if $R \vdash T$. It turns out that there always is an optimal right type, one which we will call *the* right type and which we will write $R\triangleright$, and which exactly determines the set of right types of R.

The right-guaranteeing relation $\vdash$ turns out to be a partial order on pers (although not on relations in general). That is to say, it is transitive ($A \vdash B \;\&\; B \vdash C \;\Rightarrow\; A = A ; B = A ; (B ; C) = (A ; B) ; C = A ; C \;\Rightarrow\; A \vdash C$) and antisymmetric ($A \vdash B \;\&\; B \vdash A \;\Rightarrow\; A = A ; B = (B^{-1} ; A^{-1})^{-1} = (B ; A)^{-1} = B^{-1} = B$). Of all the right types of R there is one which is least under this ordering, that is there is a per $R\triangleright$ for which both $R \vdash R\triangleright$, and $R \vdash T \Leftrightarrow R\triangleright \vdash T$.

Informally, a right type of R is a per for which the equivalence classes are classes of elements of the range of R that are treated in the same way by R. That is, x and y can only be equivalent if $\forall z.\, z\, R\, x \Leftrightarrow z\, R\, y$. Any right type must be a refinement of the coarsest equivalence relation of this kind, $\{x, y \mid \forall z.\, z\, R x \Leftrightarrow z\, R y\}$. The optimal right type is the coarsest per restricted to only those elements which it must mention because they are in the range of R – that is the relation with the smallest number of elements, and the smallest number of classes, of all right types of R. This relation is

$$\{x, y \mid (\exists z.\, z\, R\, x \;\&\; z\, R\, y) \;\&\; (\forall z.\, z\, R\, x \Leftrightarrow z\, R\, y)\}$$

Because $\forall z.\, z\, R\, x \Leftrightarrow z\, R\, y$, the condition $\exists z.\, z\, R\, x \;\&\; z\, R\, y$ is equivalent to $\exists z.\, z\, R\, x$, and says exactly that the smallest right type relates only elements of the range of R.

Define the *right view* of R by $R{>} = R^{-1} ; R$. This relation will serve us as a rough description of the range of R, which is $\{y \mid \exists x.\, x\, R\, y\}$. Clearly $R{>}^{-1} = R{>}$, but it need not itself be a type because it is not necessarily transitive: consider the relation $\Sigma = \{\langle a, a\rangle, \langle a, b\rangle, \langle c, b\rangle, \langle c, c\rangle\}$ for which $a\,(\Sigma{>})\,b \,\&\, b\,(\Sigma{>})\,c$ but not $a\,(\Sigma{>})\,c$.

The right view does put a bound on the right type, because if $R \vdash T$ then $R{>} ; T = R^{-1} ; R ; T = R^{-1} ; R = R{>}$ so $R{>} \vdash T$. Although the right view is not necessarily a type, it does always contain the type we need, and we will show that the smallest right type is

$$R\triangleright = \bigcup \{R{>} \cap T \mid R \vdash T\}$$

The attraction of this characterisation is that the family $\{R{>} \cap T \mid R \vdash T\}$ is clearly small enough to be a set, because $(R{>} \cap T) \in \mathbb{P}(\operatorname{ran} R \times \operatorname{ran} R)$.

If R is its own converse, its transitive closure $R^+ = \bigcup\{R^n \mid n \geq 1\}$ is a per. It is its own converse because each term in the union is its own converse, and $(R^+)^2 = \bigcup\{R^n \mid n \geq 1\}^2 = \bigcup\{R^n \mid n \geq 2\} \subseteq R^+$. We will need this in constructing a bound for two right types. If T and U are two pers, then $T \cup U$ is its own converse, so $(T \cup U)^+$ is a per. If $R \vdash T$ and $R \vdash U$, taking the union of the two guarantees, $R = R \cup R = (R\,;T) \cup (R\,;U) = R\,;(T \cup U)$, then by induction $R = R\,;(T \cup U)^n$, and taking a union $R = R\,;(T \cup U)^+$, so $R \vdash (T \cup U)^+$.

The right stuff

First we must show that $R{\rhd}$ is a per. It is clearly its own converse, because $R{>}^{-1} = R{>}$ and if T is a per then $T^{-1} = T$, so $R{\rhd}^{-1} = \bigcup\{R{>} \cap T \mid R \vdash T\}^{-1} = \bigcup\{(R{>} \cap T)^{-1} \mid R \vdash T\} = R{\rhd}$. To show that it is transitive, consider any two right types T and U of R, then $T \dashv R{>}$, $R{>} \vdash U$, and $T\,;U \subseteq (T \cup U)^2 \subseteq (T \cup U)^+$, so $(R{>} \cap T)\,;(R{>} \cap U) \subseteq R{>}^2 \cap (T\,;R{>}) \cap (R{>}\,;U) \cap (T\,;U) \subseteq R{>} \cap (T \cup U)^+$. Moreover $(T \cup U)^+$ is itself a right type of R, so $R{\rhd}^2 = \bigcup\{R{>} \cap T \mid R \vdash T\}^2 = \bigcup\{R{>} \cap T \mid R \vdash T\}\,;\bigcup\{R{>} \cap U \mid R \vdash U\} = \bigcup\{(R{>} \cap T)\,;(R{>} \cap U) \mid R \vdash T \,\&\, R \vdash U\} \subseteq \bigcup\{R{>} \cap T \mid R \vdash T\} = R{\rhd}$.

Having shown that $R{\rhd}$ is a type, we next show that it is a right type of R. Suppose that $R \vdash T$, and so that $R{>} \vdash T$. If $x\,(R\,;T)\,y$ there must be a z for which $x\,R\,z$ and $z\,T\,y$, and so $z\,(R\,;R^{-1}\,;T)\,y$, but $R\,;R^{-1}\,;T = R{>}$. This z is therefore a witness to $x\,(R\,;(R{>} \cap T))\,y$, so $R \subseteq R\,;(R{>} \cap T)$, but $R\,;(R{>} \cap T) \subseteq R\,;T = R$, so $R = R\,;(R{>} \cap T)$. Taking unions $R\,;R{\rhd} = R\,;\bigcup\{R{>} \cap T \mid R \vdash T\} = \bigcup\{R\,;(R{>} \cap T) \mid R \vdash T\} = \bigcup\{R \mid R \vdash T\} = R$, at least provided that every R has at least one right type.

The right type of a relation gives us another characterisation of a per. A relation is its own right type if and only if it is itself a per. One direction is obvious, because a relation equal to its own right type (which is a per) must be a per. In the other direction, if R is a per it is its own square, and its own right view, and $R \vdash R$. This means that $R \in \{R{>} \cap T \mid R \vdash T\}$ so $R \subseteq \bigcup\{R{>} \cap T \mid R \vdash T\}$. Conversely $\bigcup\{R{>} \cap T \mid R \vdash T\} \subseteq \{R{>} \mid R \vdash T\} = R{>} = R$, showing that if R is a per, $R = R{\rhd}$.

It remains to show that $R{\rhd}$ is the minimal right type of R, that is that $R \vdash T \Leftrightarrow R{\rhd} \vdash T$, for any per T. Because $R \vdash R{\rhd}$ we have that $R{\rhd} \vdash T \Rightarrow R \vdash T$ by transitivity. Notice that we need to know that T must be a per to be able to show that the other implication holds, because although $R\,;T = R \Rightarrow R{>}\,;T = R{>}$ in general $R\,;T = R \not\Rightarrow R{\rhd}\,;T = R{\rhd}$. Consider the relation $R = \{\langle a,a\rangle, \langle a,b\rangle\}$, and $T = R$ for which $R\,;T = R^2 = R$ but $R{\rhd} = \{\langle a,a\rangle, \langle b,b\rangle\}$ so $R{\rhd}\,;T = T \neq R{\rhd}$.

Suppose that $R \vdash T$, then certainly $R{>} \vdash T$, and for each U that is also a right type of R, so is $(T \cup U)^+$, so $(R{>} \cap U);T \subseteq (R{>};T) \cap (U;T) \subseteq R{>} \cap (T \cup U)^+$, and taking unions $R{\rhd}\,;T = \bigcup\{R{>} \cap U \mid R \vdash U\}\,;T = \bigcup\{(R{>} \cap U)\,;T \mid R \vdash U\} \subseteq \bigcup\{R{>} \cap (T \cup U)^+ \mid R \vdash U\} \subseteq \bigcup\{R{>} \cap U \mid R \vdash U\} = R{\rhd}$. Conversely suppose that $x\,R{\rhd}\,y$, then there is some z for which $z\,R\,y$, but $R = R\,;T$ and T is a per so $y\,T\,y$ and $x\,(R{\rhd}\,;T)\,y$. This shows that $R{\rhd}\,;T \supseteq R{\rhd}$, completing the proof that $R \vdash T \Rightarrow R{\rhd} \vdash T$.

On the other hand

It hardly needs saying, but there is a perfect symmetry between the left and right of a relation. Recall that $T \dashv R \Leftrightarrow R^{-1} \vdash T$, so defining $<R = R^{-1}>$ and $\lhd R = R^{-1} \rhd$ it can be seen that everything that has been said here about right types can be said dually about left types.

A meeting of types

A left and right type of R is just a type which is both a left type and a right type of R, that is a T for which $R : T \sim T$. Again, it turns out that there is an optimal one, which guarantees all the others. It is the smallest per which relates everything in the domain or in the range of R, but which is a refinement of both the left type and the right type of R. It will turn out to be $\bigcup\{(<R \cup R>) \cap T \mid R : T \sim T\}$.

Informally $\bigcup\{T \mid R : T \sim T\}$ is the coarsest refinement of both $\bigcup\{T \mid T \dashv R\}$ and $\bigcup\{T \mid R \vdash T\}$, and has as few classes as are needed to distinguish in the same way that R does all the elements of the domain and range. It has an additional equivalence class for all those things in neither the domain nor the range of R. The term $<R \cup R>$ excludes just this class.

We begin by formalising the idea of the smallest, coarsest mutual refinement of two pers. If U and V are pers, define

$$U \perp V = \bigcup\{(U \cup V) \cap T \mid U \vdash T \,\&\, V \vdash T\}$$

This is a per. If U, V and T are pers, $((U \cup V) \cap T)^{-1} = (U \cup V) \cap T$, so $U \perp V$ is its own converse. If each of T and T' are right types of (that is $\vdash$-greater than) both U and V, then $((U \cup V) \cap T) ; ((U \cup V) \cap T') \subseteq (T ; (U \cup V)) \cap (T ; T')$, and $T ; (U \cup V) = (T ; U) \cup (T ; V) = U \cup V$, and $(T ; T') \subseteq (T \cup T')^{+}$ which is a right type of both U and V. Therefore $(U \perp V)^2 \subseteq \bigcup\{(U \cup V) \cap (T \cup T')^{+} \mid U, V \vdash T, T'\} \subseteq \bigcup\{(U \cup V) \cap T \mid U, V \vdash T\} = U \perp V$ showing that $U \perp V$ is transitive, and so is a per.

It is, moreover, a least upper bound of U and V with respect to the guaranteeing order. That is to say, $U \vdash T \,\&\, V \vdash T$ if and only if $(U \perp V) \vdash T$. First we will show that $U \vdash (U \perp V)$. From the definition, $U ; (U \perp V) = U ; \bigcup\{(U \cup V) \cap T \mid U, V \vdash T\} = \bigcup\{U ; ((U \cup V) \cap T) \mid U, V \vdash T\}$. Now $U ; ((U \cup V) \cap T) \subseteq (U ; T) = U$, but conversely if $x \; U \; y$, then y must be in the range of both U and T, and since each is a per, $y \; U \; y$ and $y \; T \; y$, therefore $x \; (U ; ((U \cup V) \cap T)) \; y$. So we know that $U = U ; ((U \cup V) \cap T)$, and taking unions $U ; (U \perp V) = \bigcup\{U \mid U, V \vdash T\} = U$, at least provided there is some T which is a right type of both U and V.

This shows that $U \vdash (U \perp V)$, and by symmetry $V \vdash (U \perp V)$. It follows by transitivity that if $(U \perp V) \vdash T$ then $U \vdash T$ and $V \vdash T$.

Now suppose that $U \vdash T$ and $V \vdash T$, then for any other T' which is both a right type of both U and V, the composition $(T' ; T) \subseteq (T' \cup T)^{+}$ which must also be a right type of both U and V. For these relations, $((U \cup V) \cap T') ; T \subseteq ((U \cup V) ; T) \cap (T' ; T) \subseteq (U \cup V) \cap (T' \cup T)^{+}$. Therefore, taking unions of both sides, $(U \perp V) ; T = \bigcup\{(U \cup V) \cap T' \mid U, V \vdash T'\} ; T \subseteq \bigcup\{(U \cup V) \cap (T' \cup T)^{+} \mid U, V \vdash T'\} \subseteq \bigcup\{(U \cup V) \cap T' \mid U, V \vdash T'\} = U \perp V$.

Conversely, $U \perp V = \bigcup\{(U \cup V)\,;T' \mid U, V \vdash T'\} \subseteq \bigcup\{U \cup V \mid U, V \vdash T'\} = U \cup V$, since we know that U and V have at least one common right type, T. For this given type, $U \perp V \subseteq U \cup V = (U\,;T) \cup (V\,;T) = (U \cup V)\,;T$. Suppose that $x\,(U \perp V)\,y$, then y must be in the range of T, and since T is a per, $y\,T\,y$, so $x\,((U \perp V)\,;T)\,y$, showing that $(U \perp V) \subseteq ((U \perp V);T)$. We have now shown that if $U \vdash T$ and $V \vdash T$ then $(U \perp V) \vdash T$, completing the proof that $U \perp V$ is the $\vdash$-l.u.b. of U and V.

From both sides now

We can now define the left-and-right type of R by $\lhd R \rhd = \lhd R \perp R \rhd$, and we will show that this is equal each of $\bigcup\{(\lhd R \cup R \rhd) \cap T \mid R : T \sim T\}$ and $\bigcup\{(<R \cup R>) \cap T \mid R : T \sim T\}$. First of all, we know that $R \vdash T$ if and only if $R\rhd \vdash T$, and similarly for the left type, so $R : T \sim T$ if and only if $T \dashv \lhd R \,\&\, R\rhd \vdash T$. Of course since $\lhd R$ and T are pers, the former condition is exactly that $\lhd R \vdash T$. Thus, immediately from the definition $\lhd R \rhd = \lhd R \perp R \rhd = \bigcup\{(\lhd R \cup R \rhd) \cap T \mid R : T \sim T\}$.

Now $R\rhd = \bigcup\{R> \cap T \mid R \vdash T\} \subseteq \bigcup\{R> \mid R \vdash T\} = R>$, at least provided every relation has some right type. Similarly, $\lhd R \subseteq\, <R$, so $\lhd R \rhd = \bigcup\{(\lhd R \cup R\rhd) \cap T \mid R : T \sim T\} \subseteq \bigcup\{(<R \cup R>) \cap T \mid R : T \sim T\}$.

Conversely $\bigcup\{(<R \cup R>) \cap T \mid R : T \sim T\} = \bigcup\{(<R \cap T) \cup (R> \cap T) \mid R : T \sim T\} = \bigcup\{<R \cap T \mid R : T \sim T\} \cup \bigcup\{R> \cap T \mid R : T \sim T\}$. But $R : T \sim T \;\Rightarrow\; R \vdash T$ so $\bigcup\{R> \cap T \mid R : T \sim T\} \subseteq \bigcup\{R> \cap T \mid R \vdash T\} = R\rhd$ and similarly for the left-hand term, $\bigcup\{<R \cap T \mid R : T \sim T\} \subseteq \lhd R$, so $\bigcup\{(<R \cup R>) \cap T \mid R : T \sim T\} \subseteq \lhd R \cup R\rhd$. Since each element of the family in the union is a subrelation of the union itself, $R : T \sim T \;\Rightarrow\; (<R \cup R>) \cap T \subseteq \lhd R \cup R\rhd$, so $(<R \cup R>) \cap T \subseteq (\lhd R \cup R\rhd) \cap T$. Taking unions of both sides, $\bigcup\{(<R \cup R>) \cap T \mid R : T \sim T\} \subseteq \lhd R \rhd$.

This completes the proof that $\lhd R \rhd = \bigcup\{(<R \cup R>) \cap T \mid R : T \sim T\} = \bigcup\{(\lhd R \cup R\rhd) \cap T \mid R : T \sim T\}$.

The left and right type of R is a per, because it is the l.u.b. of two pers. It is a right type of R, because being a l.u.b. it is guaranteed by the least right type, $R\rhd \vdash \lhd R \rhd$, and by the transitivity of the guaranteeing operator it follows from $R \vdash R\rhd$ that $R \vdash \lhd R \rhd$. By symmetry it must also be a left type of R. It is moreover the $\vdash$-least per which is both a left and a right type, because $R : T \sim T \;\Rightarrow\; T \dashv R \,\&\, R \vdash T \;\Rightarrow\; T \dashv \lhd R \,\&\, R\rhd \vdash T \;\Rightarrow\; \lhd R \vdash T \,\&\, R\rhd \vdash T \;\Rightarrow\; \lhd R \rhd \vdash T$. This shows that $\lhd R \rhd$ exactly determines the left-and-right types of R, because $\lhd R \rhd \vdash T \;\Leftrightarrow\; R : T \sim T$.

Unsurprisingly, we now have yet another characterisation of pers: a relation R is a per if and only if $R = \lhd R \rhd$. As before if $R = \lhd R \rhd$ it must necessarily be a per, and conversely if R is a per we know that $R = \lhd R = R\rhd$, so $\lhd R \rhd = \lhd R \perp R\rhd = R \perp R = R$.

At last, nothing much

We can now define R^0 to be $\lhd R \rhd$ and know that it is a per, and that it is the best ($\vdash$-least) type for which $R^{n+m} = R^n\,;R^m$ can be extended to allow n or m to be zero. Moreover, it has the pleasant property that $T^0 = T$ for any per T, and so that $(R^0)^0 = R^0$, and by the symmetry of its definition $(R^{-1})^0 = R^0$.

In general, $(R^n)^0$ is not the same as R^0 but it is a refinement of it, which is to say that $(R^n)^0 \vdash R^0$. Since R^0 is a per, $R^0 : R^0 \sim R^0$, but $R^0 : R^0 \sim R^0 \Leftrightarrow R : R^0 \sim R^0 \Rightarrow R^n : R^0 \sim R^0 \Rightarrow (R^n)^0 \vdash R^0$. To see that $(R^n)^0 \neq R^0$, in particular consider the relation $R = \Sigma\!>$ from above. This is the union of two overlapping full relations, $\{\langle a,a\rangle,\langle a,b\rangle,\langle b,a\rangle,\langle b,b\rangle\} \cap \{\langle b,b\rangle,\langle b,c\rangle,\langle c,b\rangle,\langle c,c\rangle\}$, so $R^0 = \{\langle a,a\rangle,\langle b,b\rangle,\langle c,c\rangle\}$ is an identity relation. However R^2 is the full relation on a, b and c, and so a per, and $(R^2)^0 = R^2 \neq R^0$.

We are finally able to justify the strange claim that $R^0 = ;\{T \mid R : T \sim T\}$. What it appears we mean by it is that $R^0 \in \{T \mid R : T \sim T\}$, and that since it can absorb any of the other elements composed on either side, any composition (of a reasonable number) of members of the set must be equal to R^0. We do not think we would want to press the point though.

A very brief extensive treatment

The enthusiastic reader may care to find a neat way of showing that

$$\begin{aligned} R\triangleright &= \{x, y \mid (\exists z.\, z\,R\,x \;\&\; z\,R\,y) \;\&\; (\forall z.\, z\,R\,x \Leftrightarrow z\,R\,y)\} \\ \triangleleft R\triangleright &= \{x, y \mid ((\exists z.\, z\,R\,x \;\&\; z\,R\,y) \vee (\exists z.\, x\,R\,z \;\&\; y\,R\,z)) \\ &\qquad \& \; ((\forall z.\, z\,R\,x \Leftrightarrow z\,R\,y) \;\&\; (\forall z.\, x\,R\,z \Leftrightarrow y\,R\,z))\} \end{aligned}$$

Terms of the form $\forall z.\, z\,R\,x \Leftrightarrow z\,R\,y$ can be expressed in a pointless way by using *quotients* (or *factors*), but as it stands, the only approach that we know to work is to demonstrate equal extension by pairs of pointwise arguments.

Tall and thin, short and fat

We have dealt with empty compositions. Similar concerns arise in the case of rows and columns of components that contain no components. The relation $\mathsf{row}\, R$ can be defined by

$$\begin{aligned} &\langle a, x\rangle\ (\mathsf{row}\, R)\ \langle y, b\rangle \\ &\quad = \exists n > 0.\, \#x = \#y = n \;\& \\ &\qquad\; \exists z.\, \#z = n+1 \;\&\; a = z_0 \;\&\; (\forall i.\, \langle z_i, x_i\rangle\, R\, \langle y_i, z_{i+1}\rangle) \;\&\; z_n = b \end{aligned}$$

and represents a row of n components connected by a horizontal 'daisy-chain', at least provided we restrict the range of n to be strictly positive. Analogously, the relation $\mathsf{col}\, R = (\mathsf{row}\, R^{-1})^{-1}$ represents a column of components.

Two properties of row used often in calculations are

$$\mathsf{snd\ map}\, R \,;\, \mathsf{row}\, S \,;\, \mathsf{fst\ map}\, T \;=\; \mathsf{row}(\mathsf{snd}\, R \,;\, S \,;\, \mathsf{fst}\, T)$$

which we call 'pushing maps into row' and

$$\mathsf{fst}\, R \,;\, S = T \,;\, \mathsf{snd}\, R \;\Rightarrow\; \mathsf{fst}\, R \,;\, \mathsf{row}\, S \;=\; \mathsf{row}\, T \,;\, \mathsf{snd}\, R$$

which is 'row induction'. There are also mutual distribution (or 'abiding', above-and-beside-ing) laws: $\mathsf{row}(R \updownarrow S) = \mathsf{row}\, R \updownarrow \mathsf{row}\, S$ and $\mathsf{col}(R \leftrightarrow S) = \mathsf{col}\, R \leftrightarrow \mathsf{col}\, S$, where $\leftrightarrow$ (beside) and $\updownarrow$ (below) are the binary analogues of rows and columns respectively; and then by induction it follows that $\mathsf{row}\,\mathsf{col}\,R = \mathsf{col}\,\mathsf{row}\,R$.

Were we to extend the definitions of row and column to allow n to be zero, we would find that for any R and any x, it would be the case that $\langle x, \langle\rangle\rangle (\mathsf{row}\,R)\, \langle\langle\rangle, x\rangle$. This is a vanishingly narrow row of components, so narrow that it has no R components in it, and connects the wire at the left – the first component of the pair in the domain – to the wire at the right – the second component of the pair in the range – as if by an identity relation. The empty row does not depend on the component R, but behaves like the relation $\mathsf{snd}\,0 \,;\, swp = \mathsf{snd}\,0 \,;\, swp \,;\, \mathsf{fst}\,0 = swp \,;\, \mathsf{fst}\,0$, where 0 is the identity relation on the singleton type containing only $\langle\rangle$. If the universal identity relation is to be considered to be unimplementably large, then so surely is this relation.

More seriously, it is no longer the case that $\mathsf{row}(R \updownarrow S) = \mathsf{row}\,R \updownarrow \mathsf{row}\,S$. In particular $\mathsf{snd}\,0 \,;\, \mathsf{row}(R \updownarrow S) = \mathsf{snd}\,0 \,;\, swp \neq \mathsf{snd}\,0 \,;\, (swp \updownarrow swp) = \mathsf{snd}\,0 \,;\, (\mathsf{row}\,R \updownarrow \mathsf{row}\,S)$. This is because $\langle x, \langle\rangle\rangle\, (\mathsf{row}\,R \updownarrow \mathsf{row}\,S)\, \langle\langle\rangle, x\rangle$ only if x is a pair.

The immediate reaction to this must surely be that we can deal with empty rows, and empty columns, in a way similar to that which worked for empty repeated compositions. Perhaps we should expect the empty row of Rs to be $[T, 0] \,;\, swp = [T, 0] \,;\, swp \,;\, [0, T] = swp \,;\, [0, T]$ for some type T which captures the essence of R, such as $T = (\pi_1^{-1} \,;\, R \,;\, \pi_2)^0$. That would indeed solve the problem with row and below, because $(\pi_1^{-1} \,;\, (R \updownarrow S) \,;\, \pi_2)^0$ is certainly a relation between pairs only.

Sadly this unexpectedly breaks the apparently much more fundamental rule for pushing maps into rows. Consider the difference between $\mathsf{snd}\,\mathsf{map}\,\mathit{empty} \,;\, \mathsf{row}\,R$ and $\mathsf{row}(\mathsf{snd}\,\mathit{empty} \,;\, R)$, where empty is the entirely empty relation, which relates nothing. The component $\mathsf{snd}\,\mathit{empty} \,;\, R$ is the empty relation, whatever the value of R, so we conclude that $\mathsf{row}(\mathsf{snd}\,\mathit{empty} \,;\, R) = \mathsf{row}\,\mathit{empty}$ must be independent of R.

In contrast, $\mathsf{map}\,\mathit{empty}$ is not entirely empty. Being a map, it must be a relation between lists of equal length, and it certainly relates no lists of positive length. However it does relate $\langle\rangle$ to itself, for there seems no way of defining $\mathsf{map}\,R$ so that $0 \,;\, \mathsf{map}\,R$ is any different from 0. We are forced to conclude that $\mathsf{map}\,\mathit{empty} = 0$ and so $\mathsf{snd}\,\mathsf{map}\,\mathit{empty} \,;\, \mathsf{row}\,R = \mathsf{snd}\,0 \,;\, \mathsf{row}\,R$ is a vanishingly narrow row of Rs.

If the rule for pushing maps into rows is to remain true we can conclude that $\mathsf{snd}\,0 \,;\, \mathsf{row}\,R = \mathsf{row}\,\mathit{empty}$, that is that a zero-width row of Rs must be equal in value to a particular Ruby expression which cannot depend on R.

There seems to be no simple way out of the incompatibility of the abiding properties and the pushing of maps into rows. What we have run into here is an essential limitation of the untyped language. All our 'type judgements' are assessments of the values of expressions, and all empty maps are equal, just as all empty sets are equal. From that it seems to have followed that all empty rows need to be equal as well.

Connections

It is a little unsatisfactory that so many of the few proofs in this paper are done by arguments about points. It would be nice to be able to stand a little further back from the graphs of the relations, and perform the proofs by quoting a small number of properties of the relations themselves. Those pointwise proofs that remain seem to rely on the properties of the diagonal of a relation, that is its largest intersection with an equality relation. If necessary we would be happy enough to axiomatise a diagonalisation operation, but are reluctant to add 'the identity' and take intersections, as they do in the Eindhoven school. The diagonal of a relation would also cover the provisos that every relation has at least one right (and left) type – because the diagonal of its right (or left) view would do; and that every pair of pers has a common right type – because the union of their diagonals would do.

Hutton and Voermans [2] deals with many of the ideas about types, although in a framework in which they are happy to deal explicitly with the identity relation (for them, I) and even bigger things like the total relation on everything. They are able to use the identity relation to define (the identity on) the domain, or range, of a relation. The guarantees relation appears in their work only as a partial order on pers. Although our notations are slightly different our interpretation of pers as types is identical to theirs.

Since presenting this paper we have been shown an unpublished paper by Ed Voermans and Jaap van der Woude [3] which contains some of the results, and in particular the existence of more general least upper bounds (which are greatest lower bounds with respect to their inverted order).

The conflicting requirements of the desirable properties of empty rows and empty columns is reminiscent of the essentially partial 'above' and 'beside' operations in squiggol. Alan Jeffreys [4] shows that making horizontal and vertical concatenation of arrays total operations – rather than ones that apply only to arrays of matching sizes – inevitably leads to trouble.

References

[1] Geraint Jones and Mary Sheeran, *Circuit design in Ruby* in Jørgen Staunstrup (ed.), *Formal methods for VLSI design*, North-Holland, 1990. pp. 13–70.

[2] Graham Hutton and Ed Voermans, *A calculational theory of pers as types*, University of Glasgow Computing Science Research Report 1992/R1.

[3] Ed Voermans and Jaap van der Woude, *Relational theory of datatypes: the per version*, (unpublished).

[4] Alan Jeffreys, *Soft arrays*, in *The Squiggolist*, 1.4, June 1990.

Programming with Constructor Classes (preliminary summary)

Mark P. Jones
Department of Computer Science, Yale University
New Haven, CT 06520, U.S.A.
(jones-mark@cs.yale.edu)

Abstract

As functional programmers, we are comfortable with the idea of mapping a function across the members of a list to obtain a new list of values. But there are very similar ways of mapping functions across other kinds of data structure, so what is special about lists? Why can't we use the same name for each of these functions leaving the type system to determine which is appropriate in a particular situation? This is not just a matter of aesthetics or syntax since it would allow us to write general functions for any data structure that has an associated map function without having to repeat essentially the same definition in each case.

This paper describes a system of overloading based on the use of *constructor classes* – a natural generalization of type classes in Haskell – which provides a satisfactory solution to this problem and appears to have many other useful applications. We illustrate this with some examples using Wadler's monadic style of programming, including the first concrete implementation of monad comprehensions known to us at the time of writing.

1 An overloaded `map` function

Many functional programs use the `map` function to apply a function to each of the elements in a given list. The definition of this function in the Haskell standard prelude (Hudak et al., 1992) is as follows:

```
map            ::  (a -> b) -> ([a] -> [b])
map f []        =  []
map f (x:xs)    =  f x : map f xs
```

and it is straightforward to verify that `map` satisfies the familiar laws:

```
map id           =  id
map f . map g    =  map (f . g)
```

(For those with an interest in category theory, these observations just say that there is a *functor* from types to types whose object part maps any given type `a` to the list type `[a]` and whose arrow part maps each function `f :: a -> b` to the function `map f :: [a] -> [b]`.) Similar constructions are used with a wide range of other datatypes, as illustrated by the following examples:

```
-- Simple binary trees:
data  Tree a  =  Leaf a  |  Tree a :^: Tree a

mapTree              :: (a -> b) -> (Tree a -> Tree b)
mapTree f (Leaf x)   = Leaf (f x)
mapTree f (l :^: r) = mapTree f l :^: mapTree f r

-- A datatype for describing exceptions:
data  Maybe a  =  Just a  |  Nothing

mapMaybe             :: (a -> b) -> (Maybe a -> Maybe b)
mapMaybe f (Just x) = Just (f x)
mapMaybe f Nothing  = Nothing
```

Each of these functions has a similar type to that of the original **map** and also satisfies the functor laws given above. With this in mind, it seems a shame that we have to use different names for each of these variants. A more attractive solution would allow the use of a single name **map**, relying on the types of the objects involved to determine which particular version of the **map** function is required in a given situation. For example, it is clear that `map (1+) [1,2,3]` should be a list, calculated using the original **map** function on lists, while `map (1+) (Leaf 1 :^: Leaf 2)` should be a tree evaluated using **mapTree**.

1.1 An attempt to define map using type classes

The ability to use a single function symbol with an interpretation that depends on the type of its arguments is commonly known as *overloading*. While some authors dismiss overloading as a purely syntactic convenience, this is certainly not the case in Haskell which has a flexible type system that supports both (parametric) polymorphism and overloading based on a system of *type classes* (Wadler and Blott, 1989). One of the most significant benefits of this system is that, although each primitive overloaded operator will require a separate definition for each different argument type, only a single definition is needed for other functions described in terms of these operators.

Type classes in Haskell can be thought of as sets of types. The standard example is the class **Eq** which includes precisely those types whose elements can be compared using the (==) function. A simple definition might be:

```
class Eq a where (==) :: a -> a -> Bool
```

The equality operator can then be treated as having any of the types in the set $\{$ `a -> a -> Bool` $\mid$ `a` $\in$ `Eq` $\}$. Unfortunately, the system of type classes is not sufficiently powerful to give a satisfactory treatment for the **map** function; to do so would require a class **Map** and a type expression `m(t)` involving the type variable `t` such that $S = \{$ `m(t)` $\mid$ `t` $\in$ `Map` $\}$ includes (at least) the types:

```
(a -> b) -> ([a] -> [b])
(a -> b) -> (Tree a -> Tree b)
(a -> b) -> (Maybe a -> Maybe b)
```

(for arbitrary types `a` and `b`). The only possibility would be to take `m(t)` = `t` and choose `Map` as the set of types S for which the `map` function is required:

```
class Map t where map :: t

instance Map ((a -> b) -> ([a] -> [b])) where ...
instance Map ((a -> b) -> (Tree a -> Tree b)) where ...
instance Map ((a -> b) -> (Maybe a -> Maybe b)) where ...
```

This syntax is not permitted in the current version of Haskell but even if it were, it does not give a sufficiently accurate characterization of the type of `map`. For example, the principal type of `map j . map i` would be

```
(Map (a -> c -> e), Map (b -> e -> d)) => c -> d
```

where `a` and `b` are the types of `i` and `j` respectively. This is complicated and does not enforce the condition that `i` and `j` have function types. Furthermore, the type is *ambiguous* (the type variable `e` does not appear to the right of the => symbol or in the assumptions) and hence we cannot guarantee a well-defined semantics for this expression. Other attempts to define the `map` function, for example using multiple parameter type classes, have also failed for essentially the same reason.

1.2 Constructor classes

A much better approach is to notice that each of the types for which the `map` function is required is of the form `(a -> b) -> (f a -> f b)` where `a` and `b` are arbitrary types and `f` ranges over a set of type constructors that includes the list type constructor (which we will write as `List`), `Tree` and `Maybe`:

```
class Functor f where map :: (a -> b) -> (f a -> f b)

instance Functor List where
   map f []     = []
   map f (x:xs) = f x : map f xs

instance Functor Tree where
   map f (Leaf x)  = Leaf (f x)
   map f (l :^: r) = map f l :^: map f r

instance Functor Maybe where
   map f (Just x) = Just (f x)
   map f Nothing  = Nothing
```

`Functor` is our first example of a *constructor class*. Notice that each instance can be thought of as a function from types to types: It would be nonsense to allow the type `Int` of integers to be an instance of the class `Functor`, since the type `(a -> b) -> (Int a -> Int b)` is clearly not well-formed. In order to avoid unwanted cases like this, we have to ensure that all of the elements in any given class are of the same kind.

Our approach to this problem is to formalize the notion of *kind* writing `Type` for the kind of all types and $\kappa_1 \rightarrow \kappa_2$ for the kind of a function which takes something of kind κ_1 and returns something of kind κ_2. Instead of type expressions, we use a language of constructors given by:

$$
\begin{array}{rcll}
C & ::= & \chi & \textit{constants} \\
 & | & a & \textit{variables} \\
 & | & C\ C' & \textit{applications}
\end{array}
$$

This corresponds very closely to the way that most type expressions are already written in Haskell. For example, **`Maybe a`** is an application of the constructor constant **`Maybe`** to the constructor variable **`a`**. Each constructor constant has a corresponding kind. For example, writing `(->)` for the function space constructor and `(,)` for pairing we have:

```
Int, Float, () :: Type
List           :: Type -> Type
(->), (,)      :: Type -> Type -> Type
```

The kinds of constructor applications are described by the rule:

$$
\frac{C :: \kappa' \to \kappa \qquad C' :: \kappa'}{C\ C' :: \kappa}
$$

The task of checking that a given type expression is well-formed can now be reformulated as the task of checking that a given constructor expression is well-kinded with kind `Type`. In a similar way, all of the elements of a constructor class must have the same kind; for example, a constructor class constraint of the form `Functor f` is only valid if `f` is a constructor expression of kind `Type -> Type`.

The language of constructors is essentially a system of combinators without any reduction rules. It is not powerful enough to include a notion of abstraction; this is particularly important since it avoids the need for undecidable higher-order unification during type checking. On the other hand, it retains enough flexibility to be useful for many applications. Standard techniques can be used to infer the kinds of constructor variables, new constructor constants introduced by `data` definitions and the kind of the elements held in any particular constructor class. The important point is that there is no need – and indeed, in our current implementation, no opportunity – for the programmer to supply kind information explicitly.

The use of kinds is perhaps the most important aspect of our system, providing a loose semantic characterization of the elements in a constructor class. This is in contrast to the work of Chen, Hudak and Odersky (1992); their system of *parametric type classes* addresses similar issues to this paper but relies on a more syntactic approach that requires a process of normalization. Note also that our system includes Haskell type classes as a special case; a type class is simply a constructor class for which each instance has kind `Type`.

Returning to the original example, the following extract (taken from a session with an extended version of the Gofer system which includes support for constructor classes) illustrates how the definitions for `Functor` work in practice:

```
? map (1+) [1,2,3]
[2, 3, 4]
? map (1+) (Leaf 1 :^: Leaf 2)
Leaf 2 :^: Leaf 3
```

Furthermore, by specifying the type of **map** function more precisely, we avoid the ambiguity problems mentioned above. For example, the principal type of the expression `map j . map i` is simply

```
Functor f => f a -> f c
```

provided that `i` has type `(a -> b)` and that `j` has type `(b -> c)`.

2 Monads

Inspired by the work of Moggi (1989) and Spivey (1990), Wadler (1990, 1992) has proposed a style of functional programming based on the use of *monads*. Whilst the theory of monads had already been widely studied in the context of abstract category theory, Wadler introduced the idea that monads could be used as a practical method for modelling so-called 'impure' features in a purely functional programming language.

The basic idea is to distinguish between computations and the values that they produce. If `m` is a monad then an object of type `(m a)` represents a computation which is expected to produce a value of type `a`. These types reflect the fact that the use of particular programming language features in a given calculation is a property of the computation itself and not of the result that it produces.

Taking the approach outlined in (Wadler, 1992) we introduce a constructor class of monads using the definition:

```
class Functor m => Monad m where
   return    :: a -> m a
   bind      :: m a -> (a -> m b) -> m b
   join      :: m (m a) -> m a

   x 'bind' f = join (map f x)
   join x     = x 'bind' id
```

Notice that **Monad** is declared as a subclass of **Functor** ensuring that, for any given monad, there will also be a corresponding instance of the overloaded **map** function. On the other hand, it is not always possible (or necessary) to define a **Monad** structure for each instance of **Functor**.

By including default definitions for **bind** and **join** we only need to give a definition for one of these (in addition to a definition for **return**) to completely define an instance of **Monad**. This is often quite convenient. On the other hand, it would be an error to omit definitions for both operators since the default definitions are clearly circular.

The following declaration defines the standard monad structure for the **List** type constructor. This can be used to describe computations producing multiple results, corresponding to a simple form of non-determinism:

```
instance Monad List where
   return x = [x]
   join     = foldr (++) []
```

Another interesting use of monads is to model programs that make use of an internal state. Computations of this kind can be represented by functions of type `s -> (a,s)` (often referred to as *state transformers*) mapping an initial state to a pair containing the result and final state. In order to get this into the appropriate form for the system of constructor classes described in this paper, we introduce a new datatype:

```
data State s a = ST (s -> (a,s))
```

The functor and monad structures for state transformers are as follows:

```
instance Functor (State s) where
   map f (ST st) = ST (\s -> let (x,s') = st s in (f x,s'))

instance Monad (State s) where
   return x       = ST (\s -> (x,s))
   ST m `bind` f = ST (\s -> let (x,s') = m s
                                 ST f'  = f x
                             in  f' s')
```

Notice that the `State` constructor has kind `Type -> Type -> Type` and that the declarations above define `State s` as a monad and functor for any state type `s` (and hence `State s` has kind `Type -> Type` as required for an instance of these classes). There is no need to assume a fixed state type as in Wadler's papers.

From a user's point of view, the most interesting properties of a monad are described, not by the `return`, `bind` and `join` operators, but by the additional operations that it supports. The following examples are often useful when working with state monads. The first can be used to 'run' a program given an initial state and discarding the final state, while the second might be used to implement an integer counter in a `State Int` monad:

```
startingWith          :: State s a -> s -> a
ST m `startingWith` v = fst (m v)

incr :: State Int Int
incr  = ST (\s -> (s,s+1))
```

To illustrate the use of state monads, consider the task of labelling each of the leaf nodes in a binary tree with distinct integer values. One simple definition of this function is:

```
label      :: Tree a -> Tree (a,Int)
label tree = fst (lab tree 0)
 where lab (Leaf n)  c  =  (Leaf (n,c), c+1)
       lab (l :^: r) c  =  (l' :^: r', c'')
                           where (l',c')  = lab l c
                                 (r',c'') = lab r c'
```

This uses an explicit counter (represented by the second parameter to `lab`) and great care must be taken to ensure that the appropriate counter value is used in each part of the program; simple errors, such as writing `c` in place of `c'` in the last line, are easily made but can be hard to detect.

An alternative definition, using a state monad and following the layout suggested by Wadler (1992), can be written as follows:

```
label      :: Tree a -> Tree (a,Int)
label tree = lab tree `startingWith` 0
 where lab (Leaf n)  = incr                       `bind` \c  ->
                       return (Leaf (n,c))
       lab (l :^: r) = lab l                      `bind` \l' ->
                       lab r                      `bind` \r' ->
                       return (l' :^: r')
```

Whilst this program is perhaps a little longer than the previous version, the use of monad operations ensures that the correct counter value is passed from one part of the program to the next. There is no need to mention explicitly that a state monad is required: The use of `startingWith` and the initial value `0` (or indeed, the use of `incr` on its own) are sufficient to determine the monad `State Int` needed for the `bind` and `return` operators. It is not necessary to distinguish between different versions of the monad operators `bind`, `return` and `join` as in Wadler (1992) or to rely on the use of explicit type declarations.

3 Monad comprehensions

Wadler (1990) observed that the usual definition of list comprehensions can be generalized to arbitrary monads, of which the list constructor is just one special case. In Wadler's notation, a monad comprehension is written using the syntax of a list comprehension but with a superscript to indicate the monad in which the comprehension is to be interpreted. This is a little awkward and makes the notation less powerful than might be hoped since each comprehension is restricted to a particular monad. Using the overloaded operators described in the previous section, we have implemented a more flexible form of monad comprehension which relies on overloading rather than superscripts. At the time of writing, this is the only concrete implementation of monad comprehensions known to us.

In our system, a monad comprehension is written in the form `[| e | qs |]` where `e` is an expression and `qs` is a list of qualifiers as normal. If `qs` is empty then the monad comprehension `[| e | qs |]` is written as `[| e |]`. The implementation is based on the following translation of the comprehension notation in terms of the `return` and `bind` operators described in the previous section:

```
[| e |]                 =  return e
[| e | p <- exp, qs |]  =  exp `bind` (\p -> [| e | qs |])
```

With this notation, the `label` function can be rewritten as:

```
label      :: Tree a -> Tree (a,Int)
label tree = lab tree `startingWith` 0
 where lab (Leaf n)  = [| Leaf (n,c) | c  <- incr |]
       lab (l :^: r) = [| l' :^: r'  | l' <- lab l,
                                       r' <- lab r |]
```

Note that applying the translation rules for monad comprehensions to this definition yields the original definition in terms of **return** and **bind**. The principal advantage of the comprehension syntax is that it is rather more concise and, in the author's opinion, often more attractive.

4 Monads with a zero

Wadler (1990) observed that the comprehension notation can be extended to permit the use boolean guards as qualifiers, so long as we restrict such comprehensions to monads containing a **zero** value satisfying a small number of laws. This can be dealt with in our framework by defining a subclass of **Monad**:

```
class Monad m => Monad0 m where zero :: m a
```

For example, the **List** monad has the empty list as a **zero** element:

```
instance Monad0 List where zero = []
```

A monad comprehension involving a boolean guard can be implemented using the translation:

```
[| e | guard, qs |]  =  if guard then [| e | qs |] else zero
```

Notice that, as far as the type system is concerned, the use of **zero** in the translation of a comprehension such as **[| e | x<-xs, b |]** automatically captures the restriction to monads with a zero. There is no need to introduce any additional mechanism to deal with this.

5 Generic operations on monads

The combination of polymorphism and constructor classes in our system makes it possible to define generic functions which can be used on a wide range of different monads. A simple example of this is the *Kleisli composition* for an arbitrary monad, similar to the usual composition of functions except that it also takes care of 'side effects'. The general definition is as follows:

```
(@@)    :: Monad m => (b -> m c) -> (a -> m b) -> (a -> m c)
f @@ g  = join . map f . g
```

For example, in a monad of the form **State s**, the expression **f @@ g** denotes a state transformer in which the final state of the computation associated with **g** is used as the initial state for the computation associated with **f**. More precisely, for this particular kind of monad, the general definition given above is equivalent to:

```
(@@) :: (b -> State s c) -> (a -> State s b) -> (a -> State s c)
(f @@ g) a   = ST (\s0 -> let ST g'   = g a
                              (b, s1) = g' s0
                              ST f'   = f b
                              (c, s2) = f' s1
                          in  (c, s2))
```

The benefit of using the original generic definition is that there is no need to construct new definitions of (@@) for every different monad. On the other hand, if specific definitions were required for some instances, perhaps in the interests of efficiency, we could simply include (@@) as a member function of **Monad** and use the generic definition as a default implementation.

Generic operations can also be defined using the comprehension notation:

```
mapl          :: Monad m => (a -> m b) -> ([a] -> m [b])
mapl f []     = [| [] |]
mapl f (x:xs) = [| y:ys | y <- f x,  ys <- mapl f xs |]
```

The expression `mapl f xs` represents a computation whose result is the list obtained by applying `f` to each element of the list `xs`, starting on the left (i.e. moving from the front to the back of the list). Unlike the normal `map` function, the direction is significant because the function `f` may produce a 'side-effect'. The `mapl` function has applications in several kinds of monad with obvious examples involving state and output.

The comprehension notation can also be used to define a generalization of Haskell's `filter` function which works in an arbitrary monad with a zero:

```
filter      :: Monad0 m => (a -> Bool) -> m a -> m a
filter p xs = [| x | x<-xs, p x |]
```

There are many other general purpose functions that can be defined in the current framework and used in arbitrary monads. Unfortunately, space prohibits the inclusion of any further examples here.

6 A family of state monads

We have already described the use of monads to model programs with state using the `State` datatype in Section 2. The essential property of any such monad is the ability to update the state and we might therefore consider a more general class of state monads given by:

```
class Monad (m s) => StateMonad m s where
    update :: (s -> s) -> m s s
```

An expression of the form `update f` denotes the computation which updates the state using `f` and returns the old state as its result. For example, the `incr` function described above can be defined as `update (1+)` in this more general setting. Operations to set the state to a particular value or return the current state are easily described in terms of `update`.

The `StateMonad` class has two parameters; the first should be a constructor of kind `(Type -> Type -> Type)` while the second gives the state type (of kind `Type`). Both are needed to specify the type of `update`. Practical experience suggests that the ambiguity problems that are sometimes encountered with multiple parameter type classes do not cause any difficulty with this example.

The implementation of `update` for a monad of the form `State s` is straightforward and provides us with our first instance of `StateMonad`:

```
instance StateMonad State s where update f = ST (\s -> (s,f s))
```

A rather more interesting family of state monads can be described using the following datatype definition:

```
data StateM m s a = STM (s -> m (a,s))
```

The **StateM** monad is intended to be used to combine the features of a state monad with those of another, arbitrary, monad. For example, the constructor **StateM List Int** might be used to describe a computation which combines an integer state with the list-based form of non-determinism. Note that the first parameter to **StateM** has kind **(Type -> Type)**, a significant extension from Haskell where all of the arguments to a type constructor must be types. This is another benefit of using the system of kinds outlined in Section 1.2.

The functor and monad structure of **StateM m s** are given by:

```
instance Monad m => Functor (StateM m s) where
   map f (STM xs) = STM (\s -> [| (f x,s') | (x,s') <- xs s |])

instance Monad m => Monad (StateM m s) where
   return x          = STM (\s -> [| (x,s) |])
   STM xs `bind` f = STM (\s -> xs s   `bind`  \(x,s') ->
                                       let STM f' = f x in f' s')
```

The definition of **StateM m s** is also straightforward:

```
instance StateMonad (StateM m) s where
   update f = STM (\s -> [| (s, f s) |])
```

Support for monads like **StateM m s** seems to be an important step towards solving the problem of constructing monads by combining features from simpler monads, in this case combining the use of state with the features of an arbitrary monad **m**.

7 Other issues

In this paper, we have described a system of overloading based on the use of *constructor classes* – a natural generalization of type classes in Haskell – which appears to have many useful applications. For reasons of space, we have concentrated on practical examples motivating the use of constructor classes. The following sections touch on a number of other issues, each of which will be dealt with in more detail in a subsequent paper.

7.1 Limitations

One of the limitations of our approach is the dependence on the order of parameters on a particular type constructor. For example, we can define the functor-like behaviour of the pairing constructor in its second argument:

```
instance Functor ((,) a) where map f (v,a) = (v, f a)
```

but we cannot directly describe the corresponding functor structure in the first argument. Similar problems occur with curried functions; the function **(\y -> f x y)** can be written as **f x**, but the function **(\x -> f x y)** cannot be written without the use of an abstraction (or an equivalent notation such as sectioning) or defining a function `g y x = f x y` and writing `g y`.

The language of constructor expressions cannot be extended with abstractions without requiring the use of higher-order unification during type checking. On the other hand, we can always package up the elements of a datatype using a new datatype with a different order of parameters:

```
data Pair1 a b = P (b,a)
```

Pairs that are 'biased' towards their first argument must now be tagged with `P`. In any case, we should expect some kind of annotation would be necessary to distinguish between the two possible interpretations of `map (1+) (0,0)` as either `(1,0)` or `(0,1)`.

A much more elegant way to deal with this particular example using constructor classes is to introduce a class of bifunctors:

```
class Functor2 f where
   map2 :: (a -> b) -> (c -> d) -> (f a c -> f b d)

instance Functor2 (,) where (f `map2` g) (x,y) = (f x, g y)
```

The two possibilities mentioned above would then correspond to applying either `(1+) `map2` id` or `id `map2` (1+)` with no semantic ambiguity.

7.2 Technical aspects

The theoretical aspects of this system, including the kind system and the use of constructors, have been studied using an extension of ideas described in Jones (1992a, 1992b). All of the standard properties of the Haskell type system carry over to this more general setting. In particular, there is an effective algorithm which calculates principal types, and for which the existence of an unambiguous principal type guarantees a well-defined semantics. Decidability of the type checking process can be guaranteed by imposing some simple syntactic restrictions on the form of `instance` declarations.

7.3 Implementation details

We have already mentioned that the system of constructor classes described in this paper has been implemented as an extension to Gofer. Despite the potential overhead of the kind system, the performance of this prototype does not appear to be noticeably different to that of the original version of Gofer. Given that the Gofer system already supported the use of type classes, the changes necessary to allow the use of constructor classes were relatively straightforward. The only places where substantial modification was required were in the static analysis phase and in the unification algorithm used during type inference. In the former case, the use of kind inference to determine appropriate kinds for user defined type constructors replaces ad-hoc static checks that were needed to verify that each constructor constant appearing in a type expression had the appropriate number of arguments. Constructor class overloading is implemented in exactly the same way as before; apart from a small section of code to implement the translation of monad comprehensions, there were no changes to the back-end/code-generation phases of the Gofer system.

References

Kung Chen, Paul Hudak, and Martin Odersky (1992). Parametric type classes (Extended abstract). *ACM conference on LISP and Functional Programming*, San Francisco, California, June 1992.

Paul Hudak, Simon L. Peyton Jones and Philip Wadler (eds.) (1992). Report on the programming language Haskell, version 1.2. *ACM SIGPLAN notices*, 27, 5, May 1992.

Mark P. Jones (1992a) A theory of qualified types. In *4th European Symposium on Programming*, Rennes, France, Springer Verlag LNCS 582, February 1992.

Mark P. Jones (1992b) Qualified types: Theory and practice. D.Phil. Thesis, Programming Research Group, Oxford University Computing Laboratory, July 1992.

Eugenio Moggi (1989). Computational lambda-calculus and monads. *IEEE Symposium on Logic in Computer Science*, Asilomar, California, June 1989.

Mike Spivey (1990). A functional theory of exceptions. *Science of Computer Programming*, 14(1), June 1990.

Philip Wadler and Stephen Blott (1989). How to make ad-hoc polymorphism less ad-hoc. In *16th ACM annual symposium on Principles of Programming Languages*, Austin, Texas, January 1989.

Philip Wadler (1990). Comprehending Monads. *ACM conference on LISP and Functional Programming*, Nice, France, June 1990.

Philip Wadler (1992). The essence of functional programming. In *19th Annual Symposium on Principles of Programming Languages*, Santa Fe, New Mexico, January 1992.

Combining Monads

David J. King   Philip Wadler
University of Glasgow*

Abstract

Monads provide a way of structuring functional programs. Most real applications require a combination of primitive monads. Here we describe how some monads may be combined with others to yield a *combined monad*.

1 Introduction

Monads are taking root in the field of functional programming. Although their origins lay in the abstractions of category theory, they have a wide range of practical applications. Moggi [6] showed how they could be used to structure the semantics of computations. Since then Wadler [9, 10] adapted this idea to structure functional programs. When structuring functional programs like parsers, type checkers or interpreters, it is often the case that the monad needed is a combination of many, a so called *combined monad*.

For our purposes, we will think of a monad as a type constructor, together with three functions that must satisfy certain laws. For instance, we may have an interpreter and wish it to return, not just a value, but the number of reduction steps taken to reach the value. Later, we may want our interpreter either to return a value or an error message. Without using a monad or a similar discipline, it would be a messy undertaking to do in a purely functional programming language. If however our interpreter was written in a monadic style, we would merely have to change the monad to change what extra information the interpreter should return. An analogy can be drawn with a spreadsheet package which has rows relative to some formula. Instead of changing every element in a row we only have to change the formula to which the row is related.

For our interpreter to return the number of reductions and error messages as well it is appropriate that we use a combined monad with both properties. The construction of a combined monad is not always trivial, so it would be useful to have a systematic way of combining monads. Unfortunately, a method does not exist which combines any monad M with any monad N. However, it is conceivable that we may have a library of useful primitive monads, and for each one a technique for combining it with others. Perhaps our library could be divided into collections of monads which can be combined using the same recipe.

In this paper we will look at the class of monads containing trees, lists, bags and sets and consider how they may be combined with others. Lists will be studied first, and it will be shown that the list monad L can be combined

*Authors' address: Department of Computing Science, University of Glasgow, Glasgow G12 8QQ, Scotland, United Kingdom. Electronic mail: {gnik, wadler}@dcs.glasgow.ac.uk.

with any monad M to form the combined monad ML[1]. The list monad can be used to model a form of nondeterminism: instead of returning one value, a list of values are returned. The combined monad ML may, for instance, be state transformers of lists. Or ML may be sets of lists, perhaps a useful structure for a query system. Another practical use of this technique is to combine a parsing monad [8] with an exception monad (described in Section 2). A parsing monad has the type:

$$\textbf{type}\ Parse\ a \ = \ State \rightarrow L\ (a, State).$$

A parse may fail producing an empty list or succeed producing a list of possible parses. Combining the list part of this type with the exception monad will enable us to return either an error message or a list of possible parses.

All the work with lists is generalised in Section 7 to the tree, bag and set monads. It turns out that the monads which combine with bags and sets must hold certain properties, these are explained.

2 Combining monads

First let's look at two of the most commonly used monads and consider how they may be combined with others. Most of the notation used will be consistent with the Haskell language [4]. The monad of state transformers St has type:

$$\textbf{type}\ St\ a \ = \ State \rightarrow (a, State),$$

this says that a state transformer on type a is a function from a state to a pair consisting of a value of type a and a new state. For example, we may use a state in a type checker to hold the current substitution. The monad of exceptions Ex has the form:

$$\textbf{data}\ Ex\ a = Return\ a \mid Raise\ Exception,$$

this is a sum type with constructors $Return$ and $Raise$. This monad may be used to structure an interpreter so that it either returns a value or an error message.

Now we may combine the St monad with any other monad M:

$$\textbf{type}\ MSt\ a = State \rightarrow M\ (a, State),$$

thus forming MSt, note that M is textually substituted here. We may also combine the Ex monad with any other by defining:

$$\textbf{type}\ MEx\ a = M\ (Ex\ a)$$

There are now two distinct approaches to combining Ex with St, either:

$$\textbf{type}\ StEx\ a = State \rightarrow (Ex\ a, State)$$

or

$$\textbf{type}\ ExSt\ a = State \rightarrow Ex\ (a, State)$$

[1]The notation ML represents the combination of monad M with monad L and has nothing to do with the language Standard ML.

these have entirely different meanings. In the first model, an expression that raises an exception also returns a state. This monad may be thought of as modelling the language Standard ML, where when an exception is raised the state survives. In the second model, if an expression raises an exception then the state is not returned.

3 Monads and their comprehension

For our purposes, a monad consists of a type constructor M, an endofunctor $map^M :: (a \to b) \to M\ a \to M\ b$ and two natural transformations $unit^M :: a \to M\ a$ and $join^M :: M(M\ a) \to M\ a$, satisfying:

$$
\begin{array}{lllll}
\text{(M-1)} & map^M\ id & = & id, \\
\text{(M-2)} & map^M\ (f \cdot g) & = & map^M\ f \cdot map^M\ g, \\
\\
\text{(M-3)} & map^M\ f \cdot unit^M & = & unit^M \cdot f, \\
\text{(M-4)} & map^M\ f \cdot join^M & = & join^M \cdot map^M\ (map^M f), \\
\\
\text{(M-5)} & join^M \cdot unit^M & = & id, \\
\text{(M-6)} & join^M \cdot map^M\ unit^M & = & id, \\
\text{(M-7)} & join^M \cdot map^M\ join^M & = & join^M \cdot join^M .
\end{array}
$$

Laws (M-1) and (M-2) show that map^M is an endofunctor, while (M-3) shows that $unit^M$ is a natural transformation and similarly (M-4) shows that $join^M$ is a natural transformation. Laws (M-5) and (M-6) are the left and right unitary identities, law (M-7) is the associative property for monads.

Wadler [9] describes a comprehension for monads which is sometimes more concise and clear than the above monad functions. The comprehension has the same form as list comprehension used in functional languages like Haskell. The difference is that the structures may not be just lists, hence we tag the square brackets with a letter indicating which monad is being referred to. A monad comprehension takes the form:

$$[t \mid q]^M,$$

where t is a term and q is a qualifier. A qualifier is either empty (Λ), a generator ($x \leftarrow u$), or the composition of two qualifiers (p, q).

Monad comprehension can be defined in terms of the monad functions as follows:

$$
\begin{array}{llll}
\text{(mc-1)} & [t \mid \Lambda]^M & = & unit^M\ t, \\
\text{(mc-2)} & [t \mid x \leftarrow u]^M & = & map^M\ (\lambda x.\ t)\ u, \\
\text{(mc-3)} & [t \mid p, q]^M & = & join^M\ [[t \mid q]^M \mid p]^M .
\end{array}
$$

There are two important facts about the qualifiers, firstly that their order matters. For instance, if we define two Cartesian product functions where the qualifiers are in a different order:

$$
\begin{array}{lll}
a \times b & = & [(x, y) \mid x \leftarrow a, y \leftarrow b], \\
a \times' b & = & [(x, y) \mid y \leftarrow b, x \leftarrow a],
\end{array}
$$

where a and b range over lists. Now both forms of Cartesian product will be applied to the same arguments:

$$\begin{array}{lcl} [1,2] \times [3,4] & = & [(1,3),(1,4),(2,3),(2,4)], \\ [1,2] \times' [3,4] & = & [(1,3),(2,3),(1,4),(2,4)]. \end{array}$$

Hence, interchanging qualifiers changes the meaning that the comprehension denotes. We will see later on that if the order of qualifiers in a comprehension can be changed without changing the value that it denotes, then the monad is commutative. So, in the above case we have shown that the list monad is not commutative.

The second fact about qualifiers is that the variable part of a generator may be used in a later qualifier, but not in an earlier qualifier. For example,

$$[\, x \mid xs \leftarrow a, x \leftarrow xs \,]^M$$

the variable xs is bound by the first generator and used by the next (note, this is in fact the definition of $join^M\ a$). Reversing the quantifiers in the above comprehension will make xs a free variable.

The laws (M-5), (M-6) and (M-7) can be expressed in the comprehension:

$$\begin{array}{llcl} \text{(M-5)} & [\, t \mid \Lambda, q \,] & = & [\, t \mid q \,], \\ \text{(M-6)} & [\, t \mid q, \Lambda \,] & = & [\, t \mid q \,], \\ \text{(M-7)} & [\, t \mid (p,q), r \,] & = & [\, p, (q,r) \,]. \end{array}$$

From (mc-1), (mc-2) and (mc-3) we can derive the following which are useful for manipulating the comprehension:

$$\begin{array}{llcl} \text{(mc-4)} & [\, f\ t \mid q \,]^M & = & map^M\ f\ [\, t \mid q \,]^M, \\ \text{(mc-5)} & [\, x \mid x \leftarrow u \,]^M & = & u, \\ \text{(mc-6)} & [\, t \mid p, x \leftarrow [\, u \mid q \,]^M, r \,]^M & = & [\, t^u_x \mid p, q, r^u_x \,]^M, \end{array}$$

where the notation t^u_x means replace all free occurrences of x in t with u.

4 Composing the list monad with any other

4.1 Lists

Lists are one of the most frequently used constructs by functional programmers, and are built in to most functional languages. Lists will be denoted with the letter L. Everything we want to do with lists here can be defined in terms of the empty list and four functions. The empty list will be denoted $nil^L :: L\ a$ (we may sometimes use the notation $[\,]$). The append operation $(+\!\!+) :: L\ a \to L\ a \to L\ a$ fuses two lists:

$$[\, a_1, a_2, \ldots, a_m \,] +\!\!+ [\, b_1, b_2, \ldots, b_n \,] = [\, a_1, a_2, \ldots, a_m, b_1, b_2, \ldots, b_n \,].$$

Append $(+\!\!+)$ is associative and has nil^L as identity. Hence $(L, +\!\!+, nil^L)$ forms a monoid (in fact it is the free monoid).

The function $unit^L :: a \to L\ a$ takes an element and gives back the singleton list, thus:

$$unit^L\ a = [a].$$

The function map^L applies a function f to every element of a list:

$$\begin{array}{lcl} map^L & :: & (a \to b) \to L\ a \to L\ b \\ map^L\ f\ nil^L & = & nil^L \\ map^L\ f\ (unit^L\ a) & = & unit^L\ (f\ a) \\ map^L\ f\ (as +\!\!+\ bs) & = & (map^L\ f\ as) +\!\!+ (map^L\ f\ bs). \end{array}$$

The function $fold^L$ takes three things: an associative operator $\oplus$, an identity element e and a list:

$$\begin{array}{lcl} fold^L & :: & (a \to a \to a) \to a \to L\ a \to a \\ fold^L\ (\oplus)\ e\ nil^L & = & e \\ fold^L\ (\oplus)\ e\ (unit^L\ a) & = & a \\ fold^L\ (\oplus)\ e\ (as +\!\!+\ bs) & = & (fold^L\ (\oplus)\ e\ as) \oplus (fold^L\ (\oplus)\ e\ bs). \end{array}$$

Hence,

$$fold^L\ (\oplus)\ e\ [a_1, a_2, \ldots, a_n] = a_1 \oplus a_2 \oplus \cdots \oplus a_n.$$

The function $join^L$ appends lists of lists (also known as concatenation) and can be defined in terms of $fold^L$:

$$\begin{array}{lcl} join^L & :: & L(L\ a) \to L\ a \\ join^L & = & fold^L\ (+\!\!+)\ nil^L. \end{array}$$

A useful property of $join^L$ is that it distributes through append, that is:

$$join^L\ (a +\!\!+\ b) = join^L\ a +\!\!+\ join^L\ b.$$

It is not difficult to show that L forms a monad by using the definitions given to check that the seven monad laws are satisfied.

Homomorphism lemma

A function h that satisfies the equations:

$$\begin{array}{lcl} h\ nil^L & = & e, \\ h\ (unit^L\ a) & = & g\ a, \\ h\ (as +\!\!+\ bs) & = & h\ as \oplus h\ bs, \end{array}$$

is a homomorphism if and only if $h = fold^L\ (\oplus)\ e \cdot map^L\ g$ for some function g and operator $\oplus$ with identity e, such that $g = h \cdot unit^L$. This definition can be found in Bird's paper [3], a more general definition can be found in Spivey's paper [7].

4.2 An ML monoid

We define a special operation denoted $\otimes$ which is a kind of Cartesian product,

$$\begin{array}{lcl} (\otimes) & :: & ML\ a \to ML\ a \to ML\ a \\ a \otimes b & = & [x +\!\!+\ y \mid x \leftarrow a, y \leftarrow b]^M. \end{array}$$

The identity element for $\otimes$ is $unit^M\ nil^L$. Using our comprehension, $\otimes$ can be given in terms of the monad functions.

$$\begin{aligned}
& a \otimes b \\
& \quad = [x +\!\!+ y \mid x \leftarrow a, y \leftarrow b]^M && \text{(by definition)} \\
& \quad = join^M\ [[x +\!\!+ y \mid y \leftarrow b]^M \mid x \leftarrow a]^M && \text{(mc-3)} \\
& \quad = join^M\ (map^M\ (\lambda x.\ [x +\!\!+ y \mid y \leftarrow b]^M)\ a) && \text{(mc-2)} \\
& \quad = join^M\ (map^M\ (\lambda x.\ (map^M\ (\lambda y.\ x +\!\!+ y)\ b))\ a) && \text{(mc-2)}
\end{aligned}$$

Proposition
$(ML, \otimes, e)$ forms a monoid.

Properties of $\otimes$
For each monad function there will be a property relating it to $\otimes$, these will be useful for later proofs.

$$(\otimes\text{-}1) \quad unit^M\ a \otimes unit^M\ b \quad = \quad unit^M\ (a +\!\!+ b).$$

A list homomorphism h must distribute through append, that is:

$$h\ (a +\!\!+ b) = h\ a +\!\!+ h\ b.$$

The monad functions $map^L\ f$ and $join^L$ are list homomorphisms, however $unit^L$ is not. Using the above homomorphism lemma every such homomorphism can be expressed as the following composition $h = join^L \cdot map^L\ g$ where $g\ a = h\ [a]$. If f is a list homomorphism then:

$$(\otimes\text{-}2) \quad map^M\ f\ a \otimes map^M\ f\ b \quad = \quad map^M\ f\ (a \otimes b).$$

For ($\otimes$-3) another kind of homomorphism must first be defined:

$$h\ (a \otimes b) = h\ a \otimes' h\ b,$$

where $\otimes'$ is defined:

$$a \otimes' b \quad = \quad [x \otimes y \mid x \leftarrow a, y \leftarrow b]^M.$$

Now if f is such a homomorphism then:

$$(\otimes\text{-}3) \quad join^M (f\ a) \otimes join^M (f\ b) \quad = \quad join^M\ (f\ (a \otimes b)).$$

4.3 Folding with $\otimes$

As $(ML, \otimes, e)$ forms a monoid, we are at liberty to define a $fold^L$ operation in terms of these, it will be called *prod*.

$$\begin{aligned}
prod &:: L(ML\ a) \to ML\ a \\
prod &= fold^L\ (\otimes)\ e.
\end{aligned}$$

This function is related to the functions for monads in the following ways:

Properties of *prod*

$$\begin{aligned}
&\text{(prod-1)}\ prod \cdot unit^L && = id, \\
&\text{(prod-2)}\ prod \cdot map^L\ unit^M && = unit^M \cdot join^L, \\
&\text{(prod-3)}\ prod \cdot map^L\ (map^M\ (map^L\ f)) && = map^M\ (map^L\ f) \cdot prod, \\
&\text{(prod-4)}\ prod \cdot map^L\ (join^M \cdot map^M\ prod) && = join^M \cdot map^M\ prod \cdot prod, \\
&\text{(prod-5)}\ prod \cdot map^L\ prod && = prod \cdot join^L.
\end{aligned}$$

Interestingly, if (prod-1) and (prod-5) hold then $(ML, prod)$ forms an L-algebra as described in Barr and Wells [2]. We can prove the last four properties of *prod* by using the homomorphism lemma again. To prove that $h = prod \cdot map^L\ g$ for some given h we just have to show that h satisfies the three equations for a homomorphism.

4.4 The ML monad

Now given any monad M we can define a new monad ML:

$$\begin{aligned} unit^{ML} &= unit^M \cdot unit^L, \\ map^{ML}\ f &= map^M\ (map^L\ f), \\ join^{ML} &= join^M \cdot map^M\ prod. \end{aligned}$$

The fact that M and L are monads together with the properties of *prod* are just what we need to prove that ML forms a monad.

5 The distributive laws for monads

The definition of $join^{ML}$ defined previously was given with no justification of where it came from. In fact, $join^{ML}$ was initially defined in terms of a natural transformation $cp :: L(M\ a) \to ML\ a$ which is a Cartesian product.

$$cp = prod \cdot map^L\ (map^M\ unit^L).$$

The function $join^{ML}$ can now be defined terms of this,

$$join^{ML} = map^M\ join^L \cdot join^M \cdot map^M\ cp.$$

This can be shown to be equivalent to the previous definition of $join^{ML}$.

Properties of *cp*

$$\begin{array}{lll} \text{(cp-1)} & cp \cdot unit^L & = map^M\ unit^L, \\ \text{(cp-2)} & cp \cdot map^L\ unit^M & = unit^M, \\ \text{(cp-3)} & cp \cdot map^L\ (map^M\ f) & = map^M\ (map^L\ f) \cdot cp, \\ \text{(cp-4)} & cp \cdot map^L\ join^M & = join^M \cdot map^M\ cp \cdot cp, \\ \text{(cp-5)} & cp \cdot join^L & = map^M\ join^L \cdot cp \cdot map^L\ cp. \end{array}$$

The (cp-3) property tells us that *cp* is a natural transformation, the others are known as the distributive laws and are discussed in [1]. We can prove these properties of *cp* by using the *prod* properties. Conversely, we can prove the properties of *prod* using the properties of *cp* and defining *prod* as:

$$prod = map^M\ join^L \cdot cp.$$

6 Monad properties

The monad comprehension provides a meaningful way of describing monad properties as we showed before with the associative property for monads. In Section 3 we mentioned that interchanging qualifiers could be done with a commutative monad, thus commutativity is represented:

$$\text{(Commutativity)} \qquad [\, t \mid x \leftarrow u, y \leftarrow v \,]^M = [\, t \mid y \leftarrow v, x \leftarrow u \,]^M,$$

where x is not free in v, and y is not free in u.

We say that a monad is idempotent when:

$$\text{(Idempotence)} \qquad [\, t \mid x \leftarrow u, y \leftarrow u \,]^M = [\, t^x_y \mid x \leftarrow u \,]^M.$$

Category theorist's, for example, Barr and Wells [1] use the same name for a different concept: they define a monad to be idempotent when $join^M$ is an isomorphism. With our definition the exception monad is idempotent, whereas it is not with the category theorist's definition. Bag and set monads are commutative but not idempotent. The above properties will be used later on.

7 From the Boom hierarchy to a monad hierarchy

Similar to lists, we can define bags in terms of: nil^B, $unit^B$, $+\!\!+^B$, map^B and $fold^B$. The function $fold^B$ is the same as $fold^L$ with the proviso that its operator is associative and symmetric, and the bag union operator $+\!\!+^B$ is also associative and symmetric. Similarly, for sets the operators are associative, symmetric and idempotent. On the other end of the scale, for trees the operators need not even be associative, and need not have nil as an identity. These structures are represented in the following hierarchy, known as the Boom hierarchy, see [5].

	Trees	Lists	Bags	Sets
Associative	×	√	√	√
Symmetric	×	×	√	√
Idempotent	×	×	×	√

These structures are all finite and all form free algebraic structures. For instance, bags form the free symmetric monoid.

In the following sections we will look at the conditions needed to form MB and MS. Trivially, the combined monad MT can be formed with no extra conditions, in the same way as we formed ML. We will discover that there are a hierarchy of conditions needed on M in order to combine it with bags and sets.

7.1 Bags

To form the monad MB, where B is the bag monad and M is any monad, we must first define the Cartesian product operator on MB.

$$\begin{array}{lcl} (\otimes^B) & :: & M(B\ a) \rightarrow M(B\ a) \rightarrow M(B\ a) \\ a \otimes^B b & = & [x +\!\!+^B y \mid x \leftarrow a, y \leftarrow b]^M. \end{array}$$

To define,

$$\begin{array}{lcl} prod^B & :: & B(MB\ a) \rightarrow MB\ a \\ prod^B & = & fold^B\ (\otimes^B)\ e, \end{array}$$

where $e = unit^M\ nil^B$, the operator $\otimes^B$ must be associative and symmetric, to be used with $fold^B$. Its associativity proof is the same as the proof for $\otimes$.

Proposition
The operator $\otimes^B$ is symmetric, if M is a commutative monad.

Proof

$$\begin{array}{ll} a \otimes^B b & \\ = [x +\!\!+^B y \mid x \leftarrow a, y \leftarrow b]^M & \text{(by definition)} \\ = [y +\!\!+^B x \mid x \leftarrow a, y \leftarrow b]^M & (+\!\!+^B \text{ symmetric}) \\ = [y +\!\!+^B x \mid y \leftarrow b, x \leftarrow a]^M & (M \text{ commutative}) \\ = b \otimes^B a & \text{(by definition)} \end{array}$$

Now we can define the monad $(map^{MB}, unit^{MB}, join^{MB})$ as was done for lists, using $prod^B$ given above instead of $prod$. Therefore, we can form the combined monad MB so long as M is a commutative monad.

7.2 Sets

Using the same recipe for a third time, the Cartesian operator will be defined:

$$\begin{array}{lcl} (\otimes^S) & :: & M(S\ a) \rightarrow M(S\ a) \rightarrow M(S\ a) \\ a \otimes^S b & = & [x +\!\!+^S y \mid x \leftarrow a, y \leftarrow b]^M. \end{array}$$

where the operator $+\!\!+^S$ will be set union, but we will keep to the same notation. Now to use $fold^S$, the operator $\otimes^S$ will have to be associative, symmetric and idempotent. Proof of associativity and symmetry are the same as for lists and bags.

Proposition
The operator $\otimes^S$ is idempotent, if M is an idempotent monad.

Proof

$$\begin{array}{ll} a \otimes^S a & \\ = [x +\!\!+^S y \mid x \leftarrow a, y \leftarrow a]^M & \text{(by definition)} \\ = [x +\!\!+^S x \mid x \leftarrow a]^M & (M \text{ idempotent}) \\ = [x \mid x \leftarrow a]^M & (+\!\!+^S \text{ idempotent}) \\ = a & \text{(mc-5)} \end{array}$$

Hence, from this the monad MS can be formed so long as M is a commutative, idempotent monad.

Acknowledgements

Thanks to the Science and Engineering Research Council for funding the first author. Many thanks also to the referees: Mark Jones, André Santos and Simon Thompson for their constructive comments.

References

[1] M. Barr and C. Wells, *Toposes, Triples, and Theories.* Springer Verlag, 1985.

[2] M. Barr and C. Wells, *Category Theory for Computing Science.* Prentice Hall, 1990.

[3] R. Bird, An Introduction to the Theory of Lists. In *Logic of Programming and Calculi of Discrete Design*, Springer Verlag, 1987.

[4] P. Hudak, S. Peyton Jones and P. Wadler, editors, Report on the functional programming language Haskell, Version 1.2, *SIGPLAN Notices*, Vol. 27, No. 5, May 1992.

[5] L. Meertens, Algorithmics - towards programming as a mathematical activity. In J. deBakker, M. Hazewinkel and L. Lenstra, editors, *CWI Symposium on Mathematics and Computer Science*, Vol. 1, CWI monographs, North Holland, 1986.

[6] E. Moggi, Computational lambda-calculus and monads. In *IEEE Symposium on Logic in Computer Science*, June 1989.

[7] M. Spivey, A Categorical Approach to the Theory of Lists. In *Mathematics of Program Construction*, LNCS 375, Springer Verlag, 1989.

[8] P. Wadler, How to Replace Failure by a List of Successes. In *Proceedings of Functional Programming and Computer Architecture*, Springer-Verlag, LNCS 201, September 1985.

[9] P. Wadler, Comprehending Monads. In *ACM Conference of Lisp and Functional Programming*, June 1990.

[10] P. Wadler, The essence of functional programming. In *19'th ACM Symposium on Principles of Programming Languages*, January 1992.

Avoiding Unnecessary Updates

John Launchbury, Andy Gill, John Hughes,
Simon Marlow, Simon Peyton Jones, Philip Wadler
Computing Science Department,
Glasgow University

Abstract

Graph reduction underlies most implementations of lazy functional languages, allowing separate computations to share results when subterms are evaluated. Once a term is evaluated, the node of the graph representing the computation is *updated* with the value of the term. However, in many cases, no other computation requires this value, so the update is unnecessary. In this paper we take some steps towards an analysis for determining when these updates may be omitted.

1 Introduction

There are two obvious ways to reduce lambda expressions: outside-in or inside-out. The former is called normal-order reduction, the latter applicative-order. Neither of these mechanisms guarantee to perform fewer reductions than the other. Normal-order reduction only ever reduces terms that are definitely required, but it may end up reducing a single term more than once. On the other hand, while applicative order reduction is less likely to reduce a single term more than once, it may reduce terms unnecessarily, even to the extent of failing to terminate.

There is a popular middle ground, commonly called lazy evaluation. Semantically, lazy evaluation is equivalent to normal-order reduction—only terms which are known to be required are evaluated. Operationally, however, lazy evaluation matches exactly the applicative order behaviour in avoiding repeated evaluation. (Note that neither applicative-order reduction nor lazy evaluation is an optimal evaluation strategy in the sense of Levy [4], so both may sometimes repeat reductions.)

One common method by which lazy evaluation achieves its behaviour is *graph reduction*. When substitution takes place, a reference to an expression is substituted, rather than the expression itself. If the expression is ever evaluated, it is replaced by its value so that all other references to the term immediately see the reduced value rather than the original unreduced term. This replacement, or update, is precisely the point which distinguishes lazy evaluation from normal-order reduction. Hence, normal-order is sometimes called *tree reduction* in contrast to lazy evaluation's graph reduction.

While graph reduction supplies undoubted benefits, it also has associated costs. Updating the reference always costs instructions, and the cost of interrupting the computation at the appropriate time may be even greater. Normally of course this cost is very small when compared with the cost of recomputing a value, but it exists nonetheless. On the parallel machine GRIP [5] updates are particularly expensive because the updated node has to be flushed from local memory out to the global store. Similarly, the need for updates creates a major complication in the TIM abstract machine [2], and the presence of the *update markers* interrupts the flow of evaluation. Indeed, Fairbain and Wray used a local analysis to cut down on such update markers, but unfortunately the analysis assumed a fairly naive model of implementation and precluded more efficient alternative implementations.

In this paper we take some steps towards an analysis which detects when updates may be omitted. It is a working paper and probably contains many omissions, but nonetheless addresses an important issue in the implementation of lazy functional programming languages.

The analysis is presented in the style of type rules. This has the advantage of allowing information to flow both forwards and backwards through a program, but it has the disadvantage of being that much further from an implementation. Currently the analysis does not handle products or other data structures, but it is higher-order. Also, explicit recursion is not presented here, but we do not expect it to pose much of a problem.

2 The Language

We will use a stylised form of lambda expression extended with *let*s, plus a few other constructs for convenience. The form of expressions is a simplification of the Spineless, Tagless, G-machine implementation language (STG) [6] used in the Glasgow Haskell compiler.

The underlying philosophy of the language is that it has a direct operational reading, a sort of "abstract machine-code" for functional languages. Closures are named explicitly using *let*s, and functions accept only such closures as arguments. This philosophy is particularly appropriate for our analysis because it provides an ideal place for update annotations to be placed. Note that the *only* means of constructing closures is by using *let*s.

We make two exceptions to the rule regarding function arguments, both purely for the sake of readability: explicit numbers may also be used as arguments to functions; and primitive operations such as + may be applied to arbitrary expressions.

$$
\begin{array}{lcl}
e \in \mathit{Expression} & ::= & a \\
 & | & \lambda x.e \\
 & | & e\ a \\
 & | & \mathit{let}^i\ x = e_1\ \mathit{in}\ e_2 \\
 & | & e_1\ *\ e_2 \\
a \in \mathit{Atom} & ::= & x \\
 & | & n \\
 & & \\
* \in \mathit{Primitive} & ::= & +\ |\ \ldots \\
x \in \mathit{Variable} & & \\
n \in \mathit{Integer} & & \\
i \in \mathit{Annotation} & &
\end{array}
$$

The aim of the analysis is to discover which *let*s create closures that need to be updated and which do not. The result of the analysis is expressed as an annotation placed on the *let*. The details of the annotations will be given later.

3 Why it's difficult

Examples are often valuable for providing intuition about a problem. Furthermore, in our case they will provide an informal understanding of the STG reduction model.

Consider the program fragment,

$$\begin{array}{l} \textit{let } u = \ldots \textit{ in} \\ \quad \textit{let } v = \ u + 3 \textit{ in} \\ \qquad v + v \end{array}$$

To obtain the value of the expression, we need to know which two values to add together. The first is v. To evaluate v, we need to get the value of u. Suppose u evaluates to 5. Because graph reduction guarantees not to recompute values, u has its closure updated with the number 5. Now v can be evaluated, producing 8, and its closure updated (with the number 8).

We now have to find the value to the second argument of +, so again we need the value for v. However, as v's closure was overwritten with 8 we can obain its value immediately *and we do not have to reaccess* u. 8 is added to 8 to give the answer 16.

3.1 Hidden References

Because u was only accessed once, we could have omitted updating u's closure without causing any computation to be repeated. Note that u was only accessed once even though v was accessed twice, and v depended on u. This means that reaccessing is not necessarily transitive. Sometimes it is, however. Consider the next example.

$$\begin{array}{l} \textit{let } u = \ldots \textit{ in} \\ \quad \textit{let } v = \lambda x.u + x \textit{ in} \\ \qquad v\ 3 + v\ 4 \end{array}$$

This time v is a function which adds its argument to the value of u. Every time we use v we will need to know u's value. The problem is that even though v is already in weak head normal form (whnf) it still contains a reference to u. Thus in this example updating u's closure with its value is necessary to save recomputing that value. The next two examples show this very clearly.

$$\begin{array}{l} \textit{let } u = \ldots \textit{in} \\ \quad \textit{let } v = (\textit{let } w = u + 1 \textit{ in } \lambda x.w + x) \textit{ in} \\ \qquad v\ 3 + v\ 4 \end{array}$$

In this case, while both v and w need to be updated once evaluated, u does not because it is only used once: on evaluating $v\ 3$, w is evaluated (accessing u) and is overwritten with its value. Now all reference to u is lost, so even when v is used again, u is not reaccessed.

Contrast this with

$$\begin{array}{l} \textit{let } u = \ldots \textit{ in} \\ \quad \textit{let } v = \lambda x.(\textit{let } w = u + 1 \textit{ in } w + x) \textit{ in} \\ \qquad v\ 3 + v\ 4 \end{array}$$

Each time v is used it constructs a new closure for w (because in principle w's value could depend on x) and so continues to retain a reference to u. Thus once u is evaluated, its closure must be updated to avoid recomputing its value on a subsequent use of v. Taken together, this and the previous example show how sensitive the issue of avoiding updates is to the precise form of the expression. Denotationally the two expressions are equivalent (one is a λ-lifted version of the other) but their operational behaviour is different.

The examples have demonstrated that there are two issues to be addressed to produce a useful analysis. The first is whether a closure is duplicated or not. The second is whether duplication of a descendant closure affects the original or not. The (fairly simplistic) approach we adopt here is to assume that duplication of functions possibly duplicates closures the functions refer to, whereas duplication of an atomic value does not. Once an atomic value is reduced to weak head normal form (which for atomic values is the same as normal form) it cannot contain references to other closures which may be accessed at a later point.

4 Update-Avoidance Analysis

In the analysis we use annotated types to register when multiple accesses are possible. We are not interested in the distinction between types such as *Integer* or *Bool*, but we are interested in the level of structure present in a type, in particular whether the object is a product or a function. For simplicity we restrict ourselves to consider functions.

Types to the left of function arrows carry annotations which specify whether the function possibly duplicates its argument or not. Thus types are of the form,

$$
\begin{array}{lcl}
S, T \in \mathit{Type} & ::= & K \\
 & \mid & A \rightarrow T \\
A, B \in \mathit{AnnType} & ::= & T^{i}
\end{array}
$$

where *AnnType* is the annotated types. The annotations record whether a value may possibly be used zero, one or many times.

$$
\begin{array}{lcl}
i, j \in \mathit{Ann} & ::= & \mathit{Zero} \\
 & \mid & \mathit{One} \\
 & \mid & \mathit{Many}
\end{array}
$$

The annotations are interpreted in the following way:

Zero	Never used;
One	Certainly used no more than once;
Many	May be used any number of times.

and we assume an ordering of $\mathit{Zero} < \mathit{One} < \mathit{Many}$.

This interpretation incorporates a notion of *safe approximation*. We may end up deciding that a value could be used many times, when in fact it is only ever used once. Of course, the better the analysis is, the less frequently it will overapproximate in this way. Graph reduction is ultra-conservative in this sense in that it updates every closure whether it is used more than once or not.

$$\textit{Weak} \quad \frac{\Gamma \vdash e : T}{\Gamma, x : S^{Zero} \vdash e : T}$$

$$\textit{Cont} \quad \frac{\Gamma, x : S^{Many}, y : S^{Many} \vdash e : T}{\Gamma, z : S^{Many} \vdash e[z/x, z/y] : T}$$

$$\textit{Dere} \quad \frac{\Gamma, x : S^{i} \vdash e : T}{\Gamma, x : S^{j} \vdash e : T} \; (i \leq j)$$

$$\textit{Exch} \quad \frac{\Gamma, x : A, y : B \vdash e : T}{\Gamma, y : B, x : A \vdash e : T}$$

Figure 1: Structural rules

4.1 Structural Rules

The analysis is given in the form of type rules. Judgements are of the form,

$$\Gamma \vdash e : T$$

This is read that in the type environment Γ, we may deduce that e has type T (note, no annotation on T). Type environments are partial functions, mapping variables to annotated types. Thus each variable occurs at most once in a type environment. That is,

$$\Gamma, \Delta \in \mathit{TypeEnv} \quad ::= \quad x : A, y : B, \ldots$$

We will often write the assumptions making the annotations on the types explicit.

The structural rules given in Figure 1 define the behaviour of type environments. The weakening rule allows any variable to be introduced with a *Zero* annotation, and the contraction rule allows two occurrences of a variable to be combined so long as they both have the *Many* annotation. The renaming is present to maintain the invariant that each variable occurs once only in the type environment.

In order to allow variables with possibly other annotations to be combined, the dereliction rule allows annotations to be degraded. This clearly has the potential for losing information so should only be applied when necessary. Finally the exchange rule shows that the order of assumptions is unimportant.

4.2 The Analysis Rules

The analysis rules appear in Figure 2. The variable rule ensures that any new variables appear in the type environment with annotation at least *One* (dereliction allows this to be degraded to *Many*), and the constant rule states that numbers are an atomic type.

Var	$x : T^{One} \vdash x : T$
Const	$\vdash n : K$
Lam	$\dfrac{\Gamma, x : S^i \vdash e : T}{\Gamma \vdash (\lambda x.e) : S^i \to T}$
App	$\dfrac{\Gamma \vdash e : S^i \to T}{\Gamma, x : S^i \vdash (e\ x) : T}$
Let	$\dfrac{\Gamma \vdash e_1 : S \qquad \Delta, x : S^i \vdash e_2 : T}{\Gamma^j, \Delta \vdash (let^k\ x = e_1\ in\ e_2) : T}$
	where $j = One$ **if** $S = K;\ i$ **otherwise** $k = i$ **if** $T = K;\ Many$ **otherwise**
Prim	$\dfrac{\Gamma \vdash e_1 : K \qquad \Delta \vdash e_2 : K}{\Gamma, \Delta \vdash (e_1 * e_2) : K}$

Figure 2: Deduction rules

One pleasant consequence of only ever applying functions to variables is that the lambda and application rules are dual to each other. They have the effect of moving annotations between type environments and types.

There are essentially four variants of the let rule, depending on whether the variable being bound has an atomic type or not, and whether the term being built has an atomic type or not.

When the bound variable is of atomic type, it can contain no references to other closures once it is evaluated. So multiple accesses of the value will not propagate to the references contained in Γ, and their annotations may remain unchanged.

This is not the case for a composite structure, however. A function may contain references to other closures which are accessed *each time* the function is used. Thus all the free variables used in the definition of the function must be given an annotation at least as high as that of the function, for if the function is accessed many times, then so may any internal references.

To model these two cases we introduce an operation on type environments whose effect is to propagate annotations to every type in the environment. We define,

$$(x_1 : T_1^{i_1}, \ldots, x_n : T_n^{i_n})^j = (x_1 : T_1^{i_1 . j}, \ldots, x_n : T_n^{i_n . j})$$

where

$$\begin{array}{lcll} i \ . \ Zero & = & Zero & \\ i \ . \ One & = & i & \\ i \ . \ Many & = & Zero, & if \ i = Zero \\ & = & Many, & otherwise \end{array}$$

A similar situation arises when the term being built is of atomic type. Even if the term is bound to a variable which is used many times, none of the references used in its definition can escape. That is, none of the closures used in defining e_2 will ever be accessed more frequently than the number of accesses given in e_2. By assumption, this is already recorded by their annotation. Thus x in particular cannot be accessed more frequently than described by the annotation i, and so in this case the *let* is also annotated with i.

If e_2 is of function type, however, then there is not sufficient information present to determine whether the closure being built will only be accessed once or not. If the function is bound to a variable which is used many times, then there may be multiple accesses of x, even if it only occurs once in e_2. So in this case we are conservative and assume multiple accesses are possible, and we record this on the *let* so that an update may be performed if necessary (let^{Many} constructs an updatable closure).

5 Results

In this section we show the analysis working on the examples presented earlier.

Example 1

$$\begin{array}{l} let \ u = \ldots \ in \\ \quad let \ v = \ u + 3 \ in \\ \qquad v + v \end{array}$$

First we note that using contraction and dereliction, together with the *Var* and *Prim* rules, we have,

$$\dfrac{\dfrac{\dfrac{}{v_1 : K^{One} \vdash v_1 : K}}{v_1 : K^{Many} \vdash v_1 : K} \quad \dfrac{\dfrac{}{v_2 : K^{One} \vdash v_2 : K}}{v_2 : K^{Many} \vdash v_2 : K}}{\dfrac{v_1 : K^{Many}, v_2 : K^{Many} \vdash v_1 + v_2 : K}{v : K^{Many} \vdash v + v : K}}$$

We can use this to obtain,

$$\dfrac{\dfrac{\dfrac{}{u : K^{One} \vdash u : K} \quad \dfrac{}{\vdash 3 : K}}{u : K^{One} \vdash u + 3 : K} \qquad v : K^{Many} \vdash v + v : K}{u : K^{One} \vdash let^{Many}\ v = u + 3\ in\ v + v : K}$$

The *Many* annotation from the assumption about v has come to rest on the *let* binding v, but as v has an atomic type, its annotation is not propagated to the type environment, so u retains its original annotation.

Finally, assuming that we have some Γ for which we may infer $\Gamma \vdash \ldots : K$, we have

$$\dfrac{\Gamma \vdash \ldots : K \quad u : K^{One} \vdash let^{Many}\ v = u + 3\ in\ v + v : K}{\Gamma \vdash let^{One}\ u = \ldots\ in\ (let^{Many}\ v = u + 3\ in\ v + v) : K}$$

The final result is that u is used once only, but that v may be used more than once.

Example 2

$$\begin{array}{l} let\ u = \ldots\ in \\ \quad let\ v = \lambda x.u + x\ in \\ \quad\quad v\ 3 + v\ 4 \end{array}$$

The interesting part of this example is the binding of v. First note that we can derive,

$$\dfrac{\dfrac{\dfrac{}{u : K^{One} \vdash u : K} \quad \dfrac{}{x : K^{One} \vdash x : K}}{u : K^{One}, x : K^{One} \vdash u + x : K}}{u : K^{One} \vdash \lambda x.u + x : K^{One} \rightarrow K}$$

Following a path similar to that of example 1, we can also derive,

$$v : (K^{One} \rightarrow K)^{Many} \vdash v\ 3 + v\ 4 : K$$

Putting these together with the *let* rule gives,

$$u : K^{Many} \vdash let^{Many}\ v = \lambda x.u + x\ in\ v\ 3 + v\ 4 : K$$

Because v is not of atomic type, all the free variables involved in its binding receive v's annotation. Thus u has the annotation *Many*, so will be bound in an updatable closure.

Example 3
The final example covers the two code fragments

$$\begin{array}{l} let\ u = \ldots in \\ \quad let\ v = (let\ w = u + 1\ in\ \lambda x.w + x)\ in \\ \quad\quad v\ 3 + v\ 4 \end{array}$$

and

$$\begin{array}{l} let\ u = \ldots\ in \\ \quad let\ v = \lambda x.(let\ w = u + 1\ in\ w + x)\ in \\ \quad\quad v\ 3 + v\ 4 \end{array}$$

The analysis annotates u and v as updatable in both cases,[1] and w as updatable only in the first. When evaluating the term in the second case, a new closure w is generated each time the function v is called, and this fresh closure is only ever used once. Thus is may safely be marked as a non-updatable closure.

In contrast, in the first case, a single closure for w is generated and reused each time v is called, so requiring the closure for w to be updatable. This shows a weakness with the analysis, for if w is updated, future references to v will not refer to u, so in fact u need not be updated. However the analysis is conservative here, and is not able to distinguish between the uses of u in the two examples.

A more accurate (and presumably more expensive) analysis could keep track of the *depth* at which free variables occur in function valued expressions to determine whether references to them will remain once the function has been evaluated to whnf. Whether the relatively small gain in accuracy would be worth while or not is not clear.

6 Relationship to Linear Logic

There is obviously a close relationship between linear logic the rules presented here. The version of linear logic most closely related is *bounded linear logic* [1], where annotations are placed on the "bangs" to indicate how often a term is used. So rather than using $!T$ which describes a type that can be copied as often as required (ie. an unbounded number of times), types such as $!^n T$ are used. Such a type may be copied up to n times, but no more. The analysis presented here may be viewed as an abstraction of this as we capture two or more uses of a variable as *Many*, but retain *Zero* and *One*. One important aspect of our analysis, however, is that is deals only with banged types, and has no place for linear types.

7 Future Work

This report is a working paper, and quite a lot remains to be done. We currently have no correctness proof for this analysis. The difficulty lies in not having had

[1] Of course, as v is already in whnf, no update ever need take place. It is a simple matter to postprocess a term to remove update annotations from *lets* which bind variable to values already in whnf.

an appropriate level semantics of the STG language. The denotational semantics is too high—it doesn't distinguish between normal-order reduction and lazy evaluation—and the operation semantics is too low as it explicitly describes the heap, stack pointers and the like. New work has recently developed an intermediate level semantics [3] which, we hope, will turn out to be appropriate not merely for this proof, but for others that exploit lazy evaluation.

References

[1] Girard, Scedrov, and Scott, *Bounded Linear Logic*, J of Theoretical Computer Science, 97:1–66, 1992.

[2] J.Fairbairn and S.Wray, *A Simple Lazy Abstract-Machine to Execute Supercombinators*, in Proc. FPCA, Portland, pp 34-45, S-V, 1987.

[3] J.Launchbury, *A Natural Semantics for Lazy Evaluation*, in Proc. ACM SIGPLAN *Principles of Programming Languages*, Charleston, South Carolina, 1993.

[4] J.-J.Lévy, *Optimal Reductions in the Lambda Calculus*, in Seldin and Hindley eds., *To H.B.Curry: Essays in Combinatory Logic, Lambda Calculus and Formalism*, pp 159-191, Academic Press, 1980.

[5] S.Peyton Jones, C.Clack, J.Salkild, M.Hardie, *GRIP - a high-performance architecture for parallel graph reduction.* Proc IFIP conference on Functional Programming Languages and Computer Architecture, Portland. Springer Verlag LNCS 274, pp 98-112, 1987.

[6] S.Peyton Jones, *Implementing Lazy Functional Languages on Stock Hardware: the Spineless Tagless G-Machine*, Journal of Functional Programming, CUP, 1992, to appear.

Deforestation for Higher-Order Functions

Simon Marlow
Philip Wadler
Department of Computer Science,
University of Glasgow, Glasgow*

Abstract

Deforestation is an automatic transformation scheme for functional programs which attempts to remove unnecessary intermediate data structures. The algorithm presented here is a variant of the original, adapted for a higher order language. A detailed description of how this may be implemented in an optimising compiler is also given.

1 Introduction

Program transformation is one of the most powerful tools available to the functional compiler writer. Because of the absence of assignment and other non-referentially transparent language constructs, there are a host of correctness-preserving transformations to choose from.

In their paper, Burstall and Darlington [2] showed that recursive programs could be transformed by a sequence of small correctness-preserving transformations yielding a program that was more efficient in terms of both time and space usage. Their transformation system was characterised by the use of the *fold/unfold* system. In this system, function calls are unfolded (replaced by instantiated instances of their bodies), transformed, and folded again (the body is replaced by an instance of the head).

Unfortunately, their transformation system is not suited for inclusion in an optimising compiler, as the transformation process was guided by human intervention. The process often began with an inspirational *eureka* step from which the transformation progressed. However, many attempts have been made to specialise this type of program transformation into one that can be performed automatically.

One such method is *deforestation* [13, 14] which aims to make programs more efficient by removing intermediate data structures. Intermediate data structures (usually lists, more generally trees) are a feature of a particular programming style employed by many functional programmers, in which a stream of data flows down a pipeline being processed at each node. An example will illustrate this:

$$foldr\ (+)\ 0\ (map\ (\lambda x.1)\ xs)$$

*email: {simonm,wadler}@dcs.glasgow.ac.uk

This expression calculates the length of the list xs (by mapping each element of the list to the number 1 and then summing them). The intermediate structure in question is the list [1,1,1...] generated by the call to map. The deforestation process will transform this program into the usual recursive definition of *length*:

$$\begin{array}{l}
\textbf{letrec} \\
\quad length \;=\; \lambda xs.\ \textbf{case}\ xs\ \textbf{of} \\
\qquad\qquad\qquad\qquad Nil \quad\quad\;\; \rightarrow 0 \\
\qquad\qquad\qquad\qquad Cons\ x\ xs \;\rightarrow 1 + length\ xs \\
\textbf{in}\ length\ xs
\end{array}$$

This definition results in a faster program because the intermediate list has been eliminated. The advantage is seen in both the time (building the list cells) and space (the list cells themselves) behaviour of the program. One might argue that in a lazy functional language the original version would run in constant space and linear time anyway. While this is true, the *total* space and time used by the program are both reduced. The reduced space usage also results in a speed up as the garbage collector is invoked less often. Deforestation can never change the complexity of an algorithm, only its constant factors. There exist transformations that do change the complexity, for example the tupling algorithms by Burstall and Darlington [2], extended and automated to some extent by Chin [3].

This paper will outline a transformation system that attempts to generate definitions like the above given a program involving terms with intermediate data structures.

The original deforestation scheme [13, 14] consists of two parts. First, there is the definition of a limited class of expressions, known as treeless form. A term in treeless form uses no intermediate storage. Secondly, there is a transformation algorithm, expressed as a set of rewrite rules, which applies to any expression. Strictly speaking, it is a semi-algorithm, because it does not always terminate. It is easy to check that if the algorithm does terminate, the resulting term is in treeless form. Furthermore, if the input to the algorithm is the composition of a number of functions, each with a definition in treeless form, then the algorithm is guaranteed to terminate.

This paper generalises the transformation algorithm to a higher-order language. However, it says nothing about how to generalise treeless form. We hope it is intuitively clear that if the algorithm terminates, it does indeed produce a term that contains no intermediate structures (except where they are explicitly indicated by **let**, as explained below). However, we leave for future work a proper generalised definition of treeless form, and a generalisation of the termination result.

There are two main reasons for restricting the input to the transformer: firstly, to prevent the unfolding process from duplicating expressions, thereby making the resulting expression less efficient, and secondly to ensure termination.

Duplication of work occurs when transforming calls to functions like *square*, defined as follows:

$$square = \lambda x.\ x * x$$

Var	x, y			variable
Con	C			constructor
Term	a, b, c	$::=$	x	variable
		$\mid$	$\lambda x.a$	lambda
		$\mid$	$a\ b$	application
		$\mid$	$C\ a_1 \ldots a_n$	constructor application
		$\mid$	**case** b **of** $\{r\}$	case expression
		$\mid$	**let** $x = a$ **in** b	let expression
Pat	p	$::=$	$C\ x_1 \ldots x_n$	pattern
Alts	r	$::=$	$p_1 \to a_1 ; \ldots ; p_n \to a_n$	alternatives
Decls	d	$::=$	$x_1 = a_1 ; \ldots ; x_n = a_n$	declarations
Prog	t	$::=$	**letrec** $\{d\}$ **in** a	program

Figure 1: The Language

Now apply the function *square* to the expression $1+1$. The unfolding procedure transforms this function call to $(1+1)*(1+1)$ which may be a bad idea, since the evaluation of $1+1$ is now performed twice, whereas in the original program it was only performed once. It is for this reason that Wadler chose to restrict definitions in treeless form to those whose arguments are all *linear*, ie. occur no more than once in the body of the function. This is restrictive, however; a function may have a number of linear arguments in addition to its non-linear ones, and a great deal can be gained by unfolding such definitions. We will show how such definitions can be made safe to unfold.

In section 2 the language we use is described. Section 3 describes the basic transformation scheme, and section 5 gives an example of its operation. Section 4 introduces the knot-tying process and explains how it is used to generalise the output from the transformer into new function definitions and calls to these functions. Section 6 describes in some detail how the algorithm as a whole can be implemented in a lazy functional language. Section 7 describes some planned extensions to the algorithm.

2 The Language

The language (Figure 1) we work with is the lambda calculus extended with constructs for examining and building data structures using constructors (this approach is similar to that employed by the Haskell language [10]). Each constructor has a fixed arity, and all constructor applications are saturated: we may not write $(Cons\ x)$, though we may write $(\lambda xs.Cons\ x\ xs)$.

Case terms are used to de-construct and examine saturated constructor applications. The patterns of a case term may not be nested; algorithms to convert from nested to non-nested case terms are well known [1]. Hamilton and Jones [8] and Ferguson [6] use a slightly different approach, in that case terms are reformulated as pattern matching function definitions. The tradeoff here is that using pattern matching, while simplifying examples of the transformation system, makes the rules themselves slightly more opaque. We adopted **case** terms not only because the rules are clearer, but also because **case** is a primitive in many functional language compilers.

The language is typed using the Hindley-Milner type system [4, 9, 11]. It has polymorphic **let** and **letrec** constructs. We do not include literals such as integers and characters, since these are just special cases of the constructor mechanism.

This approach should be readily adaptable to the internal syntax used by most modern lazy functional language compilers.

3 The Transformation System

For the moment, we restrict the input to the transformer to containing a single **letrec** expression at the top level. The only functions to be unfolded are those bound by this **letrec**. This makes sense, because Deforestation is essentially a transformation for recursive programs and gives the best results when compositions of recursive functions are unfolded. We shall explain later how the transformation may be extended to cope with nested **letrec** expressions.

The transformation system comprises three mutually recursive functions, $\mathcal{T}$, $\mathcal{A}$, and $\mathcal{C}$ (Figures 2, 3, and 4). The first, $\mathcal{T}$, directs the transformation over the expression and performs all the unfolding. As it completes the unfolding, $\mathcal{T}$ passes each application to the $\mathcal{A}$ function, and each **case** statement to the $\mathcal{C}$ function. These subsidiary functions perform the major work of transformation.

The functions bound by the top-level letrec are represented by a mapping D, from variables to expressions. Strictly speaking, we should write $\mathcal{T}_D$, $\mathcal{A}_D$, and $\mathcal{C}_D$, since the functions also depend on D, but this has been omitted to allow for greater readability. The only rule which uses D is $\mathcal{T}1$.

Note the interesting duality between the two functions $\mathcal{A}$ and $\mathcal{C}$. In both cases, the rules for a variable or application on the left hand side are essentially do-nothing rules. The rules for a **case** statement push the transformation down to the branches of the **case**, and similarly for **let**. Each function also has one reduction rule — in $\mathcal{A}$ it is when a lambda-expression occurs on the left, and in $\mathcal{C}$ when a constructor application appears as the selector. The opposite case is also an error in each function; that is, it is an error to have a lambda expression as the selector to a case, and it is illegal to apply a constructor application to something. Rule $\mathcal{C}5$ is often referred to as the case-case transformation.

The correctness conditions for the three functions in the transformer can be expressed as:

$$\begin{aligned}
&\mathcal{E}\, a\,(\sigma + D) && = \mathcal{E}\,(\mathcal{T}_D\, a)\,\sigma \\
&\mathcal{E}\,(a\ b)\,(\sigma + D) && = \mathcal{E}\,(\mathcal{A}_D\, a\, b)\,\sigma \\
&\mathcal{E}\,(\mathbf{case}\ a\ \mathbf{of}\ \{r\})\,(\sigma + D) && = \mathcal{E}\,(\mathcal{C}_D\, a\, r)\,\sigma
\end{aligned}$$

Where $\mathcal{E}$ is the usual evaluation function, σ is disjoint from D, and $(+)$ is the union operator on mappings. Note that the correctness conditions for $\mathcal{A}$ and $\mathcal{C}$ are derivable from the condition for $\mathcal{T}$ and the definition of $\mathcal{T}$ as given in Figure 2.

$$\begin{array}{lcll}
\mathcal{T}\,x & = & \text{if } x \in D \text{ then } D\ x \text{ else } x & (\mathcal{T}1)\\
\mathcal{T}\,(\lambda x.a) & = & \lambda x.(\mathcal{T}\,a) & (\mathcal{T}2)\\
\mathcal{T}\,(a\ b) & = & \mathcal{A}\ (\mathcal{T}\,a)\ (\mathcal{T}\,b) & (\mathcal{T}3)\\
\mathcal{T}\,(C\ a_1 \ldots a_2) & = & C\ (\mathcal{T}\,a_1) \ldots (\mathcal{T}\,a_n) & (\mathcal{T}4)\\
\multicolumn{3}{l}{\mathcal{T}\,(\textbf{case}\ b\ \textbf{of}\ \{p_1 \to a_1\,; \ldots; p_n \to a_n\})} & (\mathcal{T}5)\\
 & = & \mathcal{C}\ (\mathcal{T}\,b)\ \{p_1 \to \mathcal{T}\,a_1\,; \ldots; p_n \to \mathcal{T}\,a_n\} & \\
\mathcal{T}\,(\textbf{let}\ x = a\ \textbf{in}\ b) & = & \textbf{let}\ x = (\mathcal{T}\,a)\ \textbf{in}\ (\mathcal{T}\,b) & (\mathcal{T}6)
\end{array}$$

Figure 2: Transformation Scheme

$$\begin{array}{lcll}
\mathcal{A}\,x\,a & = & x\ a & (\mathcal{A}1)\\
\mathcal{A}\,(\lambda x.a)\,b & = & \mathcal{T}\,(a[b/x]) & (\mathcal{A}2)\\
\mathcal{A}\,(a\ b)\,c & = & (a\ b)\ c & (\mathcal{A}3)\\
\mathcal{A}\,(C\ a_1 \ldots a_n)\,b & = & \mathit{error} & (\mathcal{A}4)\\
\multicolumn{3}{l}{\mathcal{A}\,(\textbf{case}\ b\ \textbf{of}\ \{p_1 \to a_1\,; \ldots; p_n \to a_n\})\,c} & (\mathcal{A}5)\\
 & = & \textbf{case}\ b\ \textbf{of}\ \{p_1 \to \mathcal{A}\,a_1\,c\,; \ldots; p_n \to \mathcal{A}\,a_n\,c\} & \\
\mathcal{A}\,(\textbf{let}\ x = a\ \textbf{in}\ b)\,c & = & \textbf{let}\ x = a\ \textbf{in}\ (\mathcal{A}\,b\,c) & (\mathcal{A}6)
\end{array}$$

Figure 3: $\mathcal{A}$ Function

$$\begin{array}{lcll}
\mathcal{C}\,x\,r & = & \textbf{case}\ x\ \textbf{of}\ \{r\} & (\mathcal{C}1)\\
\mathcal{C}\,(\lambda x.a)\,r & = & \mathit{error} & (\mathcal{C}2)\\
\mathcal{C}\,(a\ b)\,r & = & \textbf{case}\ a\ b\ \textbf{of}\ \{r\} & (\mathcal{C}3)\\
\multicolumn{3}{l}{\mathcal{C}\,(C\ a_1 \ldots a_n)\,\{\ldots;\ C\ x_1 \ldots x_n \to b\ ; \ldots\}} & (\mathcal{C}4)\\
 & = & \mathcal{T}\,(b[a_1/x_1, \ldots, a_n/x_n]) & \\
\multicolumn{3}{l}{\mathcal{C}\,(\textbf{case}\ b\ \textbf{of}\ \{p_1 \to a_1\,; \ldots; p_n \to a_n\})\,r} & (\mathcal{C}5)\\
 & = & \textbf{case}\ b\ \textbf{of}\ \{p_1 \to \mathcal{C}\,a_1\,r\,; \ldots; p_n \to \mathcal{C}\,a_n\,r\} & \\
\mathcal{C}\,(\textbf{let}\ x = a\ \textbf{in}\ b)\,r & = & \textbf{let}\ x = a\ \textbf{in}\ (\mathcal{C}\,b\,r) & (\mathcal{C}6)
\end{array}$$

Figure 4: $\mathcal{C}$ Function

4 Tying the knot

As it stands, the algorithm given will clearly not terminate. Unfoldings will continue to occur, producing an infinite expression tree. The key point is that this expression tree may repeat itself at regular intervals. This enables us to generate a new recursive function definition from the repeating section, and replace the infinite tree at its root with a call to this new function.

Taking the example from the introduction, and applying the transformation, stopping when we reach step (2):

$$
\begin{array}{lll}
 & \mathcal{T}\,(foldr\ (+)\ 0\ (map\ (\lambda x.1)\ xs)) & (1)\\
= & \ldots & \\
= & \textbf{case}\ xs\ \textbf{of} & (2)\\
 & \quad Nil \quad\quad\quad \rightarrow 0 & \\
 & \quad Cons\ x\ xs' \ \rightarrow 1 + \mathcal{T}\,(foldr\ (+)\ 0\ (map\ (\lambda x.1)\ xs')) &
\end{array}
$$

Now we introduce

$$f = \lambda xs.\mathcal{T}\,(foldr\ (+)\ 0\ (map\ (\lambda x.1)\ xs))$$

We can replace the expression $\mathcal{T}\,(foldr\ (+)\ 0\ (map\ (\lambda x.1)\ xs))$ in steps (1) and (2) with $f\ xs$, and we can substitute step (2) into the definition of f, to obtain the required result:

$$
\begin{array}{l}
\textbf{letrec}\\
\quad f \ = \lambda xs.\ \textbf{case}\ xs\ \textbf{of}\\
\quad\quad\quad\quad\quad\quad Nil \quad\quad\quad \rightarrow 0\\
\quad\quad\quad\quad\quad\quad Cons\ x\ xs \ \rightarrow 1 + f\ xs\\
\textbf{in}\ f\ xs
\end{array}
$$

In general, we abstract an expression e by its free variables (except primitives and those bound by a letrec) $x_1 \ldots x_n$, to generate the function

$$f = \lambda x_1.\ldots\lambda x_n.\mathcal{T}\,e$$

Now all occurrences of $\mathcal{T}\,e$ can be replaced by the appropriate call to f, and the body of f can be replaced by the transformed expression.

This is an informal description of a complicated mechanism. In Section ??, we shall describe how the system can be implemented, and in the process make much of the detail concrete.

5 An Example

As an example to demonstrate the possible scope of this algorithm, the program in figure 5 was used as the input to our implementation.

The program is an implementation of the well-known `unlines` function that splits a stream into a list of strings at line breaks. The functions **`map`**, **`foldr`**, **`compose`** (often written as '.'), **`concat`**, and **`append`** are used indirectly to define **`unlines`**. Clearly the program contains a number of intermediate structures, and we can do much better than this.

Figure 6 shows the output generated by our implementation on the above program. All the intermediate lists have been removed, and the result is much more efficient than the original.

```
letrec {
  map = \f xs ->
          case xs of {
             Nil -> Nil;
             Cons x xs -> Cons (f x) (map f xs); };

  foldr = \f a xs ->
            case xs of {
              Nil -> a;
              Cons x xs -> let { xs' = foldr f a xs; }
                           in f x xs'; };

  compose = \f g x -> f (g x);

  concat = foldr append Nil;

  append = \xs ys ->
             case xs of {
               Nil -> ys;
               Cons x xs -> Cons x (append xs ys); };

  unlines = compose concat (map (\l -> append l
                                         (Cons Newline Nil)));
} in \xs -> unlines xs
```

Figure 5: Sample Input - `unlines` program

```
letrec {
  h1 =
    \xs ->
    case xs of {
      Nil -> Nil;
      Cons x xs' -> (let xs'' = h1 xs' in h2 x xs''); };
  h2 =
    \x ->
    \xs'' ->
    case x of {
      Nil -> Cons Newline xs''
      Cons x' xs''' -> Cons x' (h2 xs''' xs''); };
} in
  \xs -> h1 xs
```

Figure 6: Sample Output

6 Implementing the algorithm

The transformation algorithm translates quite nicely into a functional program, the main problem being one of name-capture. We must ensure that all changes made to the expression tree do not re-bind any free variables, and so change the meaning of the program.

Consider rule $\mathcal{A}6$. The scope of the variable x is extended to cover the expression c. If x is a free variable of c (bound somewhere else in the program), then it will be rebound when the **let** clause moves outside. This obviously must be avoided, and there are several techniques available:

- For every situation in which name capture may occur, rename the bound variables so that they do not interfere with free ones. For instance, in the example above, x would be rebound to a variable that is not in the set of free variables of c. This method has two drawbacks: firstly, finding the free variables of an expression can be costly when performed often. Secondly, finding the free variables of an infinite expression (these occur regularly in the transformation system presented) is clearly impossible.

- Ensure that all variable names are unique, so that name capture problems do not occur. There are also problems with this idea: unfolding a function definition multiple times will certainly produce bound occurrences of variables that are non-unique. Thus we must re-bind all variables in a function definition each time the definition is unfolded. Unfortunately, we must maintain a supply of new unique variable names, and this is difficult in the face of potentially infinite transformations taking place.

- The solution which we used in our implementation is to represent the program using DeBruijn notation [5]. In this system, variables are denoted by a number, which represents the number of lambdas between the variable occurrence and the lambda which bound it. For example, the expression $\lambda f.\lambda x.f\ x$ is represented in DeBruijn notation as $\lambda.\lambda.1\ 0$. The number zero refers to the innermost enclosing lambda, 1 refers to the next, etc. This solves all problems with name capture since there are no names! The only bookkeeping that must be done is to increase or decrease the value of free variables when a part of an expression moves, to ensure that all variables still refer to the lambda that bound them. Performing substitution is now more tricky, but this can be overcome with similar techniques.

We must of course extend the DeBruijn system to include the extra constructs in our language. The **let** construct is easy; we can pretend the expression **let** $x = a$ **in** b is equivalent to $(\lambda x.b)\ a$ for the purposes of assigning numbers to variables. We can also use this technique to translate **case** and **letrec** expressions.

We choose to leave the original names of the bindings in place, as this provides a way of translating back from DeBruijn numbers to normal variable names for the purposes of displaying the output from the transformer.

Here is an example to illustrate the translation:

$$
\begin{array}{l}
\textbf{letrec} \\
\quad foldr \;\; = \lambda f.\lambda c.\lambda xs.\ \textbf{case}\ xs\ \textbf{of} \\
\qquad\qquad\qquad\qquad\qquad Nil \qquad\quad \rightarrow c \\
\qquad\qquad\qquad\qquad\qquad Cons\ x\ xs \;\; \rightarrow f\ x\ (foldr\ f\ c\ xs) \\
\textbf{in}\ \lambda f.\lambda c.\lambda xs.foldr\ f\ c\ xs
\end{array}
$$

becomes (in DeBruijn notation):

$$
\begin{array}{l}
\textbf{letrec} \\
\quad foldr \;\; = \lambda f.\lambda c.\lambda xs.\ \textbf{case}\ 0\ \textbf{of} \\
\qquad\qquad\qquad\qquad\qquad Nil \qquad\quad \rightarrow 1 \\
\qquad\qquad\qquad\qquad\qquad Cons\ x\ xs \;\; \rightarrow 4\ 1\ (5\ 4\ 3\ 0) \\
\textbf{in}\ \lambda f.\lambda c.\lambda xs.3\ 2\ 1\ 0
\end{array}
$$

Note that we cannot have any free variables in a DeBruijn expression — every variable must refer directly to its binding.

6.1 Implementing the knot-tying process

This presents easily the most complicated problem to solve in implementing the algorithm. How do we identify when to create new function definitions? Well, any infinite unfolding sequence must contain applications of rule T1, the unfolding rule. So we need to record all applications of this rule in the expression tree somehow.

In order to achieve this we will add one more term form to the language. The new object will represent the annotations to the expression tree that record unfolding operations. It takes the form **label** a b where a is the expression before unfolding takes place, and b is the same expression after unfolding and further transformations. Semantically the two expressions are identical since b is derived from a using only correctness-preserving transformations. The **label** term also maintains the invariant that no variables in a have been unfolded, whereas all variables in b have (if they have definitions in D). It follows from this that a contains no **label** terms, but b may.

We need to add some rules to the transformation system to create and manipulate **labels**. These are shown in Figure 7. The function $\mathcal{S}$ mentioned in the rules is needed to maintain the invariant mentioned above. It simply replaces every subterm of the form (**label** a b) with a, leaving the rest of the expression unchanged.. A **label** needs to be added every time a function is unfolded using rule $\mathcal{T}1$, so this has been encoded into the new version of this rule.

Now we have a transformation system that generates a labelled, potentially infinite expression tree. The knot-tying process can use the labels to identify which expressions to use to create new definitions. It is implemented as follows: firstly use a function called findloops which walks the expression collecting labels. Each new label found is checked against a list of previously collected labels. If a match is found (a label that is a renaming of the new one) then we have found a loop in the transformed expression. The new label (including the expression on its right-hand side; this will be used to create the new definition) is added to a list which is returned from findloops.

$$
\begin{array}{lll}
\mathcal{T}\,x &=& if\ x \in D\ then\ \mathbf{label}\ x\ (D x)\ else\ x \qquad (\mathcal{T}1)\\
\mathcal{T}\,(\mathbf{label}\ a\ b) & & \qquad (\mathcal{T}7)\\
&=& \mathbf{label}\ a\ (\mathcal{T}\,b)\\
\mathcal{A}\,(\mathbf{label}\ a\ b)\ c & & \qquad (\mathcal{A}7)\\
&=& \mathbf{label}\ (a\ (\mathcal{S}\ b))\ (\mathcal{A}\,b\,c)\\
\mathcal{C}\,(\mathbf{label}\ b\ c)\ \{p_1 \rightarrow a_1\,; \ldots ; p_n \rightarrow a_n\} & & \qquad (\mathcal{C}7)\\
&=& \mathbf{label}\ (\mathbf{case}\ b\ \mathbf{of}\ \{p_1 \rightarrow \mathcal{S}\ a_1\,; \ldots ; p_n \rightarrow \mathcal{S}\ a_n\})\ (\mathcal{C}\,c\,r)
\end{array}
$$

Figure 7: New Rules for Labels

We now have a list of expressions which can be made into new function definitions. The left-hand side of each label is used to find free variables of the expression and abstract them as described above. The list of labels is passed to a function **prune** which walks over both the original expression and the new function definitions. Any labels it finds are either

- a renaming of one of the labels in the list, in which case a call to the new function definition is placed in the expression in place of the label.
- not a renaming of any label in the list, in which case the label is simply replaced by its right-hand side.

The above algorithm must be implemented in a lazy functional language, since the expression tree generated by transformation is infinitely large. Together the **findloops** and **prune** functions ensure that the result is a finite expression by cutting the tree off at the points where it begins to repeat itself.

We can now extend our algorithm to include nested **letrec** expressions in the input:

$$
\begin{array}{ll}
\mathcal{T}\,(\mathbf{letrec}\ \{x_1 = a_1\ ; \ldots ;\ x_n = a_n\}\ \mathbf{in}\ b) & (\mathcal{T}8)\\
\quad = \ \text{knot-tie}\ (\mathcal{T}_{D+\{x_1 \mapsto a_1, \ldots, x_n \mapsto a_n\}}\ b) &
\end{array}
$$

The function knot-tie is assumed to perform the knot-tying process described, generating a new **letrec** in place of the old one.

7 Extensions and Further Work

The bad news is that the algorithm presented in this paper is not an algorithm: there are inputs for which it does not terminate. For some function definitions, the expression tree generated by the transformation is continually expanding and does not fall into a pattern that is recognisable by the knot-tieing process. The good news is that we have proved termination for a subset of the language presented earlier (without losing expressiveness). The language is a generalisation of *treeless form* as presented in [13, 14]; this will be published elsewhere.

There also still exists the problem of non-linear function arguments, and the duplication of work that results from substituting for these arguments during unfolding. Fortunately, we have a mechanism to make function definitions with this characteristic safe to transform.

The **let** construct can be used to emulate the function of *blazing* in Wadler's deforestation [13, 14]. The blazing mechanism is used to identify subexpressions and function arguments which are to be ignored by the deforestation process. We can simulate blazing by adding extra **lets** to protect individual expressions from being transformed.

Notice that **let** constructs are always left in place in the transformed function. An expression that is defined using **let** represents an intermediate data structure that will not be removed by the algorithm. Hence, all we need to do to protect unsafe lambda bindings from being substituted is to add an extra **let** construct:

$$\lambda x.\lambda y.\lambda z..a \Rightarrow \lambda x.\lambda y'.(\mathbf{let}\ y = y'\ \mathbf{in}\ \lambda z.a)$$

Where the variable y appears more than once in a. The algorithm ensures that unfolding and instantiation continue as normal, except that now the only occurrence of the lambda-bound y' in the function definition is the right-hand side of the **let** construct.

This still fails to tell us in general how to make a given function safe to use in the deforestation algorithm. We intend to use a form of linear logic [7] to identify function arguments which are safe to unfold, and protect others with **lets** as described in the previous section.

In this paper we have gone some way towards providing the framework for an automatic deforestation algorithm that is suitable for inclusion in an optimising compiler. Much work remains to be done.

References

[1] L.Augustsson, Compiling pattern matching, Proc. Conf on Functional Programming languages and Computer Architecture, Nancy, France, *Lecture Notes in Computer Science* 201 (Springer, Berlin, 1985)

[2] R.M.Burstall and J.Darlington, A Transformation System for Developing Recusrive Programs, *Journal of the ACM* 24(1) (1977) 44-67

[3] W.N.Chin, Automatic Methods for Program Transformation, PhD Thesis, University oF London, March 1990.

[4] L.Damas and R.Milner, Principle type schemes for functional programs, *Proceedings of the ACM Symposium on Principles of Programming Languages* 1982.

[5] N.G.DeBruijn, Lambda Calculus Notation with Nameless Dummies, *Inagationes Mathematicae*, vol.34, pp 381-392.

[6] A.B.Ferguson and P.L.Wadler, When will deforestation stop? *Procedings of the Glasgow Workshop on Functional Programming*, Rothesay, Isle of Bute, August 1988, Research Report 89/R4, Department of Computing Science, University of Glasgow, 1989.

[7] J.-Y Girard, Linear Logic, *Theoretical Computer Science* 50(1), 1-102, 1987.

[8] G.W.Hamilton and S.B.Jones, Extending deforestation for First Order Functional Programs, *Functional Programming, Glasgow 1991* R.Heldal, C.Kehler Holst, P.Wadler (Eds), Springer-Verlag, Workshops in Computing Science, 1991.

[9] R.Hindley, The principal type scheme of an object in combinatory logic, *Transactions of the American Mathematics Society* 146 29-60.

[10] P.Hudak, S.L.Peyton Jones, P.Wadler (Eds) Report on the Programming Language Haskell, Version 1.2, *ACM SIGPLAN Notices*, 27(5), May 1992.

[11] R.Milner, A theory of type polymorphism in programming, in *Journal of Computing System Science* 17 1978 348-375.

[12] Simon L Peyton Jones *The Implementation of Funtional Programming Languages* Prentice Hall, Englewood Cliffs, NJ, 1987.

[13] Philip Wadler, Deforestation: Transforming Programs To Eliminate Trees, European Symposium on Programming, Nancy, France, *Lecture Notes in Computer Science* 300 Springer, Berlin, 1988.

[14] Philip Wadler, Deforestation: Transforming Programs To Eliminate Trees *Theoretical Computer Science* 73 1990 231-248.

Hazard Algebra and the Design of Asynchronous Automata

Erik Meijer
University of Utrecht
Department of Computer Science
POBox 80.089 NL-3508 TB Utrecht The Netherlands
email: erik@cs.ruu.nl

1 Introduction

Our concern is the design of provably correct asynchronous circuits. In such circuits there may occur hazards, due to the delay of signals along wires and components. Informally, a hazard is a time interval during which the output of a circuit, or circuit component, is wrong. Hazards are hardly ever defined formally in the literature. For a synchronous circuit designer this might be no problem as he assumes the outputs of all components are correct (and stabile) by the next clock edge. Asynchronous or clockless circuits may feature hazards, even though all components are correct. So it is of vital importance for the asynchronous system designer to be able to reason formally about hazards. We shall design an algebra, a formal system, for this purpose and we shall use it to design asynchronous finite-state machines. For reasons of space most of the proofs have been omitted. These will be included in an expanded version of this paper.

Notation

The basis algebra we use is Boolean algebra with values $\mathbb{B} = \{1, 0\}$ (switching algebra) and with operations $\_$ (negation), $+$ (disjunction), and $\cdot$ (conjunction). Equality is lifted pointwise to terms containing free variables, i.e.

$$A[p] =_{\mathbb{B}} B[p] \quad \equiv \quad (\forall\, b \in \mathbb{B} :: A[p := b] = B[p := b])$$

The subscript $\mathbb{B}$ indicates that the free variable ranges over $\{1, 0\}$. Extension from a single free variable to a collection of free variables should be obvious.

2 Hazards

We are considering asynchronous circuit implementations of logical expressions. Input and output values of circuits are assumed to be in $\mathbb{B}$. We say that a circuit is *correct* for an expression A with free variables p say, if *apart from some delay* the output value of the circuit is the value that A gives for the current input values p. We do not formalize the notion of delay, but we do assume that different components/wires have different delays. A *hazard* is a time interval during which the output value is wrong, even if the delay is taken into account.

A standard example used to 'define' the notion of hazard is the circuit implementation of a 2-input data selector [3] $A = r \lhd p \rhd q = \overline{p} \cdot r + p \cdot q$. As the the output of our gedanken-oscilloscope shows, the circuit for A built according to the structure of expression A, using inverters, or-, and and-gates has a possible 1–0–1-glitch if q and r are both 1 while p switches from 1 to 0.

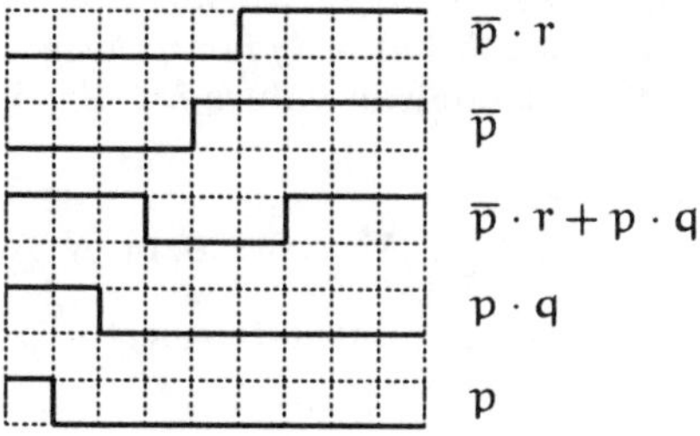

The outputs of the components for $p \cdot q$ and $\overline{p} \cdot r$ change from 1 to 0 respectively from 0 to 1, with some delay. Depending on the length of the delays the entire circuit may have a hazard as shown above. A correct circuit for $\overline{p} \cdot r + p \cdot q$ has output constantly 1 in this case.

Here the hazard is a *dip* or 1–0–1-glitch. *Spikes*, or 0–1–0-glitches are also possible, as are several glitches in succession. Traditionally, a hazard is called *static* if it is a series of glitches in an output that has to remain constant; it is called *dynamic* if it consists of a series of glitches in an output that has to change only once.

3 Conventional algebras

We intend to design an algebra by which it is possible to prove the absence of hazards in asynchronous circuits. A formal system which takes time into account is certainly going to be too complicated to be of practical use, hence a formalism in which time has been abstracted is to be preferred. However, as shown above switching algebra over $\mathbb{B}$ is too simplistic an abstraction of logic circuits.

Another possibility is the *ternary* algebra as used by Eichelberger [1] and others. Here the value set $\mathbb{B} = \{1,0\}$ is extended with a third value $\frac{1}{2}$ to become $\mathbb{T} = \{0, \frac{1}{2}, 1\}$. This new value is intended to describe the transient behaviour of logic gates. The operation of gates with respect to the transient value $\frac{1}{2}$ is determined by changing back and forth the required input of the gate and noting whether its output changes or remains fixed. Thus for example

$$\begin{array}{ll} \frac{1}{2} \cdot 1 = \frac{1}{2} & \text{since } 0 \cdot 1 \neq 1 \cdot 1, \text{ and} \\ \frac{1}{2} \cdot 0 = 0 & \text{since } 0 \cdot 0 = 0 = 1 \cdot 0. \end{array}$$

In ternary algebra we may define that an expression $A[p, q]$ has a *static-hazard* on variable p if $A = \frac{1}{2}$ when $p = \frac{1}{2}$, but A yields the same $\mathbb{B}$-value for p either 1 or 0 for some boolean value for q .

$$\begin{array}{l} \text{static hazard } (p, A) \equiv \\ \qquad (\exists\, b \in \mathbb{B} :: A[p, q := 1, b] = A[p := 0, b] \;\wedge\; A[p, q := \frac{1}{2}, b] = \frac{1}{2}) \end{array}$$

The extension from a single variable q to a collection of variables should be obvious. Similarly we define that A has a *dynamic hazard* on p when $A = \frac{1}{2}$ if $p = \frac{1}{2}$ but A yields two different boolean values for $p = 1$ resp. $p = 0$.

$$\begin{array}{l} \text{dynamic hazard } (p, A) \equiv \\ \qquad (\exists\, b \in \mathbb{B} :: A[p, q := 1, b] \neq A[p, q := 0, b] \;\wedge\; A[p, q := \frac{1}{2}, b] = \frac{1}{2}) \end{array}$$

According to these definitions the 2-input data selector $\overline{p} \cdot r + p \cdot q$ has a static hazard on p when q and r are both 1.

Not so obvious perhaps is the fact that in ternary algebra the notion of dynamic hazard is hardly useful since we can prove that for each A

$$(\exists\, b \in \mathbb{B} :: A[p, q := 0, b] \neq A[p, q := 1, b]) \;\Rightarrow\; \text{dynamic hazard } (p, A)$$

That is, the notion of dynamic hazard does not distinguish between truly occurring dynamic hazards and merely correct changes of the output. A more refined notion of dynamic hazard is wanted but this seems impossible within ternary algebra.

4 Hazard algebra

The solution to the problem of giving formal definitions of static and dynamic hazards is a quinary algebra, to be called *hazard algebra*. The domain of values is a five element set $\mathbb{H} = \mathbb{B} \cup \{\uparrow, \downarrow, \perp\}$. Informally speaking

- 1 (0) denotes a *constant high* (*constant low*) signal during an interval of time.
- A clean *rising* signal is denoted by $\uparrow$.
- A clean *falling* signal is denoted by $\downarrow$.

- $\perp$ denotes an *unknown* signal, possibly a hazard.

Fantuauzzi [2] describes a nine-valued algebra for the analysis of logical circuits that distinguishes between five different kinds of hazards instead of only one. This seems to be a little overkill. In his paper Fantuauzzi refers to a quinary algebra proposed by Lewis [6]. It might very well be the case that this quinary algebra is very similar to ours. This certainly is the case for the five-valued transitional logic of Thompson [9]. However he does not distinguish between the full ordering $\sqsubseteq$ and its refinements $\sqsubseteq_{\mathsf{P}}$ and $\sqsubseteq_{\forall}$.

The domain $\mathbb{H}$ is partially ordered as a flat cpo with $\perp$ as least element: $\perp \sqsubset \{\uparrow, \downarrow, 1, 0\}$. An equivalent formulation is $x \neq \perp \equiv \perp \sqsubset x$. As usual the ordering on values is lifted pointwise to terms

$$A \sqsubseteq_{\mathbb{H}} B \quad \equiv \quad (\forall\, x \in \mathbb{H} :: A[p := x] \sqsubseteq B[p := x]) \qquad \text{(LIFT)}$$

(Again the extension to more than one variable should be obvious). When no confusion can arise the $\mathbb{H}$ subscript is omitted.

The logical operations are extended to quinary algebra in conformity with the operational interpretation of $\uparrow, \downarrow$, and $\perp$. For example $\uparrow \cdot \downarrow = \perp$ reflects the possibility of a hazard when the inputs of an and-gate change in the opposite direction within the same time interval.

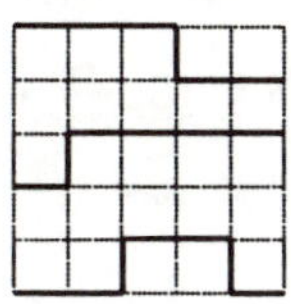

$\downarrow$

$\uparrow$

$\uparrow \cdot \downarrow$

A complete characterization of the quinary operators is given below.

$$
\begin{array}{lllllllll}
x \cdot y & = & y \cdot x & & & & x + y & = & y + x \\
x \cdot x & = & x & & & & x + x & = & x \\
0 \cdot x & = & 0 & \overline{0} & = & 1 & 0 + x & = & x \\
1 \cdot x & = & x & \overline{1} & = & 0 & 1 + x & = & 1 \\
 & & & & & & & & \\
\perp \cdot x & = & \perp \text{ if } x \neq 0 & \overline{\perp} & = & \perp & \perp + x & = & \perp \text{ if } x \neq 1 \\
\uparrow \cdot \downarrow & = & \perp & \overline{\uparrow} & = & \downarrow & \uparrow + \downarrow & = & \perp \\
 & & & \overline{\downarrow} & = & \uparrow & & &
\end{array}
$$

The static hazard example can be computed within the new algebra as follows

$$(\overline{p} \cdot r + p \cdot q)[p := \uparrow, r := 1, q := 1] = \overline{\uparrow} \cdot 1 + \uparrow \cdot 1 = \downarrow \cdot 1 + \uparrow \cdot 1 = \downarrow + \uparrow = \perp$$

In the hazard algebra, an expression $A[p, q]$ has a *hazard* on variable p if for some boolean value for q, either $p = \uparrow$ or $p = \downarrow$ makes the value of A equal to $\perp$.

$$\mathsf{hazard}\,(p, A) \quad \equiv \quad (\exists\, a \in \{\uparrow, \downarrow\}, b \in \mathbb{B} :: A[p, q := a, b] = \perp)$$

More often we use the negation of this statement, namely that an expression is *safe* for transitions of variable p.

$$\mathsf{safe}\,(p, A) \;\equiv\; (\forall\, a \in \{\uparrow, \downarrow\} :: \bot \sqsubset_{\mathbb{B}} A[p := a])$$

If $\mathsf{safe}\,(p, A)$ for all free variables p, we write $\mathsf{safe}\,(A)$.

The important question remains whether hazard-algebra is *sound*, i.e. if the circuit realization of an expression has a hazard, then it has a hazard in the algebra as well. *Completeness* means that if a hazard discovered in the algebra, the corresponding circuit has a hazard also. Completeness is not that crucial as long as not too many good circuits are ruled out. We conjecture that the hazard algebra is sound.

4.1 Facts about hazard algebra

Since a boolean expression (not containing $\bot, \uparrow, \downarrow$) takes values in $\mathbb{B}$ for each substitution of $\mathbb{B}$-values for its free variables, hazard algebra is compatible with switching algebra

$$A \sqsubseteq_{\mathbb{H}} B \;\Rightarrow\; A =_{\mathbb{B}} B$$

The converse implication does not hold. A counterexample is $A = (p+q)\cdot(\overline{q}+r)$ and $B = p \cdot \overline{q} + q \cdot r$; clearly $A =_{\mathbb{B}} B$ but substituting $p, q, r := 0, \uparrow, 0$ gives

$$A = (0 + \downarrow) \cdot (\overline{\downarrow} + 0) = \bot \;\sqsubset\; B = (0 \cdot \overline{\downarrow}) + (\downarrow \cdot 0) = 0$$

while on the other hand $p, q, r := 1, \downarrow, 1$ yields

$$A = (1 + \downarrow) \cdot (\overline{\downarrow} + 1) = 1 \;\sqsupset\; B = (1 \cdot \overline{\downarrow}) + (\downarrow \cdot 1) = \bot$$

Our hazard-algebra is no Boolean algebra, since the distribution laws do not hold in general. We do have a weak form of distribution

$$\begin{aligned} (x \cdot y) + (x \cdot z) &\sqsubseteq x \cdot (y + z) \\ (x + y) \cdot (x + z) &\sqsubseteq x + (y \cdot z) \end{aligned}$$

The familiar De Morgan laws are valid in hazard algebras, while some of the laws for negation are weakened.

$$\begin{array}{rclrcl} \overline{(x \cdot y)} &=& \overline{x} + \overline{y} & x \cdot \overline{x} &\sqsubseteq& 0 \\ \overline{(x + y)} &=& \overline{x} \cdot \overline{y} & x + \overline{x} &\sqsubseteq& 1 \\ & & & \overline{\overline{x}} &=& x \end{array}$$

The following absorption laws turned out to be quite useful.

$$\begin{aligned} x \cdot ((\overline{x} \cdot y) + z) &\sqsubseteq x \cdot z \\ x + ((\overline{x} + y) \cdot z) &\sqsubseteq x + z \\ x + ((x + y) \cdot z) &\sqsubseteq x + (y \cdot z) \\ x \cdot ((x \cdot y) + z) &\sqsubseteq x \cdot (y + z) \end{aligned}$$

We have verified these laws by writing a simple Miranda(tm)-program to do an exhaustive case analysis.

There are many occasions where a transformation of A into B preserves safety with respect to p while the two expressions are not comparable in the hazard algebra. Therefore we refine the ordering on expressions to a *ceteris-paribus*[1] ordering for changes of p only.

$$A \sqsubseteq_p B \quad \equiv \quad (\forall\, a \in \{\uparrow, \downarrow\} :: A[p := a] \sqsubseteq_{\mathbb{B}} B[p := a]) \qquad \text{(C-P)}$$

for $\sqsubseteq \in \{\sqsubset, \sqsubseteq, =, \sqsupseteq, \sqsupset\}$. When $A \sqsubseteq_p B$ holds for all p, A and B are comparable in *fundamental mode*

$$A \sqsubseteq_\forall B \quad \equiv \quad (\forall\, p :: A \sqsubseteq_p B) \qquad \text{(F-M)}$$

On the circuit level $A =_\forall B$ for example means that when operated in fundamental mode the circuits for A and B behave the same modulo delay. Fundamental mode operation means that only one input is changed at a time, and the input remains fixed until the circuit has stabilized internally.

Using the ceteris-paribus convention the definition of $\mathsf{safe}\,(p, A)$ can be written without quantifiers simply as $\perp \sqsubset_p A$. A tentative list of laws formulated using (C-P) and (F-M) is given below.

$$\begin{array}{rcll} A \sqsubseteq_{\mathbb{H}} B & \Rightarrow & A \sqsubseteq_\forall B & \\ A =_{\mathbb{B}} B & \equiv & A =_p B & ,\text{ if } p \notin A \wedge p \notin B \\ A \cdot (B + C) & =_p & A \cdot B + A \cdot C & ,\text{ if } p \notin A \vee (p \notin B \wedge p \notin C) \\ p \cdot (B + C) & =_\forall & p \cdot B + p \cdot C & ,\text{ if } p \notin B \wedge p \notin C \\ \overline{p} \cdot (B + C) & =_\forall & \overline{p} \cdot B + \overline{p} \cdot C & ,\text{ if } p \notin B \wedge p \notin C \end{array}$$

By induction on the structure of A (all basic operations are easily seen to be monotonic in their arguments) we have for all A, B, C, p the following *monotonicity* properties.

$$\begin{array}{rcl} B \sqsubseteq_{\mathbb{H}} C & \Rightarrow & A[B] \sqsubseteq_{\mathbb{H}} A[C] \\ B \sqsubseteq_\forall C & \Rightarrow & A[B] \sqsubseteq_\forall A[C] \\ B \sqsubseteq_p C & \Rightarrow & A[B] \sqsubseteq_p A[C] \end{array}$$

As a corollary we get

$$\begin{array}{rcl} \mathsf{safe}\,(p, A) \wedge A \sqsubseteq_p B & \Rightarrow & \mathsf{safe}\,(p, B) \\ \mathsf{safe}\,(A) \wedge A \sqsubseteq_\forall B & \Rightarrow & \mathsf{safe}\,(B) \end{array}$$

The above monotonicity laws are useful since many laws for $\sqsubseteq, \sqsubseteq_\forall$ and $\sqsubseteq_p$ have a simpler lhs operand than rhs operand. The laws enable us to replace an expression by a simpler one without losing safety.

5 Hazard removal

This section shows how arbitrary expressions can be made hazard-free by expanding and subsequent covering. Data selectors play a central role in this

[1] other things being equal

process. An important property of 2-input data selectors is *the fundamental mode abides law*: For all p, q not occurring in A, B, C, and D

$$(A \lhd p \rhd B) \lhd q \rhd (C \lhd p \rhd D) \quad =_{\forall} \quad (A \lhd q \rhd C) \lhd p \rhd (B \lhd q \rhd D)$$

Another law is fundamental mode distribution of $\lhd p \rhd$ over $+$ for all p not in either A, B, C, or D.

$$(A \lhd p \rhd B) + (C \lhd p \rhd D) \quad =_{\forall} \quad (A + C) \lhd p \rhd (B + D)$$

The *Shannon expansion* $pⓢA$ on variable p realizes A using a 2-input data selector controlled by p with $A[p := 1]$ and $A[p := 0]$ at the respective data inputs.

$$pⓢA \quad = \quad A[p := 0] \lhd p \rhd A[p := 1] \qquad \text{(SHANNON)}$$

Shannon expansion preserves meaning, $A =_{\mathbb{B}} pⓢA$. The abides law and the distribution law for data selectors are inherited by expansion. Idempotence of ⓢ follows from the equality $(pⓢA)[p := b] = A[p := b]$ if $b \in \mathbb{B}$.

$$\begin{aligned} pⓢ(A + B) \quad &=_{\forall} \quad (pⓢA) + (pⓢB) \\ pⓢ(pⓢA) \quad &= \quad pⓢA \\ pⓢ(qⓢA) \quad &=_{\forall} \quad qⓢ(pⓢA) \end{aligned}$$

Because of the last two laws it is safe to overload the notation for expansion over a set of variables in fundamental mode.

$$\begin{aligned} \{\}ⓢA \quad &= \quad A \\ (\{p\} \cup ps)ⓢA \quad &=_{\forall} \quad pⓢ(psⓢA) \end{aligned}$$

Expanding an expression A for each variable in A is denoted by $\boxed{A}$

$$\boxed{A} \quad = \quad \{p \mid p \in A\}ⓢA$$

In practical terms this means that A is realized using only 2-input data selectors. Total expansion expansion is idempotent and distributes over $+$, both in fundamental mode.

$$\boxed{\boxed{A}} =_{\forall} \boxed{A} \qquad \boxed{A + B} =_{\forall} \boxed{A} + \boxed{B}$$

An expression A is *expanded* if it is equal in fundamental mode to the expansion on any variable occurring in A.

$$\text{expanded}\,(A) \quad \equiv \quad (\forall\, p \in A :: A =_{\forall} pⓢA)$$

Total expansion yields an expanded term because additional expansion on variables in $\boxed{A}$ have no effect.

$$(\forall\, p : p \in \boxed{A} : \boxed{A} =_{\forall} pⓢ\boxed{A})$$

Expressions in *sum-of-product*-form are expanded if products do not contain a variable and its negation, e.g. $p \cdot \overline{p}$ is not expanded. In fact any totally expanded expression is fundamental mode equivalent to an expression in sum-of-product form. For example let A be an expression in terms of p and q then

$$\begin{aligned}\boxed{A} =_{\forall}\ & \overline{p}\cdot\overline{q}\cdot A[p:=0,q:=0]+\overline{p}\cdot q\cdot A[p:=0,q:=1]+\\ & p\cdot\overline{q}\cdot A[p:=1,q:=0]+p\cdot q\cdot A[p:=1,q:=1]\end{aligned}$$

Shannons expansion theorem can be used to provide hazard-cover for transitions of variable p. The *cover on* p *of* A is defined as

$$p\copyright A = A[p:=0]\cdot A[p:=1]$$

Adding a cover term preserves meaning, $A =_{\mathbb{B}} A + p\copyright A$, and removes hazards on p for terms expanded on p.

$$\mathsf{safe}\ (p, p\circledS A + p\copyright A) \qquad \text{(Hazard-Cover)}$$

The covering operator $\copyright$ is idempotent and commutative because $\cdot$ is commutative and idempotent. This allows overloading of $\copyright$ for covering sets of variables.

$$\begin{aligned} p\copyright(p\copyright A) &= p\copyright A & p\copyright(q\copyright A) &= q\copyright(p\copyright A)\\ \{\}\copyright A &= A & (\{p\}\cup ps)\copyright A &= p\copyright(ps\copyright A)\end{aligned}$$

Distribution over $\cdot$ is unconditional. If $A+B =_{\mathbb{B}} A$ then $p\copyright$ distributes over $+$ ceteris-paribus p. Distribution over a sum of three is pairwise ceteris-paribus p.

$$\begin{aligned} p\copyright(A\cdot B) &= (p\copyright A)\cdot(p\copyright B)\\ p\copyright(A+B) &=_p p\copyright A + p\copyright B \Leftarrow A+B =_{\mathbb{B}} A\\ p\copyright(A+B+C) &=_p p\copyright(A+B)+p\copyright(A+C)+p\copyright(B+C)\end{aligned}$$

Expansion and covering are related by the following laws

$$\begin{aligned} p\copyright(q\circledS A) &=_p q\circledS(p\copyright A)\\ p\copyright(p\circledS A) &= p\copyright A\\ p\copyright\boxed{A} &=_p \boxed{p\copyright A}\end{aligned}$$

From the last law and (Hazard-Cover) it follows that we can remove hazards on transitions of p from an expression A by first expanding A and then covering transitions of p.

$$\mathsf{safe}\ (p, \boxed{A}+\boxed{p\copyright A})$$

When two variables $\{p,q\}$ are involved we use

$$\boxed{A}+\boxed{p\copyright A}+\boxed{q\copyright A}+\boxed{\{p,q\}\copyright A}$$

which is fundamental mode equal to the following huge expression in sum-of-product form.

$$\begin{aligned} &\overline{p}\cdot\overline{q}\cdot B+\overline{p}\cdot q\cdot C+p\cdot\overline{q}\cdot D+p\cdot q\cdot E+ && (\boxed{A})\\ &\overline{q}\cdot B\cdot D+q\cdot C\cdot E+ && (\boxed{p\copyright A})\\ &\overline{p}\cdot B\cdot C+p\cdot D\cdot E+ && (\boxed{q\copyright A})\\ &B\cdot C\cdot D\cdot E && (\boxed{\{p,q\}\copyright A})\end{aligned}$$

where $B = A[p := 0, q := 0]$, $C = A[p := 0, q := 1]$, $D = A[p := 1, q := 0]$, and $E = A[p := 1, q := 1]$.

Generalizing this to arbitrary expressions, we define the hazard removal operation $\_^*$

$$A^* = \sum \{\boxed{ps©A} \mid ps \subseteq \{p \in A\}\}$$

Without proof we state that $\_^*$ removes hazards while maintaining (boolean) correctness

$$\mathsf{safe}\,(A^*) \;\wedge\; A =_{\mathbb{B}} A^*$$

The definition of A^* really hides a simple procedure that may be used when hazard covering is applied manually to an expression A in sum-of-product form: as long as $A = B + \overline{p} \cdot C + p \cdot D$ with $C \cdot D \notin B$ and $C \cdot D \neq 0$, add $C \cdot D$ to A.

6 Asynchronous Finite-state Machines

This section shows an application of our hazard algebra to the implementation of asynchronous finite state machines. In fact, Our work grew out of an attempt to formalize Peyton Jones's technique for designing asynchronous finite-state machines [4]. An *asynchronous finite state machine* consists of

- A set of inputs $\mathcal{I} = \{a, b, c, \ldots\}$.
- A set of outputs $\mathcal{O} = \{m, n, o, \ldots\}$.
- A set of states $\mathcal{S} = \{R, S, T, \ldots\}$.
- An output specification m_S which specifies for each state S and each output m a boolean expression over $\mathcal{I}$, whose value m should take when in state S.
- A transition specification K_{ST} over $\mathcal{I}$ for pairs of states S and T denoting that when the machine is in state S and K_{ST} holds a transition should be made to state T.

The transitions should be *complete* and *deterministic*. Completeness means that each state S has at least one successor state T (which may be S itself)

$$(\textstyle\sum T :: K_{ST}) \;=\; 1 \qquad \text{(COMPL)}$$

Determinacy means that in any state S at most one transition is enabled

$$K_{ST} \cdot K_{ST'} \;=\; 0, \text{ if } T \neq T' \qquad \text{(DET)}$$

From the two conditions (COMPL) and (DET) on transitions it follows that

$$K_{SR} \;=\; (\textstyle\prod T : T \neq R : \overline{K_{ST}}) \qquad \text{(SELF)}$$

Without loss of generality we therefore assume $K_{SS} = (\prod T : T \neq S : \overline{K_{ST}})$. Note that (SELF) implies (COMPL).

6.1 Circuit realization

To implement an ASFM we must encode each state in terms of the *state variables* $\mathcal{Y} = \{x, y, z, \ldots\}$. Every state is assigned a product term containing every member of $\mathcal{Y}$, each possibly negated, i.e., a characteristic vector of some subset of $\mathcal{Y}$. With n state variables at most 2^n states can be encoded.

From the specification of an ASFM and a state assignment we derive a hazard free next state function NEXT with inputs $\mathcal{I} \cup \mathcal{Y}$ and outputs $\mathcal{Y}'$, and a hazard free output function OUT with input $\mathcal{I} \cup \mathcal{Y}$ and output $\mathcal{O}$. The circuit realization of the machine is obtained by feeding the outputs of the circuit realization for NEXT back as the current state inputs of the circuits for NEXT and OUT.

For this to work properly, without hazards, a number of assumptions have to be made:

1. The "outer machine" is operated in fundamental mode, i.e. only one input variable changes at a time and remains fixed until a stabile internal state has been reached.
2. The "inner circuits" NEXT and OUT are operated in fundamental mode. Because of feedback this implies that *at most one state variable may change when making a transition from one state to another* and that the feedback delay is large enough such that the circuits have stabilized internally, and that the input is sufficiently fast. The input transition must have been completed within the feedback delay.

For each output variable m, the output function OUT contains

$$m = (\sum S, T :: S \cdot K_{ST} \cdot m_T)^* \qquad \text{(OUT)}$$

For *Moore*-type machines where the output is a function of the current state only and not of the input, space can be traded for time by using the equation

$$m = (\sum S :: S \cdot m_S)^* \qquad \text{(MOORE)}$$

for output variable m.

Next-state variables are treated the same as outputs, so NEXT contains for each state variable y

$$y' = (\sum S, T :: S \cdot K_{ST} \cdot y_T)^* \qquad \text{(NEXT)}$$

where y_T is the value of state variable y in state T.

7 Comparison with Peyton Jones

Peyton Jones uses as equation for outputs

$$m = (\sum S, T : K_{ST} \neq 0 : (S + T) \cdot m_S \cdot m_T) \qquad (\text{OUT}_{\text{SPJ}})$$

This is essentially the result of pushing $\_^*$ inside our Moore-machine equation. Formally this means we have to show

$$(\sum \mathsf{S},\mathsf{T} : \mathsf{K}_{\mathsf{ST}} \neq 0 : (\mathsf{S}+\mathsf{T}) \cdot m_{\mathsf{S}} \cdot m_{\mathsf{T}}) \quad =_{\forall} \quad (\sum \mathsf{S} :: \mathsf{S} \cdot m_{\mathsf{S}})^*$$

At this moment we lack nice algebraic laws for the $\_^*$-operator to prove this. Similarly his equation for state variables

$$y' \quad = \quad \sum \mathsf{S},\mathsf{T} : \mathsf{K}_{\mathsf{ST}} \neq 0 : (\mathsf{S}+\mathsf{T}) \cdot y^*_{\mathsf{S}} \cdot y^*_{\mathsf{T}} \qquad (\mathrm{NEXT}_{\mathrm{SPJ}})$$

where y^*_{S} is defined for arbitrary S as

$$y^*_{\mathsf{S}} \quad = \quad y_{\mathsf{S}} \cdot \overline{(\sum \mathsf{T} : \mathsf{T} \neq \mathsf{S} : \overline{y_{\mathsf{T}}} \cdot \mathsf{K}_{\mathsf{ST}})} \cdot (\sum \mathsf{T} : \mathsf{T} \neq \mathsf{S} : y_{\mathsf{T}} \cdot \mathsf{K}_{\mathsf{ST}})$$

corresponds to our equation (OUT). We believe however that our formulation is much simpler.

The following machine shows that the equations for outputs given by Peyton Jones are wrong for Mealy-type machines. The machine has a single input a, one output m and two states S and T encoded by y respectively $\overline{y}$.

$$\begin{array}{rclcrcl} m_{\mathsf{S}} & = & a & \quad & m_{\mathsf{T}} & = & 0 \\ \mathsf{K}_{\mathsf{ST}} & = & a & & \mathsf{K}_{\mathsf{TT}} & = & 1 \end{array}$$

Expanding the expression for m suggested by Peyton Jones gives

$$m \quad = \quad y \cdot a$$

which is makes the output m temporarily high just before a transition from S to T. Our equation hardwires m to 0.

8 Example

As an example we implement a so called Muller C-element. This device has two inputs a and b and one output m. If both inputs are asserted so is the output, which remains asserted until both inputs are released.

$$\begin{array}{rclcrcl} m_{\mathsf{S}} & = & 0 & \quad & m_{\mathsf{T}} & = & 1 \\ \mathsf{K}_{\mathsf{ST}} & = & a \cdot b & & \mathsf{K}_{\mathsf{TS}} & = & \overline{a} \cdot \overline{b} \end{array}$$

With two states we need only one state variable, y, and we may use the state assignment $\mathsf{S} = \overline{y}, \mathsf{T} = y$. Unfolding, expanding into sum-of-product form and simplifying (NEXT) gives

$$\begin{array}{rcl} y' & = & \mathsf{S} \cdot a \cdot b + \mathsf{T} \cdot (a+b) \\ & = & \overline{y} \cdot a \cdot b + y \cdot (a+b) \\ & = & a \cdot b + y \cdot a + y \cdot b \end{array}$$

The minimized expression is hazard-free already, so we need not apply the covering procedure. Doing the same for (OUT) shows that $m = y$. This implementation of a C-element by connecting the output of a 3-input majority circuit back to an input is well-known [8]. Compared with the two page-verification of Josephs [5], our method does surprisingly well for this example.

acknowledgements

I wish to thank Maarten Fokkinga for the many detailed comments and critisism he gave on a draft version of this paper. The remarks of the two referees are also gratefully acknowledged.

References

[1] E.B. Eichelberger. Hazard detection in combinational and sequential switching circuits. *IBM Journal of Research and Development*, 9:90–99, March 1965.

[2] Guiseppe Fantauzzi. An algebraic model for the analysis of logical circuits. *IEEE Transactions on Computers*, 23(6), June 1974.

[3] C.A.R. Hoare. A couple of novelties in the propositional calculus. In C.A.R. Hoare and C.B. Jones, editors, *Essays in Computing Science*, chapter 19, pages 325–331. Prentice Hall, 1989.

[4] Simon L Peyton Jones. A practical technique for designing asynchronous finite-state machines. Technical report, Glasgow university, 1991.

[5] Mark B. Josephs. Algebraic verification of speed-independent circuits. Technical Report PRG-TR-18-91, Programming Research Group, Oxford University Computing Laboratory, 1991.

[6] D.W. Lewis. Hazard detection by quinary simulation of logic devices with bounded propagation delays. Master's thesis, Syracuse University, New York, January 1972.

[7] Carver Mead and Lynn Conway. *Introduction to VLSI Systems.* Addison-Wesley, 1980.

[8] Charles L. Seitz. *System Timing*, chapter 7, pages 218–262. in: [7].

[9] B. Thompson. A five-valued transitional logic. November 1992.

Generating Netlists from Executable Circuit Specifications in a Pure Functional Language

John T. O'Donnell
University of Glasgow

Abstract

It is easy to write a circuit specification in a pure functional language so that execution of the specification simulates the circuit. It's harder to make an executable specification generate the circuit's netlist without using impure language features. The difficulty is that a circuit specification evaluates to a graph isomorphic to the circuit, so the specification of a circuit with feedback will evaluate to a circular (or infinite) graph. That prevents a naïve graph traversal algorithm written in a pure functional language from terminating. This paper solves the problem by requiring the circuit specification to name components explicitly. With suitable higher order functions, the naming can be achieved without placing an undue burden on the circuit designer. This approach clarifies the distinction between transformations that preserve both the behaviour and structure of a circuit and transformations that preserve the behaviour while possibly changing the structure. It also demonstrates one way to manipulate circular graphs in a pure functional language.

1. Introduction

There are plenty of special purpose digital circuit design languages, and some of them provide their own calculus for reasoning about circuits. However, an ordinary functional programming language can also be used to specify circuits. This is especially attractive since the designer can use ordinary equational reasoning within the functional language, without introducing a new calculus.

It turns out that behavioural specifications are straightforward to do in a functional language, but a subtle technical problem arises for structural specifications. As a result, it becomes difficult to generate netlists for circuits with feedback without using impure language features.

Author's address: Computing Science Department, University of Glasgow, Glasgow G12 8QQ, Britain. Email: `jtod@dcs.glasgow.ac.uk`

This paper explains the source of the problem and proposes a solution that works with a *pure* functional language. This is the first solution that has been found for the problem. Previous researchers have avoided it by various means, but that leads to other difficulties. An extra benefit is that the solution clarifies the distinction between reasoning about behaviour and reasoning about structure. It requires some extra work on the part of the circuit designer, but not much, and that could be automated within the compiler by a trivial program transformation. The paper contains a complete implementation in Haskell, including the actual netlist produced by executing an example specification.

Section 2 explains the context of this work, and shows how previous researchers avoided the problem. Section 3 explains the technical problem in detail and presents the key idea behind the solution. Section 4 then adds the full implementation details required to make the solution practical. A complete example appears in Section 5, and Section 6 discusses the results.

2. Background and related work

A circuit designer must specify both the behaviour and the structure of a circuit. Designers often write just one form of the specification, leaving the reader to figure out the other one. Textbooks on digital design commonly specify a circuit's structure explicitly with a schematic diagram, leaving the behaviour implicit. Sometimes behavioural specifications like truth tables or boolean expressions are given, assuming that the reader can figure out a structure to implement the specified behaviour.

A particularly important form of structural specification is the *netlist*, which contains enough information to build the circuit. Netlists are intended to be read by software, such as wire-wrap machines or PCB/VLSI layout packages, in order to fabricate the circuit. They are complete, precise, incomprehensible and necessary. There is no single standard netlist language, but generally a netlist must contain at least the following information:

- a list of components
- a list of wires connecting the components' ports

Sometimes the geometric locations of the components will also be specified; sometimes not.

Ideally, the designer should be able to write a single readable document that specifies both the circuit's behaviour and structure and allows analyses to be performed. Thus a single specification has several semantic meanings. In practice, this means at least using the specification to simulate the circuit and to generate its netlist. The alternative — specifying the behaviour and structure separately — is dangerous because the two specifications can become inconsistent with each other.

Three approaches have been tried for providing alternative meanings for a single specification:

1. *Collection of tools.* The traditional approach doesn't view a specification as having semantics at all. Instead, the design system provides tools that

do useful things with a specification, which is treated merely as input to the program. One consequence of this approach is that implementors of different tools find it convenient to work with different input formats, so a single circuit specification may have to appear in several different ill-defined languages, and additional tools are required to translate between them.

The second and third approaches both recognise that a circuit specification language has several alternative semantics. An ordinary programming language has one syntax and one denotational semantic function $\mathcal{E}$, so that $\mathcal{E}[\![p]\!]$ is the meaning of program p. In contrast, a circuit specification language has one syntax but several distinct semantic functions corresponding to the meanings. For example, $\mathcal{E}_b[\![c]\!]$ is the behavioural meaning of the circuit specification c (i.e. a simulation function), $\mathcal{E}_s[\![c]\!]$ is the structural meaning (i.e. a netlist), and $\mathcal{E}_a[\![c]\!]$ is the result of an analysis (e.g. c's critical path depth). These two approaches differ only in the mechanisms used to define and implement the alternative semantics.

2. *Alternative interpreters.* Each alternative denotational semantics ($\mathcal{E}_b$, $\mathcal{E}_s$, $\mathcal{E}_a$ and any others) is defined independently. This amounts to writing several interpreters or compilers for the same syntax.

3. *Alternative base functions.* This method requires only one semantic function $\mathcal{E}$ for the specification language, but it introduces several libraries containing alternative definitions of the primitive functions (logic gates, latches and the like) corresponding to the alternative semantics. Suppose that the primitive functions are $p_1, \ldots, p_n$, and the behavioural library consists of implementations $b_1, \ldots, b_n$, the structural library is $s_1, \ldots, s_n$ and the analysis library is $a_1, \ldots, a_n$. Then the alternative semantic functions are defined by incorporating the appropriate library:

$$\mathcal{E}_b[\![c]\!] = \mathcal{E}[\![\, c\ [b_1/p_1,\ \ldots,\ b_n/p_n]]\!]$$

$$\mathcal{E}_s[\![c]\!] = \mathcal{E}[\![\, c\ [s_1/p_1,\ \ldots,\ s_n/p_n]]\!]$$

$$\mathcal{E}_a[\![c]\!] = \mathcal{E}[\![\, c\ [a_1/p_1,\ \ldots,\ a_n/p_n]]\!]$$

These three approaches are not equally good. The 'collection of tools' certainly works, but it sometimes leads to incompatibilities among the alternative interpretations of a specification and it gives poor support for formal reasoning. It is much better to give explicit semantics for the alternative meanings of a circuit specification.

Alternative interpreters provide the most obvious way to define alternative semantics. However, alternative base functions are better because

- Large parts of the specification language behave the same for all the alternative meanings. With alternative interpreters the similar parts have to be reimplemented several times. That makes it harder to see the interesting parts of the semantics — the places where the semantics are different — and introduces more room for error in implementation.

- With alternative base functions, only one semantic function $\mathcal{E}$ is required and that can be the compiler for an existing programming language. For example, this paper uses Haskell as the specification language, and it doesn't need to include a Haskell compiler in an appendix: one already exists! The implementation just consists of some modules of Haskell code. Compare this with the 'alternative interpreter' approach. Writing multiple interpreters is more work, even for a toy specification language, and it is completely infeasible to use a rich language like Haskell. Furthermore, simulation is time-consuming, so an efficient compiler is needed rather than a toy interpreter. Using alternative base functions, we automatically take advantage of all the progress being made in compiler technology — unlike alternative interpreters.

The alternative base function approach is similar to 'embedding languages'. This technique is popular in the Scheme research community, where its merits are almost taken as axiomatic, but it hasn't been used much by the functional programming community.

The first computer hardware description language based on alternative semantic functions, rather than a collection of tools, was Hydra [2, 3, 4], designed and implemented by O'Donnell between 1981 and 1986. Hydra was implemented on top of Daisy, an early functional language, and it used alternative base functions to define four semantic functions:

1. A behavioural function simulated the circuit.
2. A structural function generated the netlist.
3. An analysis function calculated the critical path depth.
4. A geometric function produced a layout (this required the user to provide additional information by using geometric combining forms to specify the circuit).

Hydra's use of base functions was successful, and it made the system easy to reimplement in another functional language (in fact that was done twice).

At about the same time that Hydra was designed and implemented, Boute independently proposed the idea of giving alternative semantic interpretations to one specification [1]. Boute's 'system semantics' uses alternative interpreters. System semantics is more general than Hydra, providing for analogue as well as digital circuits. However, the original paper was only a proposal; an implementation was not given, making it difficult to evaluate the system.

More recently, Singh proposed 'nonstandard interpretation' as a new name for Hydra's 'alternative base function' technique, and used it to implement several circuit analyses for specifications in Ruby [5]. These include fault simulation and testability measures [6].

Alternative interpreters are more obvious, while alternative base functions are superior technically. But there's a catch — with alternative base functions, a problem arises in netlist generation for circuits with feedback. The next section explains the problem in detail. Previous researchers have avoided the problem rather than solving it:

- The original implementation of Hydra used an impure functional language feature, the pointer equality predicate (equivalent to the Lisp `eq` function). This is a hack that breaks referential transparency, destroying much of the advantage of using a functional language in the first place.
- Boute did not present a complete definition of a netlist generator, but his use of alternative interpreters would make it easy to program around the problem — although the advantages of alternative base functions are lost.
- Singh used alternative base functions, but restricted his specification language to combinational circuits without feedback, so the problem goes away (along with most interesting circuits).

The rest of the paper presents the first real solution to the problem, making it possible to generate netlists in a *pure* functional language using alternative base functions.

3. Motivation

This section explains the problem and the idea behind the solution. It begins by reviewing how an executable specification can produce both a simulation and a netlist and why netlist generation is hard in a pure functional language. Then it introduces the idea of named components, clarifying what it means to transform a circuit specification.

3.1 Executable specification of behaviour and structure

How can Hydra produce two different meanings — a simulator and a netlist — from one specification? The gist of the idea is simple. A circuit specification contains applications of component functions to input signals. For example, `x = and2 a b` applies the two-input `and2` gate to the inputs `a` and `b`. As far as the circuit specification is concerned, `and2` is a free variable: a user-defined function which must be defined in another module. Hydra provides several modules containing alternative definitions of primitives like `and2`. One module defines the primitives to be simulation functions, and another module defines them to be netlist generation functions. The designer executes the specification with the simulation module in order to simulate the circuit. Alternatively, running the specification with the netlist module produces the netlist. (Here is a natural application for overloading, but this paper doesn't address that issue.)

The simulation module is straightforward. Assume for now that every component has one input and one output. Each wire carries a single value called a signal, which defines the bit on the wire during every clock cycle.

```
type Signal = [Bit]
```

The inverter and latch are typical components whose behaviours are defined by

```
inv, latch :: Signal -> Signal
inv = map bit_invert
latch a = 0 : a
```

Now we can define a circuit c1 containing a latch and an inverter.

```
c1 :: Signal -> Signal
c1 x = latch (inv x)
```

This is an executable specification, and the following reduction shows how applying c1 to an input simulates the circuit. See [2] for more details on functional circuit simulation.

```
c1 [0,0,1,0,...]
  = latch (inv [0,0,1,0,...]
  = latch (map bit_invert [0,0,1,0,...])
  = latch [1,1,0,1,...]
  = [0,1,1,0,1,...]
```

The really attractive feature of c1 is that we can make it generate the circuit's netlist simply by redefining Signal, latch and inv. Instead of thinking of a signal as a sequence of bits through time, we think of it as a description of the hardware that drives a wire. So a signal may either be an input (named by a string) or the output of a component (identified by a string) whose input is some other signal.

```
data Signal = Input String | Comp String Signal
```

The components must also be redefined, using the new Signal type.

```
inv, latch :: Signal -> Signal
inv a = Comp "inv" a
latch a = Comp "latch" a
```

Now a representation of the circuit's structure can be obtained by applying c1 to a suitable input.

```
c1 (Input "w")
  = latch (inv (Input "w"))
  = latch (Comp "inv" (Input "w"))
  = Comp "latch" (Comp "inv" (Input "w"))
```

The point is that c1 simultaneously specifies the circuit's behaviour and structure. We obtain the behaviour by executing c1 with the first set of definitions of Signal, inv and latch, resulting in a circuit simulation. We obtain the structure by executing c1 with the second set of definitions, resulting in a graph that is isomorphic to the circuit. A netlist can be produced by traversing ("showing") the graph.

3.2 Feedback and circular circuits

Most realistic circuits contain feedback. Here is a simple (though unrealistic) example.

```
c2 = x where x = latch x
```

Using the behaviour module, c2 reduces to the circuit's output [0,0,...]. Using the structure module, c2 reduces to a circular graph with one Comp node that points back to itself. The definition reduces to a graph isomorphic to the real circuit, which is good. But equational reasoning also shows that

```
c2 = Comp "latch" c2
   = Comp "latch" (Comp "latch" c2)
   = Comp "latch" (Comp "latch" (Comp "latch" c2)
   ...
```

A circular graph is equal to an infinite one, so the naïve traversal falls into an infinite loop.

We can avoid the infinite loop by maintaining a list of nodes already encountered while traversing the graph, ensuring that each pointer is followed exactly once. But a pointer equality predicate, like the Lisp eq function, is needed to determine in finite time whether the current node is a member of the list of nodes already encountered. The original Hydra implementation [2] used that method, at the cost of losing referential transparency.

3.3 Identity of components

To generate netlists in a pure functional language, we need a method for determining whether two components are identical without comparing their inputs. This is more subtle than it seems. Consider the following specifications:

```
c1 x = (inv x, inv x)

c2 x = (y,y)
  where y = inv x
```

The definition of c1 suggests a pair of inverters with shared inputs. The definition of c2 suggests a single inverter whose output is shared. Yet equational reasoning shows that c1 = c2.

A definition like c1 or c2 specifies the behaviour precisely, but not the structure. This will be called a *behavioural specification*. Before trying to generate netlists, we must specify the structure unambiguously, as well as the behaviour. This will be called a *structural specification*.

Ordinary equational reasoning can be applied to either kind of specification. Using equational reasoning on a behavioural specification leaves the behaviour unchanged but may change the apparent structure (for example, transforming c1 into c2). Using equational reasoning on a structural specification changes only the notation used to describe the circuit. Transforming a structural specification might affect its readability or its hierarchical organisation, but cannot affect the actual circuit itself.

We also need a method for converting a behavioural specification into a structural specification. This definitely cannot be done by equational reasoning, since the semantics of the specification (and perhaps its type) will be changed.

Finally, we need a method for executing a structural specification to produce a graph and a traversal algorithm which produces the netlist in finite time, even for circular circuits.

The crux of a structural specification is determining whether two components are identical. It isn't enough to guarantee that two components produce the same outputs: they might or might not be identical. We do this by giving each component a unique name of type `CompName`. Two components are equal if and only if their names are equal. Furthermore, the `CompName` type will be noncircular, so any two names can be compared in finite time. The component types have to be changed:

```
data Signal = Input String | Comp String CompName Signal
inv, latch :: CompName -> Signal -> Signal
inv cn x = Comp "inv" cn x
latch cn x = Comp "latch" cn x
```

A circuit inherits its own name, and is responsible for naming its internal components. Define

```
data CompName = Base | N Int CompName
```

Now consider

```
c3 cn x = (inv (N 1 cn) x, inv (N 2 cn) x)

c4 cn x = (y1,y2)
  where y1 = inv (N 1 cn) x
        y2 = inv (N 2 cn) x

c5 cn x = (inv (N 1 cn) x, inv (N 1 cn) x)

c6 cn x = (y,y)
  where y = inv (N 1 cn) x
```

Now `c3` and `c4` specify the same circuit, which contains two distinct inverters with shared inputs. Similarly, `c5` and `c6` specify the same circuit, which contains one inverter with shared outputs. Equational reasoning shows that `c3` = `c4` and `c5` = `c6`, but `c3` ≠ `c5`. We cannot use equational reasoning to transform a two-inverter circuit into a one-inverter circuit. Using a suitable redefinition of the behavioural definition for an inverter which ignores the component name, we can show that all of `c1` through `c6` have the same behaviour.

4. Implementation

The simplified netlist generation scheme just presented illustrates the main issues, but it has several deficiencies that any practical system must overcome:

- *Explicit wires.* A netlist must list every wire explicitly, giving its source and sinks. The simplified scheme only mentions wires implicitly.
- *Multiple inputs.* A real component may take several inputs, but the simplified scheme allows only one input for each component.
- *Component pins.* Every wire connects a pin on some component to some other component pin. These pins must be identified explicitly, to enable a mechanical fabrication system to install the wires automatically.
- *Global values.* In addition to the interesting logic values carried by wires, various extra wires are needed to carry power, ground, the clock, etc. The netlist should mention these explicitly.
- *Support for generating component names.* To convert a behavioural specification into a structural one, each component must be given a unique name. We should automate the naming as far as possible, instead of making the designer do it all manually,
- *Graph traversal.* A structural specification will evaluate to a graph structure representing all the relevant information, and we need a graph traversal algorithm to convert such a graph into a finite character string expressing the netlist. The simplified scheme relies on the built-in `show`, so it will produce infinite output for a circular specification.

The following subsections present, in three stages, a complete and practical system for generating netlists solving all of these problems. The first stage is the definition of a graph data structure suitable for representing all the important details of a circuit. The second stage is a graph traversal function that extracts a netlist from a circuit graph, even if the graph is circular. The third stage develops tools for automating most of the generation of component names, and for making the remaining manual part much easier.

4.1 Representing the circuit graph

A circuit consists of wires, ports and components. A wire carries a message from a source, which drives a signal onto the wire, to a sink which reads it. Bidirectional wires are not allowed; they have to be modeled by a pair of unidirectional wires. A wire with several sinks will be treated as a set of wires.

```
type Wire = (Source, Sink)
```

Several kinds of source can drive a wire. These include constant data values; global values like power, ground and the clock; inputs to the circuit, and the output ports of components. It's good practice to treat data constants explicitly, rather than representing constant 0 as `Gnd` and constant 1 as `Vcc`. That kind of ad hoc representation would fail if the designer uses negative logic or mixed logic.

```
data Source
  = Constant Bit
  | Global String
  | Input String
```

```
  | OutPort Component Pin
  deriving Eq
```

Two kinds of sink can read the value on a wire: an output from the circuit and the input port of a component within the circuit. A component may have several input ports, so a "pin number" is needed to identify which one is the wire's sink.

```
data Sink
  = Output String
  | InPort Component Pin Source
  deriving Eq

type Pin = Int
```

We represent a component by a node containing all the information the netlist generator needs to know about it. Of course this includes the kind of component and its unique name. The inputs must also be known, since the graph traversal algorithm needs to find all the components and wires used to drive the wires connected to the components inputs.

It's interesting that the graph traversal algorithm needs to find all the inputs of a component that it knows about, but doesn't need to find the component's outputs. This means that all the arcs in the graph need to be backwards, pointing from a sink component back to the source, opposite to the direction that the information actually flows along the wire. That is why the `InPort` constructor for type `Sink` has a `Source` field.

The `CompKind` type is like an inventory part number. Here it will be defined as a string, but a more structured type should be used in practice. The inputs to a component are sinks. The component name type will be discussed later. It is essential that two component names can be compared for equality in finite time.

```
data Component = Comp CompKind CompName CompInputs

type CompKind = String
type CompInputs = [Sink]
```

4.2 Representation of the netlist

A netlist is a noncircular representation of a circuit graph, containing a list of inputs and outputs, an inventory of components and a wiring list.

```
type NetList =
  ([Source],     -- inputs
   [Sink],       -- outputs
   [Component],  -- inventory
   [Wire])       -- connections
```

4.3 Traversing the graph

The circuit graph must be traversed in order to produce the netlist, which can then be printed by a straightforward `show` function. The graph traversal algorithm needs some trivial functions for working with nodes and arcs.

```
isInput :: Source -> Bool
isOutput :: Sink -> Bool
compKind :: Component -> CompKind
compName :: Component -> CompName
compInputs :: Component -> CompInputs
```

The traversal also needs to find all the wires connected to the inputs of a component. It will follow these wires to get deeper into the graph.

```
inWires :: Component -> [Wire]
inWires = map f . compInputs
  where f :: Sink -> Wire
        f x@(InPort c p s) = (s,x)
```

Two components are identical if and only if their kinds and names are equal. If they have different names then they are distinct components — even if their corresponding inputs and outputs always carry equal values.

```
instance Eq Component where
  Comp k1 n1 x1 == Comp k2 n2 x2 = k1==k2 && n1==n2
```

The output wires of a circuit are "handles" that can be followed to find the internal components. Each time a new component is found the wires connected to its own inputs must be added to the list of handles. Following a handle will lead either to an input to the circuit or to an output port from some component, which may or may not have been encountered already.

```
follow
  :: [Source]      -- is = inputs to the circuit
  -> [Sink]        -- os = outputs from the circuit
  -> [Wire]        -- hs = handles remaining to be followed
  -> [Component]   -- cs = inventory of components
  -> [Wire]        -- ws = internal connections
  -> NetList       -- result

follow is os [] cs ws = (is, os, cs, ws)

follow is os (h@(source,sink):hs) cs ws =
  case source of
    Constant x   -> follow is' os' hs cs ws'
    Input x      -> follow is' os' hs cs ws'
    OutPort c p  -> if c `elem` cs
                      then follow is' os' hs cs ws'
                      else follow is' os' (inWires c ++ hs)
```

```
                                        (c:cs) ws'
    where is' = addSource source is
          os' = addSink sink os
          ws' = h:ws

  addSource source is =
    if isInput source && source `notElem` is
      then source:is
      else is

  addSink sink os =
    if isOutput sink && sink `notElem` os
      then sink:os
      else os
```

4.4 Component names

The simplified scheme presented in Section 3.3 required the designer to specify all the component names manually. This is tedious, and any naming errors could result in either an incorrect netlist or in nontermination of the graph traversal algorithm. Therefore it's important to simplify the task of naming the components. Two observations are useful:

1. Structuring the names makes them easier to generate. Suppose that each subsystem in the design has its own component name **cn** (even though strictly speaking it isn't a primitive component and doesn't really need one). Suppose that within the subsystem there are k components c_1 to c_k. We can give those unique names of the form 1:**cn** to k :**cn**. This is much easier than dealing with a flat namespace for the entire circuit. The structured names also lead to more informative netlists: it's easier to figure out what part of the specification produced a component in the netlist.

2. The name of a component can usually be built up by adding information to the name of one of the component's inputs (since that also must have been uniquely named). This incremental building of names can easily be automated. Of course, it is essential to avoid making a circular name definition. We can avoid that by ensuring that each equation in a **where** expression has a unique equation name consisting of the subsystem's name combined with the equation number.

Based on those observations, machinery can be defined for partially automating the name generation. We begin by defining a structured type for names. A component name becomes a list of pieces, and an outermost circuit specification can be given an empty base name.

```
  type CompName = [CompNamePiece]

  baseCompName :: CompName
```

```
baseCompName = []

data CompNamePiece
  = BlockName String  -- explicit circuit name
  | EquName Int       -- each equation is numbered
  | NodeName Int      -- nodes within rhs are numbered
  deriving Eq
```

To make netlists more readable, the designer can give a `BlockName` to important building block circuits. Block names are optional; in effect, they provide a way to put comments into a netlist.

```
block :: String -> CompName -> CompName
block x cn = BlockName x : cn
```

Each equation in a specification needs its own `EquName` to use as a foundation for components used in the right hand side. However, it's common to compose a sequence of components in the right hand side of an equation, and we can make those automatically pass `NodeNames` to each other.

```
newEquName :: Int -> CompName -> CompName
newEquName i cn = NodeName 0 : EquName i : cn

newNodeName :: CompName -> Int -> CompName
newNodeName (NodeName x : xs) i = NodeName (x+i) : xs
```

The automatic naming facility requires the inputs and outputs of a circuit to be treated differently. The input to a circuit is a `Signal`, which must be applied to a `CompName` to yield a `Source`. The output from a circuit is simply a `Source`. This means, for example, that the type of the `and2` gate changes from `Signal -> Signal -> Signal` to `Signal -> Signal -> Source`.

```
type Signal = CompName -> Source

mkInput :: String -> Signal
mkInput s = (\cn -> Input s)

mkOutput :: Signal -> Source
mkOutput x = x baseCompName
```

It's fine to pass component names from one node to the next within the right hand side of an equation, but this mechanism must be defeated when we begin a new equation. We do that with `forcename`, which forces a node `x` to use the equation name `cn` instead of the passed name `cn'`.

```
forcename :: CompName -> Signal -> Signal
forcename cn x = (\cn' -> x cn)
```

Infix operators can be used to shorten the syntax.

```
(#) = forcename
```

```
(&) :: Int -> CompName -> CompName
(&) = newEquName
```

The designer now has very little work to do in converting a behavioural specification into a structural one. Section 5 gives an example showing all this machinery in action.

4.5 Defining the primitive components

It's useful to build some tools to make it easy to define new primitive components for structural specifications. The **mkComp** function takes a complete description of the structural characteristics of a primitive component and defines a function from the component name to the component itself.

```
mkComp
  :: CompKind         -- component kind
  -> [(Signal,Int)] -- input (value,pin) assignments
  -> [Int]            -- output pins
  -> ([Source]->a)  -- [output pins] -> output grouping
  -> CompName         -- name of the component
  -> a                -- result = outputs grouped as type a

mkComp k is os f cn = f outports
  where c = Comp k cn inports
        inports = [InPort c p (x n)
                   | ((x,p),n) <- zip is cns]
        cns = map (newNodeName cn) [1..]
        outports = map (\p -> OutPort c p) os
```

The following functions can be used to convert the outports list into the right grouping of outputs.

```
mkSingleton [a] = a
mkPair [a,b] = (a,b)
mkTriple [a,b,c] = (a,b,c)
```

Now it's straightforward to define primitive components. These definitions are all higher order functions which still need to be applied to a **CompName**.

```
comp11 k x   = mkComp k [(x,0)]       [1]   mkSingleton
comp21 k x y = mkComp k [(x,0),(y,1)] [2]   mkSingleton
comp22 k x y = mkComp k [(x,0),(y,1)] [2,3] mkPair

latch   = comp11 "latch"
inv     = comp11 "inv"
and2    = comp21 "and2"
or2     = comp21 "or2"
xor     = comp21 "xor2"
halfAdd = comp22 "halfAdd"
```

5. Example: A shift register and its netlist

Here is the behavioural specification of a general shift register [2] with three bit positions `a`, `b` and `c`, defined by the shift register bit `srb` component. The shift register has a left input `li` and right input `ri`, and it also has an opcode input which tells it whether to shift to the left or right. Its circuit diagram is given below the specification.

```
sr :: Signal -> Signal -> Signal -> (Signal,Signal)

sr op li ri = (a, c)
  where a = srb op li b
        b = srb op a c
        c = srb op b ri
```

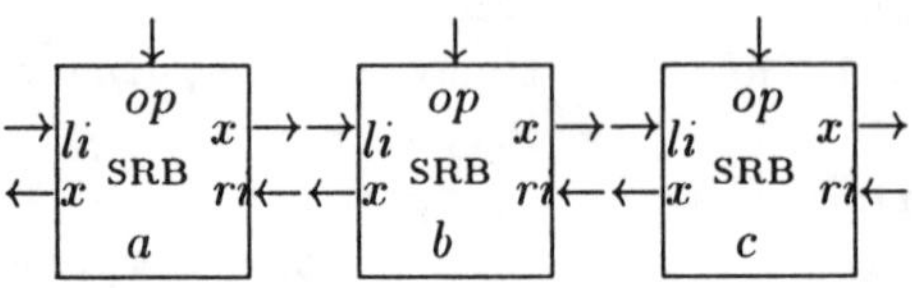

Using the tools defined in Section 4.4, it's easy to convert the behavioural specification `sr` into a structural specification `sr'`. Notice how the equations are numbered by the functions `1&cn#`, `2&cn#` and `3&cn#`, but little other change is needed. To illustrate the use of `mkComp`, the `srb` is treated as a primitive.

```
sr' :: Signal -> Signal -> Signal -> CompName
       -> (Source,Source)

sr' op li ri cn = (mkOutput a, mkOutput c)
  where a = 1&cn# srb op li b
        b = 2&cn# srb op a c
        c = 3&cn# srb op b ri

srb :: Signal -> Signal -> Signal -> CompName -> Source
srb op li ri =
  mkComp "SRB" [(op,0),(li,1),(ri,2)] [3] mkSingleton
```

Everything still works fine if we redefine `srb` as follows, using latches, logic gates and the like, but the resulting netlist is much bigger!

```
srb2 :: Signal -> Signal -> Signal -> CompName -> Source
srb2 op li ri cn = mkOutput x
  where ci = block "srb2" cn
        x = 1&ci# latch (or2 (and2 (inv op) li)
                              (and2 op ri))
```

Finally, the netlist can be constructed and converted into a string. The result of evaluating `sr'_netlist` is shown below, and could be used by an automatic circuit fabrication system, such as a wire wrap machine.

```
sr'_netlist =
  let op = mkInput "op"
      li = mkInput "li"
      ri = mkInput "ri"
  in showNetList (netlist2 (sr' op li ri baseCompName))
```

```
Inputs (3)                        Wires (11)
    1. Input ri                        1. 1_3 --> Output Outy
    2. Input li                        2. Input ri --> 1_2
    3. Input op                        3. 2_3 --> 1_1
                                       4. Input op --> 1_0
Outputs (2)                            5. 1_3 --> 2_2
    1. Output Outy                     6. 3_3 --> 2_1
    2. Output OUTx                     7. Input op --> 2_0
                                       8. 2_3 --> 3_2
Components (3)                         9. Input li --> 3_1
    1. SRB        3.0                 10. Input op --> 3_0
    2. SRB        2.0                 11. 3_3 --> Output OUTx
    3. SRB        1.0
```

Netlist produced by executing the shift register specification

---

6. Conclusion

This paper has presented the first real solution to the problem of generating netlists from executable circuit specifications with feedback in a functional programming language. The idea is to modify a behavioural circuit specification so that it gives unique names to all components. The traversal algorithm is then able to find loops in the graph by comparing any node with a list of nodes that are already known.

The component-naming approach forces a distinction between purely behavioural circuit specifications and structural specifications (which also specify the behaviour). The distinction is actually quite helpful, because the designer should know whether it is possible for a behaviour-preserving transformation to modify the circuit's structure. Both types of transformation are useful in practice.

The paper has also defined a set of tools that make it rather easy to add component names to a specification. Essentially, the designer just needs to number the equations in `where` expressions. It would be trivial to introduce a program transformation into a compiler that automates even the equation numbering. Further investigation is needed to choose the best way to automate the naming completely.

It is important to implement new ideas; otherwise it's difficult to assess them, or even to know whether they work at all. This paper has presented a complete Haskell implementation of the proposed netlist generation scheme (except for some trivial auxiliary functions omitted due to lack of space). Everything works. Section 5 contains a real circuit specification and the netlist generated by executing it.

An advantage of the naming method described here is that it requires no language extensions at all. It makes circuit specification, simulation and netlist generation possible in any pure functional language. Of course, dedicated hardware description languages and calculi offer special features that avoid the problems of component naming, but they also restrict the circuit designer to just those capabilities which they provide. It is very attractive to carry out all necessary reasoning about a circuit in a single language, with all the power and flexibility of a general purpose programming language.

References

1. R. T. Boute, "System semantics: principles, application and implementation,", ACM Trans. Programming Languages and Systems, **10** 1 (Jan. 1988) 118–155.
2. J. T. O'Donnell, "Hardware description with recursion equations," *Proceedings of the IFIP 8th International Symposium on Computer Hardware Description Languages and their Applications*, North-Holland (April 1987) 363–382.
3. J. T. O'Donnell, "Hydra: hardware description in a functional language using recursion equations and high order combining forms," *The Fusion of Hardware Design and Verification*, G. J. Milne (ed), Amsterdam: North-Holland (1988) 309–328.
4. J. T. O'Donnell and C. V. Hall, "Hydra: A digital circuit design system," Report SA/TR-4/89, Sabbagh Associates Inc., Bloomington IN (March 1989).
5. M. Sheeran, "Describing hardware algorithms in Ruby," *Declarative Systems*, North-Holland (1990) 289–303.
6. S. Singh, "Implementation of a nonstandard interpretation system," *Functional Programming, Glasgow 1989*, Workshops in Computing, Springer-Verlag (1990) 206–224.

The nofib Benchmark Suite of Haskell Programs

Will Partain
University of Glasgow

Abstract

This position paper describes the need for, make-up of, and "rules of the game" for a benchmark suite of Haskell programs. (It does not include results from running the suite.) Those of us working on the Glasgow Haskell compiler hope this suite will encourage sound, quantitative assessment of lazy functional programming systems. This version of this paper reflects the state of play at the initial pre-release of the suite.

1 Towards lazy functional benchmarking

1.1 History of benchmarking—functional

The quantitative measurement of systems for lazy functional programming is a near-scandalous subject. Dancing behind a thin veil of disclaimers, researchers in the field can still be found quoting "nfibs/sec" (or something equally egregious), as if this refers to anything remotely interesting.

The April, 1989, *Computer Journal* special issue on lazy functional programming is a not-too-dated self-portrait of the community that promotes computing in this way. It is one that non-specialists are likely to see. There are three papers under the heading "Efficiency of functional languages."

The Yale group, reporting on their ALFL compiler, cites results for the benchmarks **queens 8**, **nfib 20**, **tak**, **mm**, **deriv**, **tfib 100 40**, **qsort**, and **init**, noting that several are from the Gabriel suite of LISP benchmarks. They say that results from these tests "indicate that functional languages are indeed becoming competitive with conventional languages" [2, page 160].

Augustsson and Johnsson have a section about performance in their paper on the LML compiler [1]. They consider some of the usual suspects: **8queens**, **fib 20**, **prime**, and **kwic**, comparing against implementations of these algorithms in C, Edinburgh and New Jersey SML, and Miranda.[1] To their credit, the wondrous Chalmers hackers are somewhat apologetic, conceding that "measuring performance of the compiled code is very difficult..."

Finally, Wray and Fairbairn argue for programming techniques that make "essential use of non-strictness" and for an implementation (TIM) that makes these techniques inexpensive [10]. Though they delve into a substantial spreadsheet-like example program, they do not report any actual measurements. However, they astutely take issue with the usual toy benchmarks: "There was in the past a tendency for implementations to be judged on their performance for unusually strict benchmarks."

[1] Miranda is a trademark of Research Software Ltd.

1.2 History of benchmarking—imperative

Our imperative-programming colleagues are not far removed from our brutish benchmarking condition. Only a few years ago, "MIPS ratings," Dhrystones and friends were all the rage: marketeers bandied them about shamelessly, compiler writers tweaked their compilers to spot specific constructs in certain benchmarks, users were baffled, and no-one learned much that was worth knowing. The section on performance in Hennessy and Patterson's standard text on computer architecture is an admirable exposé of these shenanigans and is well worth reading [7].

Then, in 1988, enter the Standard Performance Evaluation Corporation (SPEC) benchmarking suite. The initial version included source code and sample inputs ("workloads") for four mostly-integer programs and six mostly-floating-point programs. These are all either real programs (e.g., the GNU C compiler) or the "kernel" of a real program (e.g., `matrix300`, floating-point matrix multiplication). Computer vendors have since put immense effort into improving their "SPECmarks," and this has delivered real benefit to the workstation user.

1.3 Towards lazy benchmarking

The SPEC suite is the most visible artifact of an important shift towards *system* benchmarking. A big reason for the shift lies in the benchmarked systems themselves. Fifteen years ago, a typical computer system—hardware and software—probably came from one manufacturer, sat in one room, and was a computing environment all on its own.

An excellent discussion about benchmarking from the self-contained-systems era is Gabriel and Masinter's paper about LISP systems [4]. "The proper role of benchmarking is to measure various dimensions of Lisp system performance and to order those systems along each of these dimensions" (page 136). A toy benchmark, of the type I have derided so far, can focus on one of these "dimensions," thus contributing to an overall picture.

Much early measurement work in functional programming was of this plot-along-dimensions style; however, the concern was usually to assess a particular implementation technique, not the system as a whole. For example, Hailperin, Huynh and Révész tried to compare systems that use strict versus lazy evaluation [5]. They went to considerable effort to factor out irrelevant details, hoping to end up with pristine data points along interesting dimensions. Hartel's effort to characterise the relative costs of fixed-combinator versus program-derived-combinator implementations was even more elaborate, using non-toy SASL programs [6].

So, can SPEC be seen as a culmination of good practice in benchmarking-by-characteristics? No! SPEC makes *no effort* to pinpoint systems along "interesting" dimensions, except for the very simplest—elapsed wall-clock time. An underlying premise of SPEC is that systems are sufficiently complicated that we probably won't even be able to pick out the interesting dimensions to measure, much less characterise benchmarks in terms of them. SPEC represents a shift to *lazy* benchmarking *of systems*.

Conte and Hwu's survey confirms that, at least in computer architecture, this shift towards "lazy, system-oriented benchmarking" is supported as a Good

Thing [3]. The trend can also be seen in some specialised areas of computing: the Perfect Benchmarks for supercomputers (Crays, etc., running FORTRAN programs) [8] and the Stanford benchmarks for parallel, shared-memory systems [9] are two examples.

2 Some serious benchmarks, `nofib`

We, the Glasgow Haskell compiler group, wish to (help) develop and promote a freely-available benchmark suite for lazy functional programming systems—called the `nofib` suite—consisting of:

1. Source code for "real" Haskell programs to compile and run;
2. Sample inputs (workloads) to feed into the compiled programs, along with the expected outputs;
3. "Rules" for compiling and running the benchmark programs, and (more notably) for reporting your benchmarking results; and
4. Sample reports, showing by example how results should be reported.

2.1 Our (non-)motivations in creating this suite

Benchmarking is a delicate art and science, and it's hard work, to boot. We have quite limited goals for the `nofib` suite, are hoping for lots of help, and are prepared to overlook considerable shortcomings, especially at the beginning.

2.1.1 Motivations.

- Our main *initial* motivation is to give functional-language implementors (including ourselves) a common set of "real Haskell programs" to attack and study. We encourage implementors to tackle the problems that *actually* make Haskell programs large and slow, thus hastening solutions to those problems.

  And of course, because the benchmark programs are shared, it will be possible to *compare* performance results between systems running on identical hardware (e.g., Chalmers HBC vs. Glasgow Haskell, both running on the same Sun4). Racing is the fun part!

- Our *ultimate* motivation for this benchmark suite is to provide "end users" of Haskell implementations with a useful *predictor* of how those systems will perform on their own programs.

  The initial `nofib` suite will have no value as a predictive tool. Perhaps those with greater expertise will help us correct this. If necessary, we will gladly hand over "the token" for the suite to a more disinterested party.

- We are very keen on (some might say "paranoid about") readily-accessible *reproducible* results. That is the whole point of the "reporting rules" elsewhere in this paper.

  Good-but-irreproducible benchmarking results are very damaging, because they lull implementors into a false sense of security.

- After the initial pre-release of the suite, which will be for (possibly major) debugging, we intend to keep the suite *stable*, so that sensible comparisons can be made over time.
- Having said that, benchmarks must change over time, or they become stale. It is difficult to brim with confidence about the Gabriel benchmarks for LISP systems; they are more than a decade old.

  Being forced to change a benchmark suite can be a mark of success. The SPEC people made substantial changes to their suite in 1992: so much work had gone into compiler tricks that improved SPEC performance results that some tests were no longer useful (notably the `matrix300` test mentioned earlier).

2.1.2 Non-motivations.

We are profoundly uninterested in distilling a "single figure of merit" (e.g., MIPS) to characterise a Haskell implementation's performance.

Initially at least, we are also uninterested in any statistics derived from the raw **nofib** numbers, e.g., various means, standard deviations, etc. You may calculate and report any such numbers—all honest efforts to understand these benchmarks are welcome—but the raw, underlying numbers must be readily available.

An important issue we are *not* addressing with this suite is inter-language comparisons: "How does program X written in Haskell fare against the same program written in language Y?" Such comparisons raise a nest of issues all their own; for example, is it really the "same" program when written in the two compared languages? This disclaimer aside, we do provide the **nofib** program sources in other languages if we happen to have them.

2.2 The Real subset

The **nofib** programs are divided into three subsets: Real, Imaginary, and Spectral (somewhere between Real and Imaginary).

The Real subset of the **nofib** suite is by far the most important. In fact, we insist that anyone who wishes to report any results from running this suite (in whatever form) must first distribute their complete, raw results for the Real subset in a public forum (e.g., available by anonymous FTP).

The programs in the Real subset are listed in Table 1. Each one meets most of the following criteria:

- Written in standard Haskell (version 1.2 or greater).
- Written by someone trying to get a job done, not by someone trying to make a pedagogical or stylistic point.
- Performs some useful task such that someone other than the author might want to execute the program for other than watch-a-demo reasons.
- Neither implausibly small or impossibly large (the Glasgow Haskell compiler, written in Haskell, falls in the latter category).

Program	Description	Origin
`anna`	Strictness analyser	Julian Seward (Manchester)
`calc`	arbitrary-precision calculator	Liang & Mirani (Yale)
`compress`	Text compression	Paul Sanders (BT)
`fluid`	Fluid-dynamics program	Xiaoming Zhang (Swansea)
`gamteb`	Monte Carlo photon transport	Pat Fasel (Los Alamos)
`gg`	Graphs from GRIP statistics	Iain Checkland (York)
`hpg`	Haskell program generator	Nick North (NPL)
`infer`	Hindley-Milner type inference	Phil Wadler (Glasgow)
`lift`	Fully-lazy lambda lifter	David Lester (Manchester) & Simon Peyton Jones (Glasgow)
`maillist`	Mailing-list generator	Paul Hudak (Yale)
`mkhprog`	Haskell program skeletons	Nick North (NPL)
`parser`	Partial Haskell parser	Julian Seward (Manchester)
`pic`	Particle in cell	Pat Fasel (Los Alamos)
`prolog`	"mini-Prolog" interpreter	Mark Jones (Oxford)
`reptile`	Escher tiling program	Sandra Foubister (York)
`veritas`	Theorem-prover	Gareth Howells (Kent)

Table 1: `nofib` benchmarks: Real Subset

- The run time and space for the compiled program must neither be too small (e.g., time less than five secs.) or too large (e.g., such that a research student in a typical academic setting could not run it).

Other desiderata for the Real subset as a whole:

- Written by diverse people, with varying functional-programming skills and styles, at different sites.
- Include programs of varying "ages," from first attempts, to heavily-tuned rewritten-four-times behemoths, to transliterations-from-LML, etc...
- Span across as many different application areas as possible.
- The suite, as a whole, should be able to compile and run to completion overnight, in a typical academic Unix computing environment.

2.3 The Spectral subset

The programs in the Spectral subset of `nofib`—listed in Table 2—are those that don't quite meet the criteria for Real programs, usually the stipulation that someone other than the author might want to run them. Many of these programs fall into Hennessy and Patterson's category of "kernel" benchmarks, being "small, key pieces from real programs" [7, page 45].

2.4 The Imaginary subset

The Imaginary subset of the suite is the usual small toy benchmarks, e.g., `primes`, `kwic`, `queens`, and `tak`. These are distinctly unimportant, and you

Program	Description	Origin
`boyer`	Gabriel suite 'boyer' benchmark	Denis Howe (Imperial)
`cichelli`	Perfect hashing function	Iain Checkland (York)
`clausify`	Propositions to clausal form	Colin Runciman (York)
`fish`	Draws Escher's fish	Satnam Singh (Glasgow)
`knights`	Knight's tour	Jon Hill (QMW)
`life`	Game of Life	John Launchbury (Glasgow)
`mandel`	Mandelbrot sets	Jon Hill (QMW)
`minimax`	tic-tac-toe (0s and Xs)	Iain Checkland (York)
`multiplier`	Binary-multiplier simulator	John O'Donnell (Glasgow)
`pretty`	Pretty-printer	John Hughes (Chalmers)
`primetest`	Primality testing	David Lester (Manchester)
`rewrite`	Rewriting system	Mike Spivey (Oxford)
`scc`	Strongly-connected components	John Launchbury (Glasgow)
`sorting`	Sorting algorithms	Will Partain (Glasgow)

Table 2: `nofib` benchmarks: Spectral Subset

may get a special commendation if you ignore them completely. They can be quite useful as test programs, e.g., to answer the question, "Does the system work at all after Simon's changes?"

3 Rules for running and reporting

Glasgow will provide the `nofib` program sources, as well as input workloads and expected outputs. (We will also provide some "scaffolding" to make it easier to run the benchmarks.)

Anyone can then run the benchmark programs through their Haskell system. The "price" for using the benchmark suite is that you must follow our rules if you report your results in any public forum, including any publication.

In the big-money-on-the-line world of the SPEC suite, the running and reporting rules are complicated and arcane. That's because there are many people who would rather be sneaky than do honest work to improve their system's performance. For now, we assume that functional programmers are more noble creatures; the `nofib` rules are therefore quite simple.

The basic reporting principle is: You must provide enough information and results that someone with a similar hardware/software configuration can *easily* duplicate your results.

The most important specific `nofib` reporting rule is: if you wish to report or publish some results from running some part of the `nofib` suite, then you must first "file" a complete set of how-I-did-it/what-I-got information for the entire Real subset of programs, in some public forum (a newsgroup, mailing list, an anonymous-FTP directory, ...). Thereafter, you may claim whatever you like, the idea being that people can look up your "filed" information and laugh at you if you're making unsubstantiated claims.

We are not insisting on these rules because we like playing lawyer. We intend as little hindrance as possible to creative, honest uses of this suite.

There are more details about the reporting rules in the version of this paper that is distributed with the suite.

4 Concluding remarks

Inattention to benchmarking is not just sloppy, it ends up as self-delusion. Assertions that various functional-languages compilers "... generate code that is competitive with that generated by conventional language compilers ..."[2] are *simply false* by any common-sense measure; what's more, when they are repeated by Respected People, they are downright harmful: they detract from the urgency of building better implementations.

By introducing the `nofib` suite of Haskell programs, we hope for an immediate payoff, simply by giving all Haskell implementors a common set of sources with which to race each other. We also hope that we are setting the foundation for a sound predictor of Haskell-system performance.

This suite follows the general trend away from "plot-the-characteristics benchmarking" and towards "lazy, systems benchmarking," of which the SPEC suite is the most prominent example. This approach to benchmarking gives the greatest credence is given to gross system behaviour on sizable, real programs.

Comments on this paper and on the `nofib` suite itself are most welcome. Contributions of substantial functional programs that could be added to the suite would be even more welcome! I can be reached by electronic mail at `glasgow-haskell-request@dcs.glasgow.ac.uk`.

Haskell-related things, including the `nofib` suite, can be retrieved by anonymous FTP from `ftp.dcs.glasgow.ac.uk`, in `pub/haskell/glasgow`. The sites `nebula.cs.yale.edu` and `animal.cs.chalmers.se` usually have copies as well (in the same directory).

An up-to-date version of this paper will be included in the `nofib` distribution. There is also a top-level `README`, which is the first file you should consult.

Acknowledgements. My thanks to John Mashey for his many fine articles in `comp.arch` that promote sensible benchmarking, and to Jeff Reilly for providing information about SPEC. Vincent Delacour, Denis Howe, John O'Donnell, Paul Sanders, and Julian Seward were among those who provided helpful comment on earlier versions of this paper. Of course, we are *most* indebted to those people who have let their code be included in the suite.

References

[1] L. Augustsson and T. Johnsson. The Chalmers Lazy-ML compiler. *Computer Journal*, 32(2):127–141, April 1989.

[2] Adrienne Bloss, P. Hudak, and J. Young. An optimising compiler for a modern functional language. *Computer Journal*, 32(2):152–161, April 1989.

---

[2] Citation withheld to protect the guilty!

[3] Thomas M. Conte and Wen-mei W. Hwu. A brief survey of benchmark usage in the architecture community. *Computer Architecture News*, 19(4):37–44, June 1991.

[4] Richard P. Gabriel and Larry M. Masinter. Performance of Lisp systems. In *Conference Record of the 1982 ACM Symposium on LISP and Functional Programming*, pages 123–142, Pittsburgh, PA, August 15–18 1982.

[5] Brent Hailpern, Tien Huynh, and Gyorgy Révész. Comparing two functional programming systems. *IEEE Transactions on Software Engineering*, 15(5):532–542, May 1989.

[6] Pieter H. Hartel. Performance of lazy combinator graph reduction. *Software—Practice and Experience*, 21(3):299–329, March 1991.

[7] John L. Hennessy and David A. Patterson. *Computer Architecture: A Quantitative Approach.* Morgan Kaufmann Publishers, Inc., San Mateo, CA, 1990.

[8] Lynn Pointer, editor. Perfect report 2. CSRD Report 964, Center for Supercomputing Research and Development, University of Illinois, Urbana, IL, March 1990.

[9] Jaswinder Pal Singh, Wolf-Dietrich Weber, and Anoop Gupta. SPLASH: Stanford parallel applications for shared-memory. *Computer Architecture News*, 20(1):5–44, March 1992.

[10] S. C. Wray and J. Fairbairn. Non-strict languages—programming and implementation. *Computer Journal*, 32(2):142–151, April 1989.

Heap Profiling of a Lazy Functional Compiler

Colin Runciman and David Wakeling
University of York*

1 Introduction

A significant problem with lazy functional programs is that they often demand a great deal of space. Multi-megabyte workstations are now commonplace, but serious users of functional programming systems have to equip even these machines with additional memory. The essence of laziness is to delay evaluation rather than compute values that may not be needed; and once values *are* computed to retain them if they may be needed again. This policy might save time, but it can easily lead to *space faults*: the accumulation or retention of large structures in memory, in ways that the programmer is unaware of, or does not fully understand, let alone intend. Hence *profiling tools*, by which programmers can obtain information about memory use in terms of the source program, are potentially of great value.

In a previous paper [5] we described the design, implementation and use of a prototype heap profiling tool for lazy functional programs. As an example application, we used `clausify`, an existing 130 line program to normalise logical formulae. The results were even better than we had hoped for: after five iterations of profiling and refinement, modifying both program and compilation rules, the cost of running the final version (measured in bytes $\times$ seconds) was less than 0.5% of the cost of running the original. However, the information from our prototype tool related to individual definitions and constructor functions, and it was not clear whether a similar technique would work for larger and more complex programs.

This paper reports on the experimental application of heap profiling to Augustsson and Johnsson's Lazy ML (LML) compiler [1]. Since our implementation of heap profiling is itself based on the LML compiler, this amounts to a boot-strapping exercise. The LML compiler extends to some 16,500 lines of code in almost 200 modules, and is by any standard a large and sophisticated piece of software. As it has been developed over a period of almost a decade, with each successive version outperforming its predecessor, the sort of dramatic improvement obtained for the `clausify` program is hardly to be expected; but equally savings of only a few percent would not be very compelling. So we set ourselves the target of *a factor of two* — halving the cost of LML compilations.

The rest of this paper is organised as follows. Section 2 reviews the design of our prototype heap profiling tool, and describes how we have modified it to deal

*Authors' address: Department of Computer Science, University of York, Heslington, York Y01 5DD, United Kingdom. Electronic mail: **colin@minster.york.ac.uk**, **dw@minster.york.ac.uk**

with larger programs. Section 3 outlines the structure of the LML compiler, identifying its main components and their role within the compiler. Section 4 describes the application of heap-profiling to the compiler, and the successive reduction of its memory consumption guided by profiling information. Section 5 discusses to what extent the kinds of space problems found in the compiler might be avoided in future programs by modifying implementation methods. Section 6 briefly considers some related and future work. Finally, Section 7 offers some conclusions.

2 A Heap Profiling System

Our heap profiling tool has two components. The first component is a modified implementation which generates profiling information during the execution of functional programs. When the programmer requests a heap profile, execution is suspended at specified regular intervals and the implementation traverses the program graph gathering information from each cell. This information is appended to a log file and execution is resumed. When execution is complete, the log file contains a profile of the graph nodes that were stored in the heap at each interval.

The second component of the tool is a program that generates a graph from a log file. Examples of these profile graphs will be found in Section 4. A profile graph shows how the amount of heap storage used by the program (measured in bytes) varies over the time that it takes to run (measured in seconds). Shaded bands are used to show how much of the total storage is associated with each identifier.

Recently, we have made our profiling tool more suitable for dealing with large programs. The modified implementation now attaches both *static* and *dynamic* tags to every cell in the heap. Static tags carry information determined at compile-time and dynamic tags carry information determined at run-time. For the static tags, space is reserved in each cell for a pointer to some tag information maintained by the compiler. For each dynamic tag, space is reserved for some tag information maintained by the run-time system. By way of example, Figure 1 shows how a list node is tagged.

In our first implementation there were only two static tags. These identified the function that produced the graph node, and the construction that it represented. When profiling larger programs, it is natural to want to extend this basic scheme. Thus, the producer is extended to a single module or a group of modules, and the construction is extended to a type. Each cell has space for one dynamic tag; in future, we plan to use this tag for the age of the node, but at the moment it is unused.

Another improvement to the basic scheme reduces the overhead of profiling by performing a garbage collection while sampling the graph.

Usually, profile graphs are automatically scaled to fill the page, and the bands are automatically shaded and ordered so as to maximise the readability of the graph. However, for the purpose of comparison it is sometimes useful to fix certain parameters across several profile graphs. In this paper, all profile graphs share a common scale, shading and ordering.

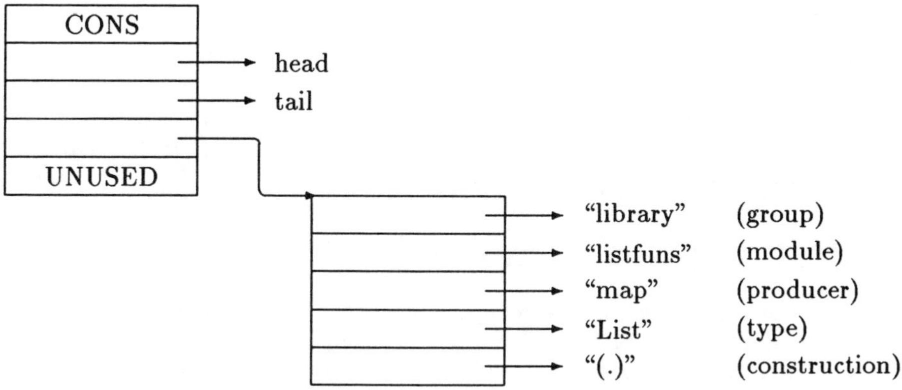

Figure 1: A tagged list node

3 An Overview of the LML Compiler

The LML compiler [1] consists of two programs which communicate via a text file. The *parser* is written in C with the aid of the Yacc parser generator. It checks the program syntax and outputs a prefix form of the parse tree. The *translator* is written in LML. It reads the prefix form of the parse tree and reconstructs it. After a number of transformations, it then produces the assembly language for the program. We are only concerned with profiling the translator, and from here on we will loosely refer to it as "the compiler".

The compiler source code is organised into 19 directories containing 198 modules; in total there are about 16,500 lines of code. In what follows, it will be useful to have an outline of the way that the compiler works. Below, a very brief description of each compiler pass is accompanied by the name of directory that contains the code for that pass.

(1) The prefix form of the parse tree is read, and the tree is reconstructed (`expr`).

(2) Conditional and ZF expressions are simplified (`curry`, `zf`).

(3) Bound and imported identifiers are renamed if necessary (`rename`).

(4) Pattern-matching is replaced by the use of case-expressions (`transform`).

(5) Type checking is performed (`type`).

(6) Expression simplifications, such as constant folding, are made (`simpl`).

(7) Simple strictness analysis is performed (`strict`).

(8) Nested functions are removed by lambda-lifting (`llift`).

(9) G-machine code is generated and optimised (`Gcode`, `Gopt`).

(10) M-machine code is generated and optimised (`mcode`, `mopt`).

(11) Assembly code is generated (`m_68000`).

Two other important components of the compiler, so far unaccounted for, are the functions in the standard library (`lib`) and the routines in the runtime system (`runtime`).

4 Profiling the Compiler

Before we can make any improvements to the LML compiler, we need to find out what makes it tick (or rather, clunk). The group profiles produced when the compiler recompiles each of its own source files are a good place to start. Leafing through them, a clear pattern emerges. Unfortunately, space precludes us from showing several of these profiles here. Instead we shall have to make do with a typical one, for the compilation of the 280 line module **hcheck** (see Figure 2). This profile shows that during a compilation taking a little over two

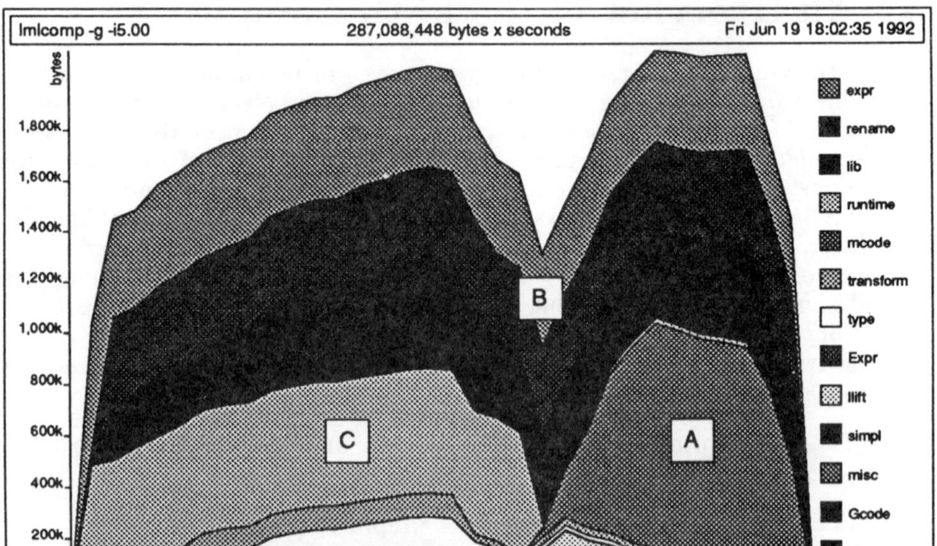

Figure 2: A group profile for **hcheck** (compiler version 0)

and a half minutes, the memory demand exceeded two megabytes at its peak, and was above one and a half megabytes for most of the time. The "bytes x seconds" figure (top centre) corresponds to the total area under the graph, and is our overall measure of cost.

A key to the various shadings used is given on the right. The boxed labels 'A', 'B' and 'C' are not present in the output from the profiler; they have been added for ease of reference to three important regions of the graph. The region labelled 'A' represents graph structure produced by the M-code generator. The region labelled 'B' includes the three topmost bands; it represents graph structure produced by the **expr** and **rename** passes, and by some standard library functions **lib**. The region labelled 'C' represents graph structure produced by the run-time system. Together these three regions account for most of the compiler's demands on heap memory. We shall now discuss each of them in turn.

Version 0

Region 'A' indicates that the M-code generator produces a large amount of graph structure towards the end of the compilation. At first, this may not seem particularly surprising: for any program written in a high level language, the machine code translation is bound to be quite large. Moreover, Johnsson's M-code generator is rather sophisticated, and so one might expect a significant amount of graph to be required to represent its internal data structures. However, this reasoning ignores the fact that the compiler is written in a *lazy* language. Since all of the clever optimisations described by Johnsson for translating G-code into M-code are *intra-functional*, and there are none which are *inter-functional*, we would actually expect G-code to be translated into M-code lazily, one function at a time. Clearly though, this is not happening. Indeed, it seems that the M-code for *every* function is generated before any assembly language is produced.

Although we could investigate further by producing a module profile restricted to the **mcode** group, it is unnecessary to do so. The profile tells us that the problem is some form of lazy pipeline blockage, and that information alone is enough for us to identify the cause. The blockage cannot be at either of the later stages in the pipeline: the M-code optimiser does little more than improve the aesthetics of the M-code, and the assembly language generator for the MC68000 is really just an elaborate pretty printer. By inspection, both are lazy, so the problem must be with the M-code generator itself. Somewhat embarrassingly, it turns out that it is one of our own modifications to the M-code generator that makes it use so much space.

Recall from Section 2 that our modified compiler attaches static and dynamic tags to every cell in the heap, and that the static tags carry information maintained by the compiler. In practice, this means that during code generation the compiler must place appropriate vectors of strings in the assembly language program, to be used at run-time when new nodes are created. This seems simple enough. However, there is a slight complication: for practical reasons it is important to ensure that neither the vectors or the strings are duplicated. Otherwise the resulting code becomes excessively large.

One way to do this is to record the vectors and strings arising during code generation in a table. When all of the M-code has been generated, any duplicates can be purged from the table and the remainder can be output along with the M-code. Another (very similar) way is to add new vectors and strings to the table only if they are not already there. This eliminates the need to purge the table before it is output. As far as coding is concerned, there is not much to choose between the two alternatives. As far as efficiency is concerned, however, the difference is rather large. The first alternative generates all of the M-code in order to create the table of vectors and strings. But none of this M-code can be output until any duplicates have been purged from the table and the correct labels for the remainder have been determined. The second alternative allows the correct labels for the vectors and strings to be determined when they are added to the table, and so the M-code can be output without delay. As Figure 3 shows, the second alternative costs 50Mbs less than the first.

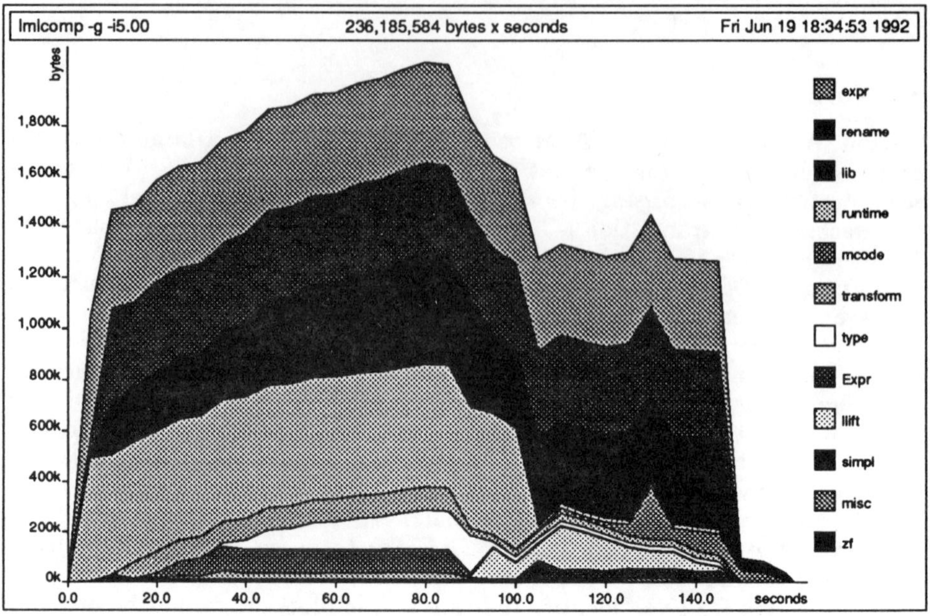

Figure 3: A group profile for **hcheck** (compiler version 1)

Version 1

Let us now turn our attention to region 'B'. Figure 4 shows a profile by type, restricted to the module groups **expr**, **rename** and **lib** that make up this region. Here we can see that half of the graph structure is of either the **List** or **Id** types. A glance at the definition of the **Id** type sheds further light on the problem:

```
type Id  = mkids String String
         + mkidi String String (Option (Modinfo # String))
         + mkid Int String String Idinfo Origname
```

Every identifier requires two strings: one is the name used by the profiler, and the other is the name used by the ordinary compiler. Usually, these names are identical; they differ only for identifiers that are renamed during compilation. Since strings are just lists of characters, Figure 4 suggests that identifiers could account for more than 90Mbs of the cost of our typical compilation. This seems rather high.

An obvious improvement would be to use a more compact string representation than the usual list of characters. Although the standard compiler affords compile-time string literals a compact representation, one cannot form

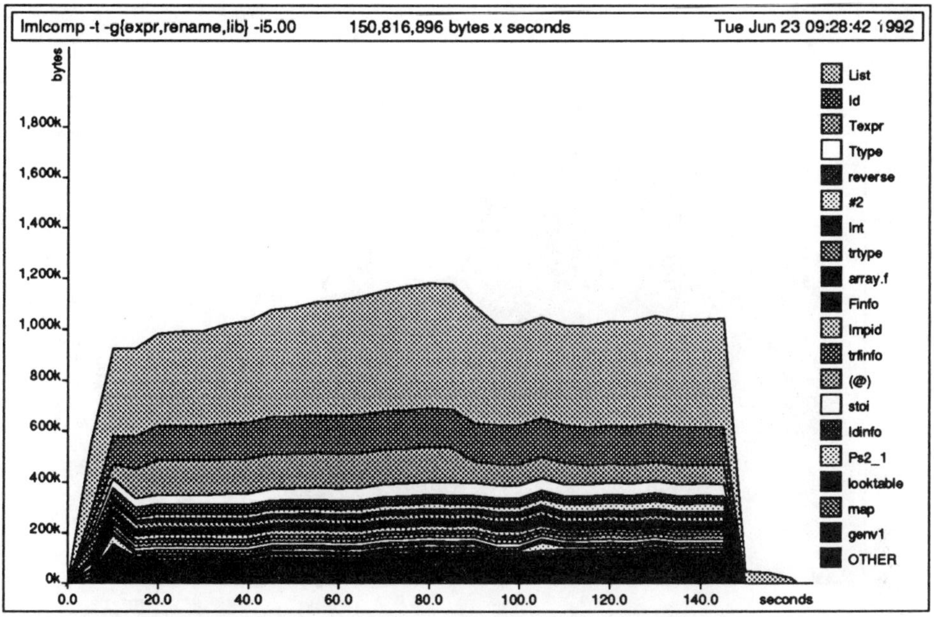

Figure 4: A type profile for the **expr**, **rename** and **lib** groups only

a compact string at run-time. Let us rectify this by introducing a primitive function

```
pack :: [Char] -> [Char]
```

Semantically, this function is the identity for finite and fully defined lists of characters. Pragmatically, it converts an ordinary list of characters into a compact one. The idea is to use this function in the compiler to pack up the name strings whenever a new `Id` is constructed. Somewhat surprisingly, using `pack` as described makes no discernible difference to the behaviour of the compiler. This is because the standard evaluation machinery causes packed strings to be unpacked. By instrumenting the run-time system to print the context in which string unpacking was performed, we discovered four operations in the compiler that cause name strings to be unpacked:

- hashing;
- comparison;
- translation to an assembly language label;
- translation to an assembly language string.

To make these operations work directly on the packed representation, we rewrote them in M-code. As Figure 5 shows, packed strings reduce the cost of compiling our example file by another 50Mbs.

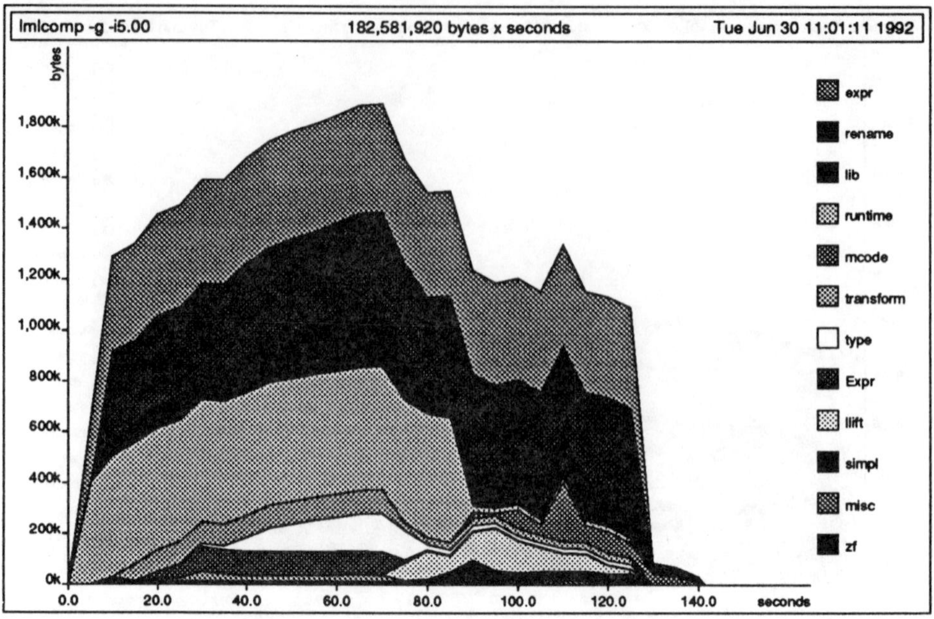

Figure 5: A group profile for the **hcheck** (compiler version 2)

Version 2

In all of the group profiles that we have seen so far, there has been a large block of graph structure produced by the run-time system (labelled 'C' in Figure 2). With the aid of a producer profile restricted to the `runtime` group (see Figure 6), we can quickly establish that almost all of this structure is produced by the built-in routine which reads the list of characters in a file.

Recall from Section 3 that the LML compiler consists of two programs, the *parser* and the *translator*, which communicate via a text file. During a compilation, the translator reads several files, but the only one of significant size is the text file created by the parser. From Figure 6 it seems that the contents of this file are retained by the translator as a list of characters for well over half the total compilation time. This is really most surprising. We would expect the translator to discard the character list in the process of constructing the abstract syntax tree. Clearly this does not happen. Yet the list is not dragged along until the very end of the compilation, so what triggers its release? In the "valley" of Figure 2 the critical computational event allowing source to be discarded is the onset of code generation. More specifically, it is the opening of the output stream for the assembly code.

Once we knew that the input stream was being retained, we made the above diagnosis by simply examining the code concerned with input and output. It looked something like this:

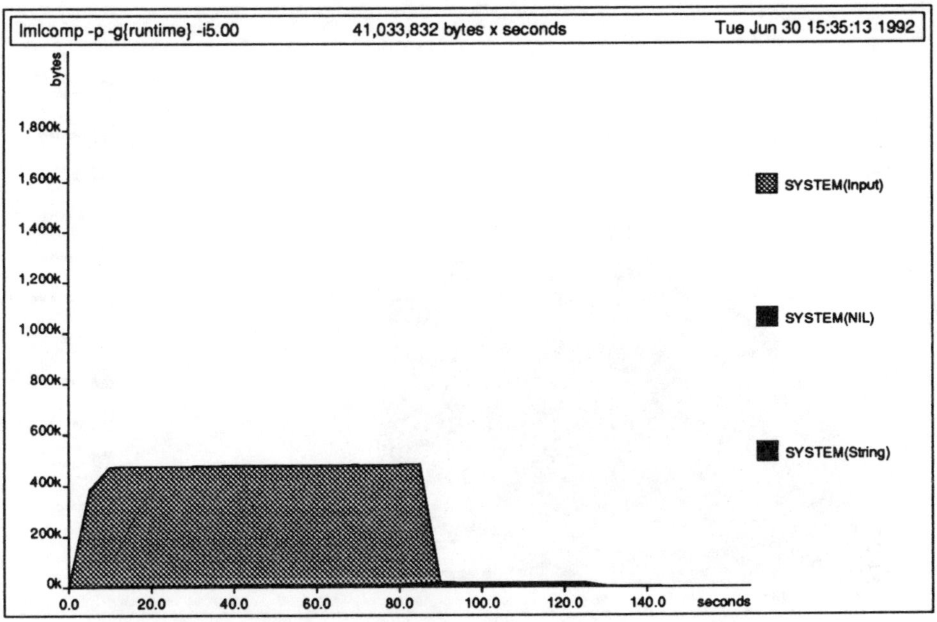

Figure 6: A producer profile restricted to the **runtime** group

```
(finput, ftype,...fasm) =
  case basename in
     No msg : fail msg
  || Yes n  : (read (n@".p"), tofile (n@".t"),...tofile (n@".s"))
  end
```

The intention here is to bind **finput** to the list of characters read from the input stream, and **ftype** and **fasm** to the streams to be used for the type and assembly language files. Unfortunately, this rather arcane piece of code suffers from a space leak caused by the implementation of lazy pattern matching. Delayed selection means that none of the components of **(finput, ftype,...fasm)** can be released until all of them have been evaluated. As a result, the list of characters read from the input stream is retained until the assembly language stream is required, which is not until well over half the total compilation time has elapsed. A fix for this particular problem is trivial: just make separate definitions of **finput**, **ftype** and **fasm**. The gain is yet another 50Mbs (see Figure 7).

5 Cure or Prevention?

Heap profiling is a diagnostic tool for programmers who want to detect, understand and hence cure space faults in their programs. Although this tool is quite effective, we are bound to ask whether the use of other techniques might prevent the introduction of space faults in the first place.

Where a space fault is due to *excessive laziness*, as with the dragging prob-

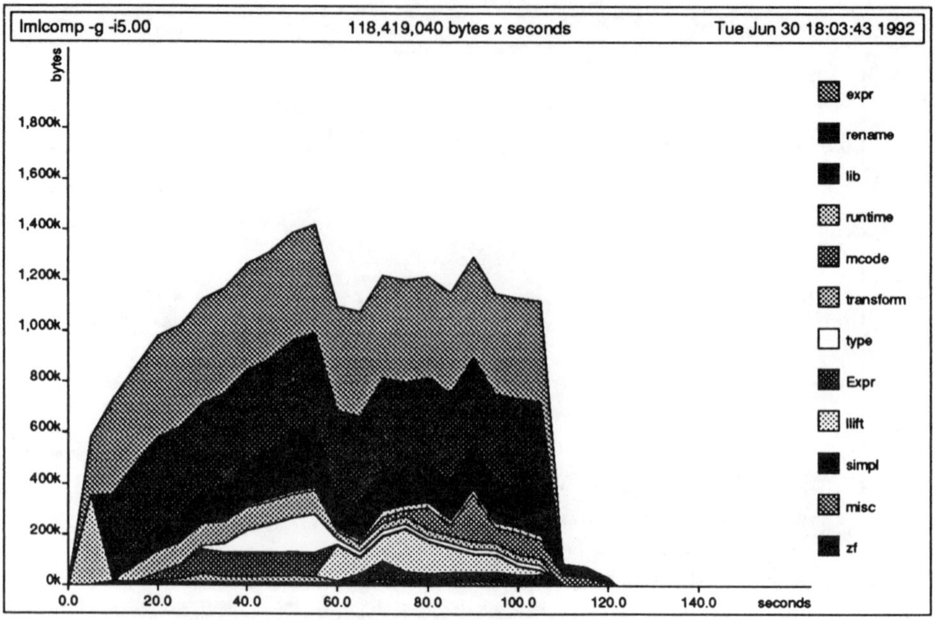

Figure 7: A group profile for the **hcheck** (compiler version 3)

lem of region 'C', it may be cured by forcing a little more evaluation in just the right place. But it is not always as easy as it was in this case to determine an appropriate source level reformulation. Many problems of this kind can be avoided at the implementation level, by introducing quasi-parallel reduction rules into the garbage collector. Wadler [10] has described such a scheme for the common case of selection from a tuple of multiple results, and this scheme is generalised in von Dorrien's *stingy evaluator* [9]. Indeed, a stingy evaluator is distributed with the LML compiler — but it is not used for the bootstrap compilation!

The fault of region 'A' was caused by a definition that was *not lazy enough*, being over-strict in a (large) argument value. To help avoid such faults, implementations might check and/or generate *strictness declarations*. Similar support for *type* declarations has been available, and widely valued, for some time. The comparison is pertinent not only because both forms of declaration can characterise useful properties of defined functions, but also because strictness analysis can be approached as a type inference problem [3].

Packed representations of character lists can bring about substantial savings in comparison with the usual "cons-cell" chains, even in the context of lazy evaluation, as Stoye [7] observed several years ago. The use of this technique to reduce the size of region 'B' might easily be dismissed as a specific low-level optimisation, not linked to any general principle. But packed strings were *already present* in the LML implementation, with lazy unpacking as the interface to normal strings, and no unpacking at all in the context of top-level concatenation. So the issue is not just whether or not an implementation employs a special representation (for example, strings, unboxed values or dictionaries) but under what circumstances, and how easily the effect can be predicted or specified by the programmer. We suggest that if a compiler is capable of using a special representation in some circumstances, the programmer should have the opportunity to specify its use in other circumstances — a form of *equal opportunity* [4]. Recall also that we chose to rewrite some string operations in M-code to avoid the unpacking machinery: an alternative approach repacks strings during garbage collection — a special case of Turner's idea [8] that expressions should revert to an earlier, smaller form when space is short.

6 Related and Future Work

Although there have been many implementations of lazy functional languages, it seems there has been comparatively little work on profiling. However, we know of at least two other profiling systems that have been constructed recently [2, 6]. In comparison with the work on these other systems, the distinctive features of our own approach include:

1. putting all the emphasis on profiling *memory space*, rather than *processor time*, and defining overall cost in byte seconds;
2. *multi-dimensional* profiling (the two dimensions in our present profiler being producers and constructions) allowing *sectioned* or *product* profiles to be obtained;
3. stressing *application* of the technique by using the profiler to reduce the costs of existing programs.

Since the Ayr workshop, Augustsson has added heap profiling, as described in this paper, to the latest version of the LML compiler.

Although various extensions and refinements of our heap profiling system could increase its effectiveness — for example, the addition of an *age* dimension by tagging graph nodes with their time of creation — we have no immediate plans to develop it further. Rather, we plan to move on from profiling memory use to profiling *parallelism*, applying similar techniques to reveal and to improve the degree of parallelism in lazy functional programs.

7 Conclusions

We claim a successful outcome from the experimental self-application of our heap profiling version of the LML compiler. A target factor of two reduction in execution cost was reached after about three week's work (and this does *not* include the reduction obtained by fixing the M-code generator fault that we ourselves had introduced!). Based on our own experiments with heap profiling, and also on the experience of a small number of other users of our system, we suspect that *most* lazy functional programs of more than a couple of pages have space faults. The diagnosis and cure of such faults are neglected problems — so much so that even rather simple techniques can lead to significant improvements. Perhaps surprisingly, similar techniques apply to both small and large programs — the compiler has more source *modules* than `clausify` has *lines* of code!

Acknowledgements

Our thanks to Lennart Augustsson and Thomas Johnsson, whose work on the LML compiler forms the basis of our own, and to Simon Peyton Jones with whom we have had some useful discussions about heap profiling. We are also grateful to the referees for their comments.

This work was funded by the Science and Engineering Research Council.

References

[1] L. Augustsson and T. Johnsson. The Chalmers Lazy-ML Compiler. *Computer Journal*, 32(2):127–141, April 1989.

[2] S. Clayman, D. Parrot, and C. Clack. A Profiling Technique for Lazy, Higher-Order Functional Programs. Technical report, Department of Computing Science, University College London, November 1991.

[3] T-M. Kuo and Mishra. Strictness Analysis: A New Perspective Based on Type Inference. In *Proceedings of the 1989 Conference on Functional Programming Languages and Computer Architecture*, pages 260–272. ACM Press, September 1989.

[4] C. Runciman and H. W. Thimbleby. Equal Opportunity Interactive Systems. *International Journal of Man-Machine Studies*, 25:439–451, 1986.

[5] C. Runciman and D. Wakeling. Heap Profiling of Lazy Functional Programs. Technical Report 172, Department of Computer Science, University of York, April 1992.

[6] P. M. Sansom and S. L. Peyton Jones. Profiling Lazy Functional Programs. In J. Launchbury and P. M. Sansom, editors, *Functional Programming, Glasgow 1992*. Springer-Verlag, Workshps in Computing, 1992.

[7] W. Stoye. *The Implementation of Functional Languages Using Custom Hardware*. PhD thesis, University of Cambridge Computer Laboratory, December 1986. Technical Report No. 81.

[8] D. A. Turner. A new implementation technique for applicative languages. *SOFTWARE — Practice and Experience*, 9(1):31–50, January 1979.

[9] C. von Dorrien. Stingy Evaluation. Licentiate Dissertation, Chalmers University of Technology, S-412 96 Göteborg, 1989.

[10] P. Wadler. Fixing Some Space Leaks with a Garbage Collector. *Software — Practice and Experience*, 17(9):595–608, September 1987.

LZW Text Compression in Haskell

Paul Sanders
Applications Research Division, BT Laboratories
Martlesham Heath, Ipswich*

Colin Runciman
Department of Computer Science, University of York
Heslington, York.†

Abstract

Functional programming is largely untested in the industrial environment. This paper summarises the results of a study into the suitability of Haskell in the area of text compression, an area with definite commercial interest. Our program initially performs very poorly in comparison with a version written in C. Experiments reveal the cause of this to be the large disparity in the relative speed of I/O and bit–level operations and also a space leak inherent in the Haskell definition.

1 Introduction

Claims for the advantages of functional programming languages abound [1] but industrial take–up of the paradigm has been almost non–existent. Two of the main reasons for this are:

- lack of proof that the advantages apply to large–scale developments;
- lack of industry–strength compilers and environments, particularly for high speed computation.

The FLARE project, managed by BT, sets out to address these issues:

> *"The effectiveness of functional programming has been amply demonstrated on a laboratory scale and it is now appropriate to scale up the experiments with a view to encouraging the wider community of applications developers to embrace this technology"* — FLARE Project Proposal.

Each partner in the project is developing examples by which to evaluate functional programming. Our example in this paper is a simplified version of the compress algorithm found as a standard application on most Unix systems. It has several key aspects which make it useful for our purpose:

*Electronic mail: **Sanders_P_M@bt-web.bt.co.uk**
†Electronic mail: **colin@minster.york.ac.uk**

- *It is widely used.* Compression programs are in use daily throughout computer using organisations. They are therefore something which most people in industry can relate to.
- *The design and use of data structures is important.* One of the largest benefits claimed of functional programming languages is the clarity that they bring to the coding of algorithms and data structures. It is therefore desirable to choose an application where data structures are important so this claim can be tested.
- *High performance is desirable.* One of the biggest criticisms of functional programming languages in the past is that programs execute so slowly that this outweighs any of the advantages their use might have. It is therefore important to choose an application where speed is of interest so that it can be judged whether or not these criticisms are still valid.

A version of the compress program has been implemented in Haskell [2] on a Sun workstation.

2 LZW Compression

There are many algorithms for data compression [3]. LZW–compression [4] is a classic being found in an advanced variant on most Unix systems as the program compress.

The algorithm works by maintaining a table of strings and associated code values which grows as the input is processed. The key feature of the algorithm is that every string in the table satisfies the prefix property, i.e. all its prefixes are also in the table. The table initially contains all the singleton strings that may be encountered with a code value for each one. The input data is taken one character at a time to find the longest initial string that exists in the table. The code for that string is then output and the process repeated on the remainder of the string. For every code produced a new entry is made to the table consisting of the matched string and next character from the input, and the code value for the new entry. Code values for new entries are determined by using a counter to store the next available code. The counter is incremented after every new table entry.

Consider compressing the string *ababcbababa* given the initial table shown in Table 1. The input data is scanned left to right starting with the *a*. This is

String	Code
a	1
b	2
c	3

Table 1: The initial string table for the example.

present in the table so an attempt is then made to find *ab*. Since it is not in the table, the code for *a*, 1, is output and the string *ab* is added to the table and assigned code 4. The *b* is now used to start the next string and the process continues as before until all the input has been consumed. The codes produced for this input are 1, 2, 4, 3, 5, 8, and 1.

Once the codes have been obtained, they need to be written to a file, ideally occupying minimal space. One method would be to turn each code into a character (taking a code to be an ASCII value). Using this method, the example would occupy 7 bytes since it produces 7 codes.

This works until the number of codes produced exceeds the maximum character value; 255 for an 8-bit character size. For our program we use a simplistic scheme whereby each code is converted into a fixed word size, 12 bits, say, and these words are taken two at a time to produce three 8-bit character codes for output. For example:

$$4,\ 11 \Rightarrow 000000000110000000001011 \Rightarrow 0, 96, 11$$

One problem remains – what to do when the number of codes exceeds what can be represented in the chosen word size ? Welch suggests[4] that entries are no longer added to the table. Our word size of 12 bits means that we will stop adding entries when we reach 4096 elements.

3 A Haskell Implementation of LZW

We shall describe only the encoding function. There are two issues involved in encode:

- how the code table should be represented;
- the encode function itself.

It is obvious that the choice of representation for the code table will have a big effect on the program's performance. We need a representation that:

- supports fast search and insert operations;
- makes economical use of storage.

In a language with side–effects we might use an array and hash function to provide fast indexing into the table. However, there is no such constant–time access structure available in current implementations of Haskell. The best we can do is use a logarithmic–time structure such as the trie [5]:

```
> data PrefixTree a b
>      = PTNil |
>        PT a b (PrefixTree a b) (PrefixTree a b) (PrefixTree a b)
```

Each element of the trie contains the prefix character, its code, a trie containing the possible extensions of that character and the two tries comprising the left and right branches of the trie node.

The encode function makes repeated calls to the function **code_string** until the input has been consumed. Presupposing the existence of **code_string** we can write **encode** as follows:

```
> type CodeTable = PrefixTree Char Int

> encode :: String -> [Int]
> encode str = encode' str first_code initial_table

> encode' [] _ _
>     = []
> encode' str code table
>     = n : encode' str' (code + 1) table'
>       where
>       (str', n, table') = code_string str 0 v t
```

Although this looks nothing out of the ordinary we shall see later that this use of matching against triples leads to a large space leak, and that this space leak is due to the semantics of tuple pattern matching in Haskell.

Coding the string entails taking the first character and locating its position in the prefix tree. The prefix tree at this position is then used to locate the next character in the string; its prefix tree is used for the following character and so on. If we cannot find an entry in a tree then we have found the longest matching substring in the table.

If we rebuild the table tree as we traverse it then we can add new entries to the table by having each recursive call return the new tree element for the appropriate branch. When we wish to add a new entry, we simply return a new tree node containing just the new element. There are three cases to consider when coding the input:

1. the input is exhausted;
2. the current character is not in the table;
3. the current character is located (on the way to matching the whole string).

The first case is trivial: if we have run out of input then we return the last code we saw together with the empty tree as we do not want to make an entry to the, now irrelevant, table.

```
>code_string :: String -> Int -> Int -> CodeTable
>                    -> (String, Int, CodeTable)
>code_string [] old_code _ _ = ([], old_code, PTNil)
```

We know if the current character is not in the prefix tree if we are given an empty tree to search in. In this case, we add the current character and code value (if there is space in the table) at the current position in the tree and return this new element along with the last code we saw.

```
>code_string i@(c:cs) old_code next_code PTNil
>        = if next_code >= max_entries
>          then (i, old_code, PTNil)
>          else (i, old_code, PT c next_code PTNil PTNil PTNil)
```

Finally, to locate the appropriate character extension in the table we use a standard binary search. If we reconstruct the tree as we search,we can perform the insertion without having to retraverse the tree. When we reach a nil node in the tree we know that this is the place where the current character should be. Inserting it into the tree is simply a matter of constructing a node for the new entry and returning this new node as part of the search.

```
>code_string i@(c:cs) old_code next_code (PT k v t l r)
>        | c < k  = (csl, nl, PT k v t l' r)
>        | c > k  = (csr, nr, PT k v t l r')
>        | c == k = (cs', n, PT k v t' l r)
>        where (csl, nl, l') = code_string i old_code next_code l
>              (csr, nr, r') = code_string i old_code next_code r
>              (cs', n, t') = code_string cs v next_code t
```

3.1 Performance Results

We are interested in two aspects of performance – how fast the program runs and how much space it uses. To enable a comparison with traditional techniques, a C version of the algorithm using the same data structures was implemented. (The real compress program uses an adaptive version of the algorithm and a sophisticated double hashing table for the codes, and so is not directly comparable; we will refer to it in the tables however to provide a reference for the order of performance we should be aiming at.)

The performance results have been obtained by running each program on three of the benchmark files from the Calgary Text Compression Corpus[1] [3]: *bib* (a bibliography – unusual English, 111Kb), *paper1* (troff source – usual English, 53Kb) and *geo* (non–ascii data file, 101Kb).

3.1.1 Performance Speed

Table 2 shows average CPU times recorded for running the programs on the benchmarks, together with the slowdown factor compared with the straightforward C version (LZWC) in each case. Timings were obtained using the built-in *time* command in tcsh on a SPARCstation IPX in single–user mode[2] We can see that the Haskell version (LZWH in the tables) is much slower than the C program. Why is our program performing so poorly? We conjecture that there are several possible reasons for this, any or all may be contributors:

- I/O is faster in C than in Haskell;

[1] Available in fsa.cpsc.ucalgary.cs: /pub/text.compression.corpus.tar.Z [136.159.2.1]

[2] The Haskell program was compiled using hbc-0.998.4 and executed with the default heap size. Sun's vanilla cc was used with the -O flag for the C programs.

File	*compress*	LZWC	LZWH	Slowdown Factor
bib	0.62	5.18	192.6	37
paper1	0.35	2.69	98.05	36
geo	0.67	4.41	248.68	56

Table 2: Comparison of compression speeds (CPU times in seconds)

- the C program is using bit–level operations unavailable to Haskell to perform the code conversions;
- there is a space leak in the Haskell program.

File I/O The C file input/output routines can access the file system directly, accessing file pointers in different ways depending on the best method for the task. In Haskell, we have no such control over how our I/O calls are translated into code. To get some idea of the relative speeds of I/O in C and Haskell, simple programs were written to copy the standard input to the standard output, these programs using only standard library calls. Statistics for these experiments are given in Table 3. The Haskell program performs the file copy approximately

File Size	C	hbc	Slowdown Factor
1Mb	1.62	11.47	7
4Mb	6.84	46.31	6.8
8Mb	13.68	92.47	6.8

Table 3: Execution speeds for file copy routine

seven times more slowly than the C program. This almost certainly accounts for some of the slowdown encountered in our compress program.

The Haskell and C programs used for this comparison are given in Appendix B.

Bit–Level Operations Our second conjecture can be tested by comparing the speeds of the code conversion routines in C and Haskell. To do this, both the LZWC and LZWH programs were altered to only produce the compression codes. Subtracting the times obtained from those in Table 2 gives the average times taken to perform the bit–level operations given in Table 4. The experiment reveals that the C routines are around a factor of five quicker than the

File	LZWC	LZWH	Slowdown Factor
bib	1.34	6.36	4.7
paper1	0.7	3.82	5.5

Table 4: Average times to perform the bit–level operations

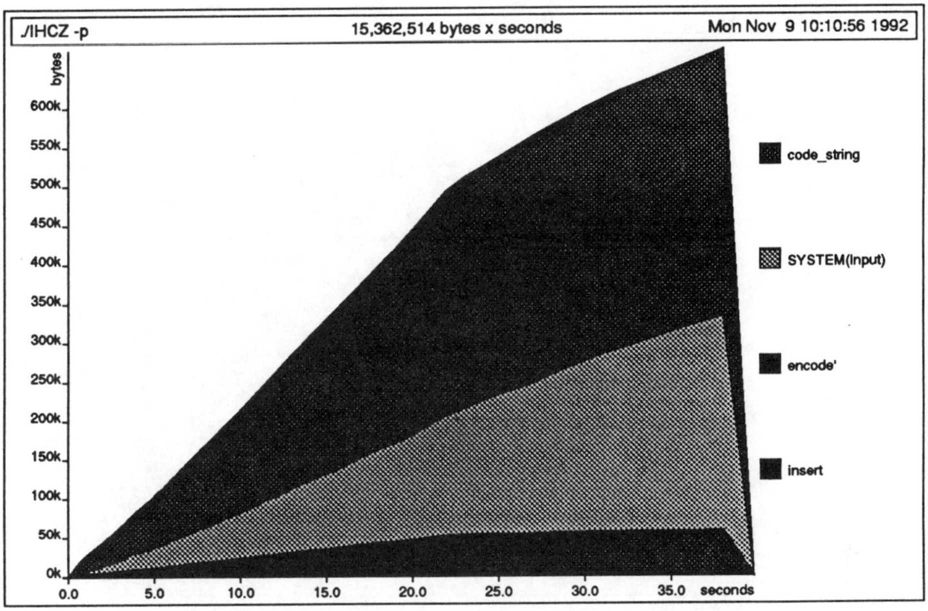

Figure 1: A producer profile for the compress program

Haskell ones. This therefore is another contributor to the poorer performance of our Haskell program.

Space Leaks One of the criticisms levelled at functional programs is the large amounts of store they consume. Moreover, it is usually impossible to find out exactly how much store is being used or what is responsible for it. Chapter 23 of [6] gives some good examples of this.

Recently, Runciman and Wakeling [7] have devised a scheme whereby the heap usage of a Haskell program may be profiled. They have extended the Haskell compiler with a profiler which allows the programmer to produce a graph of the producers of heap cells or of the constructors being produced. It is also possible to restrict the choice to specified producers and consumers thereby allowing detailed "space debugging".

A full table consists of 4096 elements, each containing one character, an Int and three prefix trees. From the M-code produced by hbc we can ascertain that a `PT` node occupies 36 bytes and a `PTNil` node 8 bytes. So a full tree would be expected to take up around 144k. The other structures in the program are, we would hope, mostly transient so the total space usage should not exceed this figure by anything other than a small amount.

Compressing a 20k file gives the space profile graph shown in Figure 1. The graph shows that the program makes a peak memory demand of 700k bytes, far more than the 144k we anticipated. Most of the space usage is due to `code_string` so we need to look at the constructions of `code_string`. This

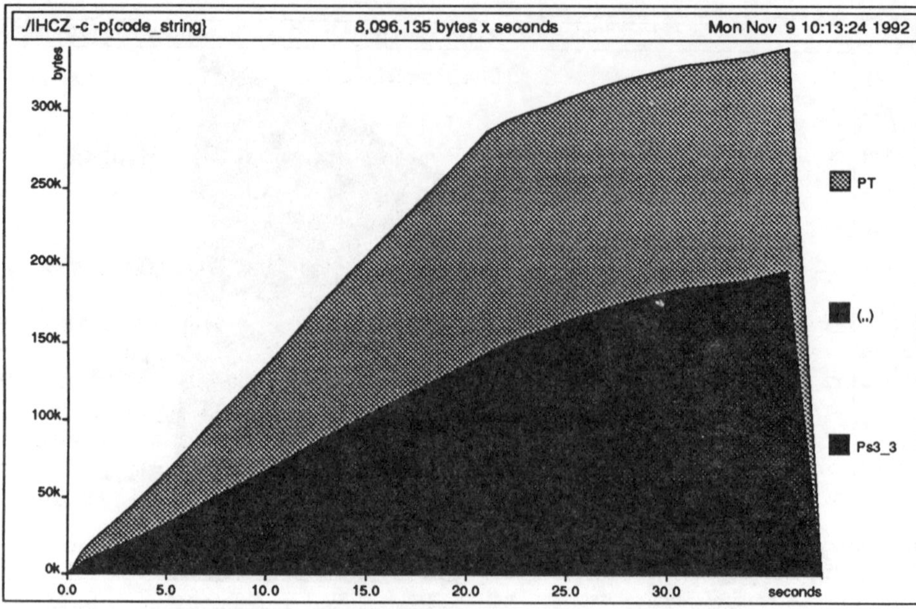

Figure 2: The constructions of code_string

graph is shown in Figure 2. We can see that the function is producing a lot of triple nodes and that these, supposedly temporary, structures occupy about the same space as the code table. It turns out that the problem lies with the triple pattern bindings in the local definitions in `code_string`, and that this is a symptom of the way in which pattern binding in Haskell is defined for tuples in a `where` or `let` clause. The Haskell manual states:

> *In both a* `where` *or* `let` *clause and at the top level of a module, the pattern* p *is matched "lazily" as an irrefutable pattern by default (as if there were an implicit ~ in front of it).*

This means that a value matched against a tuple will not be evaluated to head normal form at pattern match time but only when one of its elements is demanded. This differs from other lazy functional programming languages such as Miranda where the expression must be evaluated to tuple form before the match can succeed.

The consequence of this in space terms is that the whole of a tuple will be held on to until all of the elements of that tuple have been demanded. Consider a pair `(a, b)`. If, say, `a` is demanded early in the program it is held in store until `b` is demanded, even if `a` is no longer required and could be garbage collected. If `a` is large then this will bring a large, and needless, storage overhead to the program which uses it.

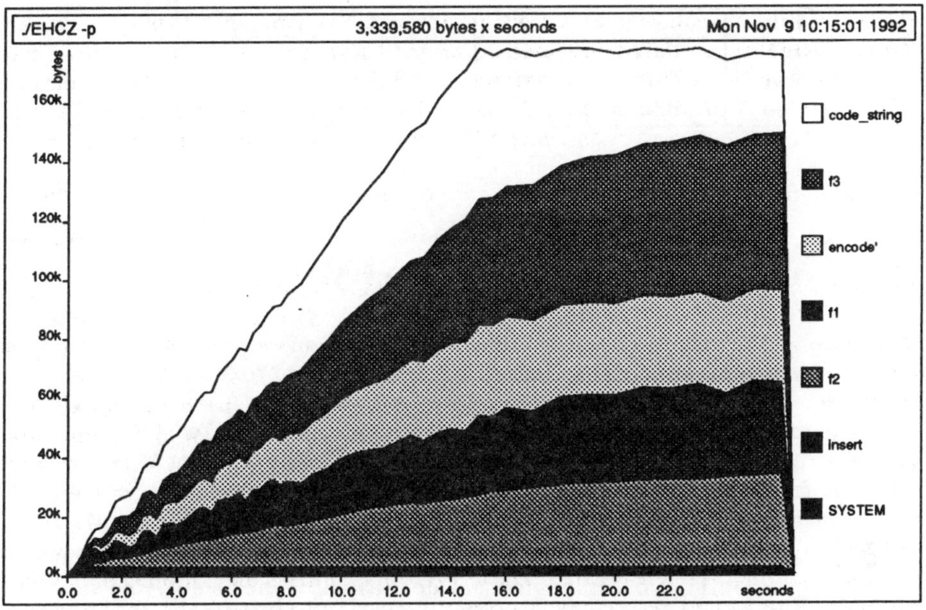

Figure 3: A producer profile for the improved compress program

It is now easily understood why **code_string** is suffering in this way. It constructs three triples, the elements of which will be demanded at different times in the program's execution, thus causing a lot of information to be stored. We need two fixes to this problem. The first is to associate each of the definitions in the local clause with a separate case of the main function. This will ensure that only one tuple closure is built for each invocation of **code_string**. Second, to force the evaluation of a triple we need to raise the pattern match to the function level, where tuples are not matched irrefutably by default. This technique is demonstrated by the new definition of **code_string** given in Appendix A.

The producer graph for this new version is shown in Figure 3. The first thing we notice is the dramatic improvement in the space usage of the program – we have reduced the space usage by over a factor of three. Furthermore, the time taken to compress the 20k file has almost halved to 26 seconds. Running this new version of the program on the benchmarks gives the timings in Table 5. It would appear that we have been successful in our eradication of the triple nodes. The maximum amount of heap space needed by the program is now around 180k bytes. A constructor profile (not included here) shows that the code table takes up approximately 140k of this. We have indeed removed the space leak.

File	*compress*	LZWC	New LZWH	Slowdown Factor
bib	0.62	5.18	110.3	21
paper1	0.35	2.69	63.25	24
geo	0.67	4.41	144.41	33

Table 5: Results of compression experiments – speed (in CPU seconds)

4 Conclusions and Future Work

In this paper we have shown the development of an implementation of LZW compression in Haskell. The Haskell program ran approximately 35–55 times more slowly than the equivalent program written in C. An investigation into the cause of the slowdown revealed that a space leak, Haskell I/O speed and the lack of bit-level operators were contributors. Taken together these elements account for almost all of the slowdown. This clearly indicates areas for future compiler research and improvement.

The space leak demonstrated a potential hazard with the Haskell pattern-matching semantics for tuples in local definitions. The irrefutable matching in a local clause can cause large space leaks where such tuples are used. In our program an innocent use of triples caused the program to use three times more space than was needed. Although cured by a simple transformation, this problem could cause much trouble for the unwary. The transformation also has the drawback of making the program less declarative, thus lessening one of the advantages of the functional style.

There is still scope for improvement in the Haskell program. A tree structure which adapts itself to the pattern of usage might prove beneficial. Trees such as the splay tree [8] and the weighted path length tree [9] which modify themselves on read and writes could improve access times to the table. Further, once the table is full it is used in a read–only manner. The current version of `code_string` builds an unevaluated tree when the table is full – a version which only matches the input to strings in the table should improve performance.

Finally, our Haskell program is over–simplified. To get a true comparison with the compress program the whole of compress should be implemented in Haskell. This entails adding the advanced features such as table clearing when the compression ratio falls, increasing the maximum bit size and outputting the codes in the same way. This will give a more sound comparison of how the performance of LZW compression in Haskell compares with the performance in real–life. Work is currently in progress to address this.

5 Acknowledgements

The authors wish to thank the referees for their comments on the draft version of this paper. Particular thanks go to Guy Argo for his many detailed suggestions for improving the program and this paper. We would also like to acknowledge the input received from David Wakeling and Iain Checkland at the University of York, and Simon Peyton Jones and Kevin Hammond at the University of Glasgow.

References

[1] J Hughes. Why functional programming matters. *The Computer Journal*, 32(2):98–107, 1989.

[2] P Hudak, S Peyton-Jones, and P Wadler (Editors). Report on the programming language Haskell. Version 1.2. *ACM SIGPLAN Notices*, 27(5), 1992.

[3] T Bell, I Witten, and J Cleary. Modelling for text compression. *ACM Computing Surveys*, 21(4), December 1989.

[4] T Welch. A technique for high-performance data compression. *Computer*, 17(6):8–19, June 1984.

[5] D Knuth. *Sorting and Searching, The Art of Computer Programming*, volume 3. Addison-Wesley Publishing Company, 1973.

[6] S L Peyton Jones. *The Implementation of Functional Programming.* Prentice-Hall International, 1987.

[7] C Runciman and D Wakeling. Heap profiling of lazy functional programs. Technical Report YCS172, University of York - Department of Computer Science, 1992.

[8] D Sleator and R Tarjan. Self–adjusting binary search trees. *Journal of the ACM*, 32(3):652–686, 1985.

[9] G Argo. Weighting without waiting: the weighted path length tree. *Computer Journal*, 1991.

A The Improved Definition of code_string

```
code_string :: String -> Int -> Int -> CodeTable
                  -> (String, Int, CodeTable)
code_string [] old_code _ _
        = ([], old_code, PTNil)
code_string ca@(c:_) old_code next_code PTNil =
        if next_code >= max_entries then
            (ca, old_code, PTNil)
        else
            (ca, old_code, PT c next_code PTNil PTNil PTNil)
code_string ca@(c:_) old_code next_code (PT k v t l r)
        | c < k  = fix-leak result1 k v t r
        where result1 = code_string ca old_code next_code l
```

```
                fix-leak (csl, nl, l') k v t r
                        = (csl, nl, PT k v t l' r)

code_string ca@(c:_) old_code next_code (PT k v t l r)
        | c > k  = fix-leak result2 p l
        where result2 = code_string ca old_code next_code r
              fix-leak (csr, nr, r') k v t l
                     = (csr, nr, PT k v t l r')

code_string (_:cs) old_code next_code (PT k v t l r)
        | otherwise = fix-leak result3 k v l r
        where result3 = code_string cs v next_code t
              fix-leak (cs', n, t') k v l r
                        = (cs', n, PT (PTE k v t') l r)
```

B I/O Benchmark Programs

The C Program:

```
#include <stdio.h>

main ()
{
  register int c;

  while ((c = getchar ()) != EOF) {
    putchar (c);
  };
}
```

The Haskell Program:

```
main = readChan stdin abort (\ f ->
          appendChan stdout f abort done)
```

Profiling Lazy Functional Programs

Patrick M. Sansom*
University of Glasgow†

Simon L. Peyton Jones
University of Glasgow

Abstract

Profiling tools, which measure and display the dynamic space and time behaviour of programs, are essential for identifying execution bottlenecks. A variety of such tools exist for conventional languages, but almost none for non-strict functional languages. There is a good reason for this: lazy evaluation means that the program is executed in an order which is not immediately apparent from the source code, so it is difficult to relate dynamically-gathered statistics back to the original source.

We present a new technique which solves this problem. The framework is general enough to profile both space and time behaviour. Better still, it is cheap to implement, and we describe how to do so in the context of the Spineless Tagless G-machine.

1 Introduction

Software engineers writing real applications often need to predict, measure and improve the performance of the parts of their programs. Lazy functional programming environments have typically provided few tools to help this process despite the fact that they are more prone to unexpected "performance bugs" than their imperative counterparts.

Conventional languages provide profiling tools such as *gprof* [3] and *mprof* [11] which attribute time usage and space allocation to source code. This enables the programmer to identify the "critical parts" of the program being developed. We are interested in developing similar tools to enable the profiling of lazy functional program performance.

Though these tools will include the identification of *time* spent in the different "parts" of the program, we are also interested in tools which identify the *space* usage. Unlike most conventional languages, functional languages provide an abstraction which hides the allocation and reclamation of data structures. This abstraction can result in unexpected spatial behaviour ranging from over-liberal allocation to so-called *space leaks* [6]. Results from Runciman and Wakeling who have developed a heap profiling tool have indicated how revealing such information can be [9,10].

An essential part of any profiler is that the profiling information gathered must be *faithful* to the normal execution. In particular:

---

*The author gratefully acknowledges the support of the Commonwealth Scholarship Commission.

†Authors' address: Dept of Computing Science, Glasgow University, Glasgow, Scotland
E-mail: sansom@dcs.glasgow.ac.uk, simonpj@dcs.glasgow.ac.uk

- The lazy evaluation order must not be modified.
- We want to profile the actual execution of programs compiled with an optimising compiler. An instrumented interpreter is not satisfactory.
- The profiling scheme must be reasonably cheap. The additional cost of profiling should not distort the information gathered about the execution.

Our approach concentrates on what we consider to be the key problem: The identification of the different program "parts" for which statistics are accumulated (Section 2). We introduce the notion of a "cost centre" which identifies the source code expressions for which we are interested in accumulating statistical information (Section 3). We go on to describe a remarkably simple implementation which keeps track of the current source expression being evaluated without modifying the lazy semantics (Section 4) and finally describe how we use this scheme to gather the profiling statistics we are interested in (Section 5).

2 Profiling Lazy Functional Programs is Difficult

The key problem in profiling any program is to relate any information gathered about the execution of the program back to the source code in a way which accurately identifies the source with which it should be attributed. Unfortunately, the very features which lazy functional languages advocate, such as higher order functions, polymorphism, lazy evaluation and program transformation, make a well-defined mapping back to the source code difficult to achieve.

A general discussion of some of the problems that lazy languages pose to profiling is given in [8]. We address the issues with respect to the mapping problem identified above.

2.1 Re-use of Functions

Polymorphism and higher order functions encourage the re-use of functions in many different contexts. In [5], the ability to provide generalised, higher order functions which can then be specialised with appropriate base functions is advocated as a major strength of functional languages. Unfortunately this heavy re-use of a small number of functions makes it harder to identify the source of observed execution costs. Suppose we wish to know the cost of the expression:

```
map (f x) l
```

Knowing that the program spent 20% of its time in the function `map` is not particularly helpful, as there may be many applications of `map` in the program. The costs of the different calls to `map` need to be attributed to their various call sites, of which this expression is one. In general we may want to attribute the cost of a function invocation to the *stack* of call sites invoking its execution.

This problem does arise in conventional languages where a routine may be called from many call sites, which are usually statically identifiable. It is normally solved by using an approximation which apportions time spent in a particular routine to its various callers [3].

2.2 Lazy Evaluation

Lazy evaluation poses the profiler with some awkward problems.

It is not necessarily clear what part of the program should bear the cost of evaluating a suspension. An expression is only evaluated if its result is demanded by some other expression. So the question arises: "Should the cost of evaluation be attributed to the part of the program which instantiated the expression or the part of the program which demanded the result?". This is further complicated by the fact that multiple expressions may demand the result with all but the first finding the expression already evaluated. If we attribute the cost to demanding expressions it should probably be shared among all the demanding expressions.

Furthermore, the nature of lazy evaluation means that evaluation of an expression will be interleaved with the evaluation of the inputs which it demands. As this expression is itself being demanded it will also be interleaved with the execution of its demander. The resulting order of execution bears no resemblance to the source code we are trying to map our profiling results to. A scheme which attributes the different execution fragments to the appropriate source expression is required. Accumulation of statistics to the different call sites is made more difficult as we do not have an explicit call stack — instead we have a demand stack.

Finally, it is essential that the lazy semantics are not modified by the profiler. In conventional languages one might measure the time taken to execute between two "points" in the source. However in a lazy language there is no linear evaluation sequence so we no longer have the notion of a "point" in the execution corresponding to a "point" in the source. One could imagine a crude profiling scheme which forced evaluation of the intermediate data structure after each phase of (say) a compiler. This would enable us to measure the cost of the each phase, but we would be measuring the cost of a different program — one which forces its intermediate data and which may be evaluating parts which need never be evaluated!

2.3 Program Transformation and Optimisation

Functional language implementations involve radical transformation and optimisation which may result in executable code which is very different from the source:

- Hidden functions are introduced by high level translation of syntactic sugar such as list comprehensions.
- Auxiliary functions and definitions are introduced as expressions are transformed.
- The combined effect of all the transformations may drastically change the structure of the original source.

It is highly undesirable to turn off these optimisations as the resulting profile would not be of the program you actually want to run and improve. As we want to be able to profile a fully optimised program, running with real data, this transformation problem must be addressed.

3 Cost centres — A practical solution

Our approach specifically addresses the problem of mapping the statistics to source code. Rather than collecting profiling information about every function in the source, we annotate particular source expressions, which we are interested in profiling, with *cost centres* which identify the expressions. During execution statistical information is gathered about the expressions being evaluated and attributed to the appropriate cost centre.

Suppose we are interested in determining the cost incurred in evaluating the expression

```
map (f x) l
```

We introduce a *set cost centre* expression construct, `scc`, which is used to annotate an expression with a cost centre. A *cost centre* is a label under which we attribute execution costs. It is represented as a literal string which, together with the module name, identifies the cost centre. For example

```
scc "foo" (map (f x) l)
```

causes the cost of the actual evaluation of `map (f x) l` to be attributed to the cost centre `"foo"`. This expression will be used as a running example throughout this section.

The `scc` expression construct encloses a static expression whose evaluation cost is associated with a cost centre identified by a *label*

`scc` *label expr*

We insist that the label is a literal string as we do not want to have to compute it at runtime. Semantically, `scc` simply returns the value of *expr*, but operationally, it results in the cost of evaluating *expr* being attributed to the cost centre *label*.

For the collected statistics to have any useful meaning we must clearly identify what we mean by the *cost incurred in evaluating an expression*. This requires us to define exactly what evaluation should be measured and where the costs of it should be attributed.

3.1 Degree of Evaluation

We are measuring the cost of a source expression. However in a lazy language the extent to which an expression is evaluated is dependent on the demand placed by the surrounding context. We do not want to affect the evaluation sequence at all — we want to measure the evaluation that is actually required by the program being executed and at the same point in time that it is required. Let's call this degree of evaluation the *actual evaluation*.

This unknown degree of evaluation results in a potential source of confusion. A programmer might be expecting to measure evaluation which never occurs. However, we are interested in identifying the critical expressions within the program, and are not concerned with potentially inefficient expressions which are never actually evaluated. If the evaluation is demanded, its cost will be measured.

The degree of evaluation also affects the cost of demanding an expression's inputs i.e. free variables. When examining the cost of a particular expression we don't want the water to be muddied by the degree of evaluation of these inputs. We just want to know the cost of executing the expression itself. The cost of evaluating any unevaluated inputs will not be attributed to the demanding expression — this will be attributed to the cost centre responsible for building the closures. In the example above the costs of evaluating `f`, `x` and `l` will not be attributed to `"foo"`. This corresponds to the intuition we have for strict languages where the evaluation of all any inputs to an expression is completed before we evaluate the expression.

3.2 Attribution of Costs

A particular cost centre is attributed with the costs of the actual evaluation demanded of all the instances of its expressions. The costs of all the function calls made by the expression are *inherited* and attributed to the enclosing cost centre. This allows us to aggregate the cost a large nest of function calls together, enabling the overall performance of the logical parts of a program to be compared without being swamped by detailed function oriented information.

In our example, the call of `map` and all the calls to `f` hidden inside `map` will be attributed to `"foo"`. Calls to `map` from other sites will be attributed to the enclosing cost centre at those sites.

3.3 Nested Cost Centres

It is possible for an expression enclosed with an `scc` annotation to have an `scc` expression within it. This might arise from an explicit `scc` sub-expression or an `scc` expression embedded in a called function. Consider the expression

```
scc "foo" map (f x) (scc "bar" (map (g y) l))
```

Should the cost of the inner `map`, be attributed to the cost centre `"foo"` as well as `"bar"`? We have adopt a very simple scheme. *Costs are only attributed to a single cost centre.* So the costs of the inner expression, `map (g y) l`, will be attributed to the cost centre `"bar"` and the cost of mapping `f x` over the result attributed to `"foo"`.

As another example consider

```
scc "foo" (map (scc "bar" (f x)) l)
```

This will attribute the cost of evaluating `f x` to `"bar"`. The cost of applying the resulting function to the elements of the list `l` will still be attributed to `"foo"` as this is not in the scope of the `scc` for `"bar"`. If we wanted to attribute the cost of evaluating the list elements to `"bar"` we would have to bring the complete application of `f` into the scope of `"bar"`. This can be done by introducing a lambda

```
scc "foo" (map  (\y -> scc "bar" (f x y))  l)
```

Here the cost of the evaluation of elements of the resulting list are attributed to the cost centre `"bar"` while the cost of constructing the list is attributed to the cost centre `"foo"`. If the list was forced but the elements never evaluated the cost of building the list would accrue to `"foo"` but no costs would accrue to `"bar"`. This level control of the attribution of costs allows us to break down the detailed costs of evaluation. However care is needed to ensure that the **scc** expressions measure what we intend.

Aggregation of costs to enclosing cost centres is possible. However:

- Collecting accurate aggregated information imposes a much greater overhead as we would need to keep track of the current call stack of cost centres.

- It is not clear that this aggregation, given our notion of user-definable cost centre with inheritance, is going to provide us with a significant improvement in the profiling information available.

For the time being we do not plan to perform any aggregation but experience may cause us to revise this decision.

3.4 Identifying Expressions

Annotation of the source code expressions with explicit **scc** expressions can be a little tedious. This is especially true when obtaining the first profile of a program as you only have an intuition, which may well be wrong, as to which expressions are consuming the time and space resources. If your program has a clear logical structure, such as the passes of a compiler, a few **scc** annotations at the top level should reveal which "parts" should be annotated further to provide a more detailed profile. Alternatively you might be more interested in determining the costs of a particular implementation of an underlying abstract data type. In this case all the functions which implement these operations would need to be annotated.

To ease this annotation overhead we provide a compiler option which annotates all the top level declarations in a module with a cost centre labelled with the name of the declaration. As the module name is also recorded with the cost centre the cost of the module as a whole can be determined by summing the costs of the individual cost centres in the module.

This is very useful when bootstrapping the profiling cycle as it enables the user to gain an overall picture of the cost distribution of their program which is essential to guide further investigate.

4 Implementation

The main idea is to keep track of the cost centre of the current expression which is being evaluated — the *current cost centre*. As costs are incurred they are attributed to this current cost centre.

We are implementing cost centres within the framework of the Haskell compiler being developed at the University of Glasgow [4]. This uses the STG-machine as an underlying abstract machine [7]. The discussion which follows attempts to provide a general description of the manipulation of cost centres. However some details of the STG-machine are required to understand the more concrete discussion about our implementation.

During compilation we statically declare a *cost centre* structure for each **scc** label encountered in the source. **scc** constructs which have the same label refer to a single cost centre. A pointer to this structure is used to identify the cost centre. A store location, **currentCostCentre** is declared, which indicates where costs should be attributed. This is actually a pointer to the appropriate structure.

The main problem with keeping track of the current cost centre in a lazy language is the interleaving of evaluation. When an unevaluated closure, or *thunk*, is entered we must ensure that

1. The costs of evaluation are attributed to the appropriate cost centre.
2. Once evaluation is complete the cost centre of the demanding expression is restored.

Consider the expression `scc "foo" (g x, y)`. The pair will be returned with the computation for `g x` suspended within it. We must ensure that the evaluation of `g x`, if it is demanded, is attributed to the cost centre `"foo"`. To enable us to do this the `currentCostCentre`, `"foo"`, is attached to the thunk, `g x`, when it is built. On entering a thunk the `currentCostCentre` is set to the cost centre stored in the thunk and the subsequent costs attributed to the thunk's cost centre. In fact, we attach the current cost centre to all heap-allocated closures as this allows us to identify which cost centres were responsible for building the various heap objects.

All that remains to be done is to devise a scheme which restores the demanding cost centre once evaluation of the thunk, `g x`, is complete. Lazy evaluation requires the thunk to be updated with its head normal form once evaluation is complete, thus avoiding repeated evaluation. At precisely this point we must restore the demanding cost centre — evaluation of the thunk is complete and control is returning to the demanding expression.

In the STG-machine an update is triggered by an update frame. This is pushed onto the stack when the thunk is entered and removed when the update is performed. This provides us with a convenient place to save and restore the demanding cost centre. We augment the update frame with the demanding cost centre. On entering a thunk

1. An update frame is pushed (as usual) which contains the cost centre of the demanding expression, i.e. the `currentCostCentre`.
2. The `currentCostCentre` is then set to the cost centre stored in the thunk being entered.

When the evaluation is complete an update is triggered by the update frame. As well as updating the closure the `currentCostCentre` of the demanding expression is restored.

For closures which are already evaluated the result is returned as normal. No manipulation of cost centres is required. The small cost of entry and return is attributed to the demanding cost centre.

In this way, costs accrue to the cost centre of the *builder* of a closure, and the *enterer's* cost centre is restored when evaluation of the closure is complete. At this point the closure is in HNF, but any unevaluated closures lying inside the returned value have recorded inside them the appropriate cost centre.

The only other time the `currentCostCentre` is changed is when an `scc` expression is evaluated. Again we have to save the current cost centre and restore it when evaluation is complete. We already have a scheme for doing this which saves the current cost centre in an update frame. The same idea is used here except that we don't push a real update frame. Instead we push a frame that appears to be an update frame but does not contain a closure to be updated. When triggered it simply restores the saved cost centre. Evaluating an `scc` expression requires

1. A "restore cost centre frame" containing the `currentCostCentre` to be pushed. This appears to be an update frame but does not actually contain a closure to update.

2. The `currentCostCentre` to be set to the new cost centre associated with the `scc` expression.

Thunks built within the `scc` expression will have this new cost centre attached so costs incured during evaluation of these closures will accrue to this centre. When evaluation of the `scc` expression is complete, the apparent update is triggered which simply restores the saved cost centre.

The sole purpose of the cost centre concept is to provide a user-definable mapping from the profiling statistics back to the source code. Time and space allocation can be attributed to the currently active cost centre using the usual clock/allocation interrupt, which samples the `currentCostCentre` register. The cost centre attached to a closure indicates which cost centre was responsible for building the closure. This allows us to profile the heap attributing the heap usage to the cost centres that were responsible for creating it.

4.1 Optimisation Revisited

It is important to avoid program transformations that change the scope of the `scc` expression, as this will change the expression which is evaluated under that cost centre. Consider the following transformation:

$$\ldots\ \texttt{scc}\ cc\ (\ldots e_{sub} \ldots)\ \ldots \quad \Longrightarrow \quad \texttt{let}\ v = e_{sub}\ \texttt{in}\ \ldots\ \texttt{scc}\ cc\ (\ldots v \ldots)\ \ldots$$

This transformation doesn't change the meaning of the expression. However, as the expression, e_{sub}, is lifted outside the `scc` expression it will result in an evaluation of e_{sub} no longer being attributed to the cost centre *cc*. In short, program transformation can move costs from one cost centre to another.

Such transformations must be avoided as we require the execution costs to be accurately mapped back to the appropriate source code cost centre. This conflicts with our goal of measuring the costs of a fully optimised implementation. We still perform the program transformations on the expressions within an `scc` expression and on expressions containing `scc` expressions. What must be avoided is performing a transformation which moves computation from the scope of one cost centre to another. That is, we must not

- Lift a sub-expression out of an `scc` expression (as above).

- Unfold a definition which was declared outside the `scc` expression, e.g.

$$\texttt{let}\ v = e_{defn}\ \texttt{in}\ \ldots\ \texttt{scc}\ cc\ (\ldots v \ldots)\ \ldots \quad \Longrightarrow \quad \ldots\ \texttt{scc}\ cc\ (\ldots e_{defn} \ldots)\ \ldots$$

It is possible to relax some of these transformation restrictions provided care is taken to preserve the appropriate cost centres. Sub-expressions can be lifted out of an **scc** expression if they carry the **scc** with them. The lifting example above becomes

$$\ldots \texttt{scc}\ cc\ (\ldots e_{sub} \ldots) \ldots \quad \Longrightarrow \quad \texttt{let}\ v = \texttt{scc}_{lift}\ cc\ e_{sub}\ \texttt{in} \ldots \texttt{scc}\ cc\ (\ldots v \ldots) \ldots$$

Definitions may be unfolded if their cost centre can be determined and the unfolded expression is annotated with this cost centre. We can also allow the unfolding of function declarations as they are in normal form and do not require any evaluation. Thus the in-lining of function declarations is not hindered. We still need to restrict the unfolding of constructor applications, which are also in head normal form, as this will result in the cost of the heap allocation of the constructor closure being moved.

In spite of the restrictions the measured cost of evaluating an identified expression will reflect the true cost of the fully-optimised evaluation of that expression. However the cost of evaluating the program as a whole may be affected by optimisations which were curtailed by the profiling requirements to identify the individual expressions of interest.

5 Gathering Profiling Statistics

Having described the mechanism by which we map the profiling statistics back to the source code we now move on to describe the statistics we actually gather. It is important to remember that any metering we do to gather the statistics should not distort the characteristics of normal execution — as it is normal execution that we are attempting to profile. Any additional actions required should be very simple and within memory, unless the profiling clock is stopped while they are being performed.

5.1 Information Available

We first identify the information which is immediately available to us.

A cost centre is represented as a pointer to a static structure. It consists of the label and module of the **scc** annotation and any statistical meters we want to accumulate for the cost centre. At every point during the execution we can identify the current cost centre. This is used to attribute execution events such as a timer interrupt or heap allocation.

Closures also contain information which can be used to profile the heap. In the STG machine, augmented with our implementation of cost-centres, each closure is laid out as shown in figure 1. The first word of the closure is the *info pointer*. It points to the *info table*; a static structure containing information about the closure. In particular it contains the code to execute when the closure is entered. When profiling we store additional *description* information in the info table indicating what the closure is. The second word points to the *cost centre* responsible for building the closure. A third word stores a *time stamp* indicating when the closure was created. From this the closures age can be calculated. These additional cost centre and time stamp words are only present when the program has been compiled for profiling. The space occupied by them is disregarded in all the profiling information gathered as the

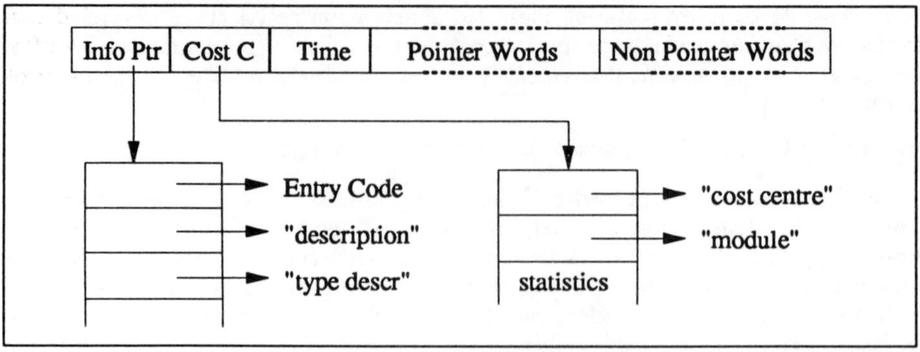

Figure 1: Closure layout

information we gather should reflect the state of affairs that would exist during normal execution.

Thus, for every heap-allocated closure we can identify:

- Which part of the program created the closure, as indicated by the attached cost centre,
- The closure's time stamp (and therefore age), and
- The data constructor or application the closure represents, as conveyed by the description and type description information stored in the closure's info-table.

5.2 Profiling Information

We now briefly describe the profiling information which we gather. There are two distinct parts of the profiling tool.

First we produce an aggregate profile reporting the execution costs of the different parts of the source program. For each cost centre we report:

- The proportion of *time* spent evaluating instances of the expression. This is an approximate measure gathered by sampling the `currentCostCentre` during execution using a 20ms clock interrupt.
- The amount of heap allocated during the evaluation of the expression instances. Whenever we allocate a closure we increment the memory counter of the closure's cost centre.

An example profiling report can be found in figure 2. It was produced for the final version of `clausify` as presented in [10].

The second part of the profiling system shows the programs heap behaviour over time. At regular intervals a heap sample produces a summary of the space occupied by live closures. This can be broken down by the producing cost centre, closure description or time stamp. In addition the heap sample can be instructed to select a sub-set of the closures to report depending on the closure's

```
        Time and Allocation Profiling Report  (Sat Jun 13 22:33 1992)

           clausify_p +RTS -H2M -K120k -S -p -hC

        total time  =        14.38 secs    (719 ticks)
        total alloc =   6,414,004 bytes   (537129 allocs)

Cost Centre  Module  scc's subcc  %time %alloc  (ticks allocs    bytes)
unicl        Main        1     0   87.8   89.6  (  631 483082 5744736)
disin        Main        1     0    8.8    6.8  (   63  36442  437304)
split        Main        1     0    3.1    3.3  (   22  16037  213820)
MAIN                     1     8    0.1    0.1  (    1    255    3268)
mapdisp      Main        1     0    0.1    0.0  (    1     40     464)
parse        Main        1     0    0.1    0.1  (    1    407    4376)
concat       Main        1     0    0.0    0.0  (    0     11     160)
negin        Main        1     0    0.0    0.1  (    0    525    5916)
elim         Main        1     0    0.0    0.1  (    0    330    3960)
```

Figure 2: Time and Allocation Profiling Report

cost centre, description and age. When execution is complete the profiles can be processed to produce a graphical visualisation of the heap's behaviour [10].

This is by no means the limit of the information one might wish to collect. Any runtime event or heap closure property of interest can make use of the cost centre mechanism to relate the information back to the different parts of the source.

6 Related Work

This work is closely related to work done by Runciman and Wakeling. In [8] they identify many of the problems profiling lazy functional languages and proposed an interpretive profiler based on source level graph reduction.

More recently they have independently proposed and implemented a heap profiling scheme that is similar to ours [9,10]. They store the *function* that produced the graph node and the name of the *construction* in each closure and produce time profiles of the heap broken up by function and/or construction. Interpreting the profiles of particular programs revealed interesting phenomena about their execution. These lead to changes to the program under investigation and the evaluation scheme used by the compiler which improved the programs' performance.

Our method differs from theirs in that it profiles evaluation *time* (not just space). A heap profile does not provide an explicit indication of which parts of the program are consuming the evaluation time. This is important because most of a program's execution time is usually spent evaluating expressions, not in the garbage collector.

Our current cost centres are similar to a technique proposed by Appel, Duba and MacQueen for SML [1]. They keep track of the *current function* being evaluated by adding appropriate statements to the intermediate code. The meter of the current function is incremented at regular timer interrupts providing an aggregate time profile of the different functions. Their work was motivated by the need to keep track of interleaved execution arising from transforming optimisations. Though this is also an issue for us: we arrived at our scheme because we can't avoid the interleaving arising from lazy evaluation.

Clayman, Parrott and Clack have implemented a profiling scheme in an interpreted lazy graph-reduction system which profiles heap usage and execution time [2]. They attribute profiling information to top-level functions marked for profiling. Unique *colours* are attached to the root of each profiled function and propagated over the graphical representation of the program at compile-time. Any costs accruing to unprofiled functions are *inherited* by the caller due to the propagation of the caller's colour. The authors have demonstrated the output of their tool for small programs.

Their notion of a unique *colour* is very similar to our notion of a cost centre. However their compile-time propagation of colours imposes a number of limitations on the inheritance profiling:

- Unprofiled functions cannot be shared by more than one profiled function.
- Separate module compilation is not possible.

These severely limits the use of inheritance profiling in large programs. Our dynamic inheritance scheme propagates cost centres at runtime using the current cost centre. This allows the cost of unprofiled functions to be inherited by many different callers residing in different modules.

7 Future Work

This work is still in an early stage of development. We have just completed the implementation of cost centres and the associated statistics gathering. We still have to evaluate the use of the profiling tool.

We are particularly interested in evaluating the dynamic cost centre model. Though we do believe that a tool which identifies source by function is adequate for small programs, we do not believe that such a tool is appropriate for large programs. The number of functions, call sites and amount of information is too cumbersome. We are planning to profile the Glasgow Haskell compiler, an extremely large Haskell program, as a practical test of the profiling tool. As well as tune the performance of the compiler we hope this will enable us to evaluate the use of our profiling tool and identify possible enhancements to the tool and any additional profiling information which would have aided the profiling task.

Bibliography

1. AW Appel, BF Duba & DB MacQueen, "Profiling in the presence of optimization and garbage collection," SML Distribution, Nov 1988.
2. S Clayman, D Parrott & C Clack, "A profiling technique for lazy, higher-order functional programs," Technical Report, Dept of Computer Science, University College London, Nov 1991.

3. SL Graham, PB Kessler & MK McKusick, "An execution profiler for modular programs," *Software — Practice and Experience* 13 (1983), 671–685.
4. C Hall, K Hammond, W Partain, SL Peyton Jones & P Wadler, "The glasgow haskell compiler: A retrospective," in *Functional Programming, Glasgow 1992*, J Launchbury & PM Sansom, eds., Springer-Verlag, Workshops in Computing, Ayr, Scotland, 1992.
5. John Hughes, "Why functional programming matters," *The Computer Journal* 32 (Apr 1989).
6. SL Peyton Jones, *The Implementation of Functional Programming Languages*, Prentice Hall, 1987.
7. SL Peyton Jones, "Implementing lazy functional languages on stock hardware: the Spineless Tagless G-machine," *Journal of Functional Programming* 2 (Apr 1992), 127–202.
8. C Runciman & D Wakeling, "Problems and proposals for time and space profiling of functional programs," in *Functional Programming, Glasgow 1990*, SL Peyton Jones, G Hutton & CK Holst, eds., Springer-Verlag, Workshops in Computing, Ullapool, Scotland, 1990.
9. C Runciman & D Wakeling, "Heap profiling of a lazy functional compiler," in *Functional Programming, Glasgow 1992*, J Launchbury & PM Sansom, eds., Springer-Verlag, Workshops in Computing, Ayr, Scotland, 1992.
10. C Runciman & D Wakeling, "Heap profiling of lazy functional programs," Technical Report 172, Dept of Computer Science, University of York, April 1992.
11. B Zorn & P Halfinger, "A memory allocation profiler for C and LISP programs," in *USENIX 88, San Francisco*, 1988, 223–237.

On Program Transformation in the Glasgow Haskell Compiler

André Santos* Simon L Peyton Jones
University of Glasgow†

Abstract

In this paper we describe a series of program transformations that are currently being implemented in the Glasgow Haskell Compiler. They are semantics preserving program transformations and therefore are perfectly suitable for incorporation in a compiler. We describe some of the transformations, how they interact and their impact on the time/space behaviour of some programs.

1 Introduction

Program transformations can considerably improve the performance of certain programs, by transforming inefficient code into more efficient versions. In other cases it can change the space behaviour of a program, making it use less memory.

The Glasgow Haskell Compiler was designed with program transformations in mind, allowing for transformation passes to be easily incorporated into the compiler. Here we will show some of the transformations that have been actually implemented and how they affect the time/space behaviour of some programs.

We initially describe the basic idea behind some transformations and how they are carried out through an example. Then we discuss some of them in more detail and present future directions for research and some preliminary results.

The Glasgow Haskell Compiler works by translating a Haskell program into the Core Language (Figure 1), which is in fact the second order lambda calculus augmented with some constructs, like `case` and `let`. The Core Language allows us to express boxed as well as unboxed values, therefore allowing many transformations usually relegated to the code generator to be expressed as Core-to-Core transformations. It is in the Core Language that most of the program transformations we will describe are carried out.

Next, the program is translated from the Core Language to Spineless Tagless G-Machine (STG) Language [4], the abstract machine used by the compiler. Only at this level the transformations start to be more specific to the implementation model we use. Finally the code is translated to C, which is used as a high level assembler.

---

*Sponsored by CAPES, Brazil.

†Authors' address: Department of Computing Science, University of Glasgow, Glasgow G12 8QQ, Scotland, U.K. E-mail: {`andre, simonpj`}`@dcs.glasgow.ac.uk`

Program	*Prog*	$\rightarrow$	$Binding_1$; ... ; $Binding_n$	$n \geq 1$
Bindings	*Binding*	$\rightarrow$	`nonrec` *Bind*	
		|	`rec` *Binds*	
	Binds	$\rightarrow$	$Bind_1$; ... ; $Bind_n$	$n \geq 1$
	Bind	$\rightarrow$	*var* `=` *Expr*	
Expression	*Expr*	$\rightarrow$	$Expr_1$ $Expr_2$	Application
		|	*Expr ty*	Type application
		|	λ *vars* `->` *Expr*	Lambda abstraction
		|	Λ *ty* `->` *Expr*	Type abstraction
		|	`case` *Expr* `of` *Alts*	Case expression
		|	`let` *Binding* `in` *Expr*	Local definition
		|	*con* $var_1 \ldots var_n$	Constructor $n \geq 0$
		|	*prim* $var_1 \ldots var_n$	Primitive $n \geq 0$
		|	*var*	Variable
		|	*Literal*	Unboxed Object
Literal values	*Literal*	$\rightarrow$	*integer* | *float* | ...	
Alternatives	*Alts*	$\rightarrow$	$Calt_1$; ... ; $Calt_n$; *Default*	$n \geq 0$
		|	$Lalt_1$; ... ; $Lalt_n$; *Default*	$n \geq 0$
Constr. alt	*Calt*	$\rightarrow$	*Con* $var_1 \ldots var_n$ `->` *Expr*	$n \geq 0$
Literal alt	*Lalt*	$\rightarrow$	*Literal* `->` *Expr*	
Default alt	*Default*	$\rightarrow$	`NoDefault`	
		|	`_` `->` *Expr*	
		|	*var* `->` *Expr*	

Figure 1: Syntax of the Core language

Pass	Action
Function Specialisation	Specialises overloaded functions used with same types/dictionaries
Simplifier I	Does some unfolding, β-reductions and some transformations
Simplifier II	Same as above with a more aggressive unfolding strategy
Simplifier III	Same as above also unfolding non-recursive functions with higher order arguments
Let-Floating	Floats let-bindings to the outermost possible position
Arg. Satisfaction Check	Reduces argument satisfaction checks in STG

Table 1: Compiler Options

2 Transformations

A lot of work has been done on techniques for transforming functional programs into more efficient ones. These techniques have sometimes resulted in the development of tools to aid the transformation process. Most of these tools, however, are dependent on user assistance and/or on very expensive analysis techniques in order to achieve good results. Therefore these techniques are not suitable for being incorporated into real functional language compilers.

We deal here with automatic semantics preserving transformations, which can be derived and carried out directly from the original program. In fact the selection of the transformations was mostly guided by inspection of the actual code generated by the compiler after each step, in small as well as large programs.

Most of the transformations we will describe are carried out in the Core Language, the language to which the original program is translated, by removing syntactic sugar and transforming out pattern matching, list comprehensions, etc. It allows us to express and exploit some ideas on unboxed values (as described in [5]), and this will be extensively demonstrated through the examples.

Some other transformations are expressed in the STG Language (STG-to-STG transformations), to which the Core language is translated immediately before code generation. The reason for having such transformations expressed as STG-to-STG transformations rather than Core-to-Core in the Glasgow Haskell Compiler is that they either exploit specific characteristics of STG or are more suitable to be done after the translations from Core to STG as this translation would expose more opportunities for transformations.

In Figure 2 we have an outline of the transformations. In Table 1 we give some more details on what each transformation pass does.

Some of the transformations described in the next sections are quite simple and widely known, but our main concern is with how they interact and how the compiled code can benefit from the different analysis/transformations. Also, although many of the expressions transformed out are very unlikely to appear in the original program, they are often found after the program is desugared to the Core Language, as we will see in the examples. One may argue that we

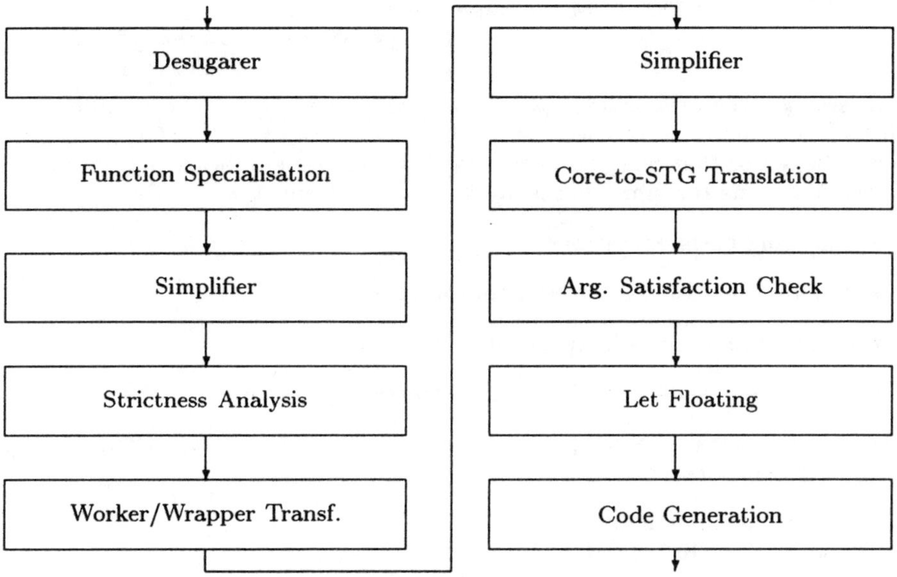

Figure 2: Transformation Passes

should avoid generating such expressions during the desugaring, but this would unnecessarily complicate this process.

We will introduce some transformations by giving an example and showing how they are used in it. The example we will use is quite simple, but the transformations that show up in it also occur very often in large programs.

3 An Example

In this section we will show how the transformations interact when generating a more efficient version of the factorial program. This will give an idea of the effect of the entire transformation sequence before we discuss some of the transformations in more detail.

A definition of the factorial function in the Core language could be

```
fact :: Int -> Int
fact = \ n -> case (n < (MkInt 1#)) of
                True -> MkInt 1#
                False -> n * fact (n - (MkInt 1#))
```

`MkInt` is used as the constructor for boxed integers. We put a `#` after a variable or value that is unboxed, as in [5].

We initially unfold the definitions of `-`, `*` and `<` to make explicit the unboxing/boxing operations on their arguments/results. The definition of `-` for example is

```
(-) = \ x y -> case x of
```

```
                    MkInt x# -> case y of
                                   MkInt y# -> case (x# -# y#) of
                                                 r -> MkInt r
```

where -# is the subtraction operation on unboxed integers. These unfoldings will lead us to many cases where we will be unboxing a value that has previously been unboxed or that has just been boxed, which are redundant operations.

The first time the simplifier is applied it transforms the code by

- unfolding basic operations
- applying β-reductions where appropriate
- avoiding redundant boxing/unboxing of values
- doing case-of-case transformations where appropriate

These and other transformations are detailed in the next section. By doing this the code is transformed to

```
fact = \ n -> case n of
                MkInt n# ->
                    case (n# <# 1#) of
                      0# -> case (fact (case (n# -# 1#) of
                                             v# -> MkInt v#)) of
                                MkInt v'# -> case (n# *# v'#) of
                                                 v''# -> MkInt v''#
                      _ ->  MkInt 1#
```

This already avoids many unnecessary boxing/unboxing operations, which is an improvement by itself. But it can do an even better job if we use a strictness analyser together with the Worker/Wrapper transformation, which will split the function in a worker/wrapper pair of functions. The idea of the Worker/Wrapper Transformation is to make minimal changes from the original functions while splitting, and let the simplifier do the rest of the job. Therefore we get an inefficient Worker/Wrapper pair which will become a more efficient one through the transformations:

```
fact :: Int -> Int
fact = \n -> case n of
               MkInt n# -> case fact' n# of
                              r# -> MkInt r#
fact' :: Int# -> Int#
fact' = \ n# -> let n = MkInt n#
                in case
                     (case (n# <# 1#) of
                        0# -> case (fact (case (n# -# 1#) of
                                               v# -> MkInt v#)) of
                                  MkInt v'# -> case (n# *# v'#) of
                                                   v''# -> MkInt v''#
                        _ -> MkInt 1#)
                   of
                     MkInt v'''# -> v'''#
```

Now the simplifier is called again to unfold the wrapper (**fact**) into the worker (**fact'**), to get the worker to call itself. By doing this we get many other opportunities for removing extra boxing/unboxing operations, case-of-case transformations, β-reductions, etc.

```
fact' = \ n# -> case (n# <# 1#) of
                    0# -> case (n# -# 1#) of
                            v# -> case fact' v# of
                                    v'# -> (n# *# v'#)
                    _ -> 1#
```

Clearly this definition is quite an improvement on the first one, by keeping the values unboxed during most of the computation.

4 Core-to-Core Transformations

Here we describe some of the transformations that are implemented as Core-to-Core transformations. The list is not exhaustive, but is intended to give a reasonable idea of the transformations carried out.

4.1 Function Specialisation Pass

The Function Specialisation Pass specialises local overloaded functions that are always used with the same types/dictionaries. An example of how it works follows.

```
f y = let double x = x + x in double (double y)
```

Assuming **plus** is the overloaded addition operation, which receives a type and dictionary as arguments, this would become (in Core)

```
f = /\ ty -> \ dict -> \ y ->
     let double = /\ ty' -> \ dict' -> \ x -> plus ty' dict' x x
     in double ty dict (double ty dict y)
```

As **double** is locally defined and called with the same type/dictionary we may transform this definition to

```
f = /\ ty -> \ dict -> \ y ->
     let double = /\ ty' -> \ dict' -> \ x -> plus ty' dict' x x
     in let double' = double ty dict
        in double' (double' y)
```

then as there is only one occurrence of **double** we inline it, obtaining

```
f = /\ ty -> \ dict -> \ y ->
     let double' = \ x -> plus ty dict x x
     in double' (double' y)
```

Some of the work of this pass could be eliminated if the typechecker already avoided these occurrences of types/dictionaries, but it is still not clear if all instances could be easily eliminated by the typechecker without further complicating it. Anyway, other transformations can introduce such expressions, which are worth transforming out.

Notice that this process is quite similar to common subexpression elimination. In general, common subexpression elimination in functional languages can generate unanticipated space leaks. In this case we do a very restricted version of common subexpression elimination, for dictionaries, so there is no such risk.

4.2 The Simplifier

The Simplifier consists itself of a series of very simple transformations. Many of these transformations deal with expressions that are very unlikely to be generated directly by a programmer, but are very often generated after desugaring Haskell to Core or by other transformation passes. It proceeds as follows:

- to guide the transformations, information is needed about the way in which each named value is *used*. This information is collected by a Substitution Analysis pass, which annotates every binder with information regarding whether it can be unfolded, removed or kept as a let-binding. The Substitution Analyser in its basic version counts occurrences of binders. If the binder does not occur in the program it is marked as not used and will be removed by the simplifier. If it occurs only once or is bound to a variable or a basic literal it is marked to be substituted (unfolded). If it occurs more than once it is marked for not being substituted, as this could possibly generate code and work duplication. Later we will discuss some more aggressive options that may unfold binders referenced more than once. In these cases we may duplicate code, but never duplicate work.

- Based on this information the program is simplified. This includes unfolding definitions, β-reductions, etc. We will describe some of them in more detail in the following sections.

- The process iterates until no more simplifications are possible. In typical programs quite a few iterations are necessary. Although we currently do not have a proof of the termination of the process, we are careful to ensure that transformations we are introducing do not interfere with the termination of the process.

Here we list some of the transformations implemented by the simplifier.

4.2.1 λ-elimination

An application of a lambda abstraction is always transformed to a `let` expression, thus:

(`\`x `->` *body*) e $\quad\Longrightarrow\quad$ `let` x `=` e `in` *body*

4.2.2 Let-elimination

A `let`-binding may be removed, unfolded or kept as a let depending on the corresponding annotation that comes from the substitution analysis pass. The three possibilities are

- binding not used: `let` x = e `in` *body* $\Longrightarrow$ *body*
- unfold the binding[1]: `let` x = e `in` *body* $\Longrightarrow$ *body*$[e/x]$
- do not unfold: No action takes place. This is the most critical decision, as we want to take as many opportunities for simplifications as possible, and unfolding let bindings is a major source of it. This is why we allow some more aggressive options for the simplifier, which will select more bindings to be unfolded.

4.2.3 Case-elimination

If a `case` expression scrutinises a (saturated) constructor application, it can readily be eliminated:

$$\begin{array}{ll} & \texttt{case}\ (C\ e_1 \ldots e_n)\ \texttt{of}\ \ldots\ C\ x_1 \ldots x_n\ \texttt{->}\ e \\ \Longrightarrow & \texttt{let}\ x_1\ \texttt{=}\ e_1\texttt{;}\ \ldots\texttt{;}\ x_n\ \texttt{=}\ e_n\ \texttt{in}\ e \end{array}$$

But a similar situation can arise in two other ways. Firstly, the `case` expression might be scrutinising a variable (or in general an expression[2]) which has already been scrutinised:

$$\begin{array}{l} \texttt{case}\ e\ \texttt{of}\ \{\ldots C\ x_1 \ldots x_n\ \texttt{->}\ \ldots\texttt{case}\ e\ \texttt{of}\ \{\ldots C\ y_1 \ldots y_n\ \texttt{->}\ body\}\} \\ \Longrightarrow \\ \texttt{case}\ e\ \texttt{of}\ \{\ldots C\ x_1 \ldots x_n\ \texttt{->}\ \ldots\texttt{let}\ y_1\ \texttt{=}\ x_1\texttt{;}\ \ldots\texttt{;}\ y_n\ \texttt{=}\ x_n\ \texttt{in}\ body\} \end{array}$$

Secondly, it might be scrutinising a variable which is `let`-bound to a (saturated) constructor application:

$$\begin{array}{ll} & \texttt{let}\ x\ \texttt{=}\ C\ x_1 \ldots x_n\ \texttt{in}\ \ldots\texttt{case}\ x\ \texttt{of} \ldots C\ y_1 \ldots y_n\ \texttt{->}\ body \\ \Longrightarrow & \texttt{let}\ x\ \texttt{=}\ C\ x_1 \ldots x_n\ \texttt{in}\ \ldots\texttt{let}\ y_1\ \texttt{=}\ x_1 \ldots y_n\ \texttt{=}\ x_n\ \texttt{in}\ body \end{array}$$

This transformation is useful when x occurs many times in its scope, so the `let` expression is not going to be eliminated. Notice that the arguments to the constructor should be variables, so that no loss of laziness occurs; this can easily be guaranteed by introducing new `let` bindings.

4.2.4 Let-floating

Many `let` bindings can be floated outwards somewhat to increase the applicability of other transformations.

$$\begin{array}{ll} & \texttt{let}\ \{x\ \texttt{=}\ \texttt{let(rec)}\ bind\ \texttt{in}\ e_x\}\ \texttt{in}\ b \\ \Longrightarrow & \texttt{let(rec)}\ bind\ \texttt{in}\ \texttt{let}\ x\ \texttt{=}\ e_x\ \texttt{in}\ b \end{array}$$

This is useful if e_x is a constructor, or even if it is a partial application (then no update is required). Also STG can allocate the two closures at once after the transformation, and before two allocations would be executed.

The only possible disadvantage would be in cases when x would not be evaluated. In this case we would have allocated one extra closure (for *bind*) that would not be allocated in the first form.

Lets can be floated out of many other expressions, like lambda abstractions, case alternatives, letrecs, etc., but in performing these floatings we have to be careful not to float bindings outside binders used by it, so we need information

---

[1] Renaming of variables is performed during the substitution process to avoid name clashes.
[2] We currently handle only the case when it is a variable.

regarding free variables of expressions. In fact we have a more general let floating pass that handles all these cases, but it is done in the STG language. As when translating from Core to STG many new lets are generated, which may also be floated out, we would need such a transformation in the STG level anyway. Thus we perform here only the simpler cases, and leave the others to be done as a STG-to-STG transformation.

When floating lets a sort of space leak may occur, when, for example, a definition is floated to the top level. In this case the definition might not be garbage collected, and therefore keep some (possibly large) amount of memory in the heap which would have been garbage collected if the definition had not been floated. This may significantly increase the number of garbage collections or even, due to th increase in memory usage, make impossible to run the problem.

Although this does not seem to be a problem for most programs, a possible solution would be not to float definitions to the top level or whenever they ae floated have the option of not updating them, that is, recomputing them whenever they are used. As can be seen there is a space-time trade off in this aspect of the optimisation, where one can either choose to share the computation and use more memory or (possibly) recompute it but save space.

4.2.5 Case-of-case

$$\begin{array}{ll} & \texttt{case (case } e \texttt{ of } p_{11} \texttt{ -> } e_{11}\texttt{;}\ldots\texttt{;}p_{1n} \texttt{ -> } e_{1n}\texttt{) of} \\ & p_{21} \texttt{ -> } e_{21}\texttt{;}\ldots\texttt{;}p_{2m} \texttt{ -> } e_{2m} \\ \Longrightarrow & \texttt{case } e \texttt{ of} \\ & p_{11} \texttt{ -> case } e_{11} \texttt{ of } p_{21} \texttt{ -> } e_{21}\ldots p_{2m} \texttt{ -> } e_{2m} \\ & p_{1n} \texttt{ -> case } e_{1n} \texttt{ of } p_{21} \texttt{ -> } e_{21}\ldots p_{2m} \texttt{ -> } e_{2m} \end{array}$$

This was first described by Augustsson in his thesis [1]. It may duplicate code, but not work.

4.3 More Aggressive Options of the Simplifier

In fact we do not have a more aggressive version of the simplifier, but a more aggressive substitution analysis, that will select more expressions to be unfolded, other than the ones we can guarantee not to increase code size (as are used only once) or duplicate work (when the bindees are variables or basic literals).

The options currently available are:

4.3.1 Selecting Candidates for Unfolding

By unfolding function definitions we do not risk duplicating work, but risk duplicating code. This option heuristically selects small functions with certain characteristics to be unfolded.

Currently the bindings selected by this option are the non-recursive ones which define functions with small and relatively simple bodies. It was observed that this class of functions when unfolded usually exposes simple transformations and β-reductions at compile time and therefore (usually) do not result in significant code duplication. As said earlier this is a completely arbitrary selection and one can find examples where it may lead to a large code increase.

By avoiding recursive functions we avoid termination problems and as the bindings are always functions, basic values or variables no risk of duplicating work is incurred.

4.3.2 Unfolding Functions with Higher Order Arguments

The aim of this is to select functions that contain high order arguments to be (possibly transformed and) unfolded, eliminating part of the higher order nature of the program.

For dealing with higher order recursive definitions we expect to incorporate an analysis and transformations similar to those described in [2] for deciding when higher order arguments can be effectively removed by transforming the definitions and then specialising the functions.

For non-recursive higher order functions we will analyse whether their unfolding will expose further reductions and unfold based on this information.

The current implementation of this simply selects non-recursive higher order functions to be unfolded. This handles the unfolding of most monad definitions which allowed us to verify that by unfolding these definitions in a program that makes heavy use of them may give a significant reduction of execution time as well as space usage. Due to the specific nature of monads, these unfoldings expose a high number of compile time β-reductions which result in not only reduction in execution time but also avoid the large code increase one would expect by doing such unfolding.

Also, reducing the higher order nature of the program we make the work of the strictness analyser easier.

4.4 Transformations based on Strictness Analysis

These currently are Worker/Wrapper transformations, which consist of exposing unboxed values to transformations as described in [5]. We will not further describe it due to space limitations, but it is presented in the reference above.

After these transformations, the simplifier is used to unfold wrapper definitions, which by themselves expose many of the transformations the simplifier handles.

Currently the simplifier is used twice (when together with the strictness analyser and the Worker-Wrapper transformation). Before the strictness analysis it simplifies the code, allowing the strictness analysis to be performed in a simpler program, possibly allowing it to do a better or faster job. After strictness analysis the simplifier will unfold wrappers and explore any further transformations exposed by this.

5 STG-to-STG Transformations

Due to space limitations we will not describe the STG language in detail. But it can be seen as a simple functional language, and the only relevant information to understand why these transformations are in the STG rather than in the Core language are specific to the fact that the Glasgow Haskell Compiler is translated into STG and the expressions that are handled by these transformations can be generated during this translation. Therefore, to avoid duplicating identical transformations in the Core Level, we decided to apply them solely in the STG language. Also some of them take advantage of specific characteristics of this abstract machine, and may not be useful transformations for other models.

5.1 Let Floating

The Let Floating pass floats out let bindings as far as possible towards the top level. By as far as possible we mean up to the point where one of its free variables is bound.

The algorithm used is similar to the one described in [6] which is used as part of the full laziness transformation.

Notice the similarity of this pass with the full laziness transformation. In fact, to have full laziness the only differences are that we would need to let-bind the maximal free expressions and also allow the insertion of let bindings between lambda-bound variables.

5.2 Reducing Argument Satisfaction Checks

STG can take advantage of transforming definitions like

```
let g = \v1 v2 -> v1 + v2                  let g = \v1 v2 -> v1 + v2
in let f = \x -> g (x+1)        ==>        in let f = \x y -> g (x+1) y
   in f 1 2                                   in f 1 2
```

In the first one we have an argument satisfaction check for `f` and another for **g**, and in the second as we know that **g**'s application is saturated (has all the arguments that g will need) we can avoid this argument satisfaction check.

6 Some Results

In this section we present some preliminary results in the use of the transformations we described in the previous sections.

Here we have the results of applying different options in some programs from a benchmark suite [3]. All measurements are in CPU seconds in a Sun 4/40.

	No Simpl.	Simpl.	Simpl. + letfloating
exp 3 8	82.7	83.0	83.2
primes	9.2	9.1	10.1
cichelli	99.5	93.6	82.1
clausify	6.1	4.1	4.2
minimax	3.1	2.6	2.3
rewrite	2.2	2.4	2.0
compress	7.5	5.5	5.4

We have not mentioned in the tables above some of the transformation passes we have described. This is due to their minimal impact on these test programs. But for programs which have the appropriate characteristics the results are quite reasonable. Most of the transformations are always beneficial (they do not impose extra overhead to the execution of a program), but a few of them may make a few programs run slower, e.g. let floating (see section 4.2.4), although this seems not to be the typical behaviour. This is the sort of problem that causes a worse performance in programs like `exp 3 8` and `primes`.

The space behaviour is also one of our targets, and although we will not present detailed results here, some transformations also significantly reduce the space requirement of certain programs, but a more detailed analysis of their impact on space usage is still to be done.

The effect on the compilation time of using the transformations above is usually minimal, and in some cases the total compilation time is even reduced, as less (or a simpler version) of the code is passed to the subsequent passes.

7 Conclusions

As expected, the initial results demonstrate that the transformations have quite different effects on different programs. As they do not rely on very expensive analysis techniques, their impact on compile time is minor, so it seems like they can be safely incorporated into the compilation process, as they may cause a reasonable gain in time/space performance.

We are currently working on extending this set of transformations and measuring their influence on the time/space behaviour of programs. This way we expect to supply sufficient information on them allowing one to select which set of transformations best suits particular applications, as well as allowing a user to select more aggressive options when he can afford to trade some extra increase in code size for a reduction in execution speed.

References

[1] L. Augustsson. *Compiling Lazy Functional Languages, Part II.* PhD thesis, Department of Computer Science, Chalmers University of Technology, S–412 96 Göteborg, November 1987.

[2] W. N. Chin and J. Darlington. Removing higher-order expressions by program transformation, February 1991.

[3] W. D. Partain. The nofib benchmarking suite. In J. Launchbury and P. M. Sansom, editors, *Functional Programming, Glasgow 1992*, Ayr, Scotland, 1992. Springer Verlag, Workshops in Computing.

[4] S. L. Peyton Jones. Implementing lazy functional languages on stock hardware: The Spineless Tagless G-machine. *Journal of Functional Programming*, 2(2):127–202, April 1992.

[5] S. L. Peyton Jones and J. Launchbury. Unboxed values as first class citizens in a non-strict functional language. In *Functional Programming Languages and Computer Architecture*, Cambridge, September 1991.

[6] S. L. Peyton Jones and D. Lester. A fully-lazy lambda lifter in Haskell. *Software – Practice and Experience*, 21(5):479–506, May 1991.

Graphical User Interfaces for Haskell

Duncan C. Sinclair*
University of Glasgow

Abstract

User interfaces are normally based on low-level trickery either within the run-time system, or in a separate program which has been connected to the stream I/O system of the language. We present a new twist to this by giving some intelligence to the outside system, which will have greater control of the interface. This has a number of benefits: it makes creating new programs easier, increases the efficiency of the resulting system, and improves the separation between the two halves of the system.

1 Introduction

Many people have written of the problems functional languages have with user interfaces, and have proposed various solutions. These solutions range from the simplistic [9], to the powerful [10], with some truly innovative possibilities explored [4,5].

These systems usually have, at some level, the functional program communicating with an external system, receiving events from the user or system, and replying with requests, telling the system what to do next. This can be done either as low-level run-time calls embedded within the language, or as an external process, connected to the input and output streams of the language. This difference is of no concern, what matters is that at some level there is a protocol between the program written in the functional language and another system which acts as its agent, creating and manipulating the interface.

Mostly, however, control is held firmly by the functional program. We wish to pursue the idea of the user interface being controlled by an external agent which has its own intelligence, and can be programmed separately from the functional program.

2 Tcl and Tk

Tcl and Tk provide a simple yet powerful programming system for developing windowing applications. We will use this system for our externally-controlled interface.

2.1 The Tcl Language

John Ousterhout's Tcl [6], which stands for "Tool command language", is a simple interpreted language, intended to be extended and embedded within an application. Its purpose is to provide a means by which systems may be controlled by users and programmed by the application writer.

*Department of Computing Science, University of Glasgow, Glasgow, G12 8QQ, UK.
E-mail: `sinclair@dcs.gla.ac.uk`

Tcl has strings as its only base type. It can arrange these into arrays or, if they are numeric, regard them as numbers. Here is a small example program to calculate the factorial of 10:

```
proc fac x {
  if $x==1 {return 1}
  return [expr {$x * [fac [expr $x-1]] }]
}
set a 10
puts stdout "The factorial of $a is [fac $a]"
```

Square brackets cause in-line evaluation. Curly brackets are a form of quoting, usually used to hold program fragments which will be interpreted in a recursive manner.

2.2 The Tk Toolkit

Tk [7], also by John Ousterhout, is a toolkit for the X Window System [8], based around the Tcl language. It allows the creation of user interfaces built out of components such as buttons, menus, and dialogs. This can either be done in a imperative language such as C, or in Tcl. One feature of this is that it is possible to write complete programs in Tcl, using Tk for its interface. It is also possible for users or external processes to control Tcl/Tk applications using the Tcl language.

Here is a very trivial Tk program, written in Tcl:

```
label .hello -text "Hello, World!"
pack append . .hello {}
```

Without going into too much detail, this creates a small label which says "Hello, World!", and displays it in a window.

This two-line script is at least an order of magnitude shorter than the equivalent in C, or any functional system where the interface to the window system is at a similar level to that of C. This makes writing user interfaces much easier than before, and with Tcl at hand no power is lost.

2.3 Multiprocessing

The programmer's first introduction to the Tcl/Tk system is through a simple shell, called `wish`. It can either be run interactively, for experimentation and debugging, or in a batch mode, submitting scripts to the interpreter. Normally, the script will set up an interface, with some action procedures to be executed when buttons or menus are activated. Once the script has been evaluated the Tcl interpreter, rather than exiting, waits for any other commands to arrive from the user or other external processes. This multiple input scheme can be thought of as some sort of multiprocessing. Such pseudo-multiprocessing can be thwarted if any "process" gives the interpreter a command which does not terminate.

2.4 Extending the Language

By modifying the `wish` shell with a little bit of C programming, we have created a new shell program which have called `swish`, with extra commands added to the Tcl language.

We have added three commands, the first, `spawnchannels`, is responsible for spawning an external process, creating three communications channels (i.e. pipes) between the existing and new processes.

The first channel feeds straight into the Tcl interpreter, allowing the external process to feed commands to the running Tcl/Tk program. This can be anything from supplying a complete Tcl program for execution, to the occasional procedure call to update state or modify the program's appearance.

The other two commands are tied to the remaining two channels, and allow messages to be sent back from the Tcl program to the external system. We partition these messages into asynchronous events (the `event` command), and synchronous replies (the `reply` command). These are sent on independent channels to help avoid deadlock, which would otherwise have to be solved by some process of selecting, separating, and buffering these messages in the external system (this is especially difficult when the external system is a functional program). One major advantage of this separation is that we can run the two systems in an asynchronous manner, which makes possible true concurrent operation.

3 Haskell with Tcl

We will now look at what happens when the external process is actually a Haskell [1] program. We chose Haskell because of its good I/O primitives, and good support from the language designers and implementors.

3.1 Process Communication

To `swish`, the Haskell program is the external process, but naturally it works the other way around from the point of view of the functional programmer. So in this section we will talk of the Tcl process as being the external process.

Using the Haskell optional request ReadChannels, and the standard AppenChan request, a Haskell program can communicate with our external process through the three channels created by the `swish` program. The Chalmers Haskell B compiler [3] also provides 'TICK' and 'TIMEOUT' channels which are useful for creating "real-time" graphical programs. Figure 1 show how this works.

We have not yet investigated the best way to structure the functional code, and admittedly early efforts have been difficult to program and read. It is for this reason that we omit a sample of what such a program looks like.

The structure of the Haskell program we use is similar to the typical event-loop found in imperative languages, but unfortunately can get complicated because of the amount of state and channels being passed between functions. Using mechanisms similar to that in the Concurrent Clean system [2], it may be possible to structure the functional program in a cleaner way.

3.2 Examples

Typically, the Haskell program takes no part in the layout of the interface, and how it works; all this is left to the Tcl program. The Haskell program deals with higher-level decisions, such as what information will appear in various windows, while the Tcl program is left to decide how this is done.

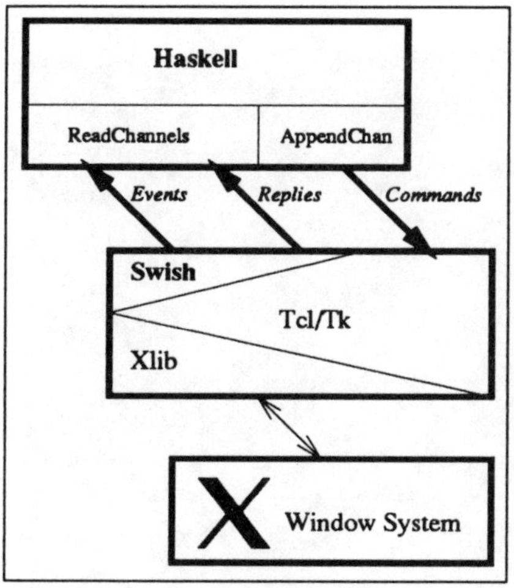

Figure 1: Communication between Haskell and Tcl/Tk

An Alarm Clock

For our first example, we have a simple alarm clock program, in which the Haskell program keeps note of what the time is, and when it should activate the alarm. Every second it advises tcl what the time is, using a procedure defined in the script that `swish` has executed. The Tcl/Tk process then updates the display, without the Haskell program knowing whether it is running an analogue or digital clock. When the user sets the alarm, the dialog is conducted exclusively within the Tcl/Tk process. When this is concluded, the Haskell program receives an 'alarm set' event, telling it when to activate the alarm.

This shows how a greater degree of separation between the interface and functionality can be reached using this method, compared with other methods where the distinction tends to be blurred.

When the alarm is activated, our Haskell program sends a command to the Tcl/Tk process to display a flashing window. This window is then completely managed by the Tcl/Tk process, flashing it every second until the user acknowledges it. Meanwhile, the Haskell process continues counting time.

A Maze Game

As a more substantial example we created a three dimensional maze game, written in Haskell, using Tcl/Tk for its interface. The general idea is for the player to completely navigate the maze, using simple commands such as turn left, turn right and move forward. An indication of the separation between the interface and the program is that the two halves were written by different people in different countries.

The Haskell program is responsible for looking after the creation of the maze, keeping track of where the player is in the maze, and the current view of the maze. It takes events such as 'left', 'right', and 'forward' and causes the display to be updated by sending to the Tcl/Tk process a list of where there are walls visible.

The Tcl/Tk program sets up the display, which includes buttons that the player uses to navigate the maze, plus a perspective view of the maze as 'seen' in the direction the

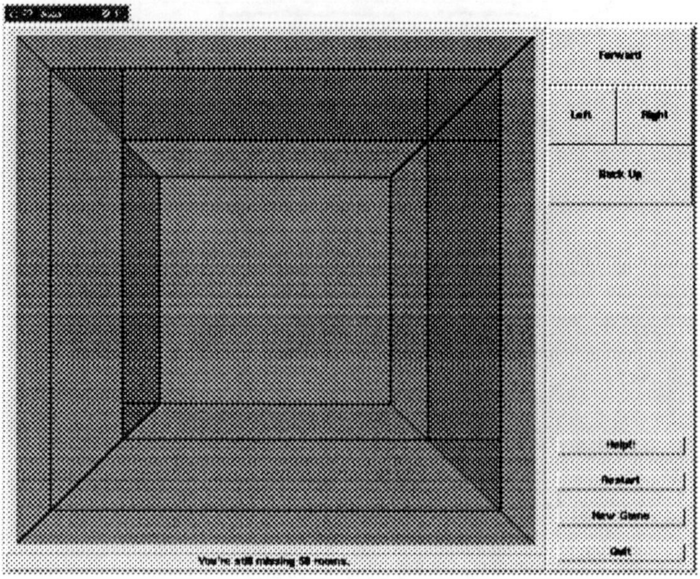

Figure 2: Functional Maze in X

player is facing. When a button is pressed by the player, the program passes on the appropriate event to the Haskell process. It also receives the list of visible walls, and updates the display accordingly.

Neither process 'knows' what the other does with messages sent, and either could be implemented totally differently, without affecting the other.

Figure 2 shows what the maze program looks like. A copy of the source may be requested from the author using electronic mail.

4 Discussion

In the abstract we claimed that our system would do three things for us: make programming the system easier, make it more efficient, and improve the modular separation between the functional program and its interface.

We claim that the Tcl/Tk system is easier to program than typical other systems for creating interfaces. One major reason for this is that the interface is written in an imperative language, which we would argue is more suited to interface creation and manipulation than functional languages. Our evidence for this is simply that we find it hard to create user interfaces within our functional programs. In our system almost all of the interface handling is transparent to the functional program.

We feel it is more efficient, simply because two heads are better than one. Even in other two-process systems what usually happens is that one process is always waiting for the other. They run synchronously, to ensure that they can predict what the next input will be. Also, the system external to the functional program is usually not smart enough to do anything useful. With our Tcl/Tk system, we can program it to do other things when not doing anything else. The flashing alarm is an example of this.

In any system it is good for the user interface to be separate from the main functionality of the program. This increases portability between systems where only the interface would need rewritten, and helps keep interface decisions out of the main body of code where it may lead to problems later. Our system clearly helps in achieving this aim by having the user interface defined in a totally different language than the main body of code. We feel that this demarcation is a good thing, with functional languages being used for the parts of the programming task to which their special abilities are suited.

Acknowledgements

Thanks to: John K. Ousterhout, the author of Tcl and Tk; Satnam Singh, for motivating me to do this; Gilbert Cockton, for motivating my desire to get it right; Patrick Sansom, who helped on a previous version of the system; and lastly Carsten Kehler Holst who motivated and implemented the Haskell part of the maze example.

Bibliography

1. P Hudak et al, "Report on the functional programming language Haskell, Version 1.2," *SIGPLAN Notices* 27 (May 1992).
2. P. M. Achten, J. H. G. van Groningen & M. J. Plasmeijer, "High level specification of I/O in functional languages," in *Functional Programming, Glasgow 1992*, J Launchbury & PM Sansom, eds., Springer-Verlag, Workshops in Computing, Ayr, Scotland, 1992.
3. Lennart Augustsson, "Haskell B. user's manual," From Haskell B distribution, Aug 1992.
4. Magnus Carlsson, "Fudgets – A Graphical Interface in a Lazy Functional Language," Draft, Chalmers University, Sweden, August 1992.
5. Andrew Dwelly, "Graphical user interfaces and dialogue combinators," ECRC, 1989.
6. John K. Ousterhout, "Tcl: An Embeddable Command Language," in *Proc. USENIX Winter Conference 1990*.
7. John K. Ousterhout, "An X11 Toolkit Based on the Tcl Language," in *Proc. USENIX Winter Conference 1991*.
8. Robert W. Scheifler & Jim Gettys, "The X Window System," *ACM Transactions on Graphics vol. 5, No. 2* (Apr 1986).
9. Duncan C. Sinclair, "Graphical User Interfaces from Functional Languages," Final Year Project, May 1989.
10. Satnam Singh, "Using XView / X11 from Miranda," in *Functional Programming, Glasgow 1991*, Workshops in Computing, Springer-Verlag, Aug 1991.

Formulating Haskell

Simon Thompson
Computing Laboratory, University of Kent
Canterbury, CT2 7NF, U.K.*

Abstract

The functional programming language Haskell is examined from the point of view of proving programs correct. Particular features explored include the data type definition facilities, classes, the behaviour of patterns and guards and the monad approach to IO in the Glasgow Haskell compiler.

1 Introduction

Haskell [Hudak *et al.*, 1992, Hudak and Fasel, 1992] is a lazy functional programming language which is likely to become a *de facto* as well as a *de jure* standard academically and commercially. It is often said that a crucial part of the appeal of functional languages is the ease with which proofs concerning functional programs can be written. It is also widely accepted that if proof is to be taken seriously, it needs to be formalised, and to be checked by machine[1].

The aim of this paper is to initiate discussion on the form that a logic for Haskell might take. It is based to some degree on the author's previous work on devising a logic for Miranda, [Thompson, 1989], which in turn builds on earlier work in the area. Implementation of the logic for Miranda is in progress at the University of Kent (funded by SERC grant GR/F 29134), and it is expected that the system will be freely available within the next year.

The paper begins with a discussion of the carrier logic for the axiomatisation, and the relation between the semantics of the language and the logic. Next types and their operators, including equality, are axiomatised. Classes are unique to Haskell, and their effect on verification is discussed in Section 4. The logical form of definitions is described next, and in particular the unfortunate interaction between pattern matching and guards is explored. IO in the Glasgow Haskell compiler is defined in terms of an IO monad – we show how the monadic approach is amenable to formal treatment in section 6. The paper concludes with a number of miscellaneous points.

One issue addressed throughout the paper is the choice of which parts of the language are amenable to formal treatment. For example, only some of the numeric types are logically tractable.

*E-mail: `sjt@ukc.ac.uk`

[1] This paradigm is different from that prevailing in mathematics, where proofs are subject to social scrutiny, but the nature of proofs about programs seems to be sufficiently different to make this sort of check highly unlikely.

2 Logic

The basic intuition behind a functional program is that expressions denote values and expressions of ground type are evaluated to give printable values or results. It seems sensible for the logic to be one of *equations* between expressions of the language. These will be written

`e ≡ f`

where `e` and `f` are Haskell expressions. The symbol $\equiv$ is used in preference to `=` and `==` for reasons which will become clear. The relation $\equiv$ is an equivalence relation, and obeys Leibniz's law: equals may be substituted for equals in terms and formulas.

Since the language is typed, so should the logic itself, making an equation of the form above invalid unless `e` and `f` have the same (or unifiable) types. (Logicians call this a *many-sorted* logic.)

Expressions in Haskell need not denote a defined value – evaluation of an expression may loop indefinitely, for instance. This phenomenon may be rendered logically in a number of ways: expressions can be permitted not to take values, giving a partial logic, or their value may be the undefined value, or 'bottom', $\perp$. The latter 'LCF' approach is adopted here, it is both simple and sufficiently expressible; further discussion of the issue can be found in [Thompson, 1989].

What should be the logic in which these equations are embedded? Lacking arguments to the contrary, the simplest option of first-order (many-sorted) predicate calculus seems appropriate. It is open whether it should be classical or constructive; note however that for simple $\forall\exists$ (or Π^0_2) statements, such as the assertion that a function from `Int` to `Int` is total, their strength is the same.

As a part of the standardisation exercise, it seems that a formal semantics for the language will emerge. This allows the possibility that the soundness of a proposed logic can be verified: every assertion or theorem of the system can be checked to see whether it is indeed valid in the formal interpretation. Soundness is clearly a minimal requirement, but can be problematic depending upon the form of semantics adopted: issues of full abstraction and the case of parallel `or` come to mind.

Again given the semantics, the converse to soundness can be examined: is every assertion validated by the semantics derivable in the logic? Such a result is unlikely in view of Gödel's incompleteness results, but *relative* completeness results have been established for Hoare logics of imperative languages.

3 Types

This section examines the way that types and operations over them are to be axiomatised.

3.1 Algebraic Types

Algebraic types can be treated in a uniform way, as they come with constructors and definition by pattern matching, but no predefined operators.

The `Boolean` type is a typical example of a simple algebraic type: it is an enumerated type. Its elements are `True`, `False` and $\perp$, and therefore theorems valid in Boolean algebra, like

```
x || not x ≡ True
```

will *fail* to be valid, since

```
⊥ || not ⊥ ≡ ⊥
```

This was taken as one justification for introducing the quantifier $\forall_{\mathtt{def}}$ in the logic for Miranda. Familiar theorems are rendered thus

```
(∀def x :: Bool)(x || not x ≡ True)
```

In a similar way, the induction principle (or elimination rule) for the type can take two forms

$$\frac{\mathtt{P(True)} \quad \mathtt{P(False)}}{(\forall_{\mathtt{def}}\ \mathtt{x} :: \mathtt{Bool}).\mathtt{P(x)}}$$

and

$$\frac{\mathtt{P(True)} \quad \mathtt{P(False)} \quad \mathtt{P(}\bot\mathtt{)}}{(\forall\ \mathtt{x} :: \mathtt{Bool}).\mathtt{P(x)}}$$

It is a matter of general principle that from the latter rule can be derived the rule of exhaustion:

```
(∀ x :: Bool)(x ≡ True ∨ x ≡ False ∨ x ≡ ⊥)
```

On the other hand, an axiom to assert the distinctness of the constructors is required:

```
(False ≢ True ∧ ⊥ ≢ False ∧ ⊥ ≢ True)
```

It is logically sufficient to assert one such axiom, as from this those at other types can be derived.

A general algebraic type like that of lists is rather more complex. The type is inhabited by finite lists like `[2,3,4]`, but also by partial lists, such as `[2,⊥,3]` and `4:⊥:3:⊥` and by infinite lists like `[1,3,..]`. Some theorems for lists are valid over the whole type

```
map (f.g) ≡ map f . map g
```

whilst others are only valid for finite lists (possibly containing ⊥)

```
reverse (reverse x) ≡ x
```

and still others are restricted to finite lists of *defined* elements

```
product x == 0 ≡ elem 0 x
```

Properly to reflect these differences, in [Thompson, 1989] restricted quantifiers and induction rules were introduced. Typical of such a rule is

$$\frac{\mathtt{P([])} \quad (\forall_{\mathtt{def}}\ \mathtt{x} :: \mathtt{a})(\forall_{\mathtt{def}}\ \mathtt{l} :: \mathtt{[a]}).\mathtt{P(l)} \Rightarrow \mathtt{P(x:l)}}{(\forall_{\mathtt{def}}\ \mathtt{l} :: \mathtt{[a]}).\mathtt{P(l)}}$$

This characterises the finite lists of defined elements. Note that often the proof of the second hypothesis will be a consequence of

```
(∀def x :: a)(∀ l :: [a]).P(l) ⇒P(x:l)
```

in which the list `l` will simply be an arbitrary list.

The *infinite* lists are described quite differently. They can be seen as members of a *greatest* fixed point, with equality over them characterised by a bisimulation-like co-induction principle [Pitts, 1992]. Pitts characterises the infinite elements as a greatest fixed point of an inductive definition, and defines the equality relation over the set of elements in a similar way. For lists the principle states that two lists `l` and `m` are equal if `l` $\asymp$ `m` for some *pre-equality* relation $\asymp$. The relation $\asymp$ is a pre-equality relation if and only if for all `l` and `m`,

$$\mathtt{l} \asymp \mathtt{m} \Rightarrow (\mathtt{l} \equiv [\,] \equiv \mathtt{m}) \vee (\mathtt{l} \equiv \mathtt{a} : \mathtt{l}' \wedge \mathtt{m} \equiv \mathtt{b} : \mathtt{m}' \wedge \mathtt{a} \equiv \mathtt{b} \wedge \mathtt{l}' \asymp \mathtt{m}')$$

The attractive feature of his approach is that it works for all algebraic types, such as solutions of

```
data LambdaModel = Fun (LambdaModel -> LambdaModel)
```

giving a characterisation of equality of these elements of a model of the untyped λ-calculus. The disadvantage of his approach is that the principle requires a *second-order* logic for its formulation, since two elements are equal if *for some pre-equality relation* .... A similar problem presents itself with induction principles, of course, and the usual expedient is to replace the characterisation by a *schema*, restricting the pre-equality relations to those which are definable in the logic.

Alternatively, mathematical induction may be used to define equality over types which appear only in the range position of a function-space constructor on the right-hand side of their definitions. For lists we have:

`l` $\equiv$ `m` if and only if $(\forall_{\mathtt{def}}$ `n :: Nat`$)$(`take n l` $\equiv$ `take n m`)

where `take` is defined in the standard prelude.

This fragmentation of the principles of induction over the type of lists seems to be unavoidable: the general principle of induction for lazy lists is too weak to include the others as special cases, since it is restricted to *admissible* predicates. [Paulson, 1987] contains details of the general rule as well as providing a good background reference to the LCF approach.

3.2 Built-in Types

Built-in types are akin to abstract types: no direct access is given to the (machine) representation, rather manipulation is through predefined operators. Axioms for these types therefore have to reflect as much of the structure of the type as is thought necessary. In the case of floating-point and complex numbers, it seems highly unlikely that any satisfactory (but sound!) axiomatisation exists, and we would argue that this part of the language be omitted from the logic[2]

It is therefore appropriate to restrict attention to the integral and rational types. Even then, giving a sufficiently abstract presentation of the fixed-precision integers, `Int`, is difficult, so we restrict attention to the full integers, `Integer`. In the Miranda logic a subtype of the integers, `Nat`, is introduced, allowing theorems on properties of natural number-functions to be expressed directly. This means that Miranda definitions have to be read as being overloaded in a limited way, but it presents no theoretical difficulties.

How are the integers and operations over them axiomatised? The system will include the *graphs* of the operations, giving their values at each argument sequence. This will not be enough to axiomatise the primitive operations, `primQuotRem` and the like, which will also be specified by their primitive recursive definitions. From these definitions can be derived the usual theorems such as associativity of `(+)`, or indeed the results themselves may be included

[2]The IEEE characterisation of floating point operations seems to be too low level to be usable in verification. It is perfect for the specification of a floating-point unit, for instance.

as primitives. (From the point of view of a logical characterisation, any built-in operation adds some uncertainty as to its precise behaviour.)

Function types are characterised by function composition, which is a defined operation, and (logical) equality between functions. Basic to functional programming is that functions are characterised by their behaviour, meaning the values they return, and that programs have the same behaviour when equals are substituted for equals. Equality on functions is given by the *extensionality rule*:

$$\frac{(\forall \texttt{x} :: \texttt{a})(\ \texttt{f x} \equiv \texttt{g x}\ )}{\texttt{f} \equiv \texttt{g}}$$

This rule is adhered to by Haskell – it is a matter of some delicacy in language design to ensure that this is the case. Tuples do *not* obey the extensionality condition. This is because

```
fst (⊥,⊥) ≡ ⊥            fst ⊥ ≡ ⊥
snd (⊥,⊥) ≡ ⊥            snd ⊥ ≡ ⊥
```

giving $(\perp, \perp)$ and $\perp$ the same components, but because of the behaviour of pattern matching over pairs, the function

```
test (x,y) = 27
```

returns 27 on (⊥,⊥) and ⊥ on ⊥. This adds a slight complication to the characterisation of equality. Any advantage of such a definition is at the *implementation* level: to check whether a member of a product type is defined (i.e. unequal to ⊥) simply requires a check that it is a pair; if $\perp$ and $(\perp, \perp)$ are identified, the pair (e_1, e_2) is defined if and only if one of the expressions e_1, e_2 is defined, so a parallel evaluation of the expressions e_1 and e_2 is required. More is said about pattern matching in general in Section 5.

4 Classes

Classes give a general treatment of *overloading* or *ad hoc* polymorphism. Functions which are polymorphic in the usual sense of parametric polymorphism are amenable to uniform treatment. At each type the same defining equation is used, with the same logical characterisation. How much will this be true of type classes; in other words, how much can logical structure be built on top of the class structure?

There seem to be two distinct cases. On the one hand, classes like `Text` and all the numeric classes will in general *fail* to share any significant properties. In the first case this is plain, but for numeric classes, it is an unfortunate truth that, for example, addition on `Int` and `Integer` behave in fundamentally different ways, even though the two types inhabit the same classes.

More optimistically, for the classes `Eq` and `Ord` the intention is that operations of equality and ordering are defined on their members. Even if the implementations are different, all equality relations should be (partial) equivalence relations on their domains; all orderings should be pseudo-partial orderings. (They will not be total since they will in general fail to be reflexive.) In the logic this could be reflected by a *logical class*.

```
logical class (Eq a) => Equality a
where
symm  is (∀ x,y :: a)( x==y ≡ y==x )
trans is (∀ x,y,z :: a)
             ( x==y ≡ True ∧ y==z ≡ True ⇒ x==z ≡ True)
```

For a type to inhabit this logical class, *proofs* of the theorems `symm` and `trans` have to be given.

The method of `derived` instantiations could be extended to the logic. A symmetrical and transitive relation on type a will be extended to a similar relation on type `[a]` by the standard definition of equality, for instance.

A similar treatment of ordering is possible.

```
class (Eq a) => DefEq a
where
defined :: a -> Bool
defined x = x==x

logical class (Ord a) => Ordering a
where
asymm is (∀ x,y :: a)
             ( x<=y ≡ True ∧ y<=x ≡ True ⇒ x==y ≡ True)
total is (∀def x,y :: a)( x<=y ≡ True ∨ y<=x ≡ True )
trans is ...
```

In these examples, the same name is given to occurrences of the same formula at different type instances: the polymorphism in the formula is parametric. The *proofs* of the formulae are defined differently at different types, an *ad hoc* overloading. It is also possible to give an *ad hoc* overloading to names with, for instance, `exhaustion`, used to name the appropriate axiom of exhaustion at each type.

```
exhaust.Bool is (∀ x :: Bool)(x ≡ True ∨ x ≡ False ∨ x ≡ ⊥)
exhaust.Nat is
     (∀ x :: Nat)(x ≡ ⊥ ∨ x ≡ 0 ∨ (∃ df y :: Nat)(x ≡ y+1))
```

Whether this mechanism has other than mnemonic value remains to be seen.

5 Definitions

Haskell definitions have the form of equations, so it is plausible that the `=` symbol of the language can simply be replaced by the ≡ of the logic. In a simple definition of the form

```
f x y = x+y*y
```

this is the case, but the addition of pattern matching, guards and scopes (in the form of `where` and `let`) makes the situation substantially more complicated. A function will be defined by a sequence of equations, and the order of these will be significant. Take the case of

```
g [13]      = 27
g (a:b:x) = 32
```

Given the argument `[bot,2,3]`, when `bot` is defined by

```
bot = bot
```

the result of evaluating `g [bot,2,3]` is undefined (at least with Gofer and the Glasgow prototype – `hbi` gives a result!). Re-ordering the equations gives the result 32 on the same argument. A thorough analysis of the sequential nature of pattern matching both within and between clauses of a definition is required to give a full rendering of a definition by pattern matching. Details of the transformation are explained in [Thompson, 1989], with the example of g above giving

```
g [13] ≡ 27  ∧  (a==a ≡ True ⇒ g (a:b:x) ≡ 32)
```

The rules mentioned cover pattern matching and guards within function definitions.

5.1 Patterns & Guards

One aspect of definitions is particularly complicated to explain; this is the interaction of pattern matching and guards. In definitions without guards, such as

$$\begin{array}{lll} f & p_1 = & e_1 \\ f & p_2 = & e_2 \\ & \ldots & \end{array}$$

if an argument matches more than one pattern, the first matching equation will be used. In the case that guards are added,

$$\begin{array}{llllll} f & p_1 & \mid & g_{11} & = & e_{11} \\ & & \mid & g_{12} & = & e_{12} \\ & & & \ldots\ldots & & \\ f & p_2 & \mid & g_{21} & = & e_{21} \\ & & \mid & g_{22} & = & e_{22} \\ & & & \ldots\ldots & & \\ & \ldots & & & & \end{array}$$

it may be possible for an argument to match p_1, but to *fail* the guards g_{11}, g_{12}, ...and so to 'fall through' to the subsequent equation. The 'entry conditions' for this equation are no longer being in the complement of the pattern p_1, since now there is the possibility of being in the unification of p_1 and p_2 combined with failing the conjunction of the guards g_{11}, g_{12}, ... In such a case the logical translation must treat the second equation in two different ways. The first gives a rewrite of the second equation to

$$\begin{array}{ll} f\ \sigma(\ p_2) & \mid\ \sigma(\ g_{21}) = \sigma(\ e_{21}) \\ & \mid\ \sigma(\ g_{22}) = \sigma(\ e_{22}) \\ & \ldots\ldots \\ \ldots & \end{array}$$

where σ is the most-general substitution unifying the patterns p_1 and p_2, guarded by the expression

$$\sigma(\ g_{11})\ \&\&\ \sigma(\ g_{12})\ \&\&\ \ldots$$

whilst the second is given by unifying the complement of p_1 with p_2.

This problem is made worse still if the first equation has local definitions given by a `where` clause. In such an eventuality, the guards will use the identifiers defined locally, and it is not enough to use the same definitions redefined to use the pattern variables given by the substitution σ, since name clashes may result with definitions local to the second equation; renaming of local definitions will be necessary in general.

A simple way of removing this problem is to add a compulsory `Else` or `True` case,

```
f p1 | g11 =  e11
     | g12 =  e12
       .....
     | True =  e1k
```

so that once a pattern is matched by an argument, the function is committed to using this pattern. Many functions have this feature, and it is not clear that the extra power of avoiding it in certain circumstances is worth the extra effort required to understand function definitions. This undesirable feature is shared by Miranda, but not by Standard ML, in which guards are replaced by the

```
if ... then ... else ...
```

expression.

One feature differentiating Haskell from Miranda is the strength of the expression language. In Miranda, functions can only be defined in a series of equations: there is no explicit lambda, and in particular, case analyses are always in the form of a series of equational clauses. This restricts the programmer somewhat, but is an advantage when explaining the language in a logical form. The description of Haskell needs to include in some way or another how the `case` and lambda expression forms evaluate: these will need a collection of *axiom schemes* to cover all eventualities. In Miranda, by contrast, the explanation is given in the logical translation of the function definitions.

5.2 Irrefutable Patterns

Haskell introduces the notion of an irrefutable pattern: a pattern which is only matched on demand. All top-level pattern bindings are irrefutable by default, and it is useful to make irrefutable the argument patterns in interactive functions (for background discussion see [Thompson, 1990]). An example is

```
f ~(a:x) = a + f x
```

This can be described either by

```
f y = (head y) + f (tail y)
```

or by

```
f y = a + f x
      where
      (a:x) = y
```

The latter seems to be more in the spirit of the definitions than does the former.

The effect of a pattern binding can be a program error – what is the effect in the logic? If an axiom of the form

```
(a:x) = e
```

is introduced, and the expression `e` evaluates to `[]`, the effect is to give

```
(a:x) ≡ []
```

which contradicts the distinctness of the list constructors, and is indeed a logical contradiction. To safeguard against this in the logic, it is necessary to write

```
matches e == True ⇒ (a:x) ≡ e
```

where `matches` has the definition:

```
matches (a:x) = True
```

This has the effect of leaving `a` and `x` undefined when `matches e` is not `True`. As patterns are explained in a similar way, by the translation from

```
f p@q = blah
```

to

```
f p = blah
      where
      q = p
```

5.3 Scopes

A local definition is given either by a `let`, giving a definition local to an expression, or a `where`, giving a definition local to the right hand side of a clause of a definition. The simple effect of a definition is a *conjunction* of the logical effect of the local and the global, with a restriction on the scope of the names involved. In other words, the logic will naturally inherit the scoping of Haskell.

The scope of some definitions in `where` clauses can be restricted to a subset of the right hand sides. Given the type

```
data mo = Eenie Int | Meenie Bool
```

definitions like

```
f :: mo -> ...
f x | isEenie x  = ... a ...
    | isMeenie x = ... b ...
                   where
                   (Eenie a)  = x
                   (Meenie b) = x
```

are common. The scope of `a` is the first equation and of `b` the second. Thus `where` is eliminated in favour of `let`.

Similarly, modules and abstract data types provide control on the visibility of definitions. This can be reflected in the logic (for ADTs, say) by making visible outside the implementation scope only those theorems which do not refer to the underlying representation.

6 Input/Output

Input/output in Haskell can be programmed by means of streams or continuations. Stream programs are simply lazy-list manipulating functions, and the methods of verifying them are inherited from lists. An advantage of the stream approach is that it introduces explicit notations for the values on input and output, but a major disadvantage is a consequence of the *absence* of interleaving information in the functions. Much work is needed to translate stream functions into descriptions of *traces* of input/output behaviour. A trace is a sequence of input and output actions of the form

```
[ r c , w c ]
```

which describes the action of reading `c` followed by writing `c`. Details of how to translate stream programs into traces can be found in [Thompson, 1990].

The Glasgow Haskell compiler supports input/output by a third, primitive mechanism: *monads*, [Peyton Jones and Wadler, 1993, Wadler, 1992]. Preliminary work suggests that a trace description of monadic IO is quite straightforward. An interaction of type

```
IO a
```

will have a trace of the form

$$([rc, wc, ...], x)$$

where `[ r c , w c , ... ]` is a trace of I/O actions and `x` is a value of type `a`. The basic operations of the monad can then be described by their traces. Getting a character, `getcIO`, which is of type `IO Char` will have traces of the form

```
( [ r ch ] , ch )
```

where `ch` is a character. `putcIO` is a function from `Char` to `IO ()`; `putcIO ch` will have the trace

```
( [ w ch ] , () )
```

The combination operator, `bindIO` has type

```
IO a -> (a -> IO b) -> IO b
```

We can describe traces of `bindIO m f` in terms of traces of `m` and `f c` (with `x` in type `a`) thus. If `(s,x)` is a trace of `m` and `(t,y)` a trace of `f x` then

```
( s++t , y )
```

is a trace of `bindIO m f`.

These trace descriptions can be seen as primitive, or can be proved on the basis of the implementations of the operations in [Peyton Jones and Wadler, 1993], assuming a suitable axiomatisation of the underlying C compiler! The simple operation of the `bindIO` functional is due to the data dependencies evident in the underlying implementation, for instance.

Whether this approach can scale up to tackle real problems is open, as indeed is the field of verifying interactive programs itself.

7 Other Issues

In discussing the interpretation of definitions, such as

```
fac x | x == 0 = 1
      | x > 0  = x * fac (x-1)
```

the equational rendering

```
x == 0 ≡ True ⇒ fac x ≡ 1
x > 0 ≡ True  ⇒ fac x ≡ x * fac (x-1)
```

implies that `fac` is a fixed point of the definition, but not necessarily the *least* one. It is open whether this needs to be incorporated – further discussion can be found in [Thompson, 1989].

8 Conclusion

The paper addresses the design of the Haskell programming language from the point of view of giving (formal) proofs of correctness of functional programs. It is evident that Haskell share the elegance and simplicity of other lazy languages, but that certain features cause difficulties for the verifier. The ability freely to combine pattern matching, guards and local definitions causes difficulties beyond the advantage gained. Classes come in two forms: ones like the numerical classes where the overloading is conventional or mnemonic, since the operations share little but name; and the others, like the equality class, in which the operations have a common axiomatisation. It is the latter form which the verifier can work with more effectively.

I am grateful to Gareth Howells and Mark Longley for discussions about

Haskell and functional program verification. The referees made useful suggestions about both presentation and content.

References

[Hudak and Fasel, 1992] Paul Hudak and Joseph H. Fasel. A gentle introduction to Haskell. *ACM SIGPLAN Notices*, 27(5), 1992.

[Hudak *et al.*, 1992] Paul Hudak, Simon Peyton Jones, and Philip Wadler (Editors). Report on the Programming Language Haskell, version 1.2. *ACM SIGPLAN Notices*, 27(5), 1992.

[Paulson, 1987] Lawrence C. Paulson. *Logic and Computation — Interactive proof with Cambridge LCF.* Cambridge University Press, 1987.

[Peyton Jones and Wadler, 1993] Simon L. Peyton Jones and Philip Wadler. Imperative functional programming. In *Twentieth Annual Symposium on Principles of Programming Languages (POPL).* ACM, 1993.

[Pitts, 1992] Andrew M. Pitts. A co-induction principle for recursively defined domains. Preprint – Computer Laboratory, University of Cambridge, 1992.

[Thompson, 1989] Simon J. Thompson. A logic for Miranda. *Formal Aspects of Computing*, 1, 1989.

[Thompson, 1990] Simon J. Thompson. Interactive functional programs: a method and a formal semantics. In David A. Turner, editor, *Research Topics in Functional Programming.* Addison Wesley, 1990.

[Wadler, 1992] Philip Wadler. The essence of functional programming. In *Nineteenth Annual Symposium on Principles of Programming Languages (POPL).* ACM, 1992.

Author Index

Published in 1990–92

AI and Cognitive Science '89, Dublin City University, Eire, 14–15 September 1989
A. F. Smeaton and G. McDermott (Eds.)

Specification and Verification of Concurrent Systems, University of Stirling, Scotland, 6–8 July 1988
C. Rattray (Ed.)

Semantics for Concurrency, Proceedings of the International BCS-FACS Workshop, Sponsored by Logic for IT (S.E.R.C.), University of Leicester, UK, 23–25 July 1990
M. Z. Kwiatkowska, M. W. Shields and R. M. Thomas (Eds.)

Functional Programming, Glasgow 1989
Proceedings of the 1989 Glasgow Workshop, Fraserburgh, Scotland, 21–23 August 1989
K. Davis and J. Hughes (Eds.)

Persistent Object Systems, Proceedings of the Third International Workshop, Newcastle, Australia, 10–13 January 1989
J. Rosenberg and D. Koch (Eds.)

Z User Workshop, Oxford 1989, Proceedings of the Fourth Annual Z User Meeting, Oxford, 15 December 1989
J. E. Nicholls (Ed.)

Formal Methods for Trustworthy Computer Systems (FM89), Halifax, Canada, 23–27 July 1989
Dan Craigen (Editor) and Karen Summerskill (Assistant Editor)

Security and Persistence, Proceedings of the International Workshop on Computer Architecture to Support Security and Persistence of Information, Bremen, West Germany, 8–11 May 1990
John Rosenberg and J. Leslie Keedy (Eds.)

Women into Computing: Selected Papers 1988–1990
Gillian Lovegrove and Barbara Segal (Eds.)

3rd Refinement Workshop (organised by BCS-FACS, and sponsored by IBM UK Laboratories, Hursley Park and the Programming Research Group, University of Oxford), Hursley Park, 9–11 January 1990
Carroll Morgan and J. C. P. Woodcock (Eds.)

Designing Correct Circuits, Workshop jointly organised by the Universities of Oxford and Glasgow, Oxford, 26–28 September 1990
Geraint Jones and Mary Sheeran (Eds.)

Functional Programming, Glasgow 1990
Proceedings of the 1990 Glasgow Workshop on Functional Programming, Ullapool, Scotland, 13–15 August 1990
Simon L. Peyton Jones, Graham Hutton and Carsten Kehler Holst (Eds.)

4th Refinement Workshop, Proceedings of the 4th Refinement Workshop, organised by BCS-FACS, Cambridge, 9–11 January 1991
Joseph M. Morris and Roger C. Shaw (Eds.)

AI and Cognitive Science '90, University of Ulster at Jordanstown, 20–21 September 1990
Michael F. McTear and Norman Creaney (Eds.)

Software Re-use, Utrecht 1989, Proceedings of the Software Re-use Workshop, Utrecht, The Netherlands, 23–24 November 1989
Liesbeth Dusink and Patrick Hall (Eds.)

Z User Workshop, 1990, Proceedings of the Fifth Annual Z User Meeting, Oxford, 17–18 December 1990
J.E. Nicholls (Ed.)

IV Higher Order Workshop, Banff 1990
Proceedings of the IV Higher Order Workshop, Banff, Alberta, Canada, 10–14 September 1990
Graham Birtwistle (Ed.)

ALPUK91, Proceedings of the 3rd UK Annual Conference on Logic Programming, Edinburgh, 10–12 April 1991
Geraint A.Wiggins, Chris Mellish and Tim Duncan (Eds.)

Specifications of Database Systems
International Workshop on Specifications of Database Systems, Glasgow, 3–5 July 1991
David J. Harper and Moira C. Norrie (Eds.)

7th UK Computer and Telecommunications Performance Engineering Workshop
Edinburgh, 22–23 July 1991
J. Hillston, P.J.B. King and R.J. Pooley (Eds.)

Logic Program Synthesis and Transformation
Proceedings of LOPSTR 91, International Workshop on Logic Program Synthesis and Transformation, University of Manchester, 4–5 July 1991
T.P. Clement and K.-K. Lau (Eds.)